Contents

Illustrations

Preface and Acknowledgements

THIS BOOK is in some ways a successor to my survey of post-war British musical plays, *A Tanner's Worth of Tune*. Alongside the British musicals that played in the West End from 1945 to the beginning of the 1970s, when what we might designate the 'Golden Age' of the musical endured a fast eclipse, there ran a constant stream of American musicals imported from Broadway. Almost without exception, these shows had enjoyed critical and commercial success in New York; this, indeed, especially the commercial aspect, was the only reason they were sent to London: to make more money for producers and writers.

This is the first book to deal specifically with the West End productions of those American shows. Even glimpses of such a history have hitherto slipped through almost any other book on either American or British musical theatre, becoming very much a forgotten aspect of the British, and by default American, theatrical past. The book deals with every Broadway musical presented in London between 1939 and 1972, in chronological order, as well as those that originated in New York off-Broadway, such as *The Fantasticks* and *Little Mary Sunshine*. I have also not allowed musicals seen only in London which had substantial American authorship, such as *Love from Judy*, *The Crystal Heart*, *The Love Doctor* and *I and Albert*, to slip through the net of forgotten productions. No stone has been left unintentionally unturned.

Countless books have been written about the Broadway musical, and very few dependable books about the British musical. Why bother with Dora Bryan, London's Lorelei Lee in *Gentlemen Prefer Blondes*, when Broadway had Carol Channing? Why trouble to discuss Anne Rogers and Ian Carmichael in *I Do! I Do!*, when New York boasted Mary Martin and Robert Preston? Need we know any more than that Judy Holliday swept all before her in the Broadway *Bells Are Ringing*? Does it matter that in the cavernous Coliseum Janet Blair followed in her wake? Or that Ethel Merman stayed home while the unknown Billie Worth was shipped to Britain to play *Call Me Madam*? In its way, one of the functions of this book is to bring back some of those faded characters standing at the back of the theatrical portrait, drawing them once more into the bright foreground. In the new light of day, many actors and personalities who have too long resided in the shadows of the negative once more emerge.

West End Broadway is also essentially a critical survey. The reception of the Broadway musical in London often differed greatly from its reception in New York, and copper-bottomed American successes (*The Fantasticks*, *Damn Yankees*, *Carnival* among them) registered as West End flops. Even the presiding goliaths Rodgers and Hammerstein suffered much critical opposition in London after their debut with *Oklahoma!* In quoting from contemporary reviews, this book for the first time brings together a critical perspective on American musicals seen in London.

As well as giving a general survey of each, I have not demurred from offering a personal opinion. I have tried to avoid the blandness that stalks through so much writing about musical theatre. Some relaxation is offered in the occasional blast of back-stage gossip, without which the musical theatre would be speechless, but the reader may be assured that the author has done his utmost to deal in facts.

The appendix brings together for the first time essential information about every American musical in London of the period, including a complete list of musical numbers, sourced from the original production's printed programmes. Textual niceties are sometimes confounded by the fact that theatrical programmes, and other printed material, contain misprints.

The staff of the Victoria and Albert Theatre Collection at Blythe House in Kensington Olympia have been unfailingly helpful and enthusiastic, scurrying back and forth between their cherished archives and the Reading Room. *West End Broadway* could not have been written without this resource. A lifetime's study of theatrical journals, notably the indispensable *Plays and Players* and the much more polite *Theatre World* under the editorship of Miss Frances Stephens, has left the author's mind stuffed with the furniture of the theatrical past. Over the years I have spoken to numberless participants in British musical theatre, and much information from these conversations has wound itself into this text. The reader will be able to distinguish my own views from those of others, and I hold myself responsible for any errors which may, unwanted, have crept in.

On this occasion, I am specially grateful for the assistance of Patricia Michael, whose West End appearances included many American musicals, among them *Once Upon a Mattress, Little Mary Sunshine, How to Succeed in Business* and *The Desert Song*. Once again, my thanks go to Judith Bruce, whose American musicals in London included *The Pajama Game, Damn Yankees* and *Wonderful Town*. Miss Michael and Miss Bruce have helpfully opened their photograph albums to me. Jan Waters, half made up for her evening's performance of *The Mousetrap* at St Martin's Theatre, told me in Dressing Room Number One of her involvement with *Do Re Mi, High Spirits* and *Show Boat*. Others whose memories invade the book include Sally Logan, the star of *Carnival*, Anna Dawson of *Little Mary Sunshine*, Doreen Hermitage of *Gone with the Wind*, Vivienne Martin of *Golden Boy, Cabaret* and *Fiddler on the Roof*, Josephine Gordon of *Camelot*, the late Dilys Laye of *The Crystal Heart*, Val May (the director of *Fiorello!*), Michael Lomax of *The Great Waltz*, and Pip Hinton of *Where's Charley?*

In the preparation of photographs, I must thank Josh Siegel. Antony Howard consented to the use of his letter to the *Stage*. Roger Fillary of the Players Theatre Archive kindly provided photographs of the London production of Antony Hopkins' and Peter Powell's *Johnny the Priest*. Mark Fox, archivist to the Really Useful Group, helpfully supplied me with the number of performances for a few elusive productions. Paul Guinery illuminated my understanding of *Love from*

Judy, and I was always heartened by his invigorating enthusiasm. Thanks are due to Stewart Nicholls, tireless in his enthusiasm for the British musical.

Michael Middeke at the Boydell Press commissioned the book, and was keen from the moment I floated the idea. 'Go away and write it,' was his advice, and three years later here it is. During its protracted birth, his blend of encouragement and subtle cajolement hit the right note. My thanks go to the production team at the Boydell Press, to Michael Richards and to Mike Webb. The book has been skilfully prepared for publication by David Roberts, whose eye has made this such an attractive object. Every effort has been made to trace the holders of copyright for material used in the book. I apologise for any omissions of acknowledgement, which the publisher will be pleased to correct in any subsequent editions.

Lastly, a fond acknowledgment of those who suffer most from the writing of a book: the author's friends. Hopefully, I have learned to fall silent when I see the glazed look that clouds the eyes of my listeners, as I regale them with another (for me) fascinating piece of information or debate relevant to *West End Broadway*. Now that the book is in print, they may check the facts, and discover whether my views are any less authoritarian or absurd than on those occasions when I hoped to beguile them with some gem drawn from a foolish lifelong obsession for musical theatre.

Adrian Wright
Norfolk, 2012

Introduction

PATRONS HURRYING INTO THE WEST END on the evening of 20 April 1964 were troubled by severe disruptions on the London Underground, a fire at Battersea Power Station having brought chaos to the Central Line and halted all traffic between Northolt and West Ruislip. The admittance of latecomers to performances of the several Broadway musicals then running in the West End must have been an irritation to those who had taken the trouble to arrive early, and getting that evening's *The Sound of Music, No Strings, How to Succeed in Business Without Really Trying* and *A Funny Thing Happened on the Way to the Forum* off to a shaky start.

Around 7 p.m. the failure of a 60,000 volt feeder at Iver in Buckinghamshire spelt disaster for the opening night of Britain's third television channel, BBC2, blacking out BBC TV Centre at Shepherd's Bush in West London. The highlight of that first night's viewing was to have been a performance of *Kiss Me, Kate* with Howard Keel and Patricia Morison, topped by a live firework display from Southend Pier. In the event, a remarkably calm Gerald Priestland sat at a table in what looked like a scout hut within Alexandra Palace and read genuine news items that might have been written for the occasion by Peter Cook. At intervals the telephone rang to inform Priestland that there was no further information. A juddering message appeared on screen confirming that there was a 'Major Power Failure', and that 'BBC2 Will Start Shortly' (it did the following day). Someone must have hastily got on to the BBC Record Library, for now an orchestral arrangement of 'You Are Beautiful', a song from Rodgers and Hammerstein's *Flower Drum Song*, provided the only entertainment. After another juddery interruption from Priestland, there was heard the strains of 'I Feel Pretty' from *West Side Story*. Then came the title song from an American musical that the British public knew nothing of, *Mr Wonderful*. By hook or by crook, the BBC was determined to make this an evening of Broadway musicals.

Kiss Me, Kate was an interesting celebratory choice for a new television channel that would have popular appeal to a more up-market viewing public than BBC1. What was it about *Kiss Me, Kate* that struck the right note (perhaps some of Cole Porter's notes), achieving popularity without vulgarity? Anyway, the *British* Broadcasting Company, starting as they meant to go on, had chosen an *American* musical over a British one, and a musical that had in the thirteen years since its London premiere achieved a sort of classicism, or at least seemed to have classicism built in thanks to its source material. The most obvious reason for the choice was that this was a musical about a theatrical company putting on a musical version of Shakespeare's *The Taming of the Shrew*, with an off-stage relationship between its leading man and woman that stormily mirrored that of Shakespeare's Kate and Petruchio. *Kiss Me, Kate* offered a shortcut to that place where popular culture collided with 'serious', and was a safe choice for the opening night of a channel that wanted to put its supposedly intellectual eggs and less demanding eggs into one basket.

In more recent years, BBC1 has shown much more interest in promoting British musicals that might unappealingly but accurately be described as global blockbusters. Massive television campaigns have been mounted by their producers to trumpet revivals of trusted old favourites of musical theatre: *Jesus Christ Superstar*, *The Wizard of Oz*, *Oliver!* among them. And where once British musicals stayed home while American musicals (those that had earned their ticket by being a financial success on Broadway) moved into the West End, the traffic has been reversed. One of the first lessons to learn is that justice plays no part in theatrical enterprise. Many of the elements that contributed to the establishment of American musical theatre had their beginnings in British musical theatre. Broadway absorbed and exploited them so effectively that London was left with little more than a desiccated carcass that until the 1970s was considered inferior in every department.[1]

The Beggar's Opera was celebrated in Britain as the work said to have made Rich gay and Gay rich when it was produced at Lincoln's Inn Fields in 1728. This was almost certainly the first London-to-New-York transfer – and this book you are holding is moving in the opposite direction. The 'gay'ness referred to the fact that the show made both its producer John Rich and its librettist John Gay wealthy, as it hopefully did the least celebrated of the trio, its arranger of traditional melodies Johann Christoph Pepusch. Presented as a ballad opera, in the twentieth century the work was increasingly presented as a musical to a public that probably did not understand, or have a care for, the difference.[2] Although it would be another 104 years before *The Beggar's Opera* was again seen in America, it established a sort of template for the musical play long before the work usually voted as the first American musical, *The Black Crook*. *The Beggar's Opera* had many of the ingredients that would be expected of the genre in the centuries ahead: a plot, characters good and bad, sexual complication, comedy (and hopefully wit), tragedy (or at least poignancy), here and there a dash of dancing, and songs, identifiable as individual numbers in a way that 'serious' opera eschewed.

Years ahead of *Oklahoma!*, *The Beggar's Opera* arrived from London as integrated as could be. It didn't even separate out the comedy from the drama, as did so many works considered as 'integrated'. *Oklahoma!* itself made a point of excluding its two leading romantic roles from any funny business, a sign that the show was probably just another operetta. *Oklahoma!*'s heroine Laurey is a classic example of a leading lady who couldn't make a cat laugh. Even more than *Oklahoma!* (complete with *dream* sequence), *The Beggar's Opera* carried a storyline through its characters and bears a striking resemblance to a stream of consciousness; no time for dreaming here. Two hundred years before *Oklahoma!* was applauded for doing all, *The Beggar's Opera* had done most. Gay and Pepusch's musical had another essential that all musicals of the future sought:

songs that an audience would remember as it wound its way home. What does it matter that in *The Beggar's Opera* Pepusch borrowed, stole or remembered, arranged and harmonised existent melodies and songs, of and in the air? It is perhaps Pepusch who starts that crucial link between the musical play's song and script. We hear 'Everything's Coming Up Roses' and we are linked instantly to *Gypsy*. We hear 'How Are Things in Glocca Morra?' and we look up for *Finian's Rainbow*. The song conjures the show, the show the song, and we place 'Were I Laid on Greenland's Coast' with *The Beggar's Opera*.

It would be absurd to embark here on a potted history of the beginnings of American musical theatre, and to attempt some sort of authoritative summary would be presumptuous, for the complex evolution of the Broadway musical cannot be sketched, but some point of embarkation may be necessary. The first exemplar of the truly American musical was most probably *The Black Crook*, 'an Original, Grand, Romantic Magical and Spectacular Drama in Four Acts' written by Charles M. Barras with music by Thomas E. Baker, produced at Niblo's Garden in New York in September 1866. There's no mention in that self-description of music, ballet or song, but the items listed in the theatre programme tell differently. Miss Milly Cavendish (from England) sang the first song of Act One, 'Early in the Morning', followed by a 'Grand Ballet' and 'Pas de Fleurs', after which Miss Cavendish sang 'Naughty, Naughty Man'.[3] These delights may have been eclipsed by the 'Grand Incantation! Introducing many Weird and Startling Effects' before the end of Act One.

Act Two revealed Mlle. Rita Sangalli (the Première Danseuses Assoluta) in the 'Splendid Pas de Naide', and the corps de ballet in a 'March of Fishes' and 'Dance of Mermaids', making way for Annie Kemp Bowler as Stalacta, Queen of the Golden Realm, who sang 'Flow On, Silver Stream' and 'The Power of Love'. The third act brought Mlle. Marie Bonfanti of the Parisian Ballet Troupe in 'An Original and Grand Dance de Amazons', and the fourth act a 'Triple Sword Combat' and, at the last, 'a Dazzling Transformation Scene, revealing the Nymphs of the Golden Realm, terminating with Stalacta's Happiness and Joy'. A year after the end of the Civil War, this was a welcome enchantment in New York, playing Niblo's Garden for 475 performances, a remarkable achievement, not least because the auditorium accommodated 3,200 patrons. It seemed that such diversion could make more money for its producers than had ever been imagined. The modesty of what was to be the American musical had been overcome, and the fact that money could be made out of it has influenced its development ever since. Indeed, Broadway musicals that were brought to the West End were only granted passage if they were considered money-makers.

Long before *The Black Crook*, writers for musical theatre recognised that it might be sensible to base their musical entertainments on established works, and preferably those for which the public had already shown a fondness. The most obvious early examples in 1796 included *The Archers, or The Mountaineers of Switzerland*, a picturesque work by William Dunlap built around the legend of

William Tell. This had an original score by the British composer Benjamin Carr, but Dunlap and Carr never collaborated again. *The Sicilian Romance* had its origin in a gothic novel by Ann Ward Radcliffe. Again, the score was original, but much altered in its transfer from London, where its music had been by William Reeves, supplanted in New York by the music of one of its producers, Alexander Reinagle. There was a British origin for *Edwin and Angelina*, an 'Opera (Musical Drama)', in Oliver Goldsmith's *The Vicar of Wakefield*. The songs were 'partly from Goldsmith, and partly original', but the show came and went in one night (a precedent that a few other Broadway shows would follow).

Throughout the century that lies between the American debut of *The Beggar's Opera* and *The Black Crook*, musical entertainments in some sort of fusion between speech and music proliferated in a confusion of disguises, as Operetta Bouffe; Opéra-Bouffon; Burlesque; Light Opera; Romantic Opera; Burleske Oper; Laughable Burlesque Burletta; Vaudeville; Operatic Romance; Opéra-comique; Romantic Burlesque; An Entirely New and Original Operatic; Dramatic, Spasmodic Burlesque; English Parlor Opera; A New and Entertaining Pièce de Circonstance; Bouffonnerie Musicale; Romantic Musical Drama; Grand Romantic Spectacle, and so on and on. Most of these would settle or coalesce or be absorbed into the 'musical', 'musical play' and 'musical comedy'. 'Opera' is a label that haunts early manifestations of American musical theatre, but it may be that the most influential of those works that might genuinely be regarded as operas had been imported from Britain. The popularity of ballad opera made way in the 1840s for that school of British opera which even in its country of origin has in our own day been repudiated.

Michael William Balfe's *The Bohemian Girl* premiered in London in 1843 and in New York the following year. There it survived a great many revivals, the last being in 1933, after which it could hardly be expected to hold the modern stage. Never mind that the piece was promoted as 'A Grand Opera'; the stirrings of the musical play are concealed within. Alfred Bunn's rudimentary libretto showed how important it would be for musicals of the future to have intelligent and skilful book writers. (Find a replacement for Mr Bunn.) Although the programme did not list separate musical numbers, *The Bohemian Girl*'s success was partly due to its easily assimilated and extractable items, among them 'I Dreamt I Dwelt in Marble Halls'. Bunn's word-smithery was laughable, but there was the semblance of cohesiveness between plot, character and music, and the music had at least been specially composed for the piece, not adapted from existing compositions. What's more, composers like Balfe were well aware of the difference between writing music and coming up with tunes, and wrote principally to please the pit. If future Broadway composers wished to succeed, they needed to learn this lesson. Dance was not completely neglected, either. Long before Agnes de Mille, attempts were being made to integrate choreography in to what passed for musical entertainment. The New York premiere of *The Bohemian Girl* lists Monsieur Martin as *maître de ballet*, and although the score has no specific dance music, such moments were present in 'The Tent of the Queen of the Gypsies' and 'A Grand Fair'.

William Vincent Wallace's *Maritana* (London 1845; New York 1848) was another British opera that had the air (or airs) of a musical about it, most obvious in such songs as 'Scenes That Are Brightest' and 'Yes Let Me Like a Soldier Fall'. Somewhere in the Theatre Royal, Drury Lane during its first performances there must have been someone saying 'Lovely music! Pity about the book!', although at the time no one much was considering that the quality of a musical's book might be of any importance. Wallace had to cope with a libretto from Edward Fitzball *and* Alfred Bunn; what today might vulgarly be called a double whammy. Both *The Bohemian Girl* and *Maritana* were produced successfully at Niblo's Garden before *The Black Crook* was dreamed of. Balfe and Bunn, with musical interpolations from 'Dr Cunnington', were back in America with *The Enchantress*, schizophrenically labelled 'A Grand Operatic Drama (Light Opera)', altered for its 1863 revival at Niblo's to a 'Grand Operatic Spectacle'. The title, of course, belied the fact that once again the libretto was, in its untutored way, integrated. Opera it may have been, but the musical items were listed for the 1846 premiere and, twenty years before *The Black Crook*, dance was again on the menu which included a 'Ballet d'Ensemble with Flute Solo', the speciality dance provided by Miss Cohen as the Spirit of Good.

Two years after *The Black Crook* the British opera *The Lily of Killarney* was effectively an operatic embryo of the musical, at least in its strong offering of take-away melodies that could survive outside the theatre, but despite Julius Benedict's 'The Moon Has Raised Her Lamp Above' and 'It Is a Charming Girl I Know', and despite the Irishness of it all (a qualification that gave the work considerable American appeal), the lily did not have great Broadway success to match that of *The Bohemian Girl* or *Maritana*. Balfe and Wallace showed they had the ability to distance themselves from the embryonic musical play in other works. Balfe's *Lurline* is a distinct musical advancement, as is Wallace's *Falstaff*, but both had dubious librettos and neither was seen in America. Nevertheless, *The Bohemian Girl* and *Maritana* provide convincing evidence that mid-Victorian 'opera' was a not too distant relation of the musical play. From 1858, with the New York production of the 'Bouffonnerie Musicale' *Les Deux Aveugles*, the works of Jacques Offenbach became a Broadway constant, enjoying an American vogue until the end of the century. Offenbach's settings of often irreligious material and the fact that his melodies were highly extractable contributed to their popularity, and his Frenchness was no hindrance.

The success of *The Black Crook* led to several revivals and the first musical sequel in Broadway's history, *The White Fawn*, presented at Niblo's in 1868. As every theatre aficionado knows, sequels are rarely made as welcome as their predecessors – catastrophe lurks. *The White Fawn* avoided it, although the massiveness of the project proved problematic. (The last act did not begin until after midnight, and an army of eighty stage-hands could not tame the scenery.)

The Parisian Ballet Troupe was again on hand to present the 'Grand Ballet of Fire-Flies', a 'Dance of Fish' and a 'Nettle-Fish Dance', Egyptian dancing and a 'Grand March'. The music was credited to Howard Glover, although interpolation allowed Miss Lizzie Wilmore to sing 'I Love the Military' from Offenbach's *The Grand Duchess of Gérolstein*, which had premiered the previous year in Paris. Early musicals benefited from the Frankenstein concept of amassing material. *The White Fawn* faded after 176 performances, but *The Black Crook* was deemed such a hit that it was exported to London. This is the show that starts the traffic from Broadway to the West End, produced at the Alhambra Theatre for Christmas 1874 and staying for six months. Would the audience at Niblo's have recognised it? The London production had transformed itself into an 'opéra bouffe' by the actor Harry Paulton, with music by Frederic Clay and Georges Jacobi. At this time Clay was one of the forerunners of British musical theatre. His opera *Court and Cottage* had been seen at Covent Garden twelve years earlier, and in 1869 he started a collaboration with W. S. Gilbert. *That* name was to be for ever associated with Arthur Sullivan, in a series of works, collectively known as 'The Savoy Operas', originally presented in London but transferred to America with tremendous success and ensuing influence on American musical theatre. Long before the twentieth century began, the American musical was about to become an art-form *and* a business. In London the American musical was a business.

Almost a hundred years on from *The Black Crook* America was still not done with Barras and Baker's old work. On 5 March 1954 a 'Musical Extravaganza in Two Acts', *The Girl in Pink Tights*, opened on Broadway. The music was said to be by Sigmund Romberg, some of whose operettas had enjoyed notable American and British success, but Romberg had died three years before *The Girl in Pink Tights* was seen; his last New York show had been the 1948 *My Romance*. Now, Romberg's music was 'developed and orchestrated' by his colleague-cum-orchestrator Don Walker. It's a jaunty, highly likeable score, but it's the plot that draws our attention here. This is a musical *about* the creation of *The Black Crook*. A Broadway musical about the making of a musical? There would be another such four years later in *Say, Darling* about the making of *The Pajama Game*. *Say, Darling* was elliptical in its references to its inspiration, but *The Girl in Pink Tights* seemed to be a recreation of the making of *The Black Crook*, showing how the American musical – that diverting amalgam of the play, the music and the ballet – was born.

Much that had happened was accidental. At Niblo's Garden, the producers of a new melodrama based on the Faust legend sat despondently through the rehearsals, awaiting what they predicted would be a flop.[4] Meanwhile, across the White Way at the Academy of Music, the Parisian Ballet Troupe was about to open in a programme of dance when a ruinous fire at the Academy left the Paris dancers theatre-less and jobless. The melodrama's producers, William Wheatley and Henry C. Jarrett, saw a possibility to enliven the dullness of their show: why not hire the Parisian Troupe and their scenery and mingle their routines into the fabric of the melodrama? The result was five and a half hours of endurance for the audience, but *The Black Crook* had helped plant a seed from which the American musical flourished. *The Black Crook* also proved that while a Broadway success might be sent to London, the less successful musicals, among them some of the most interesting – *The Girl in Pink Tights* was one such – seldom travel.

So it was that London was denied the opportunity to see *The Black Crook*'s history made into a modern musical, to hear Romberg's (or Walker's) jaunty songs, or to admire the show's Broadway star Jeanmaire as one of the Parisian Troupe, Lisette, ecstatic at being invited to ride 'Up in the Elevated Railway' or recklessly explaining 'When I Am Free to Love'. Neither would it hear 'We're All in the Same Boat' in which the melodrama company at Niblo's and the dancers at the Academy realise that their destinies are linked. Between them, they acknowledge the essential ingredients of what we now regard as the Broadway musical, whether in New York or London's West End.

> Our dramatic extravaganza
> Can be a goldmine or bonanza,
> And for the ladies we'll have a sob scene
> And for the gents something a trifle obscene.
> It's never been done
> It's something fresh
> We'll give 'em flash
> We'll give 'em flesh,
> Give them something they never got
> Dancing, Singing and a Plot.[5]

1 A 1930s attempt at glamorising Cicely Courtneidge,
whose American musicals in London spanned *Lido Lady* (1926) to *High Spirits* (1964)

1939-45

The War Years

Is your journey really necessary?
(Propaganda slogan produced by the
Railway Executive Committee)

T HEATRE-GOING in London's West End during World War II could be a perilous undertaking. In the first uncertain days it was safer to stay at home by the wireless and listen to what seemed like endless recitals of popular music played by Sandy MacPherson at the BBC Theatre Organ. It seemed that the palaces of the British and Moss Empires might soon be reduced to rubble.[1] When at 11 a.m. on 3 September 1939 the British Prime Minister Neville Chamberlain announced that his government was declaring war on Germany, the surety of continuing life juddered through the British public. My mother, who was shelling peas in the back garden of her parents' home in Norwich, abandoned the colander and ran indoors to attend the unwelcome radio broadcast. Only a pitiful percentage of the listening public would have given a thought as to what would become of the country's theatres, its writers, its actors, its composers and librettists, and its musicals. The 1930s had seen a steady trickle of such frivolities. Dotted among the plentiful British musicals were a few works from some of the masters of Broadway, such as Rodgers and Hart's *Evergreen* of 1930 (the last of three pieces written specifically for London), Rudolf Friml's operetta *The Three Musketeers*, and *Rio Rita*, and Rodgers and Hart's *On Your Toes* of 1937.

By 1939, with what the more grandiloquent historians called the gathering storm of war all around, theatrical frivolity seemed to some unnecessary and to some essential. That year no American musicals made their way into the West End, that area of London with a preponderance of theatres, among them the London Coliseum and Theatre Royal, Drury Lane, which would become the central platforms of the post-war American musical invasion. British musicals were expected merely to entertain and beguile the ear and eye for an unsophisticated while: enter Ivor Novello's Viennese-like *The Dancing Years*, the knockabout farce of *Runaway Love*, and Cicely Courtneidge in a musical comedy with plenty of revue-like opportunities for comic antics, *Under Your Hat*, at the Palace Theatre.

All theatrical activity in the West End was stopped on 4 September 1939, when the government announced a compulsory closure of all theatres. London and the provinces, deprived the balm of dramatic escapism, seemed doomed to endure a complete darkness. The *Daily Express* helpfully informed its readers that 'There is no such thing as culture in wartime', although its editors may not have considered musical theatre 'cultural'.[2] Twelve days later the government reconsidered, and theatres were allowed to reopen on 16 September, although external illuminations had to be extinguished during air-raids. This enlightened approach sustained the war effort, but was small compensation for the ensuing era of rationing, privation, emotional disruption, illicit marketing, permanent threat of attack, blackout restrictions, Anderson shelters, gas masks, soaring rates of crime and divorce, the Home Guard, evacuation of children, pea-souper fogs, queuing, the arrival of American GI's bearing gifts of ladies' nylon stockings, and Tommy Trinder insisting that the British people were 'You lucky people!'

Throughout the Phoney (or Bore) War that spread from September to the following April, and all through the Blitz (marked in the calendar as lasting from 7 September 1940 until 11 May 1941), theatres remained open, acrobats tumbled and principal boys in pantomime slapped thighs that may or may not have been encased in American nylons (introduced in 1940 but two years later almost impossible to purchase). Even as its foundations were rocked by bombing, the Windmill Theatre (the capital's home of burlesque and refined striptease) established its reputation that throughout the war 'We Never Closed'. Plunging from the stygian gloom of Shaftesbury Avenue into the artificiality of the lighted auditoriums of the theatres, dense with the fag-end mist of nicotine overdosing (smoking was almost encouraged throughout a performance), must have seemed an unearthly experience. Immediately on the announcement of war London's most esteemed Theatre Royal in Drury Lane was commandeered by ENSA, the Entertainments National Service Association, its Controller the eminent actor-manager Sir Seymour Hicks.

A more intrusive government policy might have dictated the diet of theatregoers for the duration of the war: only serious drama, perhaps, or dramas the subsidiary or main purpose of which was to instil a correct form of patriotism, or provide opiate entertainment to the wanting masses. At the end of the conflict the critic A. E. Wilson recalled how

> The war, in fact, stimulated the taste for drama, for during those long, dreary years it had proved a sovereign anodyne, a blessed relief from cares and anxieties, the gloom of the darkened streets, of dismal and oppressive shortages. It provided a temporary but healing panacea for griefs and miseries and an ideal diversion for those on leave.[3]

One such panacea was in fact titled *Diversions*, a revue seen at Wyndham's Theatre in October 1940, with no less a star than Edith Evans at its centre (its sequel, *Diversion No. 2*, played at the same theatre from January 1941). Revues, mixed bouquets of the bright and breezy, provided easily digested diversion, and there was a plentiful supply of them in 1939 after the embargo on theatrical productions was lifted. Herbert Farjeon's *Little Revue*, premiered at the Little Theatre in April 1939 and forced to close on 4 September, was the first to show itself above the parapet when it reopened on 20 September. The 'intelligent' revue thrived in the months leading up to the outbreak of war with *The Gate Revue* and *The Little Revue*, but after the commencement of hostilities revues were more intent on raucous entertaining than in exercising the senses: Sandy Powell in *Can You Hear Me, Mother?* at the Coliseum; a herd of British comedians in *Shephard's Pie*; the Crazy Gang in *The Little Dog Laughed* at the Palladium; the 'musical crazy show' *Eve on Parade* (hints of nudity) at the Garrick Theatre; Bobby Howes and Beatrice Lillie in *All Clear*; the 'intimate rag' *Black Velvet* at the Hippodrome. For the tired business man of legend, a natural port of call was *Gaieties de Montmartre*, an oasis of Gallic naughtiness and feathered boredom, at the Prince of Wales Theatre.

Although America was to join the war in 1941, declaring hostilities against Japan on 8 December and against Germany on 11 December, theatrical life on Broadway seemed almost oblivious to the circumstance. From the outbreak of World War II through 1945 the American musical not only prospered but was busy changing its form. This, after all, was the time of *Oklahoma!* and *Carousel*, of the audacity of Rodgers and Hammerstein, a period when operetta redressed itself. In 1939, there were not many signs that the American musical would come up with much except easily pleasing light-headed shows to pass a happy hour or two: more diversions.

The obvious difficulties of wartime presented a considerable obstacle to the British management that wanted to bring a show from New York, and home-grown product dominated. Perhaps remembering how successful the British operetta *The Maid of the Mountains* had been during the First World War, managements turned to reviving trusted favourites. 1940 had new productions of *The Chocolate Soldier*, *White Horse Inn* and the other long-runner of the Great War, *Chu Chin Chow*, which only managed 158 performances against its original 2,238. *Chu Chin Chow* was remarkable for being one of the very few British musicals of the first half of the twentieth century to be transferred to Broadway, where it flopped. Never mind; this in itself was an achievement, for throughout the period covered by this book the traffic is nearly all one-way – Broadway to West End.

Revivals predominate for the rest of London's war. Only one reason may have been that remnants of the original sets and costumes were still in working order. 1942 saw the second London revival of Oscar Hammerstein II and Otto Harbach's 1920s heroine *Rose-Marie* enacted twice daily with a veteran operetta leading man Raymond Newell as mountie Jim Kenyon. With so many young actors at war the West End was a paradise for ageing juveniles. The *Observer* reported, 'Pre-war splendours dazzle, the theme songs have a verve that only encores can temper, and Mr. [George] Lacy's comic cadenzas are classics of their kind.'[4] London's other American musical of 1942 masqueraded as *Wild Rose*, but was really an old Jerome Kern show, *Sally*, originally seen in the West End in 1921, in disguise: the programme promised 'A New Treatment of an Old Story' devised and staged by Robert Nesbitt. The same sort of inconsequential musical comedy plot that from 1915 had served Kern's bijou Princess Theatre musicals, this was about Sally Green, a zesty dish-washer with the spirit of a Joan of Arc who becomes a Broadway star. In its new frock of *Wild Rose* the 1942 production had several of the characteristics of many Broadway imports into the West End. The show had been written as a vehicle for Marilyn Miller, but, like many another Broadway star after her, Miller wasn't up for going to London. In this case, London did well, getting Dorothy Dickson, one of the most appealing musical stars of the period, sometimes off-note but with a sort of transatlantic glamour and allure that is almost completely gone from British theatre of our own day.

As with many shows to come, London didn't seem to mind seeing an American musical with an all-British cast, here directed by its other star George Grossmith. At the Winter Garden in 1921, audiences probably didn't realise that they were seeing a different *production*, not a restaging of the one that had opened only eight months before in New York and was still running. Different designers had been brought in for the sets and costumes, as well as a new choreographer. Another coup for Dickson and the company of several other imported American shows of the time was that they were able to set down recordings of the score (eight of the songs and an orchestral medley in the case of *Sally*). Twenty-one years later, for *Wild Rose*, even more attention seems to have been given to the old work.

If British names were wholly responsible for the new production, many were impressive. The choreographer was Robert Helpmann, already a principal dancer at Sadler's Wells Ballet and soon to become a noted actor and director, going on to stage *Camelot* at Drury Lane in the 1960s. In the same year that he directed and choreographed *Wild Rose* he also choreographed three Sadler's Wells ballets: *Comus, Hamlet* and *The Birds.* One can only wonder at what he did to revive the saga of Sally Green, but there can be no doubt that his very name on the playbill gave evidence of some care being given to the American visitor. The sets were by Ernst (sometimes Ernest) Stern, already known for his work on *White Horse Inn*, Noel Coward's *Bitter Sweet* and Rodgers and Hart's *Evergreen.* There were new costumes, too, by Frederick Dawson, and fresh orchestrations by Val Phillips, as well as textual alterations to Guy Bolton's book by the British lyricist Frank Eyton and comedian Richard Hearne. This tendency to trifle with the original American product was, perhaps fortunately, quite rare. Of most of this audiences would have been quite unaware, their concentration fixed on the most obvious aspect of the entertainment: the casting.

Casting the British production of a Broadway musical was one of the most troublesome problems facing London producers during World War II. There might be no problem if the original New York star whose performance had ensured the success of the show could be persuaded to cross the Atlantic (itself a hazardous undertaking during war), but this was not often the case. Britain had its own popular stars of musical comedy and variety, well known for keeping the curtain up, but their experience was with British material by British writers, material of a type that was known to have local appeal. The domestic repertory of British players could usually find a billet in some American musical, either in London or on tour. Still, London was lucky to see Jessie Matthews cast as the new-look Sally in *Wild Rose*, although by 1942 Matthews' successful career was beginning to slide because of increasingly inferior films, theatrical upset, relationship difficulties and mental instability. The previous year Matthews had swum across the tide of one-way traffic from New York to Shaftesbury Avenue by being signed for the lead in an American show, *The Lady Comes Across*. She did and she didn't.

Embarking on the pre-Broadway tour, the distinctions between the unlikely plot about an innocent girl (Matthews) getting mixed up with a bunch of spies and real life became blurred, and Matthews imagined that the heroine's troubles were her own. She was hospitalised and withdrawn from the production, leaving her hapless replacement to get through the three Broadway performances as best she could. More happily, Matthews stayed put for the run of *Wild Rose*, a star and a rose by any other name, although the notices did nothing for her diminishing career. James Agate noted 'sufficient wit, sparkling tunes, brilliant lighting and dazzling dresses'[5] but *Wild Rose* may have been even less of an 'integrated' musical than it had been in New York as *Sally*. The programme lists the speciality acts Johnny Nitt, Moran and Elf, and a chimpanzee named Tarzan. Crucially, the production kept Kern's fine songs, most notably 'Look for the Silver Lining', although the Act Three 'Flor Fina' ballet was by Victor Herbert, and the show's incidental music by Elsie April, at one time Noel Coward's amanuensis.

There are alternatives to finding an established star name to head up an American musical in London. Spend weeks in audition and discover a cast of complete unknowns. This may be commendable but may not appeal to the British public, always more contented to be going to see someone they already know. Another alternative looks across the Atlantic: didn't the show have a post-Broadway tour, and isn't the actor who took the lead on the road available for London? With luck, this person may also be something of a name in London, but it's unlikely the actor will have the cachet of the show's original star. Then, if nothing better suggests itself, how about the Broadway star's standby? Move forward twenty years to Richard Rodgers' *No Strings*, and read in the London programme that the leading lady at Her Majesty's Theatre is Beverly Todd, who 'at one time' played the part on Broadway. And even if an American name (of sorts) can be found to do the job in London, does that performer have the qualities that the originator of the part (for whom the script and songs may have been specifically written) possessed? Janet Blair, nice to have around and no offence taken, but playing the lead in the London *Bells Are Ringing* when Broadway had the privilege of seeing Judy Holliday? More wisely, when the exact performer could not be found to take the flight to London, producers bided their time (sometimes a decade or more) until someone else, as right in a different

"My last-thing-at-night drink
is Ovaltine"
says Pat Kirkwood

PAT KIRKWOOD writes: "*It is generally admitted that one of the brightest shows in town is 'Black Velvet' at the Hippodrome. I have been flattered by the many people who have kindly paid tribute to my own efforts to make it such a success, but I think I ought to tell you that some of the praise belongs to 'Ovaltine.' My last-thing-at-night drink of 'Ovaltine' ensures that I get a long, restful sleep and wake full of energy, ready for a busy day that ends very, very late.*"

World-wide experience shows that there is nothing like 'Ovaltine.' Its exceptional value in every emergency is being amply demonstrated to-day. After a period of nervous tension, for example, 'Ovaltine' has outstanding advantages. Its special properties rapidly soothe the nerves, quickly induce sleep and help you to gain the utmost benefit from your sleeping hours.

Prepared from Nature's finest foods, 'Ovaltine' provides concentrated nutriment to every cell and tissue of body, brain and nerves. Its pre-eminent nerve-restoring properties are largely derived from the new-laid eggs used in its manufacture. *No tonic food beverage could be complete without eggs.*

For these reasons make 'Ovaltine' your constant stand-by. Remember— '*Ovaltine' results are obtained only from 'Ovaltine.'*

P548A

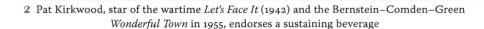

2 Pat Kirkwood, star of the wartime *Let's Face It* (1942) and the Bernstein–Comden–Green *Wonderful Town* in 1955, endorses a sustaining beverage

way, appeared on the scene: think Ethel Merman, Broadway's *Gypsy* of 1959, and Angela Lansbury's London *Gypsy* of 1974. Fifteen years to wait, but better this than enduring a miscast Rose, or a lesser one stopping off in London during a tiring tour.

London in 1942 also had two original Broadway shows, *DuBarry Was a Lady* and *Let's Face It!* The first at least offered something that had been denied the British public since the start of the war; some sophistication in the shape of a Cole Porter score. *DuBarry* – 'New York's Latest Musical Comedy' according to the programme – had taken three years to get to London, and by the time the lady arrived she had undergone alteration: from Broadway's Ethel Merman (the British had heard of her) to the West End's Frances Day (of whom Americans had probably never heard). These two leading ladies tell us something else about what can happen to a musical shipped over from America: the stardom may be equally valid, but the things that go to make up that stardom may be vividly different. Merman and Day? We might as well compare the moon with the sun. As it happens, the London run of *DuBarry* was about half that of the original Broadway production (another trend that repeats throughout the period of this book; few London editions equalled or outran the New York versions, although it's wise to remember that the London theatres used for many Broadway shows were much bigger than the Broadway houses). Perhaps audiences didn't care much for Porter's not very inspired songs, or resented Merman not being there, or was tiring of Day and the droll Arthur Riscoe, who in 1934 had already teamed for the British musical *Jill Darling*. There is always a wide choice of possible reasons for a show's failure or success in theatre, for which science offers no explanations.

Riscoe and Day were welcomed in *DuBarry*, although one critic complained that Day shouldn't waste her time with mindless frivolities but instead join the intellectual frivolities of a Herbert Farjeon revue, but nothing farther from a Farjeon idea could have been imagined than *DuBarry*. Riscoe played Louis Blore, a lavatory attendant at a smart night club. He comes into money and imagines himself to be Louis XV, transported to Versailles where his girlfriend Jenny Daly (Day) becomes the Comtesse du Barry. There were those who considered that *A Yankee at the Court of King Arthur* had already made such a plot device unusable, but the glamour and comedy brightened the dull London scene, although *The Times* complained that the show 'seems in translation from the American to have taken on an odd resemblance to Christmas pantomime'. Singling out Day's 'Katy Went to Haiti' its critic was not keen on the rest of the songs. 'Their quality, judged by the composer's past excellence, is gravely in doubt, and Mr. Cole Porter is the Rupert of the light musical stage.'[6] As much, indeed, could be said (and sometimes was) of the other Porter works that peppered the London war years.

Porter had also written the score for the second Broadway import of 1942, *Let's Face It!*, then reaching the end of its successful New York run. Herbert and Dorothy Fields concocted the book from a now forgotten play by Russell Medcraft and Norma Mitchell, *The Cradle Snatchers*. In London, it sufficiently lit the gloom to last for a year, even if the *Daily Telegraph*'s W. A. Darlington along with other critics found the plot about army wives adopting three soldiers from a nearby army base dull and bedraggled. On Broadway the show consolidated Danny Kaye's reputation after playing *Lady in the Dark*, and then Kaye ignored the American musical for thirty years until manhandling Richard Rodgers' 'Noah' musical *Two by Two*. London got Bobby Howes, the elfin diminutive whose career had embraced amusing British musicals of the 1930s, mostly by the hard-working Jack Waller (who doubled as an impresario and was co-producer with Tom Arnold for *Let's Face It!*) and Joseph Tunbridge. Howes was a survivor, and had been since the 1920s, when he'd had his first try at the transatlantic musical singing duets with Estelle Brody in Rudolf Friml's *The Blue Kitten*. Howes' career would last until the early 1960s, playing fatherly Ben Rumson to his daughter Sally Ann in the London *Paint Your Wagon*, and Finian in a Broadway revival of *Finian's Rainbow*. Howes' leading lady was another British stalwart, Joyce Barbour, a name that has mainly escaped theatrical histories, with two other formidable personalities, Pat Kirkwood and Noele Gordon, in support.

For the first half of 1943 London had to make do with more revivals, beginning with Harry Welchman's return as Pierre Birabeau and Edith Day's return as Margot in the Hammerstein–Romberg *The Desert Song*, roles they had created at Drury Lane in 1927. The operetta had already been staged just before the outbreak of war at the Garrick Theatre, featuring Sally, the donkey who had appeared in the initial production twelve years earlier. Rebellious critical observers noted that even in 1939 'the light relief provided for this version would seem to have had its day'.[7] Furthermore, the 'somewhat gruelling libretto [was] heroic in style but stammers in the telling'.[8] An earlier revival at the Coliseum in 1936 had been greeted with similar reservations, the *Observer* noting that since its premiere in 1927 'its transports seemed to me to have cooled in the interval', despite comedienne Clarice Hardwicke, 'steadying the amiable puerilities of the soubrette with her own delightfully professional art'.[9] And in 1936 *The Times* reported that Welchman 'always inclined to be sacerdotal, is now an Episcopal desperado, and Miss Edith Day has sometimes to strain after notes that once came without an effort'.[10] On this occasion, the show ran three and a quarter hours.

In April 1943 came the first London revival (twice daily, 2.15 and 6.15) of the Kern and Hammerstein *Show Boat* with, in the absence of Paul Robeson, 'Mr. Jetsam' (otherwise H. C. Hilliam) from the variety double-act Flotsam and Jetsam, brought in and blacked-up as the bale-lifting Joe. Critics noticed the difference. The cast of seventy included Bruce Carfax, Pat Taylor and the Australian singer Gwyneth Lascelles, subbed at some performances by Valerie Hay. The show was another dash of colour in the West End's blacked-out landscape, but one wonders if critics, making allowances for the difficulties, left their sharper faculties at home. *The Times* played safe by describing it as 'lavish with its dresses and chorus, and decked out as it is with a brilliance of colour and with all its flags flying it seems destined for a prosperous voyage'.[11]

Show Boat lasted until the end of the year at the Stoll, but the first London revival of *The Vagabond King*, despite some bigger names and a spectacular production from Robert Nesbitt, didn't draw the crowds at the Winter Garden, where it had originally played successfully in 1927. Operetta with a Parisian twist (the programme gives its setting as 'Old Paris during the reign of Louis XI'), the show had Friml's sumptuous melodies, and Webster Booth as the poor poet Francois Villon to sing one of the best of them, 'Only a Rose'. The less-welcome news for some was that Booth's wife and singing partner Anne Ziegler also turned up at the Winter Garden every night to play Katharine de Vaucelles. For *The Times*, Ziegler 'finicks where she should be statuesque', but Booth reminded the critic of Douglas Fairbanks.[12] At the three weekly matinees their roles were taken by Dennis Noble and Maria Elsner. Relief from the romance was offered by the 'low' comedian Syd Walker.

Londoners expected to be refreshed by *Sunny River*, a genuinely original American work, reasonably fresh from its short New York run in 1941, much redressed: new orchestrations by Alfred Reynolds, and new sets and costumes by Doris Zinkeisen, the whole directed by Maxwell Wray. This *was* a rarity – a show that had soundly flopped at thirty-six performances – trusted to turn into a success in the West End. In its way *Sunny River* marked if not the start of a new order, the end of the old. The music was by Sigmund Romberg, whose long career had only three more shows to run before it ended in 1954 with *The Girl in Pink Tights*. Oscar Hammerstein II, Romberg's librettist for *Sunny River*, was no stranger to operetta, shreds of which hung about the new show despite its being billed as 'a musical play'. Hammerstein had already collaborated with Romberg on *The Desert Song*, *The New Moon*, *East Wind* and *May Wine*, as well as with Vincent Youmans (*Wildflower*, *Mary Jane McKane* and *Rainbow*), Jerome Kern (*Sunny*, *Show Boat*, *Sweet Adeline*, *Music in the Air*, *Three Sisters* and *Very Warm For May*) and Rudolf Friml (*Rose-Marie* and *The Wild Rose*). With such a pedigree Hammerstein seemed one of the least likely established figures in American musical theatre to be at the vanguard of change in the middle of the twentieth century, but only two years after Broadway had dismissed *Sunny River* came *Oklahoma!*

Sunny River has slipped the British consciousness, but with time Hammerstein's libretto has become a little more interesting. That sunny river is the Mississippi, the very river that Joe in *Show Boat* watches rolling along. The story is set in New Orleans at the beginning of the nineteenth century; a valentine to America's past, as is *Oklahoma!*, which inhabits a period that is difficult to pin down. The cabaret singer Marie Sauvinet makes the mistake of falling for the upper-class Jean Gervais, who is in love with Cecilie Marshall. Understanding the situation, Marie moves to Paris, where she becomes an opera

3 Cockney japes in the British musical of 1944:
Lupino Lane's *Meet Me Victoria* had music by Noel Gay

diva, but eventually returns to America and rekindles her romance with Jean. She finally acknowledges that his feelings for Cecilie are eternal, and departs his life forever. When Jean dies on the battlefield of 1815 New Orleans, his two lovers unite in grief with the duet 'Time Is Standing Still'.

The components of the plot are not startlingly original. More than one operetta had brought down the curtain on a sad ending; Dorothy Donnelly and Romberg had done it in *The Student Prince*, refusing to give its lovers a blissful outcome. The death of *Sunny River*'s hero was another sadness for the audience to deal with, and one of its number during the brief London run must have been Ivor Novello (imagine him missing this opportunity to see a new Romberg–Hammerstein piece) who obviously liked *Sunny River* enough to remember it in his 1943 *Arc de Triomphe*. Novello's plot is a close cousin to Hammerstein's, and perhaps many another operetta before it. In *Arc de Triomphe* the heroine (another Marie) becomes a great opera diva, and her lover Pierre, finding success as a film star, revisits his love for Marie but sees that her life is now tied to that of her impresario. Pierre goes off to war and, like Jean in *Sunny River*, dies. Novello explained that *Arc de Triomphe* was loosely based on the life of the American diva Mary Garden; it is also based on *Sunny River*.

The last of the Romberg and Hammerstein collaborations, *Sunny River* spent most of its play looking back to musical theatre of the previous two decades, but in its opening was the suggestion of something more innovative. In lieu of a conventional orchestral medley of the show's principal melodies, the curtain went up on a 'Pictorial Overture', introducing a choreographed scene on Levee Street 1806, described as a 'Symphonic Pantomime'. Was this Romberg's idea, or Hammerstein's? When Rodgers and Hammerstein were preparing *Carousel* was it Rodgers who had the idea of starting the proceedings with the 'Carousel Waltz' or Hammerstein who said 'Dick, I did this thing with Romberg that we might try'? Further study of *Sunny River*'s score and libretto might reveal other points to show how the production may have been at the crossroads of American musical theatre. James Agate rated the piece as the best since Noel Coward's *Bitter Sweet* (London, 1929):

> ... the plot is not more nonsensical than any other [...] there is a complete absence of jazz or swing, the songs are sung, not crooned, and the singers have the voices to sing them [...] there is no tap-dancing [...] the piece keeps to its period and there is no low comedian to make gags about 'utility' trousers.[13]

One of *Sunny River*'s problems was its timing, placed as it was at the very centre of Britain's war. The wonder is that such a show managed to get to London at all. A note in the Piccadilly Theatre programme gives some ideas of the conditions it endured.

Warning of Air Raid will be given by a RED electric sign over the Orchestra

Pit. ALL CLEAR will be similarly shown in GREEN. Patrons are advised to remain in the Theatre, but those wishing to leave will be directed to the nearest official air raid shelter, after which the performance will be continuing for as long as is practicable. Should any news of particular interest be received during a performance it will be announced from the stage at the end of the succeeding scene or act of the play.

The other original American import of 1943 was more to the public's taste than Hammerstein and Romberg's tale of disappointed love. *Panama Hattie* had been a 1940 hit on Broadway, uniting Merman with Porter's songs as in *DuBarry Was a Lady*, and proved to be to London's liking. Producer Emile Littler mounted a new production, hiring the West End director of much light fare, William Mollison, backed by the choreography of Wendy Toye and the costumes of Norman Hartnell. The cast of London artists was headed by a Merman substitute in Texas-born Bebe Daniels, who had settled in Britain at the start of the war. The British felt that they 'knew' Daniels, who had sacrificed her Hollywood glamour to friendliness, being readily accessible in variety shows and with her husband Ben Lyon in the popular wartime wireless programme *Hi Gang!* Mollison had the advantage of a supporting cast that was familiar to the British: Max Wall, long unrecognised as a comic genius, and the less brilliant but endearing Claude Hulbert and Richard Hearne. Those two came trailing shows and styles of an earlier period, but Daniels was genuine war fabric. As the bombs fell, her career climbed.

Panama Hattie told the story of Hattie Maloney (Daniels), a nightclub owner in Panama, involved in an almost incomprehensible plot about German spies hoping to blow up the Panama Canal. Hattie falls for the rich divorcé Nick Bullett (Ivan Brandt), and has to win over Bullett's eight-year-old daughter Elizabeth, played by thirteen-year-old Betty Blackler from North London. On the first night (when the first half lasted over two hours) she and Daniels stopped the show with 'Let's Be Buddies', and there was another hit for Daniels in 'Make It Another Old Fashioned, Please'. The show was forced out of the Piccadilly Theatre by the doodlebugs (V-1 flying bombs) that rained on London for a few months from 13 June 1944, and began a long provincial tour.

In 1944 London heard the fourth Porter score of the war in *Something for the Boys*, which, given the timing, already sounded like a smash. There was a feeling that the long war was wrapping up, and those boys, for whom something would be made ready, were in sight of coming back and getting into civvies. Evelyn Dall bubbled in a profoundly silly plot that had begun as a story in *Reader's Digest*, its book so negligible that the theatre programme neglected to mention its authors. The only other offering was a revival of Sigmund Romberg's *The Student Prince* at the Stoll (evenings at 6.00 p.m. and four weekly matinees), with Bruce Trent, who had previously only played in *DuBarry Was a Lady* as Heidelberg's hero.[14] If there was a hint of new hope in the air, this had none. *The Times* reported 'a plentiful lack of humour [...] there are some stage entertainments which it is possible both to mock at and to enjoy. *The Student Prince*, prettily revived, is one of them.'[15] Originally presented at His Majesty's Theatre in 1926 as 'a Spectacular Light Opera', the work had been hailed by one critic as a 'hard, disarmingly efficient light opera [...] There are tenors with vibrant, gristly voices; sopranos with the zest of steam-syrens, whose more adventurous notes go in at one ear and play hell there before coming out at the other'.[16] In 1944, however, the *Daily Mail* applauded it as 'spacious, gracious, and wholly delightful'.[17] There was potency enough in *The Student Prince* to achieve almost 300 performances in a 1968 London revival.

Bebe Daniels *et al.* revived *Panama Hattie* for 100 performances at the Adelphi in January 1945 – the last wartime dose of Porter, on whom London had feasted since the start of the conflict, although the stuff had been pretty poor fare. There was a little more interest in the final revival of the war, *Irene*, directed by Mollison. Harry Tierney and Joseph McCarthy's score had first been heard in London a quarter of a century earlier, when the show had lasted a year with its original Broadway star Edith Day. Perhaps tiring of the stream of old works that London had tried to breathe new life into, *The Times* decided that 'The sentimental haze surrounding a musical comedy of 1920 is inevitably a trifle thin and uninviting', noting that 'the author of the book [James Montgomery], clutching at and entwining the Pygmalion and Cinderella themes, makes a game attempt to integrate a story with song and dance, failing, but failing heroically'.[18] James Agate asked his readers to 'Let this critic plead the triumph of Mr. Arthur Riscoe and Miss Pat Taylor over wretched material rather than report upon the wretchedness of that material',[19] while the *Evening Standard* pointed out that 'Irene is 25 years older and is not the girl she was.'[20] Nevertheless, it was Irene who saw out the American musical in London of the war years.

On 30 April 1945 Adolf Hitler committed suicide in Berlin, and the Third Reich collapsed. Victory in Europe was celebrated on 8 May. It may have seemed an opportunity for theatrical celebration, but despite pockets of relieved jubilation the nation seemed aware that the difficulties brought by the war were far from over. Diets made up of dried egg, cream concocted from margarine and vanilla, and Woolton Pie (a vegetable concoction held together by oats, topped with pastry and deputising as a meat pie), as well as the menus at the government's chain of British Restaurants – three courses for 9d – manned by such as the Women's Voluntary Service, had not weakened the public's dislike of the austere lifestyle that now settled on Britain. At least a visit to the theatre brought to the dullness of the British grind a dash of glamour, no matter how spurious. The play's the thing, yes, but a musical came with some sort of guarantee of colour and fun, and perhaps a new tune to whistle on the way home.

Might not the end of the war signal a time when the musical altered? Improved? Worked its way into the British consciousness as an art form? Offered something significant to its followers? Despite the popularity of Myra

4 Non-stop entertainment throughout the war at the 'We Never Closed' Windmill Theatre

Hess's piano recitals at the National Gallery, the war years had seen a falling-away of the role of 'serious' music. Sadler's Wells Ballet was hustled out of its Rosebery Avenue theatre and homeless bombed families moved in. At Covent Garden Opera House Wagner and Donizetti gave way to a dance hall. What did Mozart know about keeping up the spirits of a bombed Cockney? Vera Lynn and George Formby and the BBC's Light Programme knew better. The *Brains Trust*[21] regular C. E. M. Joad considered that 'the distinctive cultural expression of English genius during the years 1939 to 1941 [...] is light music'.[22] Yet there was not surprisingly a cultural abeyance in the air as the war came to its end, a reflection of what Britain itself was experiencing at what should have been a moment of monumental change. One of Mass-Observation's chroniclers, Nella Last, wrote that she felt

> as if I'd sat through a long and tedious play living only for the finale, longing for the time when I could breathe fresh sweet air, go home and do something more interesting and amusing. Instead as each player left the stage they disappeared and the lights gradually dimmed, till the last performer said 'That's all, you can go home now!' – and now the audience looked at each other uncertain of the next move – and they too, slowly dispersed.[23]

The first American post-war musical import was strangely appropriate in ways that cannot have been appreciated at the time. The musical that immediately followed the conflict into the West End, beckoning the way to a new era, was one that resolutely belonged to the war years. It was also last of a long line of knocked-up concoctions whose beginnings went back to the Edwardian era. Of course, what now happened to the American musical in London had its roots back on Broadway, but by 1947 an altered appreciation of what the musical might be would reach London. Meanwhile, while *Something for the Boys* had made its intentions clear, that last wartime show *Follow the Girls* was, well, something for the boys once again. Its cast list tells us something too, or reminds us of something we may not have noticed. It is made up of people who seem to be the audience's chums. It is as if those actors, those Pat Kirkwoods, Arthur Riscoes, Frances Days, those Richard Hearnes were on a rota, always around to be slotted into a new import in lieu of the original American performer. The end of war stopped all that. Look at any cast list after *Follow the Girls* and the casting has changed. Of course, younger performers were now able to pursue their careers once again, but there was a sea change in the way American musicals in London were cast.

For now, however, the old American musical was more or less shutting up shop with *Follow the Girls*, 'a new musical comedy' that had scored in New York, the produce of five authors, to which London added a further three in Fred Thompson, Con West and Frank Eyton's additional scenes and lyrics. This pointed to the fact that the producers realised that the material given Jackie Gleason on Broadway wouldn't do for London's Arthur Askey, that tiny bespectacled king of concert party. Askey, like his leading lady Evelyn Dall who had come to fame as a band singer with Ambrose, personified the war period; in these circumstances *Follow the Girls* was a sort of envoi. Askey had been so much part of the time, enormously popular on radio and starring in British film comedies such as *I Thank You* in which his chirpy antics were designed to lift the spirits of the beleaguered populace. Although he sustained a long career until his death, Askey's reputation, his technique, his attitude, belonged to the war years, as did Dall's sexual insouciance. It seems right that immediately *Follow the Girls* closed she went back to America.

The plot wasn't much: a striptease dancer called Bubbles LaMarr (Dall) who attracts the interest of a group of Royal Navy sailors visiting a naval base in Long Island, New Jersey, gets to perform at their serviceman's canteen. If that reads like a slack throw at burlesque, we may have it about right, but – even with the war receding – it was necessary fare, with so many years of rationing and privation still ahead of the British. As global hostility faded, British austerity flourished. *Follow the Girls* and the like answered a need. Brilliance was not attempted or achieved, but the musical was fulfilling its primary function, one from which it has never distanced itself – diversion. What other function could a musical serve?

No one was going to criticise *Follow the Girls* for what it had no need to be, but *The Times* sounded a warning that reverberates down all the years of American musicals in London. The show 'follows an American pattern without achieving American speed and slickness', and, more specifically 'Mr. Arthur Askey, in essence an English cockney clown, finds himself in what is, however much he may pretend to the contrary, an alien atmosphere.' Even Dall, 'vivacity in a band-box', was not well served, for she had 'a sense of humour which is held on a leash by the entire lack of it in the script'.[24]

When the war ended, the young woman who had stopped shelling peas on that September morning to listen to Mr Chamberlain confessing that his talks with the German Führer had failed and that as a result Britain was now at war with Germany, was six years older. A decade later, my mother travelled to London (quite an expedition in those days) to see two musicals that had been sent on from Broadway: *My Fair Lady* and *Bells Are Ringing*. The dash of theatrical excitement, *West End* type, must have been invigorating, but she subsequently barely spoke of her Lerner and Loewe experience, and she walked out of *Bells Are Ringing* at the interval. Perhaps she was bored, or didn't like the songs. Perhaps what she had seen on stage was simply too foreign, unrelated to the sort of life she and her countrymen were living. Although my intelligent mother may not have been aware of cultural niceties, she may have looked on and admired and been prepared to be entranced, only to draw back and ask, 'What has this to do with me?'

Perhaps, in its modest way, that is the question this book poses. It is simply an account, year by year, of a sort of Golden Age of American musicals that made it to the West End of London between 1945 and 1972, by which time the gold was all too apparently beginning to tarnish. Those years saw the main outpouring of the works of Richard Rodgers and Oscar Hammerstein, Jule Styne, Harold Rome, Jerry Herman, Jerry Bock and Sheldon Harnick, Harvey Schmidt and Tom Jones, Charles Strouse and Lee Adams, and others. The story of the London productions that straggled into the consciousness of British culture has not hitherto been told. Was their journey really necessary?

1939 Broadway Exports

DuBarry Was a Lady (408).

1939 Broadway Only

One of the most distinguished collaborations of the year was by Jerome Kern and Oscar Hammerstein II, ***Very Warm for May*** (59), directed by Vincente Minnelli. This was Kern's final Broadway musical, with Hammerstein's libretto thought the weaker component. Richard Rodgers and Lorenz Hart's *Too Many Girls* (249) was one of many shows of the period with a come-hither title tilted at male patrons. They might have liked the story too, something about football, and the score's one enduring hit 'I Didn't Know What Time It Was'. The fascination with Hollywood was at the centre of ***Stars in Your Eyes*** (127) with its Arthur

Schwartz – Dorothy Fields score. Buddy Ebsen, Lois January and Judy Canova lightened *Yokel Boy* (208), about a girl named January who dreams of becoming a movie star. In Hollywood, it is her childhood sweetheart who becomes the star, until both decide they much prefer mucking out on a New England farm. The short-runner of the year was *Swingin' the Dream* (13), a 'musical variation' of Shakespeare's *A Midsummer Night's Dream*. Less a book musical than a revue, the company included the Benny Goodman Sextet and Louis Armstrong as Bottom.

1940 Broadway Exports

Panama Hattie (501) and *Pal Joey* (374).

1940 Broadway Only

A sort of precursor to *Call Me Madam*, **Louisiana Purchase** (444) was a happy place for Irving Berlin's breezy songs. A bio-musical based on the life of Huey Long and the political history of Louisiana, the show was the only one of the three successes of the year to stay at home. *Cabin in the Sky* (156) had a fine Vernon Duke score, among the best numbers the title song and 'Taking a Chance on Love', but not surprisingly this celebration of Negro life in the deep South was not deemed transferable. Rodgers and Hart were back with **Higher and Higher** (108), another of their works almost unknown in Britain. Intended as a vehicle for the dancer Vera Zorina, Zorina didn't do it, her replacement proved less than stellar, and too much attention focused on one particular member of the supporting cast – a live seal.

    Hold on to Your Hats (158) could hardly have had a starrier cast, with Al Jolson, Martha Raye and Jack Whiting putting over such Burton Lane and E. Y. Harburg numbers such as 'Life Was Pie for the Pioneer' and 'Down on the Dude Ranch', completed by a selection of Al Jolson favourites. Another distinguished duo, Hoagy Carmichael (music) and Johnny Mercer (lyrics), contributed the score for *Walk with Music* (55). It had toured as *Three After Three*, then became *Ooh! What You Said* before settling on its Broadway title. It gave Hollywood star Mitzi Green the chance to do impressions of Greta Garbo and Fanny Brice. *Walk with Music* moved the critic Richard Lockridge to hope that 'Somebody will have to do something about the musical comedy book someday.'[25] The quickest failure of the year was *John Henry* (7), despite being a 'music drama' starring Paul Robeson.

1941 Broadway Exports

Lady in the Dark (467), *Let's Face It!* (547) and *Sunny River* (36).

1941 Broadway Only

The only long-running Broadway show of the year not to get a transfer, **Best Foot Forward** (326) was a happy-go-lucky affair befitting its youthful songs by Hugh Martin and Ralph Blane, heard again in the successful 1963 New York revival with Liza Minnelli. The rest of the 1941 productions quickly faded from memory. **High Kickers**, set in the world of burlesque, gave Sophie Tucker such numbers as 'Didn't Your Mother Tell You Nothing?', the indisputably appropriate 'I Got Something', and one of her biggest hits from earlier times, 'Some of These Days'. With such intelligent contributors as Vernon Duke and lyricist John Latouche, **Banjo Eyes** (126) could/should have been a shoe-in with Eddie Cantor's name on the marquee. The evening ended with a medley of Cantor's old hits. Robert Stolz, a toiler in the field of operetta, wrote the music for the fairly disastrous **Night of Love** (7).

1942 Broadway Exports

None.

1942 Broadway Only

The one commercially successful show of the year was **By Jupiter** (427), with the last Rodgers and Hart Broadway score. Rodgers and Hart wrote the book, too, about the conflict between the Amazons and Greeks; one of the most amusing Amazonians was played by the moon-faced British actress Bertha Belmore. Everything else on the calendar bombed. **Beat the Band** (68) resorted to a theatrical setting, with music by Johnny Green, while **Count Me In** (61) had one of those titles that critics make mincemeat of. It described itself as an 'All-American Musical Comedy' but seems to have been an interminable revue. The invitation sent out by **The Time, the Place, and the Girl** (13) wasn't taken up. **Once Over Lightly** (6) – actually six times lightly – and **You'll See Stars** (4) –nobody did – were the year's outright disasters. The first was an attempt at presenting Rossini's *The Barber of Seville* as an American musical, and the second a 'musical comedy' biography of Gus Edwards. **The Lady Comes Across** (3) was meant to introduce American audiences to Jessie Matthews, but opened with her substitute and closed at the end of the week.

1943 Broadway Exports

Something for the Boys (422) and **Oklahoma!** (2,212).

1943 Broadway Only

Two of the best works of the year were not seen in London until decades later, and then not in open-ended West End productions. *One Touch of Venus* (567) with its Kurt Weill–Ogden Nash score was a fantasy about a statue of Venus coming to life, and one of Weill's most delightful works. The show had an unexpected sequence about the British murderer Dr Crippen.[26] In Britain the play has been treated as opera rather than musical. As much is true of *Carmen Jones* (503), in which Hammerstein utilised Bizet's music in an updating of the story. But who now remembers *Early to Bed* (382) despite its year-long run and the music of Fats Waller? There was to be no afterlife for the first collaboration of Alan Jay Lerner and Frederick Loewe, *What's Up* (63), but it marked the start of one of the outstanding partnerships in American musical theatre. Loewe did not have a high opinion of the show, about an Eastern gentleman called the Rawa of Tanglinia who frolics in a girls' school. Briefly seen was *Hairpin Harmony* (3), the sole work of Harold Orlob. It billed as a musical farce and featured the all-female band the Hairpin Harmonettes and the Clawson Triplets.

1944 Broadway Exports

Follow the Girls (888), *Song of Norway* (860) and *On the Town* (462).

1944 Broadway Only

Mexican Hayride (481) didn't sound hopeful for Shaftesbury Avenue, but had a storming success in New York at a time when American audiences craved such inconsequence. It had a Cole Porter score, the last of his three collaborations with Herbert and Dorothy Fields, and the comedy of Bobby Clark (of the painted-on spectacles), and June Havoc to take it to success. Porter was unimpressed with the result. More refined and more successful was *Bloomer Girl* (657), with the songs of Harold Arlen and Yip Harburg. To some extent the show sat in the shadow of *Oklahoma!*, set as it was in America's Civil War past, complete with its own Agnes de Mille ballet. None of the other Arlen musicals (*You Said It*, 1931; *Life Begins at 8.40*, 1934; *Hooray For What!*, 1937; *St. Louis Woman*, 1946; *House of Flowers*, 1954; *Jamaica*, 1957; and *Saratoga*, 1959) made it to London.

   Sadie Thompson (60) was another Vernon Duke – Howard Dietz flop, based on Somerset Maugham's short story and the play *Rain*. June Havoc played Sadie, taking over from Ethel Merman who had departed the production during rehearsals. *Allah Be Praised!* had music by Don Walker and Baldwin Bergersen. *Jackpot* (69) – another of those ill-judged titles – was another disappointment for Duke and Dietz, despite Nanette Fabray and Betty Garrett at the top of the company.

1945 Broadway Exports
Carousel (890).

1945 Broadway Only

Only Rodgers and Hammerstein, the new leaders of American musical theatre, were sent to London from a year that showed the American musical theatre in a surprisingly agile condition. It might have heartened London to see Sigmund Romberg's *Up in Central Park* (504), although it suggested that American writers didn't think about the possibility of a London transfer when choosing their titles. The now forgotten *Are You With It?* (267) with music by Harry Revel and lyrics by Arnold B. Horwitt had a cast that included Joan Roberts and Dolores Gray. Kurt Weill's *The Firebrand of Florence* (43), its lyrics by Ira Gershwin, was billed as a musical, but it wasn't so much a musical as his *One Touch of Venus*. Don Walker was back as composer, with Clay Warnick, for *Memphis Bound* (36), a 'black musical' worked around *HMS Pinafore*, and indeed the score was really *by* Gilbert and Sullivan, artfully adapted for the occasion. It is not known what the management of the D'Oyly Carte Opera Company, who tightly controlled performances of the Gilbert and Sullivan operettas, thought of this. *Billion Dollar Baby* (220) had some of the credits necessary for a New York success: libretto by Betty Comden and Adolph Green, George Abbott as director, dances by Jerome Robbins, sets by Oliver Smith, costumes by Irene Sharaff. Its composer Morton Gould was less known.

Lerner and Loewe made their second attempt at a musical with *The Day Before Spring* (165). Loewe would be as disparaging about this as he had been about their previous effort, *What's Up*. The authors of *Polonaise* (113) played safe by adapting the music of Chopin for its songs. The result could hardly be other than a dated operetta, although it advertised itself as a musical. *Marinka* (165) *sounded* as if it might be an old operetta, and had music by Emmerich Kalman to confirm it. 'Treat a Woman Like a Drum' insisted one of its songs, but a decorous air hung about it. *A Lady Says Yes* (87) confusingly moved between 1945 and 1545, and between Venice, China and, finally, Washington DC. Set in a West Indian village, *Carib Song* (36) had a score by Baldwin Bergersen and his lyricist William Archibald. A 'romantic comedy with music' (quite a lot of it, by Robert Stolz), *Mr. Strauss Goes to Boston* (12), was a fantasy around the life of Johann Strauss.

1946

Song of Norway

A PICTURESQUE FANTASY on the life of Edvard Grieg, **Song of Norway** (Palace Theatre, 7 March 1946; 526) launched its creators, Robert Wright and George Forrest, into a catalogue of works that borrowed from classical composers. Perhaps because the Broadway production was still playing, Emile Littler's London edition was not a replica of the New York original, now directed by Charles Hickman, whose previous experience had been in British musicals and revues, and who would go on to another substantial West End success with *Annie Get Your Gun*. George Balanchine had devised the Broadway choreography, newly invented for London by Robert Helpmann, responsible for the Concerto Ballet and the 'Freddy and His Fiddle' sequence, and Pauline Grant, whose contributions included the Pillow Dance and the Peer Gynt Ballet. Lemuel Ayers' settings were replaced by those of Joan Jefferson Farjeon, and the costumes of Robert Davison by Frederic Dawson and Sophie Fedorovitch.

The idea of tying a composer's music to a necessarily fictionalised stage biography was not new, one of the most prominent being the Franz Schubert *Blossom Time* (known in Britain as *Lilac Time*). In London, Eric Maschwitz teamed with the composer Bernard Grun to give the treatment to Chopin (*Waltz Without End* in 1942) and Dvořák (*Summer Song* in 1956). Wright and Forrest enjoyed British success with *Song of Norway* and *Kismet*, but less luck with their only two original works seen in London, *The Love Doctor* and *Grand Hotel*. Only a year after *Oklahoma!* had been greeted as a genre-changing event on Broadway, *Song of Norway* turned the clock back to the most conventional operetta, reaching even beyond the recent example of Romberg and Hammerstein II's *Sunny River* of 1941, the Rudolf Friml-composed *The Blue Kitten* of 1925, and even Vincent Youmans' 1923 *Wildflower*. These were essentially operetta but made concessions to musical comedy, as in *The Blue Kitten*'s ragtimey 'Where the Honeymoon Alone Can See' and 'A Twelve O'Clock Girl in a Nine O'Clock Town'. *Kismet* would offer a respite from the operatic with Lalume's songs, but there was no space or reason for such abandon in *Song of Norway*.

The play followed the friendship between Grieg, his wife Nina Hagerup, and the poet Rikard Nordraak. Grieg's happy marriage is overturned when he is lured away by the diva Louisa Giovanni, but on the death of Nordraak Grieg hears again the call of his homeland and, inspired by his friend's poetry, writes the A Minor Piano Concerto, a piece that provided the crowning finale of the evening. All was melody, grace and stage splendour, with Grieg's melodies skilfully reconstructed in a score bestrided by the signature songs 'Now' and 'Strange Music'. The well-cooked hokum was served with dainty dialogue, much of it of the 'What a lovely tune! Who is that playing?' variety. Crucial to all was the resplendent orchestration of Arthur Kay and the voices, hoping to persuade

PALACE THEATRE

SHAFTESBURY AVENUE   :   LONDON, W.I

Under the Management of Tom Arnold and Emile Littler

General Manager: Francis H. Short

BOX OFFICE OPEN 10—7.30   Telephone: GERrard 6834-5

EMILE LITTLER'S

SONG OF NORWAY

Presented by arrangement with Chappell & Co., Ltd.

AN OPERETTA BASED ON THE LIFE AND MUSIC OF
EDVARD GRIEG

The choreography of the Concerto Ballet and Freddy and His Fiddle are by
ROBERT HELPMANN.   All other ballets, including the Pillow Dance and the
Peer Gynt Ballet are by PAULINE GRANT.

SYMPHONY ORCHESTRA CONDUCTED BY GIDEON FAGAN

THE OPERETTA DIRECTED by CHARLES HICKMAN

5   A question of taste? In 1946 *Song of Norway* inaugurated the London productions
involving Robert Wright and George Forrest: *Romany Love* (1947), *Kismet* (1955),
The Love Doctor (1959), *The Great Waltz* (1970) and *Grand Hotel* (1993)

audiences that they had been elevated to an operatic plane. Here was a work of concoction balanced with invention.

Wright and Forrest later claimed that the British production made unauthorised alterations to the script, music, lyrics and running order, although the sequence of numbers in the London programme matches that of the New York original. They could scarcely have complained about the British production values, or the casting. The burden fell on singers rather than actors, with many of the principals being brought in from Sadler's Wells Opera. Yorkshire-born Arthur Servent played Nordraak, John Hargreaves played Grieg, Halina Victoria played Nina and Janet Hamilton-Smith played Louisa. Thirteen years later Hamilton-Smith (who also had a singing career as Janet Bailey) would sing 'Bring Back the Axe' in the notorious John Osborne musical *The World of Paul Slickey*. The dancer and revue artist Moyra Fraser was the Spirit of Norway for the Concerto Ballet, with David Bor seated at the piano. Stephen Williams for the *Stage* noted the 'hysterical enthusiasm of its first night', proving that 'people still want [classical music] coated with sugar, sicklied o'er with a rosy cast of sentimentality and decorated as prettily as a Christmas card'. Furthermore, 'The humour is desperately poor, although it is only fair to add that the music is very skilfully arranged, and the inevitable pruning and juxtapositions are made with as much taste as possible.'[1] The production was remounted at the Palace in July 1949, when *Theatre World* announced that 'No outstanding singing or acting appears in the revival. An all round competence must be qualified by some regret that there is not just that little extra clarity in the singing which means so much to an audience.'[2] The revival was hustled out of the Palace to make way for Ivor Novello's *King Rhapsody*. As late as 1970 British audiences were flocking to such pre-war operettas as Drury Lane's *The Great Waltz*, exercising the music of Strauss (father and son) in a costume extravaganza that suggested the musical had not advanced a jot since *Song of Norway*.

It may seem depressing that even in 1970 audiences were turning out to see the sort of operetta flim-flam that had been around since the early days of the genre. In 1970, after all, audiences had much more choice, and the opportunity to be discerning, than had those in 1946. *Song of Norway* was the West End's first post-war operetta, and almost the last. Grieg's work provided ready-made lollipops that may or may not have played a part in the democratisation of classical music. Perhaps there was something 'classy' in the very use of such material, as there was in hiring Helpmann to turn choreography into ballet, and leading singers from Sadler's Wells Opera which itself was beginning to enjoy a revival of quality and interest. *Song of Norway* belonged with those who could accept the bridging of the gap between the classical and the popular, making classical music digestible and popular music respectable. The resulting concoction was ideal for consumption by those ready for middlebrow diversion at a time when cultural differentiation in Britain was, rather than being dismantled, perhaps being reinforced. This was the year when the BBC established the Third Programme, with aims and aesthetics that removed it from the more popular varieties of broadcasting. The lack of any other new product from America concentrated the public's mind, but rumours of the importance of the yet unseen in London *Oklahoma!* by the new teaming of Richard Rodgers and Oscar Hammerstein II, were circulating.

Meanwhile, it was the British musical that flourished (at least in quantity). One of the most interesting failures was ***Evangeline***, based on James Laver's novel, from which Cole Porter had fashioned his 1933 London success *Nymph Errant*. Now the British stage and screen star Frances Day played Evangeline Edwards, a role that had been taken in *Nymph Errant* by Gertrude Lawrence. Porter's score had contained some gems ('The Physician' and 'Solomon'), but for *Evangeline* Romney Brent's book and the songs of lyricist Eric Maschwitz and music of George Posford and Harry Jacobson were less memorable. Composer Vivian Ellis and librettist A. P. Herbert produced ***Big Ben***, a tribute to the fortitude of war-weary Londoners. The songs were gentle and literate, but it was only a mild success. Noel Gay, whose reputation as a composer of happy tunes was tied into the just-finished war, wrote the music for ***Sweetheart Mine***, presented, co-written by, and starring the comic Lauri Lupino Lane, hoping to repeat the luck of his pre-war hit *Me and My Girl*. Much was expected of Noel Coward's ***Pacific 1860***, written for the reopening of the beleaguered Theatre Royal, Drury Lane. Despite the exotic settings and America's Mary Martin as leading lady, there was no disguising a grave disappointment.

1946 Broadway Exports

Annie Get Your Gun (1,147) and ***Lute Song*** (142). ***Gypsy Lady*** (79) subsequently played London as ***Romany Love***.

1946 Broadway Only

A lively Broadway scene produced three exports, only one of which would have British success. The New York stay-at-homes were undistinguished except for ***St. Louis Woman*** (113), with Pearl Bailey as Butterfly singing Johnny Mercer lyrics to Harold Arlen melodies. ***Nellie Bly*** (16) celebrated the life of a dauntless daughter of America who wanted to better Phineas Fogg's eighty-day trip around the world as charted by Jules Verne; Nellie managed it in seventy-eight. The quickest casualty was ***The Duchess Misbehaves*** (5) which lost its leading man *en route* to Broadway. The hero forgot himself and imagined he was Goya; the plot recalled that of *DuBarry Was a Lady*. Orson Welles tried to outdo Nellie Bly by writing the book of ***Around the World in Eighty Days*** (75) and starring in it, but the scenic diversions could not compensate for a poor Cole Porter score. ***Park Avenue*** (72) struck more sophisticated notes, some of them sung by the British leads Leonora Corbett and Arthur Margetson in the score by Arthur

Schwartz and his lyricist Ira Gershwin (his last Broadway assignment). Based on the Cinderella story and set in the Kingdom of Nicely, *If the Shoe Fits* (20) made no impact. *Toplitzky of Notre Dame* (60) didn't sound tailor-made for the West End, and Broadway rejected this tale of Irish shenanigans in which an angel intervenes in the fortune of a football team. In its modest way, this foreshadowed the plot of *Damn Yankees*. The rest of the year offered regurgitation of old pieces, including the British *The Beggar's Opera*, now disguised as *Beggar's Holiday* (108) with Alfred Drake as a new-age gangster Macheath. Richard Tauber had a brief voice-troubled dalliance with *Yours is My Heart* (36), a version of Franz Lehár's *The Land of Smiles*.

6 Although doomed to failure in the West End in the wake of *Oklahoma!*, in 1947 the political whimsy *Finian's Rainbow* had one of the strongest scores of the post-war years

1947

Romany Love
Oklahoma!
Annie Get Your Gun
Finian's Rainbow

T HE RELIEF OF VICTORY IN EUROPE may have marked an immediate post-war euphoria in Britain, but that joyful spirit was quickly tempered by an awareness that for years to come the country would be paying for its participation in the conflict. Clothes would continue to be rationed until 1949; in June 1947 newspapers were restricted to a maximum of four pages; in September that year the taking of foreign holidays became illegal; and in an effort to save coal the government cut train services by 10%. In the age of domestic austerity, the cook Marguerite Patten would have blinked at the mention of 'quiches', then known as 'flans'. In his BBC TV *Cookery* series Philip Harben did his best to bring back enthusiasm to the kitchen, perhaps utilising the official fish of the day, the unappetisingly oily snoek. Writing in her diary kept for Mass-Observation in December 1947, Wembley housewife Rose Uttin's list of provisions made miserable reading: '1 oz of bacon per week – 3 lbs potatoes [they had been rationed only that year] – 2 ozs butter – 3 ozs marge – 1 oz cooking fat – 2 ozs cheese and 1 oz meat – 1 lb jam or marmalade per month – 1 lb bread per day ... My dinner today 2 sausages which tasted like wet bread with sage added – mashed potato – tomato – 1 cube cheese and 1 slice bread and butter.'[1] On being shown the stipulated amount of food available to British citizens, Winston Churchill pronounced it quite adequate for a day, only to be told that he was looking at the weekly amount.

Radio, the cinema and the slowly increasing availability of televisions tried to brighten the bleakness. The BBC's television transmission had been closed at the outbreak of war (at the time Mickey Mouse had been half-way through a cartoon); transmission was resumed on 7 June 1946; that afternoon those tuning in could see preparations in the Mall for the next day's Victory Parade. The significance was hardly universal, for transmission only worked within a 40-mile radius of Alexandra Palace. Viewers were offered ersatz glamour as Bobby and Sally Ann Howes introduced their guests on the BBC's *Café Continental*. The cinema promoted escapism in various forms from the Ealing's *Hue and Cry* set in the dilapidated ruins of war-torn London, the Archers' story of frustrated nuns *Black Narcissus*, the compendium *Holiday Camp* suggesting that Britain was at play in one great Butlins, and the gritty drama of *Brighton Rock* and *It Always Rains on Sunday*. The latter had Googie Withers as a sexually frustrated housewife ground down by the dullness of her existence against a setting of provincial rain-spattered streets, defunct air-raid shelters and muddy shunting-yards, with not even a glimmer of the shoddy gangster romance of *Brighton Rock*.

The rain on Sunday was an urban myth consolidated in Tony Hancock's 'Sunday afternoon' episode of his radio series *Hancock's Half Hour* eleven years later. This perception of Britain as a monochrome wasteland of ennui endured at least until the end of the 1950s; the enervating atmosphere of boredom, restriction, lack of money or choice – the perpetual sense of a grey sky glowering over post-war Britain that in 1940 George Orwell had linked to 'gloomy Sundays'.[2] In such circumstances, it seemed inevitable that the public would look to musical comedy to alleviate the general depression, although London theatre was now available almost exclusively to a metropolitan rather than cosmopolitan audience.

Fast on the heels of their previous year's *Song of Norway* and after a seven-week season in Manchester came **Romany Love** (His Majesty's Theatre, 7 March 1947; 90), another operetta with a score by Robert Wright and George Forrest fashioned from the music of Victor Herbert, notably taken from *The Fortune Teller* and *The Serenade*. With its book by Henry Myers, this had played Broadway in 1946 as *Gypsy Lady*, when *Theatre World*'s American correspondent E. Mawby Green complained that 'the new 1946 book is as dated as anything written fifty years ago and hangs like a millstone, making every joy sag'. What was more, the company's 'singing ability is quite limited and when they are not singing *Gypsy Lady* has a semi-professional air, just a notch or two above the performances given by English operetta societies'.[3] Despite its short stay in New York, impresario Jack Hylton brought the production to London with its original Broadway principals headed by Helena Bliss and Melville Cooper, now directed by William Mollison. There was nothing fresh in its story, set in Paris around the turn of the century, of the attractive gypsy Musetta (Bliss) who longs to be a lady, and is taken up for 'pygmalioning' by the actor Alvardo (John Tyers). In her new guise she conquers Paris and captures the heart of a duke's son before the lure of the caravans overcomes her and she returns to the arms of a gypsy lover. All agreed that every colour had been thrown into its mixing. 'This new American importation improves as it progresses,' reported the *Stage*. 'The opening is not too bright, but later one feels there is everything that one wants in an operetta-comedy, and that everything of the best.'[4] Of the songs, 'Springtide' was thought the most attractive, but by the end of May *Romany Love* had been replaced by the successful play *Edward, My Son*.

A few days before Rodgers and Hammerstein's first musical opened at Drury Lane, C. B. Cochran's production of A. P. Herbert and Vivian Ellis's second British musical *Bless the Bride* opened at the Adelphi Theatre. The difference between the British and American product could hardly have been more stark. The Adelphi offered a gentle valentine, a pastiche dedicated to the country's Victorian past, with occasional excursions to a France inhabited by its heart-throb leading man Georges Guétary. A. E. Wilson recognised 'the usual stuff of operetta'[5] not as a negative criticism but recommendation, and in this vein the critics and public welcomed such fulsome entertainment. Following on their modern-day *Big Ben*, the occasion seemed to mark a regression in the writers' attitude, and for inspiration Ellis turned to the work of his composer-grandmother Julia Woolf ('the Ethel Smyth of her day'),[6] notably her music for the 1888 operetta *Carina*. Woolf's music was dispensed with a charm that found its way into most of Ellis's output, in which the vigour that was very shortly to explode on stage at Drury Lane was not apparent.

An abandonment of decorum was also lacking in *Bless the Bride*, always teetering on the edge of gentility. *Bless the Bride* has shreds of academia about it, tatters of condescension, and the soon-to-be-degraded flag of Empire rule fluttered around its story of conflict between the British and French. The show seemed fashioned for a literate middle class whose occupations included occasional forays into musical theatre. It was culturally specific in its setting, too, locked into the period it fastened on, in a way that the Drury Lane show was not. It didn't matter that at Drury Lane the boys wore cowboy costumes and the girls danced in gingham; what was happening on stage was happening at that moment in some sort of timeless zone, in a way the action of *Bless the Bride* never was. The simplicity of vision of the American contender was beyond the comprehension of Herbert and Ellis. Herbert's book and lyrics were cluttered by his erudite wisdoms, his passions for Parliament, canals, reforming the Divorce Law, his achievements as novelist and revue writer, undoubtedly coloured by his education at Winchester and Oxford, and being called to the bar. Such an inspired campaigner on social issues, and eminent contributor to *Punch*, could only be a visitor to the hardened world of show-business to which Hammerstein belonged.

The actor Edward Fox recalls being taken as a young boy to the first night of **Oklahoma!** (Theatre Royal, Drury Lane, 30 April 1947; 1,548) by his parents, and his father's passionate outburst that 'This is exactly what we needed. This will lift the country's spirits and we can begin again.'[7] It is difficult to imagine such a vivid reaction to subsequent American musicals. Audiences at the British premiere of *West Side Story* would not have responded with such visceral fervour; Bernstein's piece may have been what the musical needed, but it could hardly be said to reinvigorate a sense of public being as did Rodgers and Hammerstein's first work. The timing of the British *Oklahoma!* was perfect, as if something brilliant and startling had strolled uninvited into a room crammed with dullness. The immediate post-war supply of musicals in London promised no greatness. With a little stroke of brilliance Ivor Novello had instigated his own celebration of conquest over the enemy, *Perchance to Dream*, just over two weeks ahead of the official Victory in Europe proclamation on 8 May 1945. Between this and the arrival of Rodgers and Hammerstein's usurper there had been much retreading of well-trodden paths. In June the first post-war proper musical was a British romance, *Sweet Yesterday*, mellifluously offering the husband-and-wife team of

Ann Ziegler and Webster Booth. The other offerings of the year suggested that farceurs were as much responsible for musicals as composers or lyricists. Britain provided in October *Big Boy* (an obvious reference to its sizeable comedian Fred Emney) and the following month *Under the Counter* in which Cicely Courtneidge extracted fun (but few memorable songs) from a piece that guided audiences into the prolonged era of austerity that peace had delivered them into, while the American *Follow the Girls* seemed little more than warmed-over wartime nonsense.

In the early spring of 1947 Manchester was the chosen location for an alien invasion that had been threatening since March 1943 when *Oklahoma!* premiered in New York. Now the Manchester Opera House was staging the British premiere ahead of its London opening. The usual fate of American musicals in London was to have an all-British cast. Think of the implications: Bruce Trent as that cowboy rhapsodising on the beauty of the Oklahoma morning, one of the favourite comics of the day Bobby Howes as the pedlar Ali Hakim, and Bobby's daughter Sally Ann Howes as Laurey. Then there were any number of soubrettish British actresses willing to provide the West End Ado Annie: surely Pat Kirkwood could have kept the curtain up, or Frances Day, or Evelyn Dall? The war years had been fond of such casting, some of it out of necessity; blame the times, not the producers. But something very different was happening in Manchester; the producers didn't want established names to bring their own personalities to bear on the show as Howes, Kirkwood and Day would have, and in the spirit of the just-ended war, the Yanks were coming.

The production company, H. M. Tennent Ltd., wisely held out for their arrival. Today Tennent is mostly remembered as the British establishment's producer of straight plays, but this most conservative of managements played a significant role in the post-war American musical in London, as did the man sent to London to restage the original New York production of *Oklahoma!*, Jerome Whyte. His is one of the many names that will often appear in these pages, for he was unofficially the emissary of Broadway musicals, entrusted with putting replicas of a New York show on to the West End stage, and content to take a credit inferior to that of the absent original director. This was often the way of the London productions; the American director – in the case of *Oklahoma!*, Rouben Mamoulian – stayed home while his deputy travelled to London to reproduce what had happened on Broadway, and Agnes de Mille put her feet up in New York while her stand-in Gemze DeLappe made sure London audiences saw the dances de Mille had created. The most *un*usual thing about *Oklahoma!* was that the Americans were coming to show everyone how it was done. They weren't star names. In America Harold, before he became Howard, Keel, had been third take over for the male lead; Betty Jane Watson had been the first takeover Laurey; Dorothea MacFarland had been the third Ado Annie (the second, Bonita Primrose, was to have her brief success in London in the British *Summer Song* nine years later).

On the face of it, Britain was sent a company of take-overs. It was, and the second-hand was something that those attending American musicals in Britain often had to accept in the years to come. Luckily, there was something about the potency of *Oklahoma!* that made this unimportant. This never was and never would be a star vehicle. When you think *Oklahoma!*, you don't think artists' names, you think Rodgers and Hammerstein. As future productions in Britain would attest, putting 'names' into it was a pointless exercise. It didn't matter that subsequently Rodgers and Hammerstein veered towards star vehicles. *Oklahoma!* operates in a totally different sphere, where ensemble is paramount.

Back in Manchester the first night of the provincial tour was cancelled because eight of the principals had still not arrived in town. Their freighter was located at Dungeness, so a tug was sent to rescue them. The next day they were packed into fast cars and driven to the theatre, opening that night although still registered as aliens. A first priority was to present them with ration books, their welcome to Austerity Britain. They can hardly have realised that some of the jubilation with which they would be greeted was a reaction to that very austerity, and to the weather. A severe winter bit at the end of January. Heavy snowdrifts seriously disrupted travel by road and rail. Power stations closed down because they could not get supplies of coal, which itself was in short supply. Electricity supplies throughout Britain were restricted and cut, television transmission was suspended, newspapers were forced to print less pages, and there were concerns about national food shortages so extreme that the Minister of Fuel and Power, Emanuel Shinwell, had police protection after receiving death threats. When the snow thawed, it brought floods. With *Oklahoma!* there were issues with British Equity, who often in the future would raise difficulties about incoming American artists taking roles that might have been played by the British. If things hadn't gone so well the Howes and Kirkwood might have been rushed to Manchester to take over. Realistically, one can't see any of the British dependables who had kept musicals going through the war being involved in what was a landmark event.

Sixty years on, we may still see *Oklahoma!* as a breakthrough musical, but perhaps in the sense of breaking through its time rather than as an innovative work. The *title* was innovative. American musicals had celebrated various states in their titles before (*Texas, L'il Darlin'* and *Louisiana Purchase* to name two) but no one had dared put the state's name *solus* up in lights. Imagine British musicals calling themselves *Surrey!* or *Essex!* And the show itself *was* innovative in the way it gathered together components of musical theatre and in the manner of its presentation. It was a matter of melding rather than invention, more a harvest festival than a sowing, and there is the possibility that too much has been made of the integrity Rodgers and Hammerstein brought to it.

It is most likely that the first most integrated musical plays originated with Offenbach in France and Gilbert and Sullivan in Britain. What is there not integrated about Offenbach's comic operas? They are not interrupted by irrelevancies or contaminated by inconsistency. We can't tell if this was true of Gilbert and Sullivan's initial effort *Thespis*, as score and libretto have been lost, but their second, the one-acter *Trial by Jury*, sets the Gilbertian style to which Sullivan responded that remains intact throughout the whole of their partnership. It is only the wash of absurdity, the topsy-turvydom, of Gilbert's libretto that obscures the fact that these are totally integrated works where characterisation is paramount, low comedy disallowed, scenic diversion demoted to a minimum; simply, Gilbert adopts a truth, and follows it. Here, there is no gap between drama and comedy, but a clear path, made the more probable because the plays mostly (except for *Princess Ida*) have only two settings, one for each act, confining the author to bring his action to the centre. This puts a constraint on the extraneous, which is fine by Gilbert as he never allows it. There has to be a reason for what he shows us on stage.

Consider *Patience*, an entertainment based on the cult surrounding Oscar Wilde and the nineteenth-century aesthetes. There is, of course, a plot, without which any librettist can hardly make bricks, and this, obviously, is present in *Oklahoma!*, although Gilbert's is perhaps the richer-patterned. A plot leads to characters, in whom Gilbert took a sharp, perhaps even peculiar, interest. In *Patience* we do not so much get characters as their characteristics. Even after a first scene we could probably list some of them, besides notes on their respective histories, so strikingly are they conveyed. Take the heroine: a milkmaid, humble but forthright and determined, who we learn owed much of her upbringing to an aunt. Patience has no time for the folderols of poetry or high aesthetics, but hers is a sharp intelligence which realises the demands of duty. She seems able to control her emotions, prescribing whom she will love.

Then there is Bunthorne, the cynosure of the twenty lovesick maidens who follow him about and fawn to have him recite his pretentious verses. He is the archetypal Victorian poser, knowingly putting on, practising artifice, presenting himself as something he is essentially not, and revelling in the cult of his celebrity. If we doubt the sincerity of this personality we have it confirmed by his next entrance, shiftily made when he is confident of being alone, when he admits to being an 'aesthetic sham'. Like many of the other characters in *Patience* Bunthorne is quite a complex character, with a public and private side. The same is true of Lady Jane, weighed down by middle age and seemingly unattractive and unimaginative but capable of deep feeling; there is a sort of justice that it is she finally who wins the hand of the handsome young soldier eager to find a bride. Grosvenor, Bunthorne's archenemy, who eventually transforms into an everyday, common (in every British sense) young man, has two sides too: the public and private, explained most blatantly when he begs those clamouring lovesick maidens to allow him a half-day holiday. The argument doesn't have to be limited to *Patience* either; Gilbert's librettos are full of rounded characters of depth.

Revert to the characters of *Oklahoma!* and take up your pen to make notes on Hammerstein's characters, or those characters that Hammerstein borrowed from Lynn Riggs' original play *Green Grow the Lilacs.* What does Hammerstein tell us about them, what do we know of them, what do we understand of them from the information we are given? We can see that Curly is a cowboy with fine descriptive powers, poetic in his appreciation of a field of corn, and with eyes for Laurey. By the end of the show we don't really know a lot more. We may not need to know much more, either; this, after all, is a musical play. Nevertheless, what sort of man is he? We don't know, although we suspect he's good to his mother, but there's no reason to bring her into it. Perhaps the only glimpse we get into the man is when he invades Jud's shack and conjures up a vision of what it will be like when Jud is dead. In some ways it's an understandable outburst against a man who lives with the rats and behaves like one and has an unhealthy interest in Laurey, and Curly, somehow perceiving the pathological faults of his pathetic work-mate, fires up his tirade. But is his treatment of Jud a tad cruel? It's not a trait we would casually accuse him of, for Hammerstein makes him (along with most of the other characters) inoffensive. We are disarmed, really, by the fact that some of these characters don't have many characteristics. Could it be that Curly and Laurey are little more than the standard young lovers of operetta?

Laurey? We don't get to know much about her either. Why is she with her Aunt Eller? What does she think about, except hoping to settle down one day with a decent man? What on earth would there be to talk about if one were left alone in a room with her? She seems to have no sort of history; she makes entrances and exits and sings songs. Remember that the original thought was that Mary Martin would play Laurey, and Shirley Temple was also in the frame, but neither would have given the part a second glance if it was as we have it now. *Oklahoma!* would have been put out of joint by their inclusion, as would *Carousel.* Only when Rodgers and Hammerstein began thinking around star performances did the sense of ensemble that had permeated their first two works fade. It isn't there in *South Pacific* or *The King and I* and the only reason why *Flower Drum Song* is something of an ensemble work is that it didn't start off with big names. It's all changed by the time the team winds up in *The Sound of Music* – Mary Martin again. At which point it doesn't surprise us that the Elsa Schraeder doesn't get good numbers, or at least numbers you'll be humming on the way home. She gets character stuff to sing, whereas Martin wanted hit songs, and Rodgers and Hammerstein had to oblige.

Back in Manchester, did that first night audience get close to Aunt Ella, an old woman happy to sit in the sun churning butter, and broadminded enough not to have a fit of the vapours when she looks into a kaleidoscope that Will has brought back from wicked Kansas? Buddha-like, Aunt Ella is all-understanding, autumnal in her perception, and quite able to put down any upset between those farmers and cowmen. Surprisingly, we learn and care most about two of the characters of whom we might not have expected such knowledge: Jud and Ali Hakim.

Hakim seems more able to create a reality than the duo with whom he mostly shares the stage, Ado Annie and Will, who every so often are obliged to break into song and dance. In some ways, of course, those are the moments when we start to learn rather more about them; certainly more than we learn when Curly and Laurey sing. Yes, there is some learning to be done about Curly through 'The Surrey with the Fringe on Top', but what cowboy ever waxed so lyrical or with such generalisation as in 'Oh, What a Beautiful Mornin''? This is Hammerstein speaking, not Curly, but nevertheless the trick works, as Hammerstein knew it would. Anyway, Hammerstein was indebted to much of this poesy to *Green Grow the Lilacs*:

> My indebtedness to Mr. Riggs' description is obvious. The cattle and the corn and the golden haze on the meadow are all there. I added some observations of my own based on my experiences with beautiful mornings, and I brought the words down to the more primitive poetic level of Curly's character. He is, after all, just a cowboy and not a playwright.

When Laurey joins Curly for 'People Will Say We're In Love', isn't this the sort of number that Romberg or Friml would have been delighted to have in one of their operettas of decades earlier? Close your eyes and you are retreading Jerome Kern and Hammerstein's 'Make Believe' from the 1927 *Show Boat*. It's all very well that Hammerstein deprecatingly referred to himself as the 'dope' who had written *Sunny River* with Romberg only two years before *Oklahoma!*, but the two works were not so far apart as we may imagine. The sedate open air floats around both.

Jud, of course, is the blackness in *Oklahoma!*'s heart. At first it seems it's going to be a walk-on part. A few gruff words, a few scowls, but as the piece develops, the unpleasantness intensifies. It has a sort of climax even at the end of Act One, when Laurey finds herself ensnared by Jud in the Dream Ballet. This is Hammerstein and Rodgers' *Madame Butterfly* moment, the end of Puccini's first act, when our knowledge that she and Lieutenant Pinkerton are about to make love is irredeemably darkened by the plunging orchestration. By then we know rather more about Jud because Hammerstein turns the trick by letting us into Jud's smoke house, and getting him to sing 'Lonely Room'. It's another one of Rodgers and Hammerstein's that you won't be singing on the bus, but it *tells* us. There is something real about Jud; not nice to know about, but real. He is the baddie, but a disfigured personality, one we can feel some sympathy for. His end, at if not by Curly's hand, comes swiftly just before the final curtain, and even then he is decorously taken off stage before dying. The canker removed, it is time for Curly to lead the company in a hymn of praise to the state in which they live; as someone on the production team had said to Hammerstein during the show's preparation, 'What it needs is a song about the land.'

The first night of *Oklahoma!* at Drury Lane was the first genuine sensation of our period. Youth, vitality, the simplicity of the plot, the ordinariness of the characters, the splendidly packaged songs that have retained their freshness for over half a century. A. E. Wilson wrote that

> There was such a hurricane of cheering at the end of *Oklahoma!* at Drury Lane that it seemed as if nothing less than an encore of the complete show would still it [...] The production lacked the elaborate spectacle and scenery expected at Drury Lane but who missed that when in the music by Richard Rodgers there was such tuneful delight, when there were such fresh young voices to sing it and such graceful dancing? [...] by right every member of the company should be named because this was a triumph not of stars but of a perfect ensemble and harmonious team work.[8]

James Agate in *The Times* did not agree, noting

> a whole merchant's venture in shadow without any hint of substance. The converse of the fairy tale about the Emperor's new clothes. Crates and panniers crammed with more samites and sarcenets than Ben Jonson himself could have found names for, but no emperor [although] I doubt very much whether a musical-comedy audience has any interest in the psychology of cowboys, the sex problems of six-footers, and the kind and diversity of desire under Oklahoma's elms.[9]

W. A. Darlington for the *Daily Telegraph* enthused over

> A terrific show. For drive and vitality I do not remember to have seen anything to beat it. Yet in plan it is completely simple [...] It must be conceded, I think, that the American theatre does this kind of thing better than ours. The complete precision of *Oklahoma!*, the utter clearness with which every syllable of the songs as well as the dialogue comes over, is something that our own directors would do well to imitate. The company has the homogeneity of an orchestra or a team of acrobats.[10]

Three years later, when the West End production closed, Beverley Baxter MP reminded the readers of *Everybody's* of the show's first night, in a piece titled 'Goodbye to *Oklahoma!*'.

> You must remember how weary and disillusioned we were at that time. We had passed from the war of the scorched earth to a parched peace. We were under-nourished, over-taxed, ill-clad, badgered and bothered by endless regulations; and we were tired. Then suddenly on the stage we saw vibrant youth, and felt the thrill of the open plains [...] To us in this blessed but beleaguered island there was a sub-conscious realisation of the unbounded, unexpanded vitality of this new world-power, the United States of America. *Oklahoma!* was more than a theatrical production. It was a symbol.[11]

The visual impact of *Oklahoma!* was a vital element of its success, noted by the *Stage* review of the Manchester premiere, described as 'sweetly sentimental [...] in a land of luscious cowboys and chocolate-box farmers' daughters against scenic backgrounds of the kind popular in childrens' books – the primary colours dazzling the eyes and raising the spirits to heights of enthusiasm.'[12] And once in London, the *Stage* reported 'no London production of recent years has brought to the boards a prettier group of girls or a more virile and good-looking group of men.' In all, the cast showed 'a degree of concentration that must be almost unprecedented on the London stage. Principals and chorus sing as though their whole previous lives had been merely a preparation for this supreme moment.'[13] How much of this thrill was still in place by the time the production moved (offering popular prices) to the Stoll Theatre in May 1950, with Stokely Gray as Curly and Gwen Overton as Laurey, is unknown.

A few weeks after the opening of *Oklahoma!* the American assault was reinforced by **Annie Get Your Gun** (Coliseum, 7 June 1947; 1,304), enjoying a success that many felt rivalled that of *Oklahoma!*, and outliving the Broadway run by 157 performances. The first-night reception for the new piece probably outdid that for the Rodgers and Hammerstein (who had presented *Annie Get Your Gun* in New York), but these were very different events. *Oklahoma!* was essentially an apparently innovative ensemble work that eschewed stars; *Annie Get Your Gun* used tried and tested Broadway techniques, and made no pretence of building itself around its female lead. In New York Ethel Merman's Annie Oakley had already almost passed into legend; for London, the little-known American Dolores Gray was elected. Impresario Emile Littler had never met Gray before she arrived in London with her manager-mother, brother and a Persian cat called Scheherazade (and subsequently Michael, a French poodle). Gray was to be the first post-war American musical star to establish herself in London; telling the first night audience that it was her twenty-third birthday they erupted into 'Happy Birthday'. 'Men Stand in Their Seats and Shout "You're wonderful"' headlined the *Recorder*, celebrating 'The Girl Who Has Brought "Stage Door Johnnies" back to London'.[14] The *Weekly Sporting Review* ran with 'London hails Dolores Gray in Finest Musical Ever'.[15] At least one reviewer considered that Gray and her leading man Bill Johnson were 'mishandled by director Helen Tamaris. Miss Gray in particular is put to great disadvantage by being obliged to walk like a rheumatic platypus, this as a reminder of the hick origins of Annie, and to assume the expression of a young heifer whenever her boy-friend comes in view.'[16]

Two weeks after Gray's opening night Eric Maschwitz's letter in the *Sunday Times* was an early warning of what might be happening to the American musical.

> Beginning with *Oklahoma!* a group of brilliant American producers reacted away from the Vienesse sugar-plums, the French pastry, the

7 London in the immediate post-war period made stars of its visiting American leading ladies, not least Dolores Gray in Irving Berlin's high-shooting *Annie Get Your Gun* (1947)

meaningless songs and vapid cut-to-measure stories of conventional musical comedy. Taking mostly American history for their theme, they contrived plays of character and action, introduced songs which continued the story and ballets which pointed the moral, recruited directors from the 'legitimate' theatre to give polish to dialogue and action. This genre having captivated Broadway for the past four years, there are already indications that it is becoming exhausted by imitation.[17]

Exhausted by imitation? *Annie Get Your Gun* was scarcely that, even if Anthony Cookman in *Tatler and Bystander* wrote that 'It has been acclaimed as the equal of *Oklahoma!*, but though its lyrics are at least as good and it has oodles of punch and exuberance it still lacks the extreme polish.'[18] The *New Statesman* had no doubt:

> Is *Annie Get Your Gun* a second *Oklahoma*? Emphatically not. Neither the polished production, nor the calculated freshness of décor, but a long, lavish show livelier than most of its sort because the music is by Irving Berlin, though this is interspersed with an intolerable deal of talk. A spectacular ballet excited the Coliseum to strange rapture.[19]

Ted Willis's review for the *Daily Worker* (headlined 'Not Up to *Oklahoma!*') decided

> Though this latest American musical tops the best British show of its kind it doesn't stand knee high to *Oklahoma!* which will probably retain its place as the liveliest and most original musical play until *Finian's Rainbow* gets here in the Autumn [...] This one misses all the opportunities that Rodgers and Hammerstein took so brilliantly in *Oklahoma!* and returns to something like the old formula.[20]

That 'old formula', and any number of variations on it, would be revisited countless times in the next half century, all too often without the benefit of such a rich score as Berlin provided. Berlin himself followed *Annie Get Your Gun* into London with another uncompromisingly formulaic piece built around a female star, *Call Me Madam*, once again written for Merman but re-enacted in the West End by another. Despite their various felicities, none of the actresses playing Annie in London revivals established themselves in the audience's affections as did Gray: Suzi Quatro in 1987, Kim Criswell in 1992 and Jane Horrocks in 2009.

It was perhaps appropriate that when the very final curtain fell on the last night of the show, it rose to speeches and then the company singing the title song from *Oklahoma!* According to the impresario Emile Littler, his principal artists had done more for the promotion of goodwill between England and America in the previous three years than any politician. Remarkably, its two leads had played the entire run. When after half an hour of applause the audience still refused to leave, Gray asked that the curtain be taken up again. The set had already been struck; the stage was bare. Gray and Johnson sang 'They Say It's Wonderful', and their love affair with the British public was over.

Finian's Rainbow (Palace Theatre, 21 October 1947; 55) had the misfortune to follow hard on the heels of *Oklahoma!* and *Annie Get Your Gun*, and the comparisons made by the British critics were not agreeable. Expectation was high, and the word from Broadway (where the still-running show had opened in January) encouraging, but the show's collapse was sure and quick. There was the view that the newcomer lacked the vigorous youth of *Oklahoma!* and the dominant female of *Annie*. The linear quality of its two precursors contrasted strongly with the components that made up *Finian's Rainbow*. A musical swathed in the fey, the whimsical, sporting its own leprechaun, and then assaulting the audience with political satire (*American* political satire at that, very little to do with a Britain empowering a Labour government under Prime Minister Clement Attlee) and a realisation of America's racial bigotry. It was a lot to take on after Curly's *aubade* of a weather forecast and after Miss Oakley had shot from the hip with Berlin's uncomplicated songs. Had the musical with message arrived? Were British audiences now to deal with America's social consciousness? If so, Britain was about to return to sender.

Finian's Rainbow was to be a rare show-up in London for its writers, composer Burton Lane and book writers Fred Saidy and E. Y. (Yip) Harburg (who also served as lyricist). There would be no West End production for Lane's 1940 musical *Hold On to Your Hats* or his collaborations with Alan Jay Lerner, *On a Clear Day You Can See Forever*, or *Carmelina*. As for Harburg, none of his other contributions to American musicals made it to Britain; these included *Bloomer Girl* and *Jamaica* (both composed by Harold Arlen, with Saidy as co-librettist), *Flahooley* (music by Sammy Fain, lyrics by Harburg who also collaborated with Saidy on the book), *The Happiest Girl in the World* (Harburg's words fitted to the music of Offenbach, the libretto by Saidy) and *Darling of the Day* (Harburg's lyrics set by Jule Styne). No matter, for the much-heralded *Finian's Rainbow* opened at the Palace to a bigger advance box-office than had been granted *Annie Get Your Gun*, an encouraging start for a production that had cost around £30,000. Presented under the management of Emile Littler, Bretaigne Windust's Broadway production was redirected (and lit) for London by James Gelb, retaining Michael Kidd's original choreography, the sets of Jo Mielziner and costumes of Eleanor Goldsmith. One missing component was an American company, and the British cast brought its problems. The distinguished Irish actor Arthur Sinclair was announced as Finian, but a few days before the London opening he was replaced (it was said because of illness) by Patrick J. Kelly, who was hastily flown in from New York. The role of Og had been assigned to Charles Hawtrey (later to find fame in the *Carry On* films), but his name was then out of the frame, and he was replaced by Alfie Bass. A newcomer, soprano Beryl Seton, was given the role of Sharon, played on Broadway by Ella Logan, with Alan Gilbert as Woody Mahoney. The West End first night was postponed because of 'technical difficulties', but this held back only temporarily a generally hostile press. The morning after the first performance which had been vociferously booed, Littler conferenced with the production personnel in an effort to cut and speed up the show, but the damage had been done.

Littler's team could do nothing about the plot that Harburg and Saidy devised, or the play's intense Irishness. Harburg played with two ideas: a piece about a mean-spirited senator who turns into a black man and has to face the consequences of his own racial prejudice, and a piece about a leprechaun who has the power to grant three wishes. These two strands melded to become *Finian's Rainbow*. Finian McLonergan and his daughter Sharon come from Ireland's Glocca Morra to America, to Rainbow Valley in Missitucky (the name marries the Mississippi with Kentucky). America is the Land of Promise to which Finian has brought a crock of gold he has taken from a leprechaun. By burying the gold near Fort Knox Finian believes it will increase. The dissatisfied leprechaun Og follows them, understandably concerned, because if the gold is not returned to him he will turn into a human. The corrupt Senator Billboard Rawkins means to have the gold himself, but is for a time turned into a black man. Romance intrudes when Sharon falls for Woody Mahoney, and Woody's sister 'Susan the Silent', who can only dance her feelings, eventually finds her voice and joins forces with Og, who having used up his last wish by turning Rawkins white again, realises he can never return to leprechaunhood, and can love Susan all the better because of it. Finian departs, wiser about the workings of the world. Here was a complex libretto, undercut with all sorts of insinuations that the British could scarcely identify. So *Finian's Rainbow* slipped out of the British grasp. What, after all, did audiences make of its bizarre treatment of the colour problem, an issue that Britain had yet to face up to?

The *Sphere* critic found the libretto 'altogether too elaborate. Besides being arch and winsome to a degree [...] the piece is shot with topical Americanisms that, although George Jean Nathan vouches for their wit on Broadway, sound merely vapid in Cambridge Circus. And something has gone wrong with the acting.'[21] J. C. Trewin agreed it presented 'sick of a whimsy [...] Another beautiful mornin? Not at all. Rather, let us say, a damp, misty evening with an odd moonbeam or two, the sound of the Blarney River screaming down to Bogus Bay. The leprechauns are about, and a leprechaun in the theatre is like a Colorado beetle in the crops.' Trewin noted that at curtain fall the audience at the Palace seemed 'dazed'.[22] Neither did the cast have the critics throwing their hats in the air. Kelly as the substitute Finian was 'a tactful, if somewhat dim figure of the hero'.[23] Beverley Baxter MP noted that Kelly had seemed 'puzzled by the cold silence of the audience', while Seton 'has one of those singing voices which makes a girl's friends say she ought to go on the stage'.[24] The *Stage* complained that in Kelly there was 'little boisterousness one felt might have helped the evening along', but it passed the rest of the cast as fit for purpose, with a special commendation for the dancer Beryl Kaye who was singled out for the best notices, and went on to repeat her role on Broadway. Dancing seems for many to have been the main feature of the production, with Kidd's routines almost stopping the show.

Its Irishness was not its only problem; that maelstrom of whimsy had much to do with the British rejecting it. The American whimsical musical has not had a happy time of it in London; much more sensible to keep such pieces as *Flahooley* (dolls that sing) and *Three Wishes for Jamie* from catching the boat over. Was there ever a more whimsical piece than *The Fantasticks?* – an ever-running phenomenon in America, and twice critically trounced in the West End. British critics were equally dismissive of British whimsy, of which there was a fair amount about in the 1950s, courtesy of such writers as Julian Slade and Donald Swann.

It seems contrary that two years later London would welcome Lerner and Loewe's *Brigadoon,* and what could be more whimsical than to have a Scots village come to life only once in a hundred years for a day, go back to sleep, and be especially reawakened before the next century came round by something as intangible as the power of love? Nevertheless, it was wise of *Brigadoon* to eschew satire or social awareness, for that, and the greenness of it all, is what had startled the British in *Finian's Rainbow.* The pity of the show's reputation in Britain is that such a brilliant score has been so undervalued. Consider its string of wonders, not least its immediate standouts 'How Are Things in Glocca Morra?', 'If This Isn't Love', the translucent 'Look to the Rainbow', and the lazy eroticism of 'Old Devil Moon'. Few Broadway scores can offer the depth of melody Lane presents, and Harburg is so distinctive a lyricist, with a style of intricate rhyming that is everlastingly playful. That facility is found in the other, iridescently witty manner of this score: the childrens' roundabout joyfulness in which Harburg rhymes his surreal way through 'When I'm Not Near the Girl I Love' and 'Something Sort of Grandish'. London would not again hear a lyricist with such unmistakable verve. Ultimately, it was left to a little revue, *Look to the Rainbow,* seen briefly at the Apollo Theatre in 1985, to celebrate Harburg's contribution to American musical theatre.

So far as the London critics were concerned, the closure of *Finian's Rainbow* was no more than a mercy killing. Littler blamed the broadcast of a bad review by the BBC, but audiences at the Palace in 1947 were faced with a number of dilemmas. Since the war had begun, there had been no musical play (and wasn't that one of the problems – proposing musical *plays* in place of musical *comedies?*) that challenged its onlookers. *Finian's Rainbow* had more than one challenge in its armoury. The satire on economics that threaded the plot must have seemed of little interest to the British: was this American or Irish satire, American or Irish economics? For an audience still enduring rationing, Og's crock of gold was removed to the realms of fantasy, and it seems that neither book, music or lyrics or production could seduce a British audience.

The fact that the show's villain was changed into a black man may also have presented difficulties in the Britain of 1947, on the threshold of social change brought about by immigration. The following year the *SS Empire Windrush* delivered 450 Caribbean immigrants to Tilbury Docks. They had left their homes in search of a better life, lured by the labour shortage Britain was suffering in the aftermath of war. After two days of doubt (would the politicians let them disembark?) they began their British lives, many of them in the employ of the National Health Service, London Transport and British Railways. The *Windrush*'s passengers had prised open a door to immigration that would radically affect the culture of Britain. Of course, none of this was known at the time of *Finian's Rainbow*, but those first black newcomers trying to find lodging in London were often confronted with the discouraging 'No Blacks. No Irish' sign in the window. Finian and his rainbow had brought both. In America, it is estimated that around five million blacks, partly because of the activities of the Ku-Klux-Klan, left the South for more hospitable destinations between 1940 and 1970. How can any of this mattered to a harmless, prettily presented musical? Did its potential audience sit at home pondering the ethics of its plot, or the moral implications of buying a ticket and sitting through it? Perhaps it just read the dreadful reviews and booked for *Oklahoma!* Perhaps the British simply couldn't cope with Harburg's lyrical shenanigans? Whatever the reasons for its collapse, *Finian's Rainbow* was a chastening reminder that the Broadway musical in London was not guaranteed success.

The show was to make two more British attempts. A bid for London was obvious in the revival of *Finian's Rainbow* which opened on Boxing Day 1957 at the New Shakespeare Theatre, Liverpool. Directed by Sam Wanamaker, with décor by Audrey Cruddas, and new choreography by Beryl Kaye, this had Shani Wallis as Sharon, Bobby Howes as Finian, Ivor Emmanuel as Woody, and Harold Lang as Og. Kaye repeated the role of Susan Mahoney that she had played on Broadway as a take-over and in the original London production. A revival seen in New York for twenty-seven performances in 1960 had Jeannie Carson as Sharon, Biff McGuire as Woody, and Bobby Howes as Finian, and these three were reunited for a new production directed by Robert Helpmann opening in Blackpool in March of the following year, with Patricia Porter as Susan and the Irish actor Donal Donnelly as Og. The original orchestrations by Robert Russell Bennett and Don Walker were replaced by those of Peter Knight, with sets and costumes by Berkeley Sutcliffe, and Kidd's choreography replaced by that of Malcolm Clare. Despite the provenance, strong cast and high production values, there was to be no London showing.

The booing that the first British *Finian's Rainbow* had attracted at its first night seems to have been the first manifestation of this type of audience dissatisfaction since the end of the war. It is much more rare to hear such an insolent audience reaction in our own times, when even a strongly expressed criticism to one's companion may result in the threat of assault from an eavesdropping neighbour.

In the case of *Finian's Rainbow* the booing may have occurred or started in the gallery, where the Gallery First Nighters sat. These disciples of London theatre religiously attended every West End premiere. Although they sat high at the very back of the auditorium, and had paid far less for their tickets than those in the stalls and dress circle, it was from here that roars of approval or cries of disapproval rained down on performers. The clarity of such messages propelled onto the stage, like some godly verdict, would sometimes be sadly missed in the coming years.

Waving the flag for the British musical, the Vivian Ellis – A. P. Herbert Victorian pastiche **Bless the Bride** found itself held up as the equal of *Oklahoma!*, although its crafted graciousness clung to an earlier era. Otherwise, the only domestic product was **The Nightingale**, an unassuming 'oriental' offering by Michael Martin-Harvey and Sax Rohmer, with music by Kennedy Russell.

1947 Broadway Exports

Street Scene (148), **Finian's Rainbow** (725), **Brigadoon** (581) and **High Button Shoes** (727).

1947 Broadway Only

Allegro (315), Rodgers and Hammerstein's small-town America experiment in originality, failed to live up to its expected brilliance, but its bravery was notable. The rest was dross: comedienne Nancy Walker in **Barefoot Boy with Cheek** (108), **Music in My Heart** (124) built around the music of Tchaikovsky, and the quickly overcome **Louisiana Lady** (4).

8 *High Button Shoes* (1948) was the first Jule Styne to reach the West End,
but crucially left behind its Broadway leading man

1948

Lute Song
High Button Shoes

Lute Song (Winter Garden, 11 October 1948; 24) was notable mainly for its décor by Robert Edmond Jones, and the London debuts in an American musical of the twenty-eight-year-old Yul Brynner and Dolly Haas, the German star most remembered for the 1936 film *Broken Blossoms*. Based on the Chinese play *Pi-Pa-Ki*, the book was by Sidney Howard and Will Irwin, lyrics by Bernard Hanighen, and music by Raymond Scott. The American production of 1946 had only a modest run with Brynner and Mary Martin leading the cast in this graceful retelling of a play that had first been seen in Peking in the early fifteenth century. When the intelligent Tsai-Yong (Brynner) is commanded to leave his wife Tchao-Ou-Niang (Haas) and move to Peking, where he must be judged against the finest scholars of his country, he leaves her a lute. At Court Tsai-Yong enters the imperial service and marries a princess. Tchao-Ou-Niang becomes a nun and falls into poverty. Happily, the princess realises she can never have her husband's love, and reunites him with Tchao-Ou-Niang.

The *Stage* critic noted 'with special pleasure the Buddhist temple scene in the final act, with priests seeking alms with all the persistence of an English vicar raising funds for rebuilding the parish hall and with some vigorous and harmonious accompanying music'.[1] In Britain *Lute Song* was consigned to history after its brief run, but in 1959 Haas recreated her London performance for a New York repertory revival. The West End production, mounted by Albert de Courville, may have happened because in May 1948 the sets, costumes and drops from the New York production were sold by a receiver.

Firing on noisy cylinders from mainstream Broadway came **High Button Shoes** (Hippodrome, 22 December 1948; 291), the first book musical to have a score by Jule Styne, many of whose shows would be seen in Britain: *Gentlemen Prefer Blondes*, *Bells Are Ringing*, *Gypsy*, *Do Re Mi*, *Funny Girl*, *Bar Mitzvah Boy* and *Sugar*, renamed for London *Some Like it Hot*. Val Parnell presented Jack Hylton's production of *High Button Shoes*, described in the theatre programme as a 'New Song and Dandy Show'. It was a replication of the New York staging, although credits for the sets (Broadway: Oliver Smith; West End: Alick Johnstone) and costumes (Broadway: Miles White; West End: Alec Shanks and Slade Lucas) differed. George Abbott (co-author of the book with Phil Silvers) had directed in New York, but in London the credit was for 'The Production reproduced for England by Archie Thomson', with Jerome Robbins' original choreography reproduced by Fred Hearn.

Based on Stephen Longstreet's novel *The Sisters Liked Them Handsome*, *High Button Shoes* set its story in 1913 New Jersey, where fly-by-night chancer Harrison Floy makes a killing by selling swamp land belonging to the Longstreet family. Floy gets away to Atlantic City, but the money is stolen from him. Although he retrieves the cash, he loses it making a bet on a football match. His bad luck continues, but Floy gets away. The Broadway production was still running when the West End production premiered, but America had at least sent two performers to be the show's stars. Lew Parker's last Broadway musical had been the 1945 *Are You With It?*, but he was unknown in Britain, as was his fellow American Kay Kimber, whose only Broadway credit was a small role in the 1942 *By Jupiter*. Neither had their name above the title. The remainder was a British cast that included Joan Heal whose career would mostly be in British musicals, Sidney James, Jack Cooper and Hermene French. As the elder Longstreets, James and Kimber had two of the show's best numbers, 'Papa, Won't You Dance with Me?' and 'I Still Get Jealous'. Whether the British cast regularly managed to get six encores at each performance for the latter (the Broadway cast did) is unknown. The *corps de ballet* included a girl called Audrey Hepburn, and among the chorus was Alma Cogan, on the brink of a short but brilliant career. One of the items she appeared in was one of the most successful, the 'Bathing Beauty Ballet' in Act Two, renamed from the Broadway version the 'Mack Sennett Ballet'.

There was booing from the gallery at the first night. The *Stage* thought Parker (who was 'a sort of American Arthur Askey') 'works hard, but is sometimes defeated by the poverty of his lines'.[2] The *Stage* didn't think too much of Kimber either. Frances Stephens in *Theatre World* praised the dancing and chorus work, which demonstrated 'once and for all that an English chorus can display every bit the same verve and vivacity previously thought to be a unique attribute of the Americans'. She cared less for the show itself. 'The story behind the show is extremely trite [...] and unfortunately there is a sad falling away in the second act. [...] it is a great pity that the show itself lacks the quality merited by the real care lavished on the production.'[3] *High Button Shoes*, high-octane stuff as it was, proved hard work for the cast contracted to play it twice nightly, at 6.00 p.m. and 8.30 p.m. Things might have been better if Broadway's Floy, Phil Silvers, had taken the boat over. Silvers *breathed* high-octane, and asking another to impersonate him was making intolerable demands on the human frame. Silvers once again stayed home when his Broadway hit *Do Re Mi* transferred to London in 1961.

An interesting glimpse into the thinking of British producers at this time is found in an article Robert Nesbitt wrote for the *Stage*. Nesbitt had just returned to London after seeing seven musicals on Broadway, and his first insistence was that 'there is no "musical" which could be transferred exactly as it stands to the West End with certain success'. That need for 'certain success' shouldn't surprise; the man, after all, was a producer, but more attention should be paid to the finer detail of Nesbitt's comments. His definition is a little confusing, as three of the seven 'musicals' were revues: *Make Mine Manhattan*, *Angel in the Wings* and *Inside U. S. A.* starring Beatrice Lillie, which Nesbitt thought would reach Britain. It didn't. That left four musicals proper. He described *Look Ma, I'm Dancin'* as 'delightful burlesque', and thought it a candidate for transfer. This 'and *High Button Shoes* are nearer to London's taste, being pure entertainment, with no attempt to put over a message'. Nesbitt had rather more difficulty with the two most interesting shows he saw. *Brigadoon* was 'a serious Scottish fantasy' which 'makes little or no bid to be amusing'. As for Rodgers and Hammerstein's *Allegro*, 'such pretentious material seems out of place in the book of a large scale "musical"', and here was 'a musical show with a message!'[4]

In the event, neither *Look Ma, I'm Dancin'* or *Allegro* made it to London, but *High Button Shoes* and *Brigadoon* did. Nesbitt may have been surprised by the fact that the 'serious Scottish fantasy' enjoyed such solid West End success, running far longer than the Broadway original. Perhaps British audiences were more open to seriousness in musical theatre than West End producers imagined. He may have been right about *High Button Shoes* being to London's taste but was the London production up to the mark of the Broadway original? He didn't anticipate the boos, and it didn't run for half as long as *Brigadoon*. Meanwhile, one wonders if Nesbitt and his fellow producers ever bothered to consult a dictionary as to the meaning of the word 'serious'.

Yet one can understand Nesbitt's viewpoint, illuminated against the background of a ground-down British society, where social changes effected by the war were being exacerbated by the prevailing conditions of everyday life. Perhaps unhelpfully, the Ministry of Information commissioned a short documentary, *What a Life!*, to convince the depressed British cinema-going public that things were, in the words of a Cicely Courtneidge song, 'looking up'. One of *What a Life!*'s screenwriters, Richard Massingham, asked the production meeting, 'Really, what is there to be cheerful about these days?'[5] Unable to find anything, the film ended up accentuating the unending drudgery of living in Britain, and was condemned in the House of Commons for spreading yet more gloom.

The year offered four British musicals. Eric Maschwitz and his composer Hans May came up with the operetta **Carissima**, where the song titles ('Venice in Spring', 'Two in a Gondola', 'Far in the Blue') tell you all you need to know. The piece was totally undeserving of its two televised performances, one of them inexplicably starring Ginger Rogers. By now the 'musical farce' **Bob's Your Uncle** seemed washed up from the previous decade. A chance for such seasoned comics as Leslie Henson and Vera Pearce to show their skills, it had music by Noel Gay. **The Kid from Stratford** did at least have a reasonably original idea which was something to do with Shakespeare, but in truth it was an excuse for little Arthur Askey (Britain's Lew Parker?) to bumble through some adventures. The most unusual entry was **Cage Me a Peacock**, adapted from his novel by Noel Langley, who had been one of the screen-writers for *The Wizard of Oz*. Ancient Rome was its diverting location, and unusually the music was by a female composer, Eve Lynd.

1948 Broadway Exports

Where's Charley? (792) and *Kiss Me, Kate* (1,077).

1948 Broadway Only

The long-runner of the year was *As the Girls Go* (420). The idea was a good one – what if a woman became the American President? – but critics felt that the show slackened into burlesque. The other reasonable runners were Alan Jay Lerner and Kurt Weill's *Love Life* (252), which charted an American marriage through 150 years.[6] That little bundle of noisy fun Nancy Walker was the main reason for *Look Ma, I'm Dancin'* (188), in which she played an heiress who takes over a ballet company. *My Romance* (95) and *Magdalena* (88) did not achieve wide popularity. *My Romance* was the last score proper by Sigmund Romberg (although *The Girl in Pink Tights* carried his name in 1954), but even its plot about a prima donna in love with a priest labelled it as old-fashioned operetta. *Magdalena* was another Robert Wright–George Forrest musical adaptation, this time based on the compositions of Villa-Lobos, but it lacked the tunefulness and appeal of their more successful work. There only remained *Hold It!* (46) about a boy who enters a beauty contest as a girl, *Sleepy Hollow* (12) which recklessly followed into the theatre just vacated by six years of *Oklahoma!*, and *Heaven on Earth* (12). This boasted characters who lived in a tree, a pixie, apparently brilliant sets and a late score by Jay Gorney, composer of the song 'Brother, Can You Spare a Dime?'

1949

Brigadoon

WHAT IS IT about Scotland that inspires so individual an emotional response in the arts? The bonny braes, the swirling kilts, the lonely mountains, the land of mist pressed onto canvas by countless Victorian painters of oils and onto paper by Edwardian watercolourists, transmuted into an approximation of Scottish music by Donizetti's *Lucia di Lammermoor* and Rossini's *La Donna del Lago* out of Walter Scott; all is airy romance. Alan Jay Lerner knew the whiff of this wild country, and although histories of American musicals tell us that **Brigadoon** (His Majesty's Theatre, 14 April 1949; 685) was probably the fault of Frederick Loewe, who introduced Lerner to the German story *Germelshausen*,[1] there were probably other influences at work. Lerner professed an interest in the works of James Barrie, he of the whimsical, sentimental 'time' play. Did Lerner also know J. B. Priestley's 'time' plays? Perhaps *They Came to a City* in which a group of disparate characters wander into a world they know nothing of, where second chances await. A Scots version of this would have had them wandering over the magic bridge that led to Brigadoon. There were those (its Broadway director Robert Lewis was one) who found *Brigadoon* whimsical and sentimental; yes, but brilliant. Barrie's appeal to Lerner was not only that he was Scots, but that he played with time, unfixed it, moved the barriers of the possible, made way for the never-on-earth. *Peter Pan* is the obvious example: the boy who will not grow old, who doesn't want to grow old, and couldn't grow old if he wanted to. The second star to the right doesn't lead to everlasting happiness, but to the tragedy of being caught somewhere beyond human emotion, aware of dying as 'an awfully big adventure', intent on believing in fairies (and clap your hands if you agree).

Other Barrie works trick with time even more considerably. In *Dear Brutus* a group of discontents at a country house gathering look out into the garden and see it has turned into a forest. It's an enchanted one, we know, as they one by one wander into it through the French windows as the curtain comes down on Act One. For the next Act we are in the forest, where Barrie gives the discontents their second chances. When the curtain falls on Act Two it's looking hopeful; they've had their second chances for happiness, and it's up to them to take them back to life. Back in the house for Act Three, with the enchanted wood vanished, the surprising thing is that no one seems altered by the experience. No one, that is, except one of the characters – the most difficult, the most unlikely. Much the same happens at the end of *Brigadoon*, for the hero has been transformed, forgiven for the past, when the peripatetic place swallows him up. One of the greatest endings in American musicals, and one to strike in the bone of our emotion.

9 The best American musical of the 1940s? The delightful
Brigadoon's first London production at His Majesty's Theatre

Back in Brigadoon (it's a place name as well as a title) Tommy Albright is much nicer to know than the principal malcontent of *Dear Brutus*; it's just that he's engaged to a girl who isn't the right one, and weary of life in New York. Cue Tommy and his chum Jeff taking a walking holiday in the Highlands. For some reason known only to Alan Jay Lerner, the year is 1935, and their map-reading isn't up to scratch: they can't find where they are, and it makes even less sense when an uncharted town emerges from a surrounding fog. Brigadoon has its cross-section of humanity: Jean MacKeith who is to be married to Charlie Cameron, and is also loved by Harry Ritchie, and Fiona, who pretty soon goes walking through the heather on the hill with Tommy, about to discover that Fiona is the right girl in the wrong place. The problem is that she, along with the rest of the town, comes to life only one day in a hundred years. It's not a promising situation. We have strayed into Sleeping Beauty territory, the sort of world discovered in James Hilton's *Lost Horizon*, when there are prices to be paid if someone crosses the boundary into the real world.

The age-old battle of head and heart ensues, and, of course, when the Brigadoon May morning comes to an end and Fiona is taken back to another hundred-year sleep – she must be a relative of Barrie's *Mary Rose*, who one day wandered into the garden for an unconscionable number of years – we can hardly blame Tommy for taking the next plane back home. Cue a scene in a New York bar, where the sort of lazy jazz music you would never hear in Brigadoon is being played. Tommy's girlfriend breezes in and starts to catch up on their relationship. We dislike her because she is shallow and hard-edged, and we tell ourselves that if this is the sort of girl Tommy was once attracted to, he's now a reformed character; after his visit to Brigadoon he's after sweetness and light, even if it's on a centenary basis.

Clumsy as this reversion to our world may seem, it's necessary, not only to give us a breather after so much heather intoxication, but to demonstrate how facile Tommy's American future will be unless he acts decisively. Not that we doubt he'll run a mile from that spiky dame; we know the ending of the scene as soon as she walks through the door. We would have no faith in him if he decided to forget the sway of the kilt. The scene becomes necessary because we have to see Tommy's weakness and strength: it's the going back, the journey, the conscious decision, made more thrilling because we know when he (and Jeff who chums along) gets back to Scotland there will be no hope of another sighting of Brigadoon; try again in a hundred years' time. But Lerner turns the legend's screw. Tommy's arrival has awakened the town's elder, kindly old Mr Murdoch. He tells Tommy that love makes anything possible, 'even miracles'. He leads Tommy over the bridge as the orchestra builds to a fortissimo conclusion.

That ending tells us in a stroke (the last of the evening) that this isn't operetta. It can't be: if it was operetta Fiona would at the final moment have appeared on the bridge, and Tommy would have rushed to her. No, the last we see is of Tommy walking slowly towards his Nirvana. Jeff, as well he might be, is speechless; just as well, as Lerner isn't about to give him any more dialogue. It's up to us to appreciate how *he* must be feeling. Tommy has gone, walked out of the real world into a better one. The fact that Fiona is not there at the last representing his ultimate wish suggests that overpowering as is his love for her, it is his quest for a different, more ecstatic life, that has compelled his decision. It's tosh, of course, and one might say that in different hands from Lerner's it would have been unbearable tosh, except that its American (and British) director Robert Lewis recognised the tosh that apparently permeated Lerner's original script. How much of what was seen on Broadway and in the West End was made the more palatable by Lewis we will never know. Sentiment, of course, was not eradicated, and was an essential make-up of the work, but there is a balance of elements in *Brigadoon* that is organic (compare the jostling of elements in *On the Town*, where everything seems less happily integrated). Perhaps *Brigadoon* was merely lucky to get away with its whimsy, for the whimsical in American musicals has often doomed their chance of a British success. Two years earlier London had dismissed *Finian's Rainbow*, and in the 1960s it was unconcerned with *Carnival* and *The Fantasticks*, while various other whimsies stayed in America. The same was true of Lerner and Loewe's first two collaborations, *What's Up* and *The Day Before Spring*; *Brigadoon* gave London its' first taste of their work.

The *Brigadoon* cast was a mix of British, Scots and American. Philip Hanna as Tommy Albright seemed an unlikely choice for leading man, with no previous experience in stage musicals. *Theatre World* reported that he had been voted 'top daytime reader in television' in America, where he regularly was watched by 80 million viewers. Working for commercial radio stations, his good looks and charm lifted him into television, where he became the pin-up boy salesman, selling soap and cigarette lighters from the comfort of an armchair as doting housewives wrote their cheques. After this striking debut, Hanna repeated his role in New York in 1950. A notable tennis player, he reached the third round of the men's singles at Wimbledon during the run; 'Looker On' in *Theatre World* swooned: 'He was idolised by the sporting public in the afternoon and the theatre-going crowds at night.' Despite his personable debut, he never played London again, and was succeeded by the British Bruce Trent.

Sadler's Wells soprano Patricia Hughes played Fiona, with American Hiram Sherman (succeeded by Lionel Murton) making his West End debut as Jeff, and soubrette Noele Gordon as Meg. An outstanding component of *Brigadoon* was its choreography. An expert in Highland dancing and a Scots dancing champion, James MacGregor Jamieson had already played Harry as a take-over in the Broadway original, and would repeat the role for the 1950 New York revival. For London he restaged Agnes de Mille's choreography, continuing this through various revivals up to 1991. He was succeeded in London by Paddy Stone. Partnering Jamieson, Noelle De Mosa also attracted excellent notices.

The notices were mixed. For Richard Findlater the piece was brought off with 'such brilliant buoyancy [...] Most English musicals are just as absurd and much less entertaining. The book mixes whimsy and sophistication: it has apparently been written (London contemporaries such as *Belinda Fair* are merely found).'[2] The *Spectator* found the music 'on the whole poor, and save for Mr Hanna there is no one to redeem it'. As for the plot, it 'need not be explored too deeply, especially as it involves not only faith in things mystical but also a firm grasp of mathematics'.[3] The *Manchester Evening News* agreed. 'The music is rhythmic rather than tuneful. There is nothing here that the legendary office boy will want to whistle.'[4] The dances were much praised. *Punch* noted 'dancing of a peculiarly dramatic kind and in a production [...] of outstanding adroitness and polish'.[5] Anthony Cookman discovered 'the effect of a dream fantasy. The dances do not lack vigour, but they achieve at their best a gliding grace, which keeps us aware that the gaiety, for all its forthrightness, is of the air airy rather than of the earth earthy. It is life, but life raised to a new power, as in a day dream.'[6] Harold Hobson verified the successful fusion of elements, with 'a book more than customarily intelligent, sentimental tunes with a sharp enough tang not to be sickly, and many Highland dances reinvigorated with transatlantic energy'.[7]

Only two years after Rodgers and Hammerstein had impacted on London, there was critical dissension about the movement of musical theatre in Britain. Frank Jackson in *Reynolds News*, having noted on the first night 'when the lunatic, sycophantic, ill-mannered applause died away', wrote 'What a pitiful comment it is on the current situation in musicals that we should have to import from Broadway a musical with its story set in the Scottish Highlands!'[8] But couldn't British producers and British writers have come up with a Scots musical as well as Americans? As early as 1859 New York had seen *Rob Roy*, 'An Operatic Drama' with music by Henry Bishop, whose works included Scottish 'operas' such as *The Heart of Midlothian* and *Montrose*, these three based on Walter Scott. *Rob Roy*, which had first played Edinburgh in 1825 as *Rob Roy MacGregor*, billed as a 'Grand Spectacular Romance with songs and dances', these including a 'Grand Scotch Ballet', a Grand Battle Tableau between English soldiers and Highlanders, and 'Auld Lang Syne'. A hundred years before *Brigadoon*, New York had proved receptive to the Scots siren.

It was London's good fortune that Lewis remained personally responsible for the London transfer. He realised that authenticity in setting and costume and atmosphere would be more important than in New York, and hired a production assistant, the singer Ian Wallace (later one of the two male stars of the Drury Lane *Fanny*). Wallace told Lewis that if as Lerner insisted the year in the reawakened Brigadoon was 1749, there could be no kilts, as at that time the kilt was banned. For London the 'modern' scene towards the end of the play was established as 1935, thus reverting to 1735 when kilts were all the rage. Wallace pointed out that the common folk down at MacConnachy Square were dressed in Royal Stuart Tartans. Wallace instructed the chorus and principals on the Scots sound, and Bunty Kelley advised Lewis on kilts, pipes and various props. The care that went into the London *Brigadoon* earned Lewis *The Times'* accolade that his treatment had been scrupulous. In fact, the *Stage* rated it above *Oklahoma!*: 'the most distinctive, and in many ways the most distinguished, of all the large-scale musical plays that have reached us from America since the war was ended.'[9]

It would not be too long before two British musicals chose Scotland as their setting: Alan Melville and Charles Zwar's gentle valentine *Marigold* and Jack Waller and Joseph Tunbridge's *Wild Grows the Heather* (adapted from Barrie, although not from one of his time plays), and in 1953 Broadway used J. M. Barrie's *What Every Woman Knows* as the basis for the Scotland-set *Maggie*.

The pontificating Beverley Baxter MP expressed dissatisfaction:

> In the realm of musicals we are unhappily in a bad way. The impact of *Oklahoma!* was a death sentence on the traditional English musical comedy despite the gallant rearguard action of *Bless the Bride* and the invincibility of Mr. Ivor Novello. Like beggars at the gate, we wait for the crumbs from our rich uncle's table.[10]

Baxter's comment is facile and unthinking, but it is interesting that he should feel so threatened only two years after the arrival of *Oklahoma!* The 'gallant rearguard action' effected by A. P. Herbert and Vivian Ellis in *Bless the Bride* was merely a retreat into operetta, a form that Novello had bent to his own demands since *Glamorous Night*. Baxter was blaming the Americans when he might as well have blamed the war that had swept away a generation of British composers and performers, with no place awaiting them in the post-war atmosphere, this aggravated by the almost total lack of British managements to build a British musical theatre. What Baxter termed 'traditional musical comedy' in fact survived, in various guises, up to the end of the 1950s, although its reputation was never to equal that of its American counterpart. Meanwhile, America was not averse to sending over its own variants of 'traditional musical comedy'. Rodgers and Hammerstein, Jerry Herman, Richard Adler and Jerry Ross, Bock and Harnick; in their ways, all were traditionalists.

The British musicals of 1949 were more plentiful than Broadway imports. The mild **Belinda Fair**, a costume piece by Eric Maschwitz and composer Jack Strachey, had Adele Dixon as an eighteenth-century woman enlisting in the army and falling for her colonel. Without the comedy of Cicely Courtneidge **Her Excellency** would probably not have enjoyed its modest success. A. P. Herbert and Vivian Ellis' follow-up to *Bless the Bride*, **Tough at the Top**, was a perhaps unconscious effort to bring off a Novello-type Ruritanian extravaganza, but it misjudged the technique and misfired with critics and public. Even less mourned was the quickly discarded **Roundabout**. The piece had started life as *Hat in the Air*, but no titfers were tossed when the show reached the West End. Triumphing was Ivor Novello's last romantic operetta **King's Rhapsody**, proving that Ruritania could still bring commercial success.

1949 Broadway Exports

South Pacific (1,925) and *Gentlemen Prefer Blondes* (740).

1949 Broadway Only

Two of the three New York productions were of interesting and well-crafted pieces. *Miss Liberty* (308) was a romance built around the sculpting of the Statue of Liberty, with a charming Irving Berlin score that concluded with a stirring setting of 'Give Me Your Tired, Your Poor', while *Lost in the Stars* (281), with its theme of racial tension in South Africa, had a brilliant score by Kurt Weill. By its very title *Texas, Li'l Darlin'* (293) never seemed a contender for export.

10 In the year of *Carousel*, British musical theatre was still producing costume pieces that verged on operetta, as in *Dear Miss Phoebe*, one of many British adaptations from the works of J. M. Barrie

1950

Carousel

R ODGERS AND HAMMERSTEIN'S *Oklahoma!* had such an ecstatic
reception in America and Britain that their next collaboration **Carousel**
(Theatre Royal, Drury Lane, 7 June 1950; 566) presented a considerable
challenge. Through the years several composers had considered adapting
Ferenc Molnár's 1909 Hungarian play *Liliom* for the musical stage, among
them Puccini, Lehár, Kálmán and Weill, but it was Rodgers and Hammerstein
who wrested the rights from Molnár's grasp. It may have seemed unlikely
material for a 'light' musical work (some of those composers would have
brought weightier considerations) but here was Hammerstein's 'time' play, his
one go at a 'second chance' play. *Liliom* is cousin to J. M. Barrie's *Dear Brutus*,
and cousin to J. B. Priestley's *An Inspector Calls*, when time coils back and
forth to bring those who knew a young woman to a proper recognition of
her death, and to *One Touch of Venus*,[1] when magic out of Shakespeare's *The
Winter's Tale* turns stone to warm flesh. The second chance is there again
in 1955 for *Damn Yankees* when a pot-bellied ordinary Joe gets the chance to
be a rippling muscled baseball hero, and in the sometimes brilliant *Steel Pier*[2]
of 1997 where a young dead pilot gets a rebate on Time to help out a hapless
marathon dancer. Above and beyond them all, *Brigadoon*, bridging forgotten
Time and present day together in the name of that stalwart of musical theatre,
Love.

Molnár's play had at first seemed a flop, but international productions and
film versions made its reputation. The simplicity of the story must have had
a natural appeal to Hammerstein. The virile young carnival barker Liliom
falls in love with a maid, Julie, who becomes pregnant by him. Misguidedly
imagining that taking part in a street robbery will help him support Julie and
the baby, Liliom is foiled, and to escape capture fatally stabs himself. In death
he is stationed temporarily in Purgatory, pleading with his celestial master to
be allowed to return to earth for a day to see his child, a daughter. After serving
time in Hell, Liliom is granted his wish and meets his daughter, but when she
rejects him he slaps her across the face. It is a disappointing act from a man who
already had the reputation of being a wife-beater, but who has in fact (as Molnár
and Hammerstein insist) only ever struck Julie once. The slap, Liliom's daughter
tells her mother, did not hurt, but felt like a kiss. Julie accepts this, and Liliom
returns to realms above.

In 1930 the surreal elements of Molnár's play were memorably visualised in
Frank Borzage's film version, with its sometimes breathtakingly effective set
pieces, not least when the locomotive drives into Liliom's room to collect him
from his deathbed.[3] Forever whizzing about the head of the film is the convoluted
switchback of the fairground and the various fizzing trains riding back and forth

between Heaven and Earth and warmer places, and the space-age attendants in their Mercury-winged apparel. Such other worldly moments are necessarily dispensed with in Hammerstein's more mundane representation of the unknown. Hammerstein also dispenses with the Carpenter, an upright smartly dressed gentleman who regularly as clockwork comes to ask Julie to accompany him to a gathering, and is refused, only to go through the same procedure the next week. When Liliom returns to earth all those years later he is surprised to see the Carpenter still calling, still asking, and Liliom is gratified to see him still being politely refused. This is such a delightful touch, underlining Julie's utter steadfastness to the wanting Liliom; it is disappointing that Hammerstein saw no use for the Carpenter. Here and there, perhaps *Carousel* could do with a few nuances.

In fact, Hammerstein's libretto cleaves closely to Molnár's play after shifting the action from Budapest to small-town New England America. Because the original location guaranteed little exoticism, nothing is lost by the transition, and Hammerstein knew that he (and his audiences) would feel a natural warmth towards a more 'homey' American setting. The Theatre Guild's production directed by Rouben Mamoulian was restaged for London by Rodgers and Hammerstein's dependable emissary Jerome Whyte, who would see this function through to the team's final *The Sound of Music*. Whyte had the advantage of the original New York credentials: choreography by Agnes de Mille, sets by Jo Mielziner, costumes by Miles White, and the orchestrations of Don Walker. American principals were imported. Stephen Douglass was an experienced Billy, having played the role as a take-over in the original Broadway production, on tour and in the 1949 New York revival. He would return to London in the 1967 *110 in the Shade*. Douglass was succeeded by the Canadian baritone Edmund Hockridge, who would go on to be the leading man in several Broadway imports, playing Sky Masterson in *Guys and Dolls*, Aristide Forestier in *Can-Can* and Sid Sorokin in *The Pajama Game*.

London's Julie, Iva Withers, had played in the chorus of the Broadway run before taking over the role from the original Julie, Jan Clayton. The performances of Douglass and Withers were much appreciated, but neither became established as London names: only with *South Pacific* did 'star' names begin to dominate Rodgers and Hammerstein musicals. Withers subsequently claimed that throughout her time in the Broadway production her leading man John Raitt had never spoken to her (considering her a chorus girl), Hammerstein did not care for her, and she had only ever been regarded as a take-over artist. She was followed in London by LaVerne Burden, who seems to have had no other Broadway credits. Similarly forgotten is Margot Moser, who had already played Carrie Pipperidge in the 1949 New York revival, and who in 1961 was a take-over Eliza Doolittle in the original *My Fair Lady*, but otherwise spent much of her career as a standby to the better known.

Carousel was greeted with less acclaim in London than in New York. Even the tactful Frances Stephens, editor of the not always incisive *Theatre World*, cautioned her readers.

> The long-awaited successor to *Oklahoma!*, while having all the superb technique and lovely music and costumes one had anticipated, was in some ways a disappointment. Naturally, it was not to be expected that there would be the same exciting impact which came with first sight and sound of *Oklahoma!*, a musical that was so astonishingly different for London eyes and ears [...] The story inclines to impinge too much on the smooth running of the show, particularly in the second act, when the sentiment is also inclined to clog. The chief delight in the end remains with the superb ballets, the magnificent chorus singing, and lovely haunting melodies.[4]

Later in the run, *Theatre World Annual* insisted that

> it would be idle to pretend that *Carousel* attained over here the tremendous popularity of its two illustrious predecessors [*Annie Get Your Gun* and *Oklahoma!*]. The Rodgers music was as haunting as ever and the Hammerstein book just as workmanlike. Agnes de Mille's choreography once again adorned the whole, and there was the same colour and vitality. There was also a greater delicacy of touch, and this combined with a certain sentimentality of approach, probably detracted from the universal appeal of the piece.[5]

Elsewhere the *Stage* criticised the wordiness of Hammerstein's dialogue, noting that 'the general key [of music] is minor, psychologically if not technically', and decided that 'the carousel may be said to revolve somewhat slowly, albeit with some exhilarating occasional turns of speed'.[6] In the *Daily Telegraph* George W. Bishop declared much of the music 'a finely orchestrated background to the action',[7] and Philip Hope-Wallace's *Guardian* notice noted some weak stretches of melodrama and thought that it was the dancing, notably the ballet, that gave the piece its vitality.[8] There was a consensus that the pace was dragged by the sentimental passages.

Such criticism may be meaningless alongside the continued British popularity of *Carousel*, enhanced by Nicholas Hytner's 1992 production for the Royal National Theatre, vastly preferable to Henry King's stodgy film version of 1956.[9] Just as it helped Billy Bigelow, time has elevated Rodgers and Hammerstein's second chance piece to the status of masterpiece. Indeed, *Time* itself pronounced it 'the Best Musical of the Twentieth Century'. In its beginnings, the mild criticisms were mostly intended for Hammerstein. Perhaps the indisputable genius of *Carousel* resides in its score, with Hammerstein so often bowed in prayer and Rodgers seemingly in adoration.

Stylistically the songs have parted company from *Oklahoma!* (and seem to exist in a different sphere from anything Rodgers wrote with Hart); eloquence and a brand of settled loveliness sets the work apart. There are the uncommon prayers of 'You'll Never Walk Alone' (falling into common usage in Britain when Liverpool Football Club claimed it for its anthem), and 'If I Loved You'. Much has been made of the expansiveness of the latter, exemplified by the 'Park Bench Scene' between Billy and Julie, although the construction of the sequence, with its interplay of dialogue and song, is not particularly original. Hammerstein had used such tricks effectively in *Show Boat* two decades earlier, just as Jerome Kern had teamed with Howard Dietz in the accomplished 'Wishing Well Scene' in their 1924 *Dear Sir*, producing eight dramatic minutes of material. Somewhere in the distillation, in Hammerstein's perfect shaping of verse, Hammerstein's fastidious tidy penmanship, does the secret of Rodgers and Hammerstein's enduring success have its origin?

If in *Carousel* Rodgers climbs to the organ loft the elevation is balanced by a lack of intellect, with which Hammerstein's characters have little truck. Being simple home-loving folk, they have a direct claim on their emotions: witness 'Mr Snow' and 'When the Children Are Asleep'. There seems little point in losing sleep about the attractiveness of a carnival barker: 'What's the Use of Wond'rin?'. Anyway, Molnár's hero is a gift to Hammerstein, whose natural and likeable inclination is to make something good out of anything dubious. Hammerstein's reactions are poetic but simple, and the natural world holds no mystery that cannot be clearly defined. Thus, the arrival of Spring is greeted with a completely organic effulgence, 'June Is Bustin' Out All Over', and communal celebration in 'A Real Nice Clambake', a revised version of a number originally intended for *Oklahoma!* Most eloquent is 'The Carousel Waltz', written as prelude to the play proper, in stead of an Overture, fairground music of a strange grandeur to set the dumb show of Hammerstein's puppets in motion. Nothing else in the score comes near inhabiting the frenzied automaton-like excitement of that waltz; what follows is a score of great quietude and guarded emotion, broken by the troubled urgency of Billy's great 'Soliloquy', as neat, tidy and poetic as anything Hammerstein wrote.

Few passages in books about Rodgers and Hammerstein do much to illuminate the process Hammerstein employed to adapt his source material. Even before Rodgers sat down at the piano to stare at his lyrics, it was Hammerstein's task to whip up magic, enchantment. Is it possible he wanted to draw off most of the otherworldly elements that clung about *Liliom*? During the pre-Broadway tour, the musical's 'heavenly' scene took place in a cosy New England homestead, with Mr God playing the harmonium as Mrs God sat comfortably listening. Rodgers objected to such a domestic depiction of the great unknown, and Hammerstein agreed to rewrite the sequence, reaccommodating the heavenly sequence in a starlit void. He was also concerned with the musical's ending, which he thought might be too downbeat, but was heartened by seeing the effectiveness of a similarly 'down' ending to *Song of Norway*. Meanwhile, he was involved in bringing the first post-war 'serious' American musical to London.

The year's British product was not without interest. Noel Coward's first attempt to distance himself from operetta, *Ace of Clubs*, was a little-appreciated piece about some gangsters and a nightclub in a twee version of Soho. It was reminiscent of too many British 'B' movies. John Toré was the sole author of a musical romance set in gold-digging South Africa, *Golden City*. J. M. Barrie's Regency charmer *Quality Street* became *Dear Miss Phoebe* by librettist Christopher Hassall and composer Harry Parr-Davies, enjoying a mild success. The hit was *Blue for a Boy*, a last gasp for the sort of musical farces that had been written for British comedians before the war. There was still mileage in the formula, proved by its twenty-month run. *Music at Midnight* had a book by Guy Bolton married to the music of Offenbach and Hans May.

1950 Broadway Exports

Call Me Madam (644) and *Guys and Dolls* (1,200).

1950 Broadway Only

The New York stay-at-homes were an undistinguished bunch. The shortest lived were *Happy as Larry* (3) about an Irish tailor who magically goes back in time, and *The Barrier* (4), a 'musical drama' bordering on opera and starring Lawrence Tibbett. Only marginally less disastrous were *The Liar* (12), from the play about a sixteenth-century lothario by Carlo Goldoni, and *Great to Be Alive!* (52). Better might have been expected of the two moderately successful stay-at-homes, *Arms and the Girl* (134) and *Out of This World* (157). The plot of the first (Nanette Fabray enlisting in the army disguised as a man) recalled the plot of the British *Belinda Fair*, but *Arms and the Girl* also had the benefit of its leading man Georges Guétary. The songs had lyrics by Dorothy Fields and music by Morton Gould. *Out of This World* was dressed to the nines in Agnes de Mille's production, but Cole Porter's songs were clearly inferior to much he had written before. Two of them ('I Am Loved' and 'Cherry Pies Ought to Be You') were subsequently heard in the 1959 London production of *Aladdin*.

1951

Kiss Me, Kate
South Pacific

Two days before the London premiere of *Kiss Me, Kate* (Coliseum, 8 March 1951; 501) Ivor Novello died in London, and with him an era of successful British musical plays. Such crowds as lined the route of his funeral cortège had never before turned out for a composer. His main popularity as the creator of musical plays began when he wrote *Glamorous Night* for the Theatre Royal, Drury Lane in 1935, followed by his other substantial successes *Careless Rapture, Crest of the Wave* and *The Dancing Years*, the wartime *Arc de Triomphe*, the musical that effectively marked the end of World War II (*Perchance to Dream*), *King's Rhapsody* and *Gay's the Word*. Novello's was a pre-eminence accentuated by the fact that he was not only the show's composer but its book writer (and sometimes lyricist), and star, and *raison d'être*. No other British practitioners had earned such consistent commercial success or public acclaim. After the war Vivian Ellis and A. P. Herbert had summoned up the nostalgic *Bless the Bride*, which in 1947 had held out admirably against *Oklahoma!*, but there could be no disguising its intrinsic backwardness, and nothing they subsequently wrote lasted long. Noel Coward's musicals had gone into the shades after the great success of his 1929 *Bitter Sweet*. In truth, most of the composers associated with British musicals of the period meant little or nothing to the domestic public: Kenneth Leslie-Smith, Manning Sherwin, Hans May, Eve Lynd, Harry Parr-Davies, George Posford.

With Novello gone, the already triumphant progress of American composers, heralded after the war by the debut of Rodgers and Hammerstein, allowed no competition through the 1950s, with long-established American composers Irving Berlin and Cole Porter ending their London careers with more than a whimper. Porter's name had been especially prevalent in wartime London, with scores for *DuBarry Was a Lady* and *Let's Face It!* (both 1942), *Panama Hattie* (1943) and *Something for the Boys* (1944). His subsequent Broadway scores for *Mexican Hayride, Seven Lively Arts* and *Around the World in 80 Days* had not been heard in London, and it seemed as if the quality of these was far distant from that of his earlier works. Then, opening in New York in 1948, came *Kiss Me, Kate*, with songs that resonated with Porter's style and sophistication, hung on a show about actors putting on a musical show based on a Shakespeare show: basically, the useful format for incorporating 'on-stage' numbers, inducing an artificiality that is somehow crucial to *Kiss Me, Kate*, the story of an American tour of a new musical comedy based on Shakespeare's *The Taming of the Shrew*. Its Petruchio and Katharine are Fred Graham and Lilli Vanessi, stars whose amatory fireworks reflect the tensions of the characters they portray.[1] There is also the secondary romance of the show's flirtatious soubrette Lois Lane and her gambler boyfriend Bill Calhoun, mixed up with some crooks (in London Sidney James and Danny Green) whose unlikely knowledge of the Bard bursts forth in 'Brush Up Your Shakespeare'.

Jack Hylton's presentation had the Broadway credits of choreography by Hanya Holm, sets and costumes by Lemuel Ayers and the possibly reduced orchestrations of Robert Russell Bennett, restaged for the West End by Sam Spewack (who co-wrote the book with Bella Spewack) from John C. Wilson's original direction. Hylton's production had the advantage of Patricia Morison, who had created the role of Lilli in New York opposite Alfred Drake, but it would be four years before Drake took London by storm in *Kismet*; now the Fred was Bill Johnson. It was Morison, who had been offered the part after the Broadway producers had approached Mary Martin, Jeanette MacDonald and Lily Pons, who caught the public's attention, as did Julie Wilson as Lois with two of the show's best items, 'Why Can't You Behave?' and 'Always True to You in My Fashion'. In August 1951 the British Valerie Tandy took over from Wilson, and in December Morison was replaced by Helena Bliss.

Ayers' décor ensured that *Kiss Me, Kate* was a visual delight, but the run of just over a year suggests that London was not overexcited, despite the splash of costumes, the wit of the lyrics, the excellent cast and the variety and quality of the songs. *Theatre World* decided that

> as the songs are by Cole Porter, and he is at his brilliant best, the musical aspect of *Kiss Me, Kate* gives us the best score, with some of the cunningest lyrics, that London has heard for many years. And as these are sung with assurance and often inspiration by Patricia Morison, Bill Johnson and Julie Wilson, we can be satisfied that we are getting full value for our money. I think the authors of *Kiss Me, Kate* are asking a good deal of their cast, by expecting them to be able not only to sing these gems of Porter's but also to play scenes from *The Shrew* [sic] with equal conviction. We have too high a Shakespearean standard in this country and, as a result, these scenes are sometimes lame and laboured and one awaits the next musical number impatiently.[2]

The *Stage* found much to enjoy in the performances but noted 'some disillusionment' as it struggled to see what was happening on stage 'through the rising smoke clouds from thousands of cigars and cigarettes in the packed, hot theatre', remarking that

> The book lacks the 'punch' and coherent effectiveness that we have come to expect from big American musicals. Even more disappointing in a sense is the music of Cole Porter. One's impression is that his aim was to adapt his musical pen to the Italian idiom that is, of course, appropriate to the legend of Petruchio and Katharine. At any rate, several of the principal numbers, while often graceful, are rather more sentimentally operatic in

manner than is entirely suited to a light entertainment of this kind. In the matter of really catching numbers Mr. Porter is less inventive than usual, though there are a few tunes which tickle the ear most agreeably.[3]

This was the tenor of many reviews including *Socialist Leader*, which concluded that 'the plot is flimsy and the humour thin and unoriginal. Although the music and songs are good, they are nothing outstanding.'[4]

The piece has enjoyed various London revivals. In 1970 Peter Coe's production for Sadler's Wells Opera met with mild enthusiasm. Most of the principals were cast from the company's stock, headed by Emile Belcourt and Ann Howard, with Judith Bruce imported from the world of musicals to play Lois. In the *Guardian* Philip Hope-Wallace praised her 'enormous verve' but was less impressed with London's major opera house staging a musical to please a public that might fight shy of opera: 'for myself it seems a downward extension of the repertory'. As for the work itself, he thought that 'Broadway and Merrie England had been here 'not quite happily yoked together', suggesting that 'even the most enjoyable American musicals have always contained yawning stretches of flat comedy'.[5] This despite Coe's having tipped old British music-hall routines into the Spewacks' libretto. The managing director of Sadler's Wells, Stephen Arlen, pointed out that he had received only one complaint about *Kiss Me, Kate* being brought into the company's repertoire; when Gounod's *Faust* had been announced there had been fifty. Coe's production reappeared the following Christmas season to even less acclaim. The *Evening News* found it 'A tepid kiss from Kate [...] it is too tame [...] No New York verve.'[6]

Bolstered by the commercial success of *Les Misérables*, in 1987 the Royal Shakespeare Company staged its own production of the musical shrew, starring Paul Jones and Nichola McAuliffe. Perhaps the choice of a musical play written around one of the Bard's plays would forestall some of the criticism that might be levelled at the obvious commercialism of the venture? Nevertheless, Eric Sams considered that

> *Kiss Me, Kate* is likely to be unfamiliar to most theatregoers; indeed, its spoken style sounds far more dated than the Shakespeare material it borrows. I think the book should have been treated with far more simplicity and restraint [...] Whenever the work is shown the respect due to a masterpiece of its genre it responds with genuine warmth, and so does the audience.[7]

In 2001 the 1999 New York revival directed by Michael Blakemore opened at the Victoria Palace, with Americans Brent Barrett and Marin Mazzie as the quarrelsome lovers. The occasional repertory production has also tussled with the grandness of the Spewack–Porter work. When the director Clare Venables staged it for Norwich Playhouse in 1996 she thought *Kiss Me, Kate* 'such a naff idea. And so there's a problem about that and about the way it's written. It's not really Shakespeare. It's little bits of Shakespeare and saying "Oh, look, isn't Shakespeare's language funny?"' Venables hated the medieval costumes of the original too: 'I think virtually the first thing I said was "I'm not going to have all those tights and pointed shoes."'[8] It is, however, into that twilit world between modernism and medievalism that *Kiss Me, Kate* has been thrust.

The disparity between the British and American critic is highlighted by the reception Rodgers and Hammerstein's fourth work (only Broadway had seen their third, *Allegro*) received on either side of the Atlantic. In New York the notices were loud in praise. Richard Watts Jr hailed 'an utterly captivating work of theatrical art [...] one of the finest musical plays in the history of the American theatre'.[9] Howard Barnes for the *Herald Tribune* declared it 'a show of rare enchantment. It is novel in texture and treatment, rich in dramatic substance, and eloquent in song'. In the *World-Telegram* William Hawkins wrote, 'This is the ultimate modern blending of music and popular theatre to date, with the finest kind of balance between story and song, and hilarity and heartbreak.'[10] In New York the work was festooned with honours, including the Pulitzer Prize for Drama, the first musical to be awarded the prize since the 1931 *Of Thee I Sing*.

Directed for Broadway by Joshua Logan (who also produced alongside Rodgers, Hammerstein and Leland Hayward), **South Pacific** (Theatre Royal, Drury Lane, 1 November 1951; 802) marked the writers' move away from ensemble theatre pieces (all three of their earlier collaborations) to a star-based formula, one that would be carried on by *The King and I* and *The Sound of Music*. Broadway's marquee had Mary Martin and Ezio Pinza; for the West End, Martin and Wilbur Evans. For Martin it was a return to Drury Lane after Noel Coward's *Pacific 1860*; indeed, when Rodgers and Hammerstein first mentioned *South Pacific* her heart must have sunk at the recall of the Coward débâcle. Evans, a Broadway veteran from *By the Beautiful Sea* and *Up in Central Park*, was making his London debut, although Georges Guétary, a Broadway player who had made his name in London with *Bless the Bride*, had been the preferred choice. The casting of British singer Muriel Smith as Bloody Mary marked the beginning of her association with Rodgers and Hammerstein; she would go on to play Lady Thiang in London's *The King and I*, and dub Juanita Hall's voice for Bloody Mary's songs in the *South Pacific* movie. The only actor to appear in the American and British productions *and* the 1958 movie was American actor Ray Walston, who would go on to originate major roles in some Broadway musicals including *House of Flowers* and most notably *Damn Yankees* in which he appeared as the satanic Applegate (and once again he couldn't be bettered for the movie).

The British reception for *South Pacific* illustrated the disparity between American and British critical reaction that was by now well established. The British critic might be prepared to throw a hat in the air for the Rodgers and Hammerstein songs, but responses were guarded. It is well to remember, too, that long runs are no guarantee of audience enjoyment; some of *South Pacific*'s prolonged West End stay can be traced back to the vast publicity campaign that had preceded then accompanied it. The *Stage* claimed that no British play had ever enjoyed the 'overpowering advance publicity' generated by both *Kiss Me, Kate* and *South Pacific*, discouraging for the home-grown British musical with no facility to whip up enthusiasm for domestic product, and perhaps overemphasising the qualities of the interlopers. There seemed no doubt as to the efficacy of Martin and those songs, but as for what linked them

> All this [plot] is told in tolerably sophisticated dialogue, but between the songs there are too many dull passages [...] there is too much story, and the story [...] is neither very good in itself nor of a character likely to appeal to British audiences as it has done to Americans. For it is not very easy for us to be interested in a complicated and not over-exciting yarn about the American-Japanese conflict in the South Pacific during what the programme calls 'the recent war' or indeed in yet another colour-bar problem.[11]

Interestingly, this notice also complained of the lack of 'big' scenes and of spectacle, especially odd when one considers the locale. This problem, indeed, is almost accentuated in the much-criticised movie, when vivid colour filters are inflicted at various key points, suggesting that even on celluloid the locale doesn't count for much. Meanwhile at Drury Lane, the *Queen* thought it 'disappointingly slow and not very dramatic'.[12] *The Times* concurred, thinking the settings and themes of the piece of little concern to the British and finding the 'pace is something between the deliberate and the ponderous. *Oklahoma!* carried its story along on the wings of song and dance [*South Pacific* almost completely dispensed with dance] but the musical and the narrative parts of this show are not much more closely integrated than in the average English musical play.'[13] The extended headline for the *Daily Express* review gave the thumbs down: 'Alas, Some Not Entirely Enchanted Evening. *South Pacific* Has Melody, Ideas – But No Wonder Touch'. Noticing that the first-night audience had been slow to applaud, John Barber had 'hoped for a musical *play* – a play described by the producer as "a deep emotional experience". I GOT a *42nd Street 'Madame Butterfly'*. Barber's praise for Martin was solid, but her leading man gave 'a leaden performance. I thought of an old uncle with the fire gone out'. Despite 'brilliant overtones in a smooth, tepid show' this was 'the weakest of all the Hammerstein-Rodgers musicals'.[14]

The gallery cheered when Martin sang 'I'm Gonna Wash That Man Right Outa My Hair' and did so on stage (no subsequent production would dare omit this trademark moment), but Beverley Baxter MP in the *Evening Standard* announced 'I would not place *South Pacific* in the same street as *Oklahoma!* It is contrived – skilfully but laboriously – whereas *Oklahoma!* just came busting out',[15] and W. A. Darlington could not see the piece being as popular as it had been in New York.[16] Part of the difficulty was that the trumpeting had been overdone. The *Illustrated London News* hinted at such: 'For Mary Martin's sake, and for the Rodgers songs, we welcome *South Pacific*; but we might have welcomed it twice as loudly if we had not been told, from New York, that it is four times as good as it is.' Furthermore, 'Its plot lunges into dullness […] and it is short of those spectacular flares, those swoops and swirls, that we look for now at Drury Lane.'[17]

This is a peculiarly British criticism; somehow the Lane's reputation was above the game, and its history and reputation for grandeur demanded a certain brand of musical entertainment. No New York theatre held such exalted rank or made such demands as the Lane. Yet since the war, when the Novello shows specially sculptured for that theatre had ended and turned to other theatres, the Lane had obligingly accommodated its productions rather than insisting on the blatant spectacles – the flares, swoops and swirls – on which its personality had been built. Spectacle is not a word one associates with *Oklahoma!* or *Carousel*, but at least *South Pacific* brought a lushness of locale in Jo Mielziner's settings. The very title, after all, promised tropical heat, the coolness of lagoon. But how much of the promise came true? One wonders how much the setting of the piece mattered to Rodgers and Hammerstein. Of one thing is certain: no Broadway musical ever set out with 'How will it suit Drury Lane?' as its mantra, and more than one American import set out on its boards would prove eminently unsuitable.

South Pacific marked a sea change in the Rodgers and Hammerstein canon. It is easy to forget that this was their first modern, contemporary musical. Both *Oklahoma!* and *Carousel* had seemed (despite what any programme note told you) to belong to some unidentifiable, pliable past; *South Pacific* was now. That 'now' was, however, essentially American; its preoccupation with American war and the colour question. Such modernity meant that dream sequences were dispensed with, and choreography almost negligible, presumably in a striving for some sort of up-to-the-moment reality. A sort of exoticism was at work again, and there was a clear appeal in its source material, James Michener's *Tales of the South Pacific*. The heat rose up from its pages, as well as an opportunity to have girls in swimwear and a stage full of sailors, ideal as a male chorus for a musical: pure macho. In this, however, they were out of date, for in 1950 the Coliseum had staged the Broadway play *Mister Roberts* (co-authored and directed by *South Pacific*'s Broadway director), a comedy about bored and frustrated sailors on a US cargo ship during World War II in the South Pacific. It seems likely that Rodgers and Hammerstein, via Logan's connections, were influenced by this piece. The young salts of *Mister Roberts* act very much in the way of *South Pacific*'s salts, losing the compass point whenever a girl ('dame') comes in view. They seem almost always just about to break into 'There Is Nothin' Like a Dame'. They become overheated while watching the girls on shore take a shower, just as Nellie shampoos in *South Pacific* (and the audience can take a peep at her on stage). Logan's idea of a sailor in the South Pacific is Hammerstein's idea of a sailor in the South Pacific. It was seemingly shared by Rodgers: 'Boys in the Navy are boys in the Navy, and there's not much that you can write for them except songs that are fun to sing.'[18]

There we are! It's not a particularly encouraging comment from a composer supposed to be at the forefront of changing the face of the American musical in the mid-twentieth century. The words and music for the sailors of E. M. Forster, Eric Crozier and Benjamin Britten's opera *Billy Budd* are far from fun; even the British musical *Scapa!*[19] had sailors ruminating on the wonders of the world ('Seagull in the Sky'). Logan and Rodgers and Hammerstein's and *South Pacific*'s sailors do everything you might expect a conventional and uncomplicated but theatrical sailor to do. Essentially, they are the comic relief (and what a relief from all that talk), working up a frenzy of testosterone over those dames and helping Nellie through 'Honey Bun'. However, just as Logan had introduced a stage full of beefcake into *Mister Roberts*, so it was reintroduced into *South Pacific*. In a world without the Chippendales, when the male body in various states of undress inhabited such magazines as *Health and Physique* and *Health and Efficiency*, with homosexuality rooted in an illegal subculture, perhaps *South Pacific* was the first post-war American musical with a subtext that appealed to gay theatregoers. Rodgers and Hammerstein, but probably not Logan, would have been appalled. Rodgers and Hammerstein musicals have always been straight down the line.

Another development in *South Pacific* is the importance of its children. Now, they begin the show with a cute duet, 'Dites-moi' (in French, if you please; something to make the audience feel as if it is intelligent enough to be sung at in a foreign language). After this, there seemed to be no stopping them. They were out in numbers marching through Rodgers and Hammerstein's next work *The King and I*, complaining about their elders' irritating ways in *Flower Drum Song*, and transmogrifying into the spookily cute, wearing white ankle socks and clothes made from curtains in *The Sound of Music*. The younger generation may have been a by-product of Hammerstein's essential 'goodness'. Didn't Beverley Baxter MP salute Hammerstein 'who is a most generous and lovable creature' and who 'has constituted himself the poet of the inexpressive'?[20]

Whatever the particulars, it may be that the London production of *South Pacific* was hampered in various ways. One of the difficulties Martin faced was in adapting to her new leading man, who generated less excitement than his Broadway predecessor. But something else went very wrong once the company arrived in London, as Rodgers discovered when he arrived at Drury Lane to find rehearsals in disarray. Logan had radically altered the staging from the Broadway production, so much to its detriment that Rodgers thought the show might last a couple of weeks. Martin proceeded to have hysterics (perhaps re-enacting one of the dressing-room scenes she had thrown, in the same dressing room, during *Pacific 1860*), insisting that the original staging be reinstated. The West End *South Pacific* had a troubled gestation. After a year Martin was replaced by Julie

Wilson; the *Stage* reported that 'she plays with no attempt to dog the footsteps of her illustrious predecessor'. [21]

The British musical ploughed on, seemingly ignorant of the changes wrought by Rodgers and Hammerstein. Novello's last completed work *Gay's the Word* tweaked his operetta formula by folding it with comedy material for Cicely Courtneidge. The other star vehicle of the year, *Zip Goes a Million*, was tailor made for the comedian George Formby by Eric Maschwitz and composer George Posford. *And So to Bed*, Vivian Ellis's musical on the life of Samuel Pepys, was discreet and tasteful in miniature, a world away from the ungainly *Rainbow Square*, with music by Robert Stolz.

1951 Broadway Exports

The King and I (1,246) and *Paint Your Wagon* (289).

1951 Broadway Only

Top-runner of the year was a Phil Silvers' vehicle *Top Banana* (350), followed by the pleasantry of *A Tree Grows in Brooklyn* (270). This adaptation of Betty Smith's novel was notable for its central performance by Shirley Booth and attractive score. *Make a Wish* (102) went along happily with Hugh Martin's jaunty songs, but the distinctive *Flahooley* (40) had the more interesting libretto and score. Billie Worth starred in the curtailed *Courtin' Time* (37), and another period romance, *Seventeen* (180), was inoffensively charming.

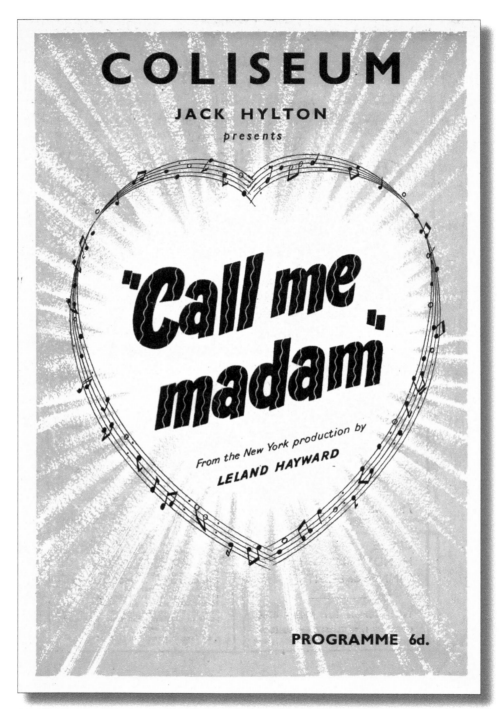

11 The West End production of Irving Berlin's political fantasy *Call Me Madam* made a star of American Billie Worth at the Coliseum in 1952

1952

Call Me Madam
Love from Judy

A*nnie Get Your Gun* had been such a London success, running several months longer than on Broadway, that London had the right to expect Irving Berlin's next musical, but the 1949 *Miss Liberty*, a diverting entertainment fictitiously centred on the building of the Statue of Liberty, had been thought unexportable after a muted response in New York (indeed, one of its songs had insisted that it was 'Only for Americans'). It wasn't often that audiences sitting through a Broadway musical in Shaftesbury Avenue had a sense of *déjà vu*: what *did* **Call Me Madam** (Coliseum, 15 March 1952; 485) recall? Oddly, it may have been a British musical, *Her Excellency*, which had opened in the West End in 1949. Her Excellency was Frances Maxwell, supposedly Britain's first female ambassador, sent to a mythical part of South America to secure an important meat contract for Britain. Once installed, she falls for the handsome American ambassador. The reason for *Her Excellency* was the antics of its star, Cicely Courtneidge, in a variety of escapades, in which the songs of Manning Sherwin and Harry Parr-Davies were merely incidental. It seems unlikely that Berlin knew of *Her Excellency*, and anyway the inspiration for both *Her Excellency* and *Call Me Madam* was begun in 1949 when President Harry Truman appointed the wealthy socialite Perle Skirvin Mesta as America's ambassador to Luxembourg.

Mesta had not only handed Howard Lindsay and Russel Crouse the idea for a topical musical, but handed Berlin the title for one of its best numbers with the name she was known by, 'The Hostess with the Mostes' on the Ball'. In this if nothing else, *Call Me Madam* emanated from real life. From the facts of the case it was only a short journey to the plot of *Call Me Madam*, with party-giving Sally Adams appointed ambassador to the mythical principality of Lichtenburg, where her unusual approach to her duties makes a strong impression. She is taken (shades of *Her Excellency*) with Lichtenburg's foreign minister Cosmo Constantine, with whom she falls in love. A subplot charts the romance of Adams' assistant Ken Gibson with the principality's Princess Maria.

On Broadway the show had the benefit of Ethel Merman, who three years before had been one of the principal reasons for the success of *Annie Get Your Gun*. There was no chance that Merman would sign for Jack Hylton's London production, for which the less stellar Billie Worth was hired, along with her husband Donald Burr, who would play Pemberton Maxwell. Hylton's coup was to sign the distinguished Austrian actor Anton Walbrook, well known in Britain as a film star, as Constantine.[1] When Walbrook took three months out to fulfil a film contract, his role was taken over by Burr until his return. Audiences may have felt short-changed in missing Walbrook's particularly continental sophistication, although sophistication is not a quality one associates with

Call Me Madam. Bizarrely, Hylton commissioned a song for Walbrook from Sandy Wilson, the British creator of *The Boy Friend*. Although it was written, the number seems never to have been used, and anyway what would the Berlin estate have thought about such a prank?

Opening just as his presentation of *Kiss Me, Kate* was about to close, the London *Call Me Madam* confirmed Hylton's post-war commitment to the Broadway musical, including some of the most challenging and innovative. The roll call of his management is impressive: *Romany Love* (1947) through *Annie Get Your Gun* (1947), *High Button Shoes* (1948), *Kiss Me, Kate* (1951), *Call Me Madam* (1952), *Wish You Were Here* and *Paint Your Wagon* (both 1953), *Pal Joey* (1954), *Wonderful Town* (1955) and Hylton's final throw *Camelot* (1961). During this period Hylton also championed revues featuring the Crazy Gang, a group of British comics who seemed never to have been anything but elderly, and some British musicals, one Italian and one South African. The British musical was outmoded and apparently impotent compared to the insistent influence of its American counterpart. Visiting London in 1952, the critic Mawby Green wrote

> The British-made stage musicals never cease to amaze us. Each time we re-visit London we hope the pattern will have changed. But no, we always find a mythical kingdom, the leading comedian chuckling around in his underwear or masquerading mischievously in skirts; the costumes scissored in a style that doesn't do anything for anybody, while the dance routines, without a kick of originality, are lashed out frantically all over the stage. There is never a musical number melodious enough to remember, and the book, well, just a prop to hang the title on.[2]

It was time for the *Stage* to reflect.

> Plots in musical plays are regarded far more seriously since we made a habit of importing our musical fare from the States. The book of *Call Me Madam* would almost pass as a straight play, dealing as it does with feasible facts of contemporary life, in the framework of a satire on American foreign policy. The heroine's cosy telephone conversations with President Truman, addressed as Harry, bring an air of authenticity to the story [...] *South Pacific* is a story which might have been the experience of any nurse serving with the United States Navy. There is also comment on the colour question for those playgoers who like to think, even at musical shows.[3]

This is fairly desperate stuff because the writer sets the bar so low. Would *you* care to sit through the book of *Call Me Madam* in the guise of a straight play? It might work, in the manner of a mild-mannered Noel Coward comedy. We may search without success for those 'feasible facts of contemporary life' that were evident to the editor of the *Stage*, who also detects 'satire', although not to the strength with which it would be served up in Britain in the 1960s and beyond. Political satire with music was what happened at Stratford East when *Mrs Wilson's Diary*, Joan Littlewood's theatrical cartoon of the then Prime Minister Harold Wilson and his devoted wife Mary, became such a hit of the moment. This was properly disrespectful, something the writers of *Call Me Madam* would never have contemplated. Much sharper political satire than anything *Call Me Madam* put up had been seen on Broadway in the 1930s with *Of Thee I Sing* and *Let 'Em Eat Cake*. Anyway, London had already rejected political satire in post-war musicals by turning its back on *Finian's Rainbow*. As for those cosy telephone chats with 'Harry' Truman, by the time of the London revival of the show these were cringingly embarrassing; we knew the White House would never have accepted a call from Noele Gordon, who was no more than the owner of a (on a good day) two-star Midlands motel.[4] And what's that about *South Pacific* being something that might have happened to any nurse? Their mothers would wish it so. Pearl among these comments is the praise given *South Pacific* because it 'comments' on the 'colour question', something that *Finian's Rainbow* had done more forcefully, and that Hammerstein had already dared do in the 1920s with *Show Boat*. The truth is that his comments on the same question a quarter of a century later are no more strongly argued.

As for those 'playgoers who like to think, even at musical shows' we can only hope the writer's tongue was in cheek. Oddly, there isn't much in British criticism about thinking, not when it comes to musical theatre, although if thinking was to be expected it was probably in the direction of American rather than British product. Sympathetic as one may be to any exercising of the brain, *Call Me Madam* is hardly a work to stir such activity. The impression it leaves behind is one of stolidity, broad humour, romance uncluttered by hate, vengeance or unfaithfulness, songs that slip in and (luckily for Berlin's bank balance) out of context. It may be that audiences in 1952 rocked themselves with laughter at the political chicanery revealed on stage (the British would do it all over again while watching the BBC TV comedy *Yes, Minister* and the puppets of *Spitting Image*) but Lindsay and Crouse's play was all innocence, when defaulting politicians in musical theatre land were regarded more as cads than villains.

Call Me Madam is merely a variant on the old 'Find the Lady' card trick that you might see being played out as you stroll the broadwalk. Send a *man* as ambassador to Lichtenburg and the curtain doesn't even rise on this story. The comedy is ready-made because it's a woman in politics, it's overlooking everything the suffragettes ever did. In *Annie Get Your Gun* the lady has a rifle; in *Call Me Madam* she has an attaché case. The politics of *Call Me Madam* is not nuclear button but soft centre. Nevertheless, Hylton and his production team were nervous about how the British public would take to so apparently liberal a dose of the American type. Within hours of completing negotiations with its Broadway producers Hylton flew to New York with his production team headed by director Richard Bird and choreographer George Carden. Together they stared at the Broadway production, directed by George Abbott and choreographed by Jerome Robbins, and considered whether the political content needed adjustment for London. They decided it didn't. Audiences consulting their programmes at the Coliseum saw a 'note from Uncle Sam' intended to ease them into the frame of mind that would make *Call Me Madam* palatable to the British.

Philip Hope-Wallace for the *Guardian* found the pulse slow and the jokes incomprehensible, reporting a 'friendly, indeed an almost doggedly fanatical, reception [...] This preference for things when American, which in the native style would cause little stir, is an interesting social phenomenon, a side effect perhaps of our own social revolution in which American classlessness (as we see it) is an appealing feature'. Nevertheless, he thought the piece 'old-fashioned', its leading role 'filled more or less by Miss Billie Worth' (whom he likened to Pat Kirkwood), and 'the dances, the sets and the book are undistinguished and unpoetic as British pantomime'.[5] The critic for the *Queen* was offended by swaying painted canvas drops, and 'exceptionally unattractive costumes'.[6] Peter Fleming thought that Worth 'goes energetically through the repertoire of a comedienne without actually being comic, except in the very broadest sense of that word'.[7] Frances Stephens decided that

> The American political satire is no obstacle at all to the enjoyment of this first rate piece of entertainment. In any case one would endure an evening of the most incomprehensible Governmental back-chat for the pleasure of seeing magnetic Billie Worth, who among the visiting stars of American musicals bids fair to become second only to Mary Martin in the affections of British audiences. She has the same extraordinary vitality and the same rich sense of comedy.[8]

Worth had come from Broadway after playing in the previous year's *Courtin' Time*, and was to have probably her finest moment with *Call Me Madam*. Ten years later Britain was less enthusiastic about her return with fellow American Bill Shirley in a 'new' American musical, described as 'a blending of musical and revue', *Yankee Doodle Comes to Town*. The newness of the piece didn't extend to its score, made up from existent songs. After a rocky first night at the Bristol Hippodrome in November 1962, the show meandered through a provincial tour *en route* to London but gave up on the road.

Following her dismissal from the television soap-opera *Crossroads*, in 1983 Noele Gordon played Adams in a provincial Roger Redfarn revival at the Victoria Palace. The home-grown cast was not up to the 1952 standard, but the formidable Gordon's first appearance was greeted with rapture by coach-loads of her doting admirers, applauding vociferously when she turned on stage to face them with the unanswerable line 'I'm back!' Peter Hepple in the *Stage* was in line with others, finding it 'very dated indeed'. As for the leading lady, she 'attacks the part [...] as if her life depends on it [...] there is a glorious indomitability about

Noele Gordon that makes her sail triumphantly through a piece which with the exception of Irving Berlin's music and lyrics creaks in every joint.'⁹ Thirty years earlier, having understudied Worth in the first West End production, Gordon took the role in the first national tour, but her 1983 *Call Me Madam* was off after seven weeks.

In September the first post-war manifestation of the No Man's Land musical, belonging wholly neither to London or Broadway, arrived with **Love from Judy** (Saville Theatre, 25 September 1952; 594). The co-mixture of New York and London was always a matter of authorship: part British, part American, and not necessarily in that order. Where a significant input (usually the score) was by American hands, they may legitimately be considered at least part American. They veer to Broadway, they collide in Shaftesbury Avenue. Almost without exception, that is where No Man's Land musicals stayed, for transfers to New York were rare (sensibly, as it is unlikely they would have thrived). In many cases these hinterland works have been overlooked partly because – evidently – they are not Broadway products. However, they are often the products of writers whose other works were usually produced on Broadway, and who had been an important factor in their creation.

The transatlantic component of *Love from Judy* was its score by Hugh Martin, with Jack Gray as co-lyricist. Jean Webster's sentimental novel *Daddy Long Legs* was adapted by Eric Maschwitz, a hard-working journeyman in the world of British musicals, whose other (genuinely British) musicals included *Zip Goes a Million, Happy Holiday* and *Summer Song*. After the gaiety of a Mardi Gras opening, the scene moved to a grim orphanage (a more memorable orphanage sequence started the Charles Strouse – Lee Adams *Annie* of later years). Eighteen-year-old orphan Jerusha (Judy) Abbott consoles the younger inmates who have not been allowed to see the carnival. Jerusha is rescued by the kindness of a patron, Jervis Pendleton, who underwrites her education. Not knowing his role in her life and imagining her patron to be an elderly gentleman, Judy falls in love with her Daddy Long Legs.

Despite the pleasantries of *Love from Judy* it seems unlikely that it would have enjoyed substantial success without Jean Carson. Emile Littler planned to put one of his favoured soubrettes into the title role, but Maschwitz was determined to promote Carson, who had already made an impression in London in Noel Coward's *After the Ball* and in pantomime at the Casino. Carson was reluctant to sign; a reluctance to get involved with any project seems to have been one of her estimable characteristics. After all, some shows she was talked into proved disappointing: her dalliance with *Finian's Rainbow* and the British short-runner *Strike a Light!* in 1966. Maschwitz had written five pleading letters before she agreed to play Judy. 'Jean Carson takes her place among the West End stars', wrote the *Stage* critic after the first night. 'She has a quality of her own: a charming combination of strength and softness.'¹⁰ A fortnight later the *Stage* celebrated how 'she restored our waning faith in the possibility of a new English leading lady being comparable to those brilliant visitors from America who have delighted us for the last few years'.[11] A full recording of the London first night confirms the proficiency and professionalism of all concerned, not least Carson in a triumphantly confident performance. For her it truly was a night of sudden radiance.

And yet for Carson, *Love from Judy* proved to be a poisoned chalice. Her reputation was made, but fossilised when Littler would not release her from the production. Shortly after the 500th performance, she collapsed with exhaustion, and was replaced for a time by understudy June Whitfield. By the time Carson left the show during its post-West End tour in March 1955, she had been with the production for two and a half years. Littler had kept her tethered to her post because he sensibly realised that it would be almost impossible to replace her. It was: Jillian Comber (who would go on to a career as a BBC *Crackerjack* girl) took over. During Carson's two and a half year sentence, no offers had come her way, no writers banged at her door, no producers wanted to nurture her. She left London after signing a contract with the National Broadcasting Corporation of America, and the West End had effectively seen the end of her.

The Canadian Bill O'Connor (who also stayed through to the tour) was Daddy Long Legs, with strong support from Adelaide Hall in one of those 'black' roles so familiar to British audiences – she had just played one such in the previous year's *Kiss Me, Kate*. Her reward was two extraneous numbers, 'Kind to Animals' and 'A Touch of Voodoo', both vaguely Broadway in feel, and the sort of songs that had usually been handed to black singers whose colour did not allow them major roles or numbers that were essential to the show's plot. Johnny Brandon (himself to be part-author of a No Man's Land musical, *Cindy*) and Audrey Freeman had the light comedy roles, with June Whitfield getting two numbers of her own, 'Here We Are' and 'Dum Dum Dum'. All were pleasant, as was Carson's first number 'I Never Dream When I'm Asleep' and 'Daddy Long Legs', beyond which she had little to sing except in encouraging the chorus to 'Go and Get Your Old Banjo'.

All were in Martin's happy manner, without lingering in the memory as had his numbers for the film *Meet Me in St. Louis*. London knew nothing of Martin's earlier scores: *Best Foot Forward*, *Look, Ma, I'm Dancin'*, and *Make a Wish*. Martin's easily-digested music inhabited the sound-world of an earlier decade, and there was simply nothing in *Love from Judy* to jump the footlights. Think for a moment of the songs of the shows that were in the air around this time: *Carousel, Kiss Me, Kate, South Pacific, Call Me Madam*, and the truth is bared. Who now remembers any of the numbers in *Love from Judy*? This is not altogether Martin's fault. In a way, all those songs (and there are rather too many of them) work well enough. Maschwitz may just be the more culpable. He was one of the few toilers in the field who genuinely seemed interested in setting up a school of identifiably British musicals. He gets alpha-plus for effort, but there is at the back of so much of his stuff the feeling that he yearns to ape the

American. Maybe, but he still remains one of the champions of a British West End against Broadway West End.

Love from Judy was probably the highlight of Maschwitz's career in musicals. Identifying it as 'a new American musical, cast in Britain', Kenneth Tynan decided, 'It sang (let us all pray) a requiem over the corpse of middle-aged musical comedy' and noted Carson's success as 'without parallel in recent years'.[12] For *Punch*, '*Love from Judy* is the nearest we have come to challenge American supremacy in this field. It hasn't the all-in magic of *Oklahoma!* (I doubt if that will ever be repeated), but its taste is better and its attack more astringent than those of recent imports from Broadway.'[13] It was, however, not musical enough for some of the public. Mrs Mary Stevens of Bushey wrote to ask of the periodical *Everybody's*

> What has happened to the old musical comedy that was really a *comedy*? The musical shows of today take themselves so seriously, what with people dying all over the place in *Carousel* and grim battle scenes in *South Pacific*. Now, in *Love from Judy*, we are supposed to be entertained by orphanage girls on their hands and knees scrubbing floors. Had it not been for vivacious Jean Carson I'd have walked out of the theatre from sheer depression.[14]

For most, *Love from Judy* manifested as a British musical, the only other home grown entry of the year being the mildly diverting **Bet Your Life**. Starring frolicsome Arthur Askey as a psychic jockey, its words were by Alan Melville, its music by Kenneth Leslie-Smith and Charles Zwar.

1952 Broadway Exports

Wish You Were Here (598).

1952 Broadway Only

Lashings of Irish whimsy arrived in **Three Wishes for Jamie** (92), with a distinguished leading man in John Raitt and some pleasing songs by Ralph Blane. **Buttrio Square** (7) survived a traumatic gestation only to be trashed in New York. Perhaps remembering Hammerstein's translation of Bizet's *Carmen* into *Carmen Jones*, less skilful authors turned Verdi's *Aida* into the spectacularly staged **My Darlin' Aida** (89). The action was moved to a Civil War-torn Tennessee in the 1860s, but the lack of extractable melodies in the source material proved unhelpful.

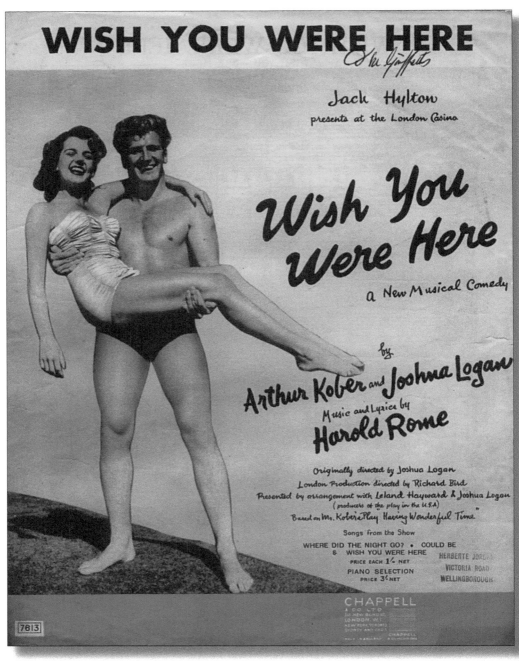

12 It might have been sponsored by Butlins: Harold Rome's love song to the American summer camp, *Wish You Were Here*: Joe Tiger Robinson scoops up a bathing beauty in the 1953 London production at the Casino

1953

Paint Your Wagon
Guys and Dolls
The King and I
Wish You Were Here

O F THE FOUR AMERICAN MUSICALS to arrive in London in 1953, only one may be said to have been a critical success. The rest, including Alan Jay Lerner and Frederick Loewe's *Paint Your Wagon* (Her Majesty's, 11 February 1953; 478), had cooler welcomes. After *Brigadoon* the public may have had high expectations of the writers' new piece, one that would seem to be an odd one out in a list that suggested sophistication: *My Fair Lady, Camelot* and *Gigi*. Here was a saga of cowboy-miners, with camp-fire songs such as 'Wanderin' Star' and 'They Call the Wind Maria'. Little prettiness was involved in the gold-mining story set in the mid-nineteenth century North California settlement of Rumson. Jennifer Rumson has the dubious honour of being the only woman in town. Her kindly, illiterate widower father, Ben, buys a wife from a Mormon. The marriage is not a happy one, and Jennifer, in love with the Mexican Julio Valveras, runs away. So does Ben's wife. Jennifer returns as an educated woman. Events are enlivened when the stagecoach brings ladies of pleasure into Rumson, but gold is discovered elsewhere and the miners and their molls move on to a new settlement, leaving the dying Ben and the faithful Jennifer awaiting the return of her lover. When an exhausted Julio returns, it is to the sound of the wagons leaving Rumson.

Restaged for London by Richard Bird, the Her Majesty's production replicated the original Oliver Smith sets and costumes by Motley, with Agnes de Mille's choreography reproduced by her assistant Mavis Ray, and musical direction by Cyril Ornadel. Pleasing to the British public, the show ran six months longer than the Broadway original, although it has never been revived in New York or London. Much attention was focused on the pairing of veteran Bobby Howes as Ben with his daughter Sally Ann Howes as Jennifer. Bobby Howes belonged to *British* theatre of the 1930s, some shreds of which hung about his daughter's technique. His career had dipped four years earlier when he had told the heckling gallery to 'Shut up' at the first night of the British musical *Roundabout*, after which managements blacked him. Sally Ann would go on to a long career in musicals, including the three home-growns *Bet Your Life, Romance in Candlelight* and *Summer Song*, and Broadway engagements that included taking over from Julie Andrews in *My Fair Lady*, and, both unseen in London, leads in *Kwamina* and *What Makes Sammy Run?* The American Ken Cantrill (Julio) had played the lead in the Australian production of *Brigadoon*, but subsequently seems to have vanished from musicals until the off-Broadway *The Athenian Touch* in 1964.

Anthony Cookman's review for the *Tatler* presaged the coming of the 'Make Our Garden Grow' finale in *Candide*.

> [*Paint Your Wagon*] rises gently to a climax of lively, almost frantic gaiety, holds this note for a good long while and then drops slowly and confidently to a quiet ending. In this ending there glimmers the ghost of an idea – the Voltairean idea that in the cultivation of our domestic garden there is perhaps more real satisfaction than in a lucky strike of gold in California.[1]

Philip Hope-Wallace considered 'it is the choreobantic crowd which carries the show, and among them Laurie Payne [playing Jake Whippany] singing to banjo stood out as something authentic sounding in an evening of much synthetic gaiety'.[2]

After attending a performance of *Paint Your Wagon* (not from choice) the composer William Alwyn remembered the affection he felt for the British musicals he had occasionally visited in the past.

> These English so-called 'musicals' have been ousted by the American 'musical' show. I have only suffered one, and a more pernicious evening I have never spent. Everything was very loud and very dull, and a tune was made to stick in one's memory by sheer persistent reiteration – 'plugging'. It is a solemn thought that if only something is done often enough and loud enough, it implants itself indelibly on the mind. I can still remember the 'hit' tune from the show (*Paint Your Wagon*), while music of a subtle beauty heard quite recently has left only an impression – a passing fragrance like a flower.[3]

With its strong storyline and score *Paint Your Wagon* was a substantial contribution to the Broadway musical in London, and if one suspects that the plot's milieu is not its creators' natural territory, the quality of the songs is palpable. Ben Rumson's 'Wanderin' Star' breaks out of everything else, a hymn to human restlessness, and 'I Talk to the Trees' now seems a precursor to *My Fair Lady*'s 'On the Street Where You Live'.

The outstanding work of the year was **Guys and Dolls** (Coliseum, 28 May 1953; 555), in effect a run at least equal to the Broadway production of 1,200 performances, for the Coliseum was twice as large as the 46th Street Theatre. *Paint Your Wagon* had retained its Broadway production components for London but taken on a British cast, the whole restaged by Richard Bird; *The King and I* similarly presented a British cast, with the original production restaged by Rodgers and Hammerstein's emissary Jerome Whyte, and restaged choreography; *Wish You Were Here* thought it could also get away with an all-British cast (it couldn't), with Richard Bird again brought in for a restaging of the Broadway production. True, George S. Kaufman's New York direction for

Guys and Dolls was restaged in London by Arthur Lewis, but the most essential members of the first Broadway company were brought over. What alternative was there if the piece was to succeed? The Broadway originals were headed by Vivian Blaine, Sam Levene, Stubby Kaye, Tom Pedi and Johnny Silver, with Jerry Wayne joining the cast as Sky Masterson, and, as Miss Sarah Brown, Lizbeth Webb, well known in the West End from her roles in Vivian Ellis and A. P. Herbert's *Big Ben* and *Bless the Bride*.

Guys and Dolls, the most street-wise American musical to have reached London since the end of the war, came extraordinarily close to expressing the humanity of the common man. No other American musical to reach London had quite done that, although elements of such intent can be discerned. *Oklahoma!* may have broken bounds, but that was a work that hovers on the edge of fantasy, not least in its insistent ballet sequences. Loesser's remarkable achievement was to transpose the cracking prose of Damon Runyon's characters, principally from his short story 'The Idyll of Miss Sarah Brown', into a score of scintillating brilliance. Abe Burrows and Jo Swerling's book has a unique tonal quality copied from Runyon, and reflected with ingenuity through Loesser's lyrics. The elegance of language used by *Guys and Doll*'s disreputables is astonishing, besides which it lends the thing a strange beauty, never distancing us from those who seem to speak so ponderously, but drawing them closer to us.

We know that these people are unreal, but they *seem* real, having all the characteristics of real people. At first glance much of the score may seem rollicking and even brash, and there is nothing especially original about the 'show within the show' numbers 'A Bushel and a Peck' and 'Take Back Your Mink'. 'Sit Down, You're Rockin' the Boat' is conventionally gold-plated Broadway, but its context and setting and verses stir the concoction; a gospel celebration that also celebrates Nicely-Nicely Johnson's simple decency. Look again at the score, and all the songs do much the same thing, telling us all we need to know about the human beings moved about before us. The Broadway musical would struggle to come up with another score so rich: luscious love songs in 'I'll Know' and 'I've Never Been in Love Before', innocent abandon in 'If I Were a Bell', heart-breaking vignettes of the human condition in 'Adelaide's Lament' (and how cleverly Loesser extends our understanding of Adelaide's steadfastness in the deeply moving 'Sue Me').

Kenneth Tynan (who thought this was the first occasion that most of the audience at the Coliseum would have heard a fugue, heard in the show's first song 'Fugue for Tinhorns') wrote 'I am ready to up and drop on my knees before Frank Loesser [who] may be the best light composer in the world. In fact, the chances are that *Guys and Dolls* is not only a young masterpiece, but the Beggar's Opera of Broadway.'[4] Noting the 'childlike innocence of the characters', *Punch* found the piece 'topsy-turvy but wholly consistent. *Guys and Dolls* is dry as a bone and charming as a fairy tale. In the simpler parts of its attack one is now and again surprisingly reminded of Gilbert and Sullivan.'[5] Perhaps so, but although Gilbert offers heightened characters who, like those in *Guys and Dolls*, bear a trace of artificiality about them, he never gives them a blood supply. Accentuating the innocence, *The Times* considered the theme 'highly moral'. It is, and not simply because of the Salvation Army; strip away that strand of the story and the essential morality that Burrows and Loesser portray is undisturbed, perhaps even accentuated. Nevertheless, the *Sunday Telegraph* found many faults with the writers' moral stance, and 'despite its numerous striking incidental merits [it is] an interminable, an overwhelming, and in the end intolerable bore'.[6] The London performances were much appreciated, with Blaine singled out for praise. Her understudy Joyce Blair got to play Adelaide during her tenure, but when Blaine left the cast she was replaced by another American, Jacqueline James, whose only Broadway credit was in the chorus of *Texas, Li'l Darlin'*. Webb stayed with the show until its close, but the various Americans were replaced: Wayne by Edmund Hockridge, and Levene by Sidney James.

When after two years at the Lane *South Pacific* closed, it made way for **The King and I** (Theatre Royal, Drury Lane, 8 October 1953; 926), a new Rodgers and Hammerstein supposedly adapted from Margaret Landon's novel *Anna and the King of Siam* but in fact largely based on Talbot Jennings and Sally Benson's script for the film. Both were taken from the diaries of Anna Leonowens, the title of which told the plot of Rodgers and Hammerstein's musical: *The English Governess at the Siamese Court*. Gertrude Lawrence recognised the possibilities of the story as a musical vehicle for herself, and commissioned the score from Irving Berlin. When he withdrew from the project, Rodgers and Hammerstein took over; a thesis could probably be written on the different work Berlin would have produced.

That this was the first of the Rodgers and Hammerstein works to be based on a real-life story gave the piece a built-in gravitas. These people existed in a way that those of *Oklahoma!* and *Carousel* and *South Pacific* did not, although their 'reality' was artificial. The characters experienced another Rodgers and Hammerstein culture clash (in *Oklahoma!* the farmer and the cowman, the evil Jud and the wholesome Curly; in *Carousel* the living and the dead; in *South Pacific* the discordant cultures of America and the East); now, it was British propriety, fair play and understatement against the authoritative dictatorship of Siam. Anna Leonowens is the English governess who goes to the Siamese court to teach the King's children, and it is their developing relationship, never turning into a love affair, that guides the plot.

The score has the mark of being written for Lawrence, in that Anna's songs are the lightest confections: 'I Whistle a Happy Tune' (artful because it introduces a featherweight emotion when darker forces await; this is the sort of song that would eventually find its natural home in *The Sound of Music*), 'Getting To Know You', 'Hello Young Lovers' and the galvanising 'Shall We Dance?'. The best of the score was in its fine ballads, 'I Have Dreamed',

'We Kiss in a Shadow' and in Lady Thiang's 'Something Wonderful', drenched in melancholia.

One of the audition hopefuls was the leading lady of earlier decades, Evelyn Laye. Hammerstein had built up Laye's hopes by asking her to apply, but she was rejected in favour of the British actress Valerie Hobson. By this time Hammerstein and Rodgers were more personally involved in casting the London productions overseen by Jerome Whyte. *The King and I* was the first of their shows in Britain to open with an all-British cast, and Hammerstein was wary. John Van Druten, who had directed the show on Broadway (restaged for the West End by Jerome Whyte) informed Hammerstein that his London contacts thought it incredible that Hobson had got the part. Hammerstein's waspish response was that 'We are aware of some of the British public and press believing that they should cast *The King and I* but we still believe we should cast it, and I think it will all die down if she is as good in the part as we think she will be, and if she isn't there is nothing that we can do about it.'[7] Hammerstein was determined not to allow British leading ladies of a certain age through the stage door. If casting was left to the British he felt sure who would end up playing Lady Thiang.

> I mean the lady who played all of Ivor [Novello]'s plays and sings out of the side of her mouth. [Obviously Olive Gilbert, Novello's contralto (and housekeeper) for whom Novello always wrote a supporting role in his musicals.] This is why we do not leave the job to English producers any more. Dennis Hoey would have automatically been cast as the Kralahome and Tuptim would be Doris Day.[8]

The casting of Hobson, who had no experience of musicals, was a surprise to many. Perhaps the fact that Gertrude Lawrence, the original Broadway Anna, was well known for not being much of a singer, and not always on the note, had led the British producers to find another such. Many of the notices felt the lack of Lawrence. Caryl Brahms wrote

> As for Anna – the modest, sober and conscientious Victorian Englishwoman who tries to turn the Siamese Palace into the nicest kind of co-educational boarding school – she has been dipped in pink icing. Miss Hobson is a vision of loveliness when in smiling repose. But she does not breathe life into a line, nor find its natural flow and rhythm. She does not speak. She orates in ringing tones. I could hear her songs quite clearly from the last seat in the front row of the stalls, but maybe that was just my luck.[9]

Hobson couldn't sing, but neither could she 'put over' with something worldly-wise and humane in the way Lawrence did, and she had no experience of the musical stage. Treading carefully through the notes via her treble warbling, Hobson would have been an embarrassment in a minor British musical, but in

The King and I she had an undoubted success. During the run, she married the politician John Profumo, whose wish it was that she should give up the stage. Hobson didn't want to, but arranged her exit from the production when she fell pregnant. Knowing that she would never again have such a role, she announced that it would be her last.

Hammerstein's fears about the casting of Lady Thiang were unfounded. The role went to Muriel Smith, who had just finished playing Bloody Mary in *South Pacific* at the Lane, and the two young lovers to whom Anna said hello were played by Doreen Duke and Jan Muzurus. More notable was the Kralahome of Martin Benson, so impressive that he was given the role in the film version. But one wonders what had alerted Rodgers and Hammerstein to the problem of British casting? Presumably there had been issues with the London casting of their previous shows, and we may propose some candidates as we glance through theatre programmes: Edmund Hockridge replacing Stephen Douglass in *Carousel*, Joyce Blair going on for Mary Martin in *South Pacific*? The problem, of course, was not peculiar to Rodgers and Hammerstein; incorrect casting had weighed down many a London production. Take Pat Kirkwood in *Wonderful Town*, Ian Wallace and Robert Morley in *Fanny*, Janet Blair in *Bells Are Ringing*, Belita in *Damn Yankees*, Cicely Courtneidge in *High Spirits*, Max Bygraves in *Do Re Mi*, and possibly the entire cast of *Flower Drum Song* (and that was Rodgers and Hammerstein). In its way the casting of *The King and I*, effectively of musical unknowns, was a brave and novel step, and the long run attests to its good sense. Interesting, too, that none of the principals ever subsequently made a dent in musical theatre.

On Broadway, Yul Brynner's name was originally in small type below the title over which Lawrence soared. The first performances put paid to that. Today we remember *The King and I* by way of Brynner, not least because he immortalised the role on film. Brynner is the actor more strongly linked to a Rodgers and Hammerstein *stage* role than any other, perhaps more remarkable because his was not a singing part. (In fact, Brynner and Herbert Lom were showing the way to Rex Harrison several years before he was supposed to have invented his way with a tune.) Mary Martin may have created Nellie Forbush and Alfred Drake Curly, but their associations with *South Pacific* and *Oklahoma!* fade beside Brynner's with *The King and I*. Confronted with Brynner's performance, by his *reputation*, Lom, no matter how proficient his attempt, could offer only something that seems to have been an impersonation not only of the troublesome Siamese monarch but of the actor who had created him. Nevertheless, Lom had excellent notices, but who remembers his King today? Such was the general lot of the British casts of American musicals. Lom went on to one of the most famous films of his career, *The Ladykillers*, but no more musicals.

On 10 October 1973 Roger Redfarn's British revival opened at the Adelphi Theatre, running for 260 performances, with Peter Wyngarde's King cast opposite the Anna of Sally Ann Howes and, lastly, Patricia Michael. The abiding appeal of the piece was proved by the London Palladium production of 3 May 2000, headed by Elaine Paige and Jason Scott Lee, succeeded by Josie Lawrence and Paul Nakauchi (and then Keo Woolford). Opening to a 7 million pound advance, the show ran until 5 January 2002.

'There's nothing nicer than people, is there?' asked one of the songs in *Wish You Were Here* (Casino, 10 October 1953; 282), nudging its audience towards its air of enforced gaiety. Here is Broadway's celebratory hymn to the delights of the summer camp: in English translation, read Butlins. The script was amended for London, so that British audiences might imagine they were getting a taste of the knobbly knees competitions and beauty pageants available at Skegness or Bognor. Faced with the evidence of its London manifestation, its New York success is a little bewildering. Perhaps in America it was treated as a genuine musical; nobody could have taken the Casino production seriously, not least because it boasted the biggest on-stage swimming pool since the days of *White Horse Inn*. Ready to dive into it were chorus girls wearing what passed for skimpy and silky in 1953, and boys in speedos.

The biggest boy of all was Joe 'Tiger' Robinson as Harry 'Muscles' Green in a rare musical appearance. Robinson's previous acting experience had been in the 'health' film *Fit as a Fiddle*, and he subsequently had a substantial role in *A Kid for Two Farthings*; his later movies included *Ursus and the Tartar Princess*. At a time when newspaper advertisements promised to turn the puniest specimen into Mr Atlas, Robinson looked, but didn't sound, like the man who might kick sand in your face. Joshua Logan directed for Broadway, passing responsibility to Richard Bird in London. Even the choice of theatre was a warning: the Casino, offering a diet of pantomimes and variety-based revues for the tired business man. And what of the sound quality endured by audiences in such palaces at this time? The *Stage Yearbook* tells us the theatre had a 'Two turn-table reproducer available for use by visiting companies [which] can be switched either to front-of-house speakers or to movable stage speakers. Reproducer includes a microphone available for the use of visiting companies.'[10] What horrors assaulted the ears of London's theatregoers? Critics of the period were constantly complaining of severe over-amplification and appalling sound quality.

Plays and Players was doubtful about a work that

> comes with an enormous reputation from America and we sit back slightly mystified at it all, listening to a book which is as banal as any that has crossed the Atlantic, and to a score that has one rather reminiscent tune. There must be something wrong. What is it? Presentation? Cast? Or is the play, like some local wine, untranslatable?[11]

In the case of *Wish You Were Here*, presentation, cast and play were all lost in translation. Yet the piece had respectable beginnings, beginning with Arthur Kober's play *Having Wonderful Time* (itself suggesting that everything about this story might be scribbled on the back of a postcard), but as several British critics made clear a wonderful time was not enjoyed by all. However, jollity was obligatory at Karefree Summer Camp, 'where friendships are formed to last a whole lifetime through', although many might have preferred a more casual liaison. Still, the piece had credence: Logan as director, sets by Jo Mielziner, Don Walker's orchestrations.

The casting of Jack Hylton's management didn't help. The leading ladies, Shani Wallis and Elizabeth Larner, were from the Hylton stable, proficient but out of their natural milieu. As romantic male lead Bruce Trent was respectably stolid, and entrusted with the show's repetitive title song. Today, the show's comedy seems tiresome, although it had Dickie Henderson Junior, ersatz American variety performer, as a 'social director'. (What did British audiences think that might be?) Then there was Christopher Hewett, specialist in camp characterisation, playing the campest camper of them all, Pinky Harris. All were diminished by that damned swimming pool, without which *Wish You Were Here* would have been even duller. Its musical director, Cyril Ornadel, recalled the first night as

> a very elegant white-tie affair. The audience sat in stony silence throughout most of the first half of the show. When we came to the swimming pool sequence at the end of the first half, one or two of the swimmer dancers, probably through first night nerves, 'misdived', causing water to splash over the orchestra pit and the first three rows of the stalls. The brass spluttered a bit, the saxophones played on, the strings stopped playing, and the beautifully dressed ladies and gentlemen of the audience got soaked. There was very little applause at the interval or, indeed, at the end of the show. The press notices were awful.[12]

Strangely, the songs were by Harold Rome, writing his first Broadway musical play score, as unlike his subsequent scores as one could imagine. Had he been Frank Loesser one might have excused these songs on the ground of versatility, but it would have been only an excuse; even in its songs, *Wish You Were Here* was only now and then diverting. When it departed the Casino, and that wretched pool removed to who knows where, audiences were offered the Moscow State Puppets. And what did *they* look like from the back seats of a 1,800-seater?

British musicals continued unlucky, although **The Glorious Days** was only a musical of sorts, being the story of a wartime ambulance driver whose concussion results in her becoming Nell Gwynn, Queen Victoria, and a 1920s flapper. These stupendous impersonations were performed by the much-loved star Anna Neagle. Another musical of sorts was **Lucky Boy**, 'a play with music', the sole work of Ian Douglas, but its good fortune ran out after three performances. Another dying ember of the knockabout musical farces that had peppered British musicals before the war was the hastily disposed of **Happy as a King**, cooked up by Austin Melford and its star Fred Emney. The British musical had been warned to stay clear of titles that included 'Glorious', 'Lucky' or 'Happy'.

1953 Broadway Exports

Wonderful Town (559), *Can-Can* (892) and *Kismet* (583).

1953 Broadway Only

The musical satire *Hazel Flagg* (190), its plot already known from the film *Nothing Sacred*, followed the adventures of a girl who becomes a national heroine when she is diagnosed as fatally ill; she isn't. Jule Styne's music wasn't his best. Rodgers and Hammerstein had one of their least popular works in *Me and Juliet* (358). Dolores Gray had a brief fling with *Carnival in Flanders* (6) and British Betty Paul played the title role in *Maggie* (5), unsuccessfully adapted from J. M. Barrie's play *What Every Woman Knows*.

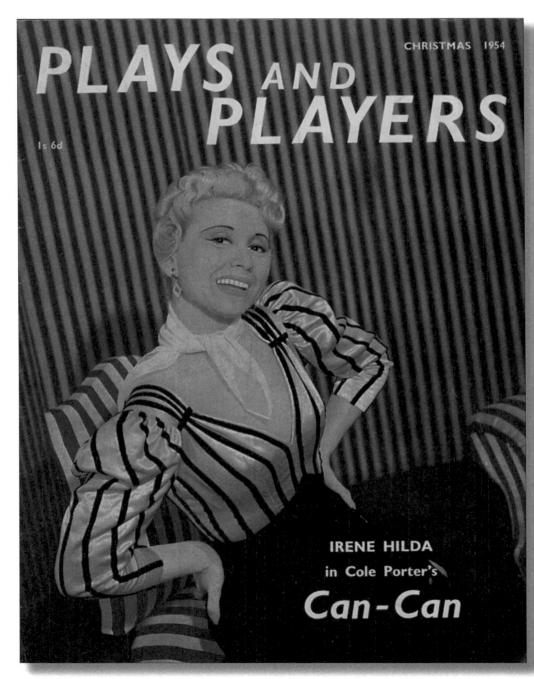

13 Just one of a number of forgotten leading ladies of American musicals in London, Irene Hilda,
loving Paris in Cole Porter's *Can-Can* at the Coliseum in 1954

1954

Pal Joey
Can-Can

T HANKS BE TO JACK HYLTON, impresario to several innovative London-Broadway productions of the 1950s, for one of the finest of the period, ***Pal Joey*** (Princes Theatre, 31 March 1954; 245). The run wasn't long, the notices were mixed, and Hylton might have been forgiven for his disappointment at a time when other musicals, of much less appreciable quality, ran longer. Delayed *en route*, it had taken fourteen years to reach the West End, and times had changed. The New York opening had been on 25 December 1940, a date on which something sweet and light and drenched with human kindness might have been expected. Lorenz Hart could not be expected to conform, but *Pal Joey* seems particularly wayward, especially sour, grandiloquently decadent, elegantly seedy. Even for 1954, the blatant sexual knowingness of 'Den of Iniquity' was daring; when Princess Margaret attended one of the performances the lyrics had to be changed so as not to offend the royal ear.

Blame it on the story's milieu; the sort of nightclubs you wouldn't want your mother to know about, people your mother wouldn't wish you to know. Low-life isn't merely an add-on in *Pal Joey*; it's the bread and butter of it. Neither is it Rodgers and Hart's richest score in that it yields few standards: count 'Bewitched' and 'I Could Write a Book' and you're almost done. Otherwise, a great deal of time is taken up by the bump-and-grind of what passes for nightclub entertainment: 'That Terrific Rainbow' (belted out, indeed, by a character called Gladys Bumps), 'Chicago', 'The Flower Garden of My Heart' and 'Plant You Now, Dig You Later'. In their way, these numbers are a trap into which the unwitting production may fall: listen to the cast recording of the 1980 London version to hear how the red light has been ignored. You wouldn't want to sit through this night after night.

In its way, *Pal Joey* has never been particularly happy in its time; it has mostly seemed out of it. By 1940 Hart and Rodgers were struggling to maintain their partnership – or more accurately Rodgers was struggling with Hart's unpredictability – although finally they had their greatest commercial success with *By Jupiter* (1942). A year later Hart was dead from alcoholism, only five days after a revival of the team's *A Connecticut Yankee* had opened in New York, and a few months after the premiere of Rodgers and Hammerstein's *Oklahoma!* In that work there was no trace of the bitter aloes with which Hart invested Rodgers' music; witnessing the wholesome neatness, the vaulting romanticism, of the Hammerstein effect on his old partner must have had a devastating effect on Hart. The bystander poet, ready with the wry take, the *double entendre* lyric, had been rendered redundant by Hammerstein's Byronic insistence on the good and healthy, the corn as high as the elephant's eye, the cleanliness of many a new day, the simple enchantment of an evening, the human desire that a walk would never be taken alone. Such expressions would have been unthinkable to Hart. His words would have stuck in the craw of Curly and Laurey and Aunt Eller; even Ado Annie, who might have been expected to subscribe to Hart's emotional outspokenness, lacked the profundity that Hart would have given her.

London would probably not have seen the work until decades after its Broadway showing had it not been for a studio recording made by CBS in 1950. Produced by Goddard Lieberson, the orchestra directed by Lehman Engel with specially commissioned orchestrations by Ted Royal, this had Vivienne Segal and Harold Lang on top form, and led directly to the New York 1952 revival. So it was that when *Pal Joey* arrived in London, the British had begun its addiction to Rodgers and Hammerstein, already having taken *Oklahoma!*, *Carousel* and *South Pacific* to its bosom. Death strode through all these works, but the presiding comfort offered by Rodgers and Hammerstein had never been attempted by Rodgers and Hart, and audiences seemed not to want to go back to that lack of reassurance, that feeling that Hart knew too well what went on in the dark corners of the mind. Hammerstein never gave the impression that he had caught the audience with its trousers down; Hart questioned romanticism. In a way Rodgers and Hammerstein put the American musical in cardigan and slippers, not least in Britain, where few of the abundant national relevances in their works had the same resonance when re-enacted on Shaftesbury Avenue. Hart references American culture in a very different way from Hammerstein, and does not try to put a fluffy bow on love. Search through *Pal Joey* and there is little of the valentine to be found. The edges are hard, and the sadness is circular. Those first three Rodgers and Hammerstein shows have resolve in their endings, the happy curtain fall with the Oklahomans throwing their hats and cares into the air. Our pal Joey just looks forward to the new trick, the next bed to spend a night in.

It is in Oklahoma, where the wind comes right behind the rain, where the American musical is supposed to have changed for ever. Countless people attest that the musical set in that territory turned the page, marked the moment when plot and songs were first properly integrated, when the Broadway musical insisted it would no longer tolerate the mish-mash, the marbled pudding of musical theatre with plums inserted here and there, the intolerance of psychological consideration; *Oklahoma!* harvested the corn that had long been in need of bringing in. Gerald Bordman masterfully sums up the significance of the piece with its rejection of 'wit and patently polished sophistication for a certain earnestness and directness'.[1] Three years before Curly walked on stage to carol a beautiful morning, *Pal Joey* was behind closed curtains, a glass of rye at its hand, a loosened tie at Joey's throat, his eyes seldom exposing themselves to anything as expansive and healthy as an open sky. Just at the moment when Hitler had plunged the world into an unspeakable chaos, Rodgers and Hart (but blame Hart) offered a musical brought up from the under-belly of low-life.

The relevance of *Pal Joey* to the American musical is seminal, a deeply shadowed epic of the emotionally restless. It must have been difficult for Hart to sit through that first night of *Oklahoma!* He must have felt that Rodgers had betrayed everything he and Hart had stood for, must have felt himself at the door of something which to Hart was simply inexplicable. To Hart, Hammerstein's dull humour must have been repugnant, and Rodgers' response to Hammerstein's lyrics suddenly foreign. Something about Hammerstein turned Rodgers hymnal. It's there in 'Oh What a Beautiful Morning', 'Many a New Day', 'People Will Say We're In Love'; this music, these words, could never have come from Rodgers and Hart. Hart's was a very different sort of honesty to Hammerstein's, and in *Pal Joey* the truthfulness can seem almost to hurt as it reflects back at us some of the less attractive aspects of being human.

Adapted by John O'Hara from some *New Yorker* short stories, *Pal Joey* is Joey Evans, a freeloading nightclub singer-dancer who is attracted to the virtuous Linda, but begins an affair with the older, worldy-wise Vera Simpson, who not only sets up an apartment for her new young beau but installs him in his own nightclub 'Chez Joey'. Ultimately, Vera and Linda unite in understanding, each offering the other to 'Take Him', before both desert their two-timing lover. No matter, for at curtain-fall Joey is making it with a new girl, giving her the old line 'I Could Write a Book' with which he had first ensnared (or bewitched) Linda. Newly directed by Neil Hartley, the London production retained Oliver Smith's sets and Miles White's costumes from the New York 1952 revival, with Hans Spialek's orchestrations now in collaboration with Don Walker.

Wisely, Hylton's production did not suffer from an all-British casting as would his *Wonderful Town*. Carol Bruce had taken over from Segal during the US tour, and Harold Lang had been the original 1952 Joey. Both proved invaluable to the London edition, although before long Lang was deported and replaced by another US tour survivor, Richard France. The Broadway actors at the Princes had brought something essential with them for a show that needed New York sensitivities to breathe life into it, not least Lang with probably the most directly sexual male performance in a London musical. Ronald Barker considered that 'Harold Lang, as the boy who oozes sex from every pore, would be a formidable rival to any of this sort seen in the Elephant and Castle area. The continual leer, the curled lip, the broad shoulders make him the most repulsively attractive specimen of virility to cross the Atlantic.'[2] Despite this allure the London *Pal Joey* centred on Bruce's much praised Vera, but the lack of a full cast recording has left only a sketch of these performances. In support were the British Sally Bazeley as wholesome (rare in this company) Linda, and Jean Brampton as Gladys Bumps.

The piece has been much revived. Philip Hedley's production for the Oxford Playhouse Company opened the 1976 Edinburgh International Festival and briefly toured. Pat Kirkwood was a glamorous Vera, delivering a memorable 'Bewitched' opposite the Joey of Bob Sherman, with Patricia Hodge as Linda and

Anna Quayle as Melba, but London didn't call it in. In August 1980 a scaled-down version premiered at the New Half Moon Theatre before transferring to the West End. Sian Phillips made a sultry Vera with none of Segal or Bruce's vulnerability, and her 'Bewitched' showed how incomparable Segal had been merely by serving the lyric rare. Segal sang it; Phillips pulled it apart. Reduced orchestrations from a team of four took the work further from its original strengths. In Rodgers' centennial year of 2002 Kathryn Evans was an assured Vera in Phil Willmott's production for Nottingham Playhouse. The 1957 film altered the plot and messed the score.

Can-Can (Coliseum, 14 October 1954; 394) became Cole Porter's second most successful musical after *Kiss Me, Kate*. In New York it had been a personal success for Lilo as La Mome Pistache, and Gwen Verdon as Claudine. Britain's replicated production did not leave behind such distinct memories, as the headlines after its first night testify. 'But this just isn't Paris' (*Daily Mail*),[3] 'Smart, Slick, Empty' (*Daily Express*),[4] 'Paris Eludes Mr. Porter' (*Tatler*).[5] *Punch* noted that the first funny moment occurred two and three-quarter minutes before the curtain fell, just as the audience was putting its coat on. Even the ballet, despite the presence of dancer Gillian Lynne, was 'utterly tasteless'.[6]

Several of the songs would stay in the repertoire, among them 'C'est Magnifique', 'It's All Right With Me', and the reason for the show, 'I Love Paris'. Then, of course, audiences had to sit through an inevitable Can-Can, surely one of France's less welcome exports, but even here Porter imposes a new melody on it that seems neither good Broadway pastiche nor veritable Moulin Rogue. Bad enough to have this pidgin-Englished parleyvoo-ing book by Abe Burrows underpinning Porter's music and lyrics performed on Broadway, where at least it would have been done with panache, but on Shaftesbury Avenue the Gallic atmosphere wasn't as convincing – a problem that *Fanny* would also experience. Here and there an accordion broke into the proceedings, and there was a high-kicking chorus line of girls and a very bad song called 'Montmart' that Porter should have thought better of, and some praised low comedy from Alfred Marks. Then there was 'Never, Never Be An Artist', a song of such awfulness that one has to check on its authorship. Perhaps this was Burrows fault. After all, as he had set the story in Paris, and travelled it to Montmartre, they were more or less obliged to have a scene with artists painting in the square. But the song simply disfigures the score; one puts it aside because it doesn't hold together, and in the hands of actors who could do with a lesson in style the problem is exacerbated.

At least Irene Hilda had proper qualifications, a sort of lightweight Edith Piaf with allure. It was her glamour, rather than her small voice, that impressed. It was her one London engagement. Opposite her was the manly presence of Edmund Hockridge, who by now had cornered the market in unmistakably heterosexual leading men with a voice to fill a big theatre. *Punch* thought him 'vocally a big gun, but a gun of unnecessarily heavy bore' and the show 'the heaviest freight to cross the Atlantic for a very long time'.[7] Earlier in 1954 a

British musical, *Wedding in Paris*, had provided London with another excursion to the French capital. The place was awash with ooh-la-la. In fact, *Wedding in Paris*, one of the dullest of musicals with the most uninspired of scores, made *Can-Can* seem like a masterpiece, instead of what is mostly was: a colourful show with a handful of standards. Maurice Chevalier brought his stock Parisian charm to the film version in 1960, but the result, even with Shirley MacLaine and Frank Sinatra, had little interesting about it. A revival at the Strand Theatre in 1988 had a revised book by Julian More, but excited few onlookers.

Two British musicals strode through the 1950s and beyond: Sandy Wilson's **The Boy Friend** and Julian Slade and Dorothy Reynolds's **Salad Days**. Wilson's tidy pastiche of 1920s musical comedies relied on American songs for its inspiration. The gossamer lightness of *Salad Days* offered a naïve abandonment that despite its many detractors took it to colossal success. **Wedding in Paris** had Anton Walbrook and Evelyn Laye as its senior citizens, but the songs of Sonny Miller and Hans May were Tin Pan Alley dross. Noel Coward's **After the Ball**, an adaptation from Oscar Wilde's *Lady Windermere's Fan*, suggested that Coward and Wilde were uneasy bedfellows. This was eclipsed by **Happy Holiday**, a classic folly of adaptation, taken from Arnold Ridley's comedy-thriller *The Ghost Train*.

1954 Broadway Exports

The Pajama Game (1,063), *Peter Pan* (152) and *Fanny* (888).

1954 Broadway Only

An intriguing mix of the old-fashioned and the brave, **The Girl in Pink Tights** (115) was Sigmund Romberg's final Broadway score, while **By the Beautiful Sea** (270) was a period piece meant to re-establish Shirley Booth as a musical star after the success of *A Tree Grows in Brooklyn*. For Truman Capote's adaptation from his novel **House of Flowers** (165) the atmospheric music was by Harold Arlen. **The Golden Apple** (173) was made up from Homer's *Iliad* and *Odyssey*. **Hit the Trail** (4), about a touring operetta company during the Nevada Gold Rush, starred the operetta favourite Irra Petina, but speedily took its own advice.

1955

Wonderful Town
Kismet
The Pajama Game

MANY INTERESTING BROADWAY SHOWS of the first half of the 1950s flopped, but at least New York had been offered the opportunity to consider them; London was denied. How would British audiences have responded to *A Tree Grows in Brooklyn*, a sensitive adaptation of Betty Smith's novel with songs by Arthur Schwartz and Dorothy Fields, and a classic turn in 'He Had Refinement' by Shirley Booth as Cissy? Was the idea of a transfer ever considered? Did it not happen because Booth may have been unavailable? And did the producers sensibly conclude that a transfer without her would be unwise? Or *Flahooley*, a likeable piece about puppets in which Barbara Cook and Yma Sumac got to sing some of the Sammy Fain–Yip Harburg numbers? It is unlikely the British would have taken to this; subsequent whimsies such as *Once Upon a Mattress* and *The Fantasticks* would be sent packing. Or *Hazel Flagg*, with its second-division Jule Styne music, based on the much better film *Nothing Sacred* about a girl who becomes famous because it is thought she is dying. How about the much more radical musical made up from Homer, *The Golden Apple*, with its rich score by Jerome Moross (among its plentiful songs 'Windflowers' and 'It's the Going Home Together').

Of the three shows imported in 1955 the first was the most interesting, much of it brilliantly inventive, and only occasionally conventional. **Wonderful Town** (Princes Theatre, 23 February 1955; 207) took its title from the song 'New York, New York' in *On the Town*, another score by Leonard Bernstein and his lyricists Betty Comden and Adolph Green. They shouldn't have been credited with *Wonderful Town*, for Leroy Anderson had been signed as composer and Arnold B. Horwitt as lyricist, although Anderson and Horwitt were not first choices: the producers wanted Frank Loesser or Irving Berlin. When Anderson and Horwitt couldn't make it work, Comden and Green were brought in, but insisted on Bernstein as composer. Bernstein had promised his mentor Serge Koussevitsky that never again would he write another musical, but in the event needed no persuasion to start work. It took the team four weeks to turn a first draft from Ruth McKinney's stories of New York life for the sisters Sherwood into a Broadway musical. In the 1930s McKinney and her sister Eileen had moved from sleepy Ohio to no. 14 Gay Street in Greenwich Village, a one–room basement apartment on top of Christopher Street's subway. It was their six-month tenure in New York that inspired McKinney's tales, first published in the *New Yorker* and subsequently as a book, and then made into the play *My Sister Eileen* by

Joseph Fields and Jerome Chodorov, who also wrote the book for *Wonderful Town.*

The result was a score of exultant vitality and attack, and one that was perhaps surprisingly very much lyric-led. Everywhere in *Wonderful Town* Bernstein's music is a *reaction* to Comden and Green's words, except probably in the love songs, which, though no doubt considered necessary, do not much enrich the experience. The three writers were re-enacting the partnership they had enjoyed as 'The Revuers', writing and playing and singing artful artless comedy and satirical numbers. Compare Ruth's 'One Hundred Easy Ways to Lose a Man' in *Wonderful Town* to 'Inspiration', a Comden-Green lyric for the 1947 *Bonanza Bound.*[1] In tone, construction, absurdity, it's the same song, unmistakably Comden–Green, or Green–Comden. This is something that the new show definitely benefited from in what is their most satirical mood. 'One Hundred Easy Ways' uses the verse–chorus–punch-line model to allow Ruth to list various techniques for washing a man out of her hair; 'Inspiration', using the same technique, tells how the great composers were moved to write their melodies. (Rimsky-Korsakov's 'Flight of the Bumble Bee' was supposedly inspired by a troublesome insect in the composer's garden.) Both lyrics are ridiculous and friendly in a way that trademarks them Comden and Green. To this, Bernstein is accommodating and of secondary importance, for in *Wonderful Town* it's the words that come first, in every sense. An obvious example is 'Conversation Piece', when the characters endure an awkward social occasion. It's a paean to embarrassment: after another yawning gap in the flow of talk one of them comes up with 'I was re-reading *Moby Dick* the other day.' Imagine Oscar Hammerstein coming up with such a line! Lorenz Hart, perhaps, but then Rodgers would not have woven it into the sort of tapestry that Bernstein was able to create.

The McKinney stories were the hook on which Comden and Green hung another mythical representation of New York, of the school of *Bells Are Ringing* and *On the Town.* If we were to believe them, we would think New York rather like an English village – cosy and suffused with friendship and care for the fellow American. Bernstein's association with that viewpoint was broken by *West Side Story*, whose gang warfare, racial prejudice and social dilemmas would have been complete anathema to Comden and Green. The truth is that McKinney had provided ideal material for them through which they could promulgate their perpetual fanciful vision of home. Perhaps this skewered their work's chance of success in Britain at a time when even the British musical was thinking about throwing away the rose-tinted spectacles when it came to depicting London or British society. The British production didn't measure up to the American, and anyway Britain wasn't in the mood for Bernstein or Comden and Green messing about with what the British thought a musical should be. (This would have to wait for *West Side Story*, but of course this didn't bring Comden and Green with it.) One wonders what audiences at the Princes made of this score. Though it is difficult to realise it now, this was musically 'modern' in a way that few other

14 Greenwich Village reaches the West End in the 1955 *Wonderful Town*, with Shani Wallis as Eileen Sherwood, Judy Bruce as Violet and Pat Kirkwood as Ruth Sherwood

musicals had dared to be. The Broadway shows of the previous year were expectedly conventional: there was nothing challenging in *Fanny*, or the explicit nostalgia of *By the Beautiful Sea*, and how might it be expected of Romberg in *The Girl in Pink Tights* – his 56th and final musical – or the pedestrian *Hit the Trail!* But a show that included 'Conversation Piece': wasn't this the musical being too clever by half?

The Broadway original was replicated by Richard Bird, directing an all-British cast with Pat Kirkwood's name above the title in the role originally played by Rosalind Russell. Kirkwood recalled that at her audition (without a piano) Fields and Chodorov told her she could sing much better than their American leading lady. She could, but this didn't mean she had Russell's other qualities. Kirkwood's talent was promoted by a glamorous, almost purring, persona; there was no spike. This alone must have taken the edge off performances at the Princes; what craft had this cast to put over the style? Kirkwood, by her own admission, had never played comedy, being one of many leading ladies who could not make a cat laugh. Kirkwood played Ruth 'with vivacity but without the intellectual grasp demanded by the part'.[2] Ronald Barker felt the British production 'suffers because the principals do not have the acting ability to bring the wit from the lines'.

Kenneth Tynan thought the piece triumphed in the teeth of the English cast. As for Kirkwood, 'long martyrdom to English musical comedy has evidently withheld from her the news that American musicals can survive without recourse to brave, apologetic smiles at the audience. For all her gallant trouping, she robs the part of the caustic intellectual dignity which Miss Rosalind Russell gave it in New York.'[3] The *Stage* unequivocally dismissed Kirkwood who 'simply does not fit this bill',[4] while *The Times* considered that she 'attacks every song and every passage of dialogue with a verve that is quite irresistible'.[5] Philip Hope-Wallace wrote that 'the general effect is of a hard-working road company dealing with something outside its familiar idiom. The accents alone are enough to set any Hollywood addict's teeth on edge.'[6] Another problem was the theatre's crude over-amplification. Barker's opinion of the work itself was high: 'one of the best half a dozen musicals to come out of America during the last twenty years [...] wit, form and striking originality [...] the score is a joy [...] devastatingly clever'.

Shani Wallis, another Hylton artist mostly cast in British productions of American musicals, played Eileen, with the little-known Dennis Bowen as male romantic lead Robert Baker (*Plays and Players* thought he 'might have strayed in from a less successful show'),[7] and the characterful Sidney James as Wreck, throwing himself so much into the part of his obsessive footballer that on 9 May he knocked himself unconscious during his number. While in London for the final rehearsals, Bernstein picked out Judy Bruce from the chorus to play the kind-hearted street-walking Violet. The illuminated marquee of the Princes only bore one name in bulbs: the show's presenter Jack Hylton.

The show settled down to a moderate success, and as Kirkwood explained it 'became a sort of cult show. It was way above the heads of most of the British public and way ahead of its time.'[8] If anything, *Wonderful Town* was very much *of* its time in the way it handled its themes and characters, and in its voice, but towards its end the British company agreed to take a pay cut to help keep it afloat. Kirkwood's role was strenuous, and Hylton milked her for all she was worth. After eight months in the saddle, she told him she needed a holiday, to which he readily agreed. She would go on holiday the very next week, but he asked her to keep this from the rest of the company. At the matinee of the last day before she was due to fly off, complete exhaustion overcame her, and she was taken home. Her first understudy was unwell, and her second understudy hadn't learned the part. The third understudy, Bruce, who had watched Kirkwood's every move at every performance from the wings, took over that evening. Kirkwood left for her agreed break. She explained that

It was some time before I could begin to enjoy the holiday as I was still in a state of exhaustion, but Hubert [Gregg, then her husband] was so caring and patient that I was on my feet a week later. Then I had a nasty shock: my agent in London called to say that JH [Jack Hylton] had put up the

15 Judy Bruce in her dressing room at the Princes Theatre on the night she took over from Pat
Kirkwood for what was left of the run of *Wonderful Town*

notice for *Wonderful Town*. Then I realised the reason he had asked me not to mention my holiday to the rest of the cast. He had planned to put the blame on me for closing, because I had, apparently, 'walked out of the show' [...] I was much distressed, especially as 'someone' had informed the press that 'Pat Kirkwood, who collapsed at the Prince's Theatre on Saturday, arrived in Paris on Monday'.[9]

The seventeen-year-old Bruce headed the cast for its last two weeks.

A 1986 revival at the Queen's Theatre boasted a leading lady whose acting ability outstripped her singing. Maureen Lipman had the intelligence needed for Ruth, but it was still an impersonation of an American character in an all-British company. The modest production (adding an unnecessary exclamation mark to the title) had new musical arrangements by Michael Reed, but was otherwise unremarkable. The truth was that in 1955 the piece had been modern and completely of its time, and the British hadn't warmed to it; by 1986 it was a period piece.

The next offering was another Hylton presentation, but this time he had signed the three original American stars. This gave it a genuine shot of Broadway, all too obviously denied to the year's other imports. The good sense of the transatlantic performer's arrival was reflected in its run, slightly longer than Broadway's 583. **Kismet** (Stoll Theatre, 20 April 1955; 648) was the third of the Robert Wright–George Forrest musical adaptations to reach London; Broadway had held on to their 1948 *Magdalena* worked up from Villa-Lobos. In 1911 *Kismet* had been a thoroughly respectable play by Edward Knoblock before Wright and Forrest brought it back into prominence as one of their most successful musical adaptations, first presented by the Los Angeles and San Francisco Light Opera Company. They fashioned three successful popular songs from the music of Alexander Borodin: 'Stranger in Paradise', 'And This Is My Beloved' and what might have been a description of the show itself, 'Baubles, Bangles and Beads'. Probably not since *Chu Chin Chow* in 1916 had London been subjected to such a parade of ostentatious orientalism. And if the supporting cast was made up from the British, the jewels in the crown had been plucked from New York.

The Koh-i-Noor was Alfred Drake, one of the strongest leading men of the twentieth century, a performer of stature although physically small, memorably voiced and sexually compelling. It was a combination ideal for *Kismet*'s poet-beggar Hajj. Drake seems to have been an artist with a direct line of communication to an audience. *Plays and Players* saw a man who was

well built. He has a kind, round face, and eyes that sparkle with the joy of living. But as soon as he comes on to the stage he assumes the appearance of a towering giant. His big personality is projected into the auditorium with enormous power [...] It is, perhaps, the way he makes movements and words fit each other that is his greatest asset. In the West End so many performers in musicals can either sing, dance or act, but few can do more

than one. Drake can do all three with equal ease. And he does not need a
microphone to send his voice to the gallery. [...] There is no star nonsense
with him.[10]

Sandy Wilson was equally impressed by

> the overpowering performance of Alfred Drake, an actor of such colossal
> nerve and conceit that he could pulverise the audience into enjoying all the
> nonsense that was going on around him [...] Alfred Drake was aggressively
> heterosexual, but his performance in *Kismet* was the essence of camp. If
> *Kismet* had ever taken itself seriously, it would have been a bore; but it was
> ridiculous, and we laughed at it, and it ran and ran.[11]

For the *Sketch* Drake was 'Douglas Fairbanks re-born'[12] and for *Punch* 'a
personality with voice, poise, dash, huge authority and the most talkative pair
of hands in the West End of London'.[13] Tudor Davies had the unenviable task
of taking over when Drake's contract ended. *Kismet* was also noteworthy in
introducing two distinguished leading ladies, Doretta Morrow as Marsinah and
Joan Diener as Lalume. Morrow had already played Broadway as Kitty in *Where's
Charley?* and Tuptim in *The King and I*, and would return to London for the 1959
Aladdin. Diener made a startling British debut. Twenty-three years later, when
she returned to London in the same role, Sandy Wilson recalled that 'the extent
of her vocal range was only matched by that of her superstructure'.[14]

Hylton brought in Elizabeth Larner when Morrow's work permit expired, but
by this time Diener had long departed London, to be replaced by her understudy
Sheila Bradley. According to Bradley, three months after the opening, Diener
had taken an unscheduled holiday and was sacked by Hylton. (What was it
with Hylton and his star's holiday arrangements?) Diener's version was that in
early August she had been out of the show because of tonsillitis, and a doctor's
certificate was sent to Hylton. She moved into a nursing home but, perhaps
without informing Hylton, took herself off to Paris and the Mediterranean to
continue her recuperation. On returning to the theatre on 31 August for the
matinee performance she was denied access to the theatre; her name had been
taken off her dressing-room door. Hylton claimed that she had broken her
contract by 'disappearing' from London, and dismissed her. Bradley's version
was that 'Hylton just told [Diener] not to bother to come back. He was a nice
little man, but tough, like a little terrier. You never wanted to do the wrong thing
by him.' After her unexpected stardom Bradley went on to a successful career in
Australia, and was the first Australian Nancy in *Oliver!* Diener would return to
London for the 1978 revival of *Kismet* at the Shaftesbury Theatre, and for *Man of
La Mancha*. The West End might have welcomed Drake back as the great actor
Edmund Kean in *Kean*, a rare original musical by Wright and Forrest seen in
New York in 1961. The Broadway recording shows Drake's range and charisma;
what a richness this would have added to Shaftesbury Avenue, but no one was

prepared to take the chance with this musical about one of England's most legendary actors, even when headed by an equally legendary star.

It may be easy to scoff at *Kismet*, but Philip Hope-Wallace recognised its efficacy: 'It has everything to please British taste: everything which adorned *Chu Chin Chow* and adorns yearly the Ali Baba pantomime at the Puddlecombe Grand [...] There is the garish Near Eastern scenery, all bilious pink and orange [and] slushy music rinsed out of Borodin's opulent scores'.[15] The *Sunday Times* thought that 'Ablaze with twinkling midriffs, this is the sort of show which cries out to be seen or better still kept on ice'.[16]

How to tarnish the great success of the original, greatly praised production? Do it with a generous public subsidy, with inferior forces, and personnel who know little of the genre? At a time of extreme financial and artistic difficulty, the English National Opera staged a revival at the Coliseum in 2007. The barn of an old theatre must have had a distinct feeling of *déjà vu* as once again it hosted a big American musical. On this occasion, however, those involved in its production appeared clueless. The *Independent* heralded *Kismet*'s rebirth in an article headed 'An exercise in very poor taste':[17] here, after all, was an old musical set in Baghdad, and in 2007 the Iraq War was a despised phenomenon to most of the British public, and one that effectively killed off the popularity of one of Britain's most popular Prime Ministers, Tony Blair. Anthony Holden decided that

> For any British theatre to choose this particular moment to mount a jaunty musical set in Baghdad, hailing the Iraqi capital as 'the home of joy, merriment and pleasure', might well seem in the direst taste. For England's state-subsidised, self-styled national opera company to do so, as British troops continue to lay down their lives there every week, borders on the obscene.[18]

Not only that, but 'It is as surprising as dispiriting to see respected conductor Richard Hickox lending a vestige of respectability to this unlicensed pillaging and downgrading of themes by a Russian composer intent on disowning coarse Western influences.'

The work was scorned as dated (hardly surprising, as it had begun life a century before), production, choreography (the choreographer Javier de Futos fled shortly before opening night), and performances derided. Some praise found its way to Michael Ball as Hajj, although not all were impressed ('irredeemingly vulgar' according to Anthony Holden).[19] In an effort to bring some New York panache to the role of Lalume, Broadway's Faith Prince was imported, but no flags were put out. Another setback was new material contributed by Kit Hesketh-Harvey, whose track record with musicals was discouraging. One critic thought it 'about as alluring as an Arabian night at Woolworths'.[20] ENO's achievement had been to obliterate any recognition of the many fine qualities of *Kismet*: its skilful reassortment of its musical sources, its tasteful and agile lyrics, its luxurious Arthur Kay orchestrations, its glamour. The ENO had also overlooked its subtlety and complexity. It is unaccountable that it subsequently had good notices for a revival of *On the Town*, another dismal experience that misfired in every direction.

The Coliseum proved a happier venue for the last Broadway transplant of 1955: **The Pajama Game** (Coliseum, 13 October 1955; 588), a replication of the 1954 Broadway edition, with George Abbott and Jerome Robbins' direction reinstated by Robert E. Griffiths, and Fosse's choreography reproduced by his assistant Zoya Leporska, who choreographed a short-lived Broadway revival in 1973. Lemuel Ayers' sets and costumes were intact, as was the strong Don Walker orchestration. The show was the debut of a new writing partnership in Richard Adler and Jerry Ross's music and lyrics, buttressed by a book by Broadway veteran George Abbott working in collaboration with Richard Bissell, whose book *7½ Cents* was the basis of the musical. Adler and Ross brought something quite new and distinctive, bright, breezy, strong, uncomplicated songs, their lyrics adequate but rarely remarkable, their music confident and recallable. Its youthfulness and energy marked it out. Many of the numbers were widely heard outside the theatre, most notably 'Hey There!' (a love song sung by the hero to his dictating machine), 'Hernando's Hideaway', 'Steam Heat' and 'Once a Year Day'.

The songs were probably the best thing about *The Pajama Game*, a story of industrial strife in the Iowan Sleep Tite Pajama Factory, complicated by the fact that the handsome young superintendent of works, Sid Sorokin (Edmund Hockridge) who has just arrived in Cedar Rapids ('A New Town Is a Blue Town') falls for one of the factory workers Babe Williams (Joy Nichols), although she resists a mutual attraction ('I'm Not At All in Love'). British critics were more impressed by the appearances of Max Wall as Hines with the title song, 'I'll Never Be Jealous Again' and 'Think of the Time I Save'. Most of them tactfully overlooked the negative reception Wall was given at his curtain-call on the opening night. The British popular press had exposed the breakdown of his marriage, and vilified his association with a younger woman. As he took his curtain call, some of the audience threw vegetables. That audience had no idea it was in the presence of a genius.

On stage with Wall was a curate's egg of a cast, headed by Hockridge, manly but uninteresting despite his many appearances in American musicals. The Australian Nichols, on the other hand, was a find, but this was to be her only West End musical. She departed for New York, where she played a number of small roles in musicals, and after understudying Patricia Routledge in *Darling of the Day* ended as a sales assistant. More solid success was had by Elizabeth Seal in the soubrette role of Gladys originally played by Carol Haney. She seemed made for the Fosse dances, and the future looked bright for a British performer with such leggy talents. The stars stayed with the show until its closure on 9 March 1957. Britain was subsequently denied the opportunity to see *Say, Darling*,

16 Seen celebrating after the first night of *The Pajama Game*,
left to right: Joy Nichols, Hal Prince, Judy Bruce and unidentified friend

another musical made up from Bissell's novel of the same name about his involvement with *The Pajama Game*. With lyricists Comden and Green and composer Jule Styne, *Say, Darling* was on Broadway for 332 performances.

The Birmingham Repertory Theatre revival of 1999 is sometimes remembered as having had bad reviews; they were not all so. A cherished directorial achievement of Simon Callow, the best of it was probably the imagination behind the production. How many artists collected by the Tate and the New York Museum of Modern Art have designed a West End musical? Frank Stella's black and white settings for the factory floor, interrupted with startling gashes of colour, promoted this revival to highly interesting, even if one wondered why Stella couldn't have been employed on a more worthy project, or a show more receptive to his ingenuity? With musicals crying out for reinvention, this was almost a waste of talent. The choreography was by the artistic director of Birmingham Royal Ballet, David Bintley. The casting was on the debit side. The television personality Ulrika Jonsson had opened at Birmingham as Babe, but pulled out before London, admitting that her voice (and possibly audiences) would not stand the strain. She was replaced by Leslie Ash, an actress best known on television, making her musical debut. Graham Bickley stepped into

Hockridge's role without inducing excitement, along with a stand-up comic John Hegley, 'an unfunny embarrassment' according to the *Daily Mail*[21] in the Max Wall role. The only consistent praise was for Anita Dobson as Mabel, but 'when the fourth lead is the best thing in the show, you know it is in trouble'.[22] The *Daily Express* found 'one or two moments of poetry, but this over-groovy production with its jazzed up score and furiously funky visuals in the end smacks of bad faith. It looks striking but, as they say, you can't hum the sets.'[23] Adler left no doubt as to what he thought of what Callow had done to his old show: he found it 'unexciting, desultory, garish, unsexy [...] I hated it.'[24] The revival threw in the towel on 18 December 1999. A downsized production was mounted at the Union Theatre in April 2008.

British musical theatre of 1955 was a parade of fast-closing productions, none of which could compete with Broadway imports. *The Burning Boat* was a three-act romance set in a music festival at a Suffolk seaside town (obviously Aldeburgh). Despite its interesting score with music by Geoffrey Wright, it was off in a few days. Peter Greenwell's *Twenty Minutes South*, the mildly amorous adventures of young London suburbans, never took hold, a fate shared by Donald Swann's bucolic *Wild Thyme*. Little sympathy was extended to *Romance in Candlelight*, cobbled together by Eric Maschwitz and Hans May, or *A Girl Called Jo*, adapted from the novels of Louisa M. Alcott. In a talk given to the Arts Theatre Club in December, Vivian Ellis complained that those in control of British theatres were incapable of creating original British musicals 'so they fell back on American. England has now become the forty-ninth state, receiving the touring companies of Broadway hits.'[25]

1955 Broadway Exports

Plain and Fancy (461) and *Damn Yankees* (1,019).

1955 Broadway Only

Silk Stockings (478) had songs by Cole Porter, and easily outran Rodgers and Hammerstein's *Pipe Dream* (246), a clumsy attempt at a John Steinbeck musical with opera singer Helen Traubel as an unlikely brothel keeper. Sammy Fain wrote the music for an old-fashioned effort, *Ankles Aweigh* (176). Less successful were *Seventh Heaven* (44) and *The Vamp* (60) starring Carol Channing as Bronx-born Flora Weems who becomes a star of silent movies.

1956

Plain and Fancy
The Threepenny Opera
Fanny

T HE FIRST ENTRY OF THE YEAR tried to do for Pennsylvania what *Oklahoma!* had done for Oklahoma, and it was appropriate that ***Plain and Fancy*** (Theatre Royal, Drury Lane, 25 January 1956; 217) should have no exclamation mark: timidity was at its heart. It seemed to creep into the vastness of Kean's old playhouse, twice as large as the theatre it had inhabited in New York and unsympathetic to the play's unpretentiousness, and having opened there was subject to constant rumours that it was about to close. From the outset there were rumours that the show had been slotted into the Lane for a limited season. *Plays and Players* thought it

> like a day on the village green, naive, old fashioned, yet somehow compelling our interest in its trivial theme. Wide eyed and innocent, it almost pleads for our affection [...] So try as we will, we cannot feel displeased with the show, and though 'Young and Foolish' is the only touch of melodic felicity in the whole score, the staging makes full compensation.

The play was 'slightly reminiscent of *Oklahoma!*', although without the latter's virile punch in music and characterisation'.[1] To some it seemed that the great age of the American musical, at least that wave of solid, confident entertainment that had been crossing the Atlantic for almost a decade, was beginning to dim. Along with *Fanny*, *Plain and Fancy* has not stayed in the British memory, never a completely dependable faculty. True, *Plain and Fancy* is no masterpiece, but it has its good side.

What's more, the show had a sort of purpose about it. As a story of the Amish people, residing in 'Dutch' Pennsylvania, it beckoned audiences into a completely different world from their own – one that in the 1950s was almost uknown to the British public – and contrasted it with the big city expectations of two supposedly sophisticated (at least in musical comedy terms) visitors from New York, Ruth Winters and Dan King. The plot was in touch with the show's simple attitudes. Finding themselves in the quaint environ of Bird-in-Hand, Ruth and Dan (not lovers, but they end up as more than just good friends at curtain-fall) are exposed to the strict traditions of the clean-living Amish. Rules of behaviour may be clearly set down, but life even for the Amish has its emotional complexities. Katie Yoder is engaged to marry Ezra Reber, but is really in love with his brother Peter. Dan pleads with the boys' father to release Katie from her obligation, but is firmly reminded of the Amish principles in 'Plain We Live', a stern rebuttal of high living which must have had some curious reactions in the plush stalls of Drury Lane. Never mind. Katie gets the correct brother, and Dan and Ruth are together at curtain-fall.

Visually, the work had much going for it. Raoul Pene Du Bois's inventive, clear lines accentuated the folksy glamour; a clever touch was the slight colour enhancement of the true Amish dress, allowing suggestions of colour without sacrificing too much authenticity. Its original Broadway director Morton Da Costa directed the replication, with Helen Tamaris's choreography notable in the ballet sequences such as 'By Lantern Light' and ultimately in a Carnival Ballet when Ezra goes temporarily off the rails, drinks whisky and washes up at a fairground where the temptations of dance halls and floosies threaten. At least he's proved what an unsuitable match he would be for Katie, and the gaudy scene (in which the show still manages to preserve its demure demeanour) is essential because it brings into even sharper focus the Amish credo. Ruth struggles to come to terms with how these people live; *her* natural reaction is to put over a number called 'It's a Helluva Way to Run a Love Affair'. Ruth isn't all snappy one-liners and her dawning understanding of the differences (with the Amish getting the better deal) in 'City Mouse, Country Mouse' allows her a charm number. But the main delights of this score are found in its lilting love songs, 'Follow Your Heart' and the signature 'Young and Foolish'.

The composer Albert Hague, whose other most remembered musical *Redhead* never came to Britain, caught the spirit of the piece perfectly. His lyricist was Arnold B. Horwitt, whose words had been heard in the 1948 revue *Make Mine Manhattan*. His words for *Plain and Fancy* were serviceable but hardly distinguished; in partnership with Hague's melodies the result might have been something from twenty years back. The American production had opened almost exactly a year before and run the whole year through, supported by good notices. Brooks Atkinson found it 'interesting if uneven musical comedy. With such genuine characters as the substance of the show, can't the authors find anything better for a second act than the old staples of Broadway? [...] The authors have not sustained the grave beauty of the first act.'[2]

Anthony Cookman found the Lane's production 'all charm, deep, rich, thick bucolic charm with tall milk churns, monster pumpkins and red-roofed barns sticking out everywhere to lengthen the impression of slow rural peace'.[3] Indeed, the finale had the company posing behind many of the Amish artefacts, as if ready for a yard sale. The critics were sympathetic but not in buying mood. 'Much of the night is tedious', wrote J. C. Trewin, but he didn't find it vulgar in the manner of other American imports: 'it is just simple, with a thinly ingratiating charm that soon wears off [...] Drury Lane invites us to a banquet and then offers a hunk of bread and cheese.'[4] *Punch* thought the play didn't tell the audience enough about these people, sympathised with Shirl Conway and Richard Derr, whom it considered had been used by the authors as stooges, thought 'the lyrics are pedestrian and the music only average' and was heartened that 'the cast does not include a single representative of those awful bull-roaring

tenors with a Vesuvian emission of treacle'. It saw, too, that in *Plain and Fancy*
the American musical had come full circle back, theatrically, to *Oklahoma!*[5]
For R. B. Marriott *Plain and Fancy* was 'the most appealing production seen at
Drury Lane since the American invasion began in '47'.[6]

The fact that *Plain and Fancy*'s theme (outsiders breaking into what was
effectively a closed American community) resembled that of the British musical
of the same year *Summer Song* (with Dvořák spending time among American
lumberjacks) has gone unrecognised. The difference is that Hague and Horwitt
took their theme seriously, making something of a documentary musical, while
in London Eric Maschwitz and his collaborators worked up an old-fashioned
musical comedy built around music that Dvořák had unknowingly already
written for them. Having taken on the job of writing a musical about the
Amish, the writers meant to make it worthy of them. They need not have done
so, especially as the Amish are not allowed to attend theatrical performances,
which undermines the veracity of the following story. Wanting to make sure they
had done it right, the producers asked an Amish family, the Zooks, to see and
approve it before its Broadway opening. The Zooks made the journey from their
home town of Intercourse and – so we are told – found nothing to complain of.

Unlike *Fanny* there wasn't a name in *Plain and Fancy* that British audiences
recognised. As the sophisticated urbanites from the Big Apple Shirl Conway and
Richard Derr, both from the original Broadway edition, shared top billing. In
New York Conway had been fourth billed below Derr and Barbara Cook, who
despite her several Broadway roles never appeared in a stage musical in Britain.
Conway had played the West End in the British *Carissima* in 1948, another
musical for which Maschwitz had been largely responsible. *Carissima* was
obvious codswollop, but in some ways it had been more aggressively 'modern'
than *Plain and Fancy*, and had a scene in which an aeroplane landed on stage,
making it the *Miss Saigon* of its day. British audiences may have recognised
Derr from some minor movies but neither he nor Conway were star names
and neither returned to another musical on Broadway. It may be that their
performances in *Plain and Fancy* were two of the best to be seen in the history
of American musicals in London. R. B. Marriott thought Conway 'brilliant'
with 'perfect timing' and that 'Together, Miss Conway and Mr Derr display a
technical accomplishment and rapport that reminds one of the Lunts'.[7] There
was a welcome for new names among the cast, notably American Joan Hovis
as the impressionable Hilda Miller, captivatingly singing one of the score's
freshest items 'This is All Very New to Me', and American Jack Drummond and
Grace O'Connor (recently a Dublin telephonist) as Peter and Katie. Hovis went
on to play in two Broadway shows, *The Country Wife* and *Love Me Little*, but
Drummond and O'Connor seemed to vanish from theatrical history.

Pity poor *Plain and Fancy*, which had never expected to be shunted into
Drury Lane, although it almost certainly wouldn't have fared better elsewhere.
Too much plain and not enough fancy, perhaps, for there was no need of great

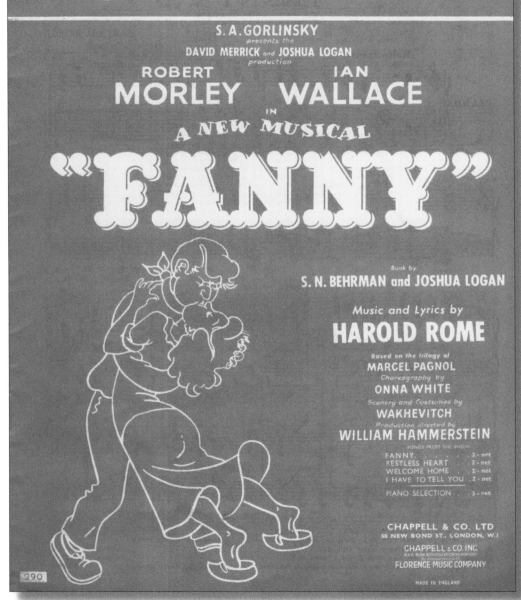

17 Marcel Pagnol's romance set to music by Harold Rome: the Theatre Royal Drury Lane's *Fanny* (1956) offered Robert Morley his only role in musicals

spectacle except for a set-piece in 'How Do You Raise a Barn?'. Conway and Derr must have walked onto that stage and thought 'Wow!' or, if they had any sense, 'Oh no!'. This was the show that had the unenviable task of breaking with the Rodgers and Hammerstein Drury Lane tradition. Since 1947 the Lane had done nothing *but*: *Oklahoma!*, *Carousel*, *South Pacific* and *The King and I*. So far as London audiences were concerned, Hague and Horwitt might have been a gentleman's outfitters in Jermyn Street. Overnight the Lane had lost the brand it had linked itself to for a decade, and now the public stayed home. *Plain and Fancy*'s producer Prince Littler would have pulled it off but had nothing to replace it with. Business worsened when Conway and Derr returned to the States and were replaced in July 1956 by British Roberta Huby and Bruce Trent. On average the show lost £1,500 a week, a total loss of £40,215.00 by the time of its closure, wiping out a nest-egg of £35,000 that the Lane had accumulated since the war. Edward Goring in the *Daily Mail* reported that

> last night stage folk were saying the days of the long run for a big American show in a huge theatre are over. The post-war boom which kept *Oklahoma!* and *Annie Get Your Gun* going for years is finished. Besides, the new shows are not as good. Even *The King and I* was not doing so well when it was kept on for a second year.[8]

Perhaps the Lane and the British public had become too dependent on Rodgers and Hammerstein. As *The King and I* sickened towards the end of 1955 there were plans to bring over their latest, *Pipe Dream*, which had opened on Broadway in November and closed after seven months. Surely it was never seriously considered? This is Rodgers and Hammerstein at their dullest, basically a chamber work with no spectacle, no chorus, a pedestrian story and dreary songs. Besides, this was about Cannery Row low life, courtesy of John Steinbeck's novel *Sweet Thursday*, inhabited by a madam who tended local prostitutes in 'The Happiest House on the Block'. It was disastrous to hand such material to Hammerstein, for whom all had to be normal as blueberry pie. Even so, letting degenerates loose at the Lane was never going to happen, at least in 1956. The British musical was waking up to kitchen-sink drama, unleashing a spate of Soho musicals that lived out a brief fashion until the end of the decade. The home-grown product that was *Expresso Bongo*, *Fings Ain't Wot They Used T'Be* and *The Crooked Mile* would make *Pipe Dream* look prim. It was. And if the show had ever reached the Lane, who would have been signed for the 'madam' role, played in New York by the Metropolitan Opera star Helen Traubel? Constance Shacklock? Muriel Smith? *Pipe Dream*, like the 1953 *Me and Juliet*, proved disappointing, and there would be no London booking; Rodgers and Hammerstein's association with the Lane was broken, and their subsequent imports *Flower Drum Song* and *The Sound of Music* were homed at the Palace Theatre. It was Hague and Horwitt who bore some of the fall-out from the change, and the next show to be put into the Lane, *Fanny*. Sometimes it seemed that the fault of the shows that were to follow was simply that they were not Rodgers and Hammerstein.

The real pity is that Britain wasn't getting *more* shows like *Plain and Fancy* and *Fanny*; being drip-fed only solid commercially successful American musicals was not good for the digestion. The producers' plan, after all, was never to present a panorama of the most interesting of American product, but to make money; we needn't suppose that Jack Hylton or Prince Littler or H. M. Tennent were in the least interested in the American musical as a genre – their interest was commercial. Come to think of it, was all that Rodgers and Hammerstein good for us, for our understanding of what was happening in the American musical? Especially after *The King and I*, when the team favoured regression over progression. The West End was being offered a *Reader's Digest* of the American musical, the most likely excerpts, designed not to move forward appreciation but to fill the producers' coffers. Wouldn't it have been more refreshing to have been offered some of the *other* American shows of the past few years, the ones that never got a passport? The sorbet between the heavier courses. Make room for *The Golden Apple* or *The Girl in Pink Tights*. On the other hand, perhaps most British playgoers wanted to be spared stuff that had already had the Broadway thumbs-down. When *Plain and Fancy* gave up, it left behind a truncated London cast recording. The three juvenile leads were allowed to sing their numbers in the studio, but because of contractual arrangements Conway and Derr were unable to participate. Nothing a telephone call over the seas might have sorted out, surely, but instead of Conway we have another cast member, Virginia Somers, standing in for her, and there is no sign of Derr's songs.

At ease masquerading as opera or musical was the British premiere of **The Threepenny Opera** (Royal Court Theatre, 9 February 1956, then Aldwych Theatre 21 March 1956; 140) by Bertolt Brecht and Kurt Weill. It had first been seen in Berlin in 1928, marking the 200th anniversary of the work on which it was unashamedly based, playing New York in an English version in 1933. Now it was presented as 'A Soho musical', in its way a precursor of the spate of 'Soho' musicals that were popular at the end of the decade, its action transposed, according to the theatre programme, to a period 'on the threshold of the twentieth century'. Marc Blitzstein's book followed the adventures of the beguiling villain Macheath, more affectionately known as Mack the Knife, who marries Polly Peachum but is sent to Newgate Prison. He escapes, assisted by another lover, Lucy Brown, but is captured and sentenced to death, only to be pardoned at the final moment, when he has mounted the scaffold.

'You are about to see an opera for beggars', the theatre programme warned. 'Since this opera was conceived with a splendour only a beggar could imagine, and since it had to be so inexpensive even a beggar could afford it, it is called *The Threepenny Opera*.' The work had its beginnings in John Gay's 1728 British piece *The Beggar's Opera*, which had first played New York in 1750. In Britain *The Beggar's Opera* proved resilient. There was a notable production by Frederick

Austin at the Lyric, Hammersmith, which managed a remarkable 1,469 performances. Other British revivals were mounted by the Royal Shakespeare Company in 1963, and by Prospect Productions in 1968. Gay's original libretto was reworked by Brecht as *Die Dreigroschenoper* and then fashioned into an English version by Blitzstein. This opened in New York at the Theatre De Lys in 1954 for a ninety-five performance run, reopening there the following year for 2,611 performances, with a distinguished cast headed by Weill's widow, Lotte Lenya. The London theatre programme made no mention of the work being based on Gay's play.[9]

Ronald Sanders has written that

> There was an 'off-Broadway' renaissance taking place, a reaction on the part of a lively and idealistic theatre culture downtown against a Broadway establishment going sour, and *The Threepenny Opera* became a major expression of the phenomenon – indeed, the success of *The Threepenny Opera* down on Christopher Street was a kind of historic revenge for Broadway's rejection of it over twenty years before. But both the production and the translation had been rather different in 1933, whereas both were outstanding in 1954 and a major source of the success.[10]

Inevitably, without an off-West End, *The Threepenny Opera* could not hope to hold on for a protracted run, but it marked the stirrings of an alternative theatre, or at least musical theatre (stirrings that made few ripples). It had a halo of remarkable credentials, as though only those who innately subscribed to its milieu, philosophy and style had been invited to contribute. The décor was by Caspar Neher, the life-long associate of Brecht who had designed the original 1928 production at the Theater am Schiffbauerdamm. Neher's assistant was the designer Ekkehard Grübler. The musical director and pianist of the eight-piece band working with Weill's original orchestrations was Berthold Goldschmidt, an émigré composer whose works had been declared non-Aryan and decadent by the Nazi regime.[11] The assistant musical director, playing harmonium in the pit, was Geoffrey Wright, an underrated composer of forgotten revue songs, the remembered 'Transatlantic Lullaby', and the short-lived musical *The Burning Boat*. The dances were arranged by the Norwegian Tutte Lemkow. Blitzstein's libretto stood at the centre of his work in musical theatre, to which he also contributed scores for *The Cradle Will Rock* (1937), *Regina* (1949) and *Juno* (1959). There was a felicity about some of the cast, too, with Bill Owen as the scrawniest Cockney Macheath of all time, Ewan MacColl bringing authenticity as The Street Singer, Daphne Anderson as Polly Peachum and Lisa Lee as her mother, Maria Remusat as Jenny (especially good in 'Pirate Jenny' and 'Solomon Song'), and Georgia Brown as Lucy. The following year Brown took over the same role in the New York production.

The critical reaction was mixed. Ivor Brown found the proceedings 'mainly sombre' and 'fusty fun in 1956'. Weill's music 'had a mixture of the menacing with the melodious' and Bliztstein's text 'contained a lavish helping of heavy-handed indecency which was propelled at the audience in a heavy-handed way'. He continued,

> I understand that Herr Brecht has a theory that actors should act actors acting and not humanity being human. If there is any value in this, I was unable to discover it. The result seemed to emerge as an orgy of boiled 'ham'. There were toy figures and poses. There was rumpus galore. Amid the dingy scenic squalor was the 'blueness' of humour. [...] All this had been critically hailed as 'immensely exciting' [but] I only got a yawn from this funeral shuffle performed on the dead body of the once exciting *Beggar's Opera*.[12]

For *Theatre World* the late arrival of *The Threepenny Opera* 'has value as an ice-breaker and as pure entertainment but, after so many years, it has lost all force as disruptive satire'. 'H.G.M.' wanted more.

> Considering that the stage is given over for three hours to thieves and beggars, punks and whores, it is surprising that so little is said to damage the structure of society. The little that is said is taken from 'whence it comes', for are we not a Welfare State, governed from the bottom up, with the Under-dog rampant? In Berlin between the wars, there was real grievance, want and bitterness, and an element of savage despair is preserved in Kurt Weill's music, which is sour, nostalgic, taunting and defiant [and which would have an echo in *Cabaret*].[13]

In a roundup review that embraced *Plain and Fancy* as well as the British musical *Summer Song* Frank Granville Barker thought *The Threepenny Opera* made the others 'simpering affairs' in comparison. Some of his observations seemed pertinent to much of what would follow in American-British musical theatre of the coming decades, noting

> Brecht's dramatic method, which insists that what happens on stage is sheer make-believe. His characters are not real: they are parts played by actors who are frequently made to step outside them. The pretence of acting is thrown aside, and the audience is assured that life is not really like the charade they have been watching.
>   Such a technique is alien to our players, who have worshipped for years at the shrine of Stanislavsky, striving their utmost always to identify themselves completely with the characters they play. It is to [the director] Sam Wanamaker's eternal credit that he has been able to throw aside his old allegiance to Stanislavsky and make this revolutionary piece of theatre the most exciting musical in London.[14]

They are words that those concerned in the writing, production and staging of musical theatre should heed, for the relationship between reality and fantasy remains a significantly misunderstood, unexplored, unconsidered, essential component of the art, too often airbrushed from the mind by a blatant superficiality. The issue is brilliantly, although hardly totally satisfactorily, solved by the very nature of *The Threepenny Opera*, which simply removes itself from the real world, drawing in its neck like a retiring tortoise. Nevertheless, the late arrival of Brecht and Weill's masterpiece marked a clear break with the middle-class preoccupations of the West End, and may be said to have been a catalyst in transforming the attitudes of British theatregoers. Despite its all-star cast, a 1972 revival at the Prince of Wales Theatre seemed less relevant or shocking.

It was the tail-end of the year by the time the next Broadway success opened. *Fanny* (Theatre Royal, Drury Lane, 15 November 1956; 347) is undeserving of the neglect into which it has fallen. In its way, it was a folly: an attempt to squeeze Marcel Pagnol's trilogy of plays – *Marius*, *Fanny* and *César* – into a two-and-a-quarter-hour musical, adapted by S. N. Behrman and Joshua Logan, its Broadway director. Frankly, any transition to theatre was going to lose something, take on the character of a different beast. Suggestion must play the larger part. A broadening has to be endured. Simplicity, already a component of the many-layered Pagnol works, must be simplified. The responsibility of the songs – words and music by Harold Rome – is to carry all this forward, for only in the heightened atmosphere of its score can such a work succeed or fall. Rome, of course, is the composer of the impossible, seemingly intent on taming the inconquerable. Who else would have taken on the mammoth dimensions of either Monsieur Pagnol or Margaret Mitchell's *Gone with the Wind*, challenges of Everest proportions? *Fanny* may be one of the unsung masterworks of the twentieth century, but it is one that many critics, in London and New York, were ready to dismiss as of little worth.

Steven Suskin's *Opening Night on Broadway* gives it straight: the New York critics' reaction to *Fanny* was one rave, two favourables, two mixed and two unfavourables. No pans. In Britain, enthusiasm was muted. This may be no more than appropriate; for much of its time the musical *is* muted, its colours and tone lacking brilliance. Walter Kerr hinted at one or two of *Fanny*'s problems, problems which followed it to London. On Broadway, Kerr found it

> subdued and attenuated. In part this is due to the simple fact of its musicalization for Broadway: spread a simple, fairly folksy comedy out to the dimensions of a vast and glittering proscenium and something of its simplicity is bound to vanish. A batch of chorus boys and chorus girls offering gifts to a baby on its first birthday is more curious than an affecting picture. Nor do the young lovers of the piece, pleasantly played and sung by William Tabbert and Florence Henderson, seem to be in Marseilles; they seem to be downstage. Ezio Pinza has an appealing episode during which he tries to teach his errant son how to make vermouth cassis

without too much seltzer. *Fanny*, I think, has too much seltzer. It is often difficult to taste the wine.[15]

The span of *Fanny* suggests epic, but the story is a simplicity. The picture is of a Marseilles waterfront, picturesque but *louche*, Arab girls apt to twist their bodies into provocative poses, testosterone-filled young bucks of sailors. Yet at the centre of these colours is the strong relationship between two middle-aged friends, the kindly café owner César and the sailmaker Panisse. César's son Marius is in love with Fanny, but the call of the sea lures him from her side. The pregnant Fanny is abandoned, but Panisse offers to take her as his wife. Years after, Marius returns from sea. The attraction between Fanny and her lost sailor is as strong as ever, but César will not allow such catastrophe to affect Panisse. Fanny and Marius's son Césario goes in search of Marius, now working in a petrol station in Toulon. Césario tells Marius that he too wants to go to sea, but Marius persuades him not to make the same mistake. When Césario returns to Marseilles, it is to find Panisse on his deathbed, attended by the faithful César. Panisse's last wish is that Fanny should now marry Marius, ensuring that Césario is brought up by two kindly parents.

The differences between the American and British productions are striking. In New York the show was presented by Logan and, making his production debut, the notorious David Merrick; in Britain S. A. Gorlinsky made his debut as a theatrical producer, alongside the H. M. Tennent management. London's was no mere replication of the New York original, with a new director in William Hammerstein, and new choreographer, Onna White, replacing Broadway's Helen Tamaris. There were new sets and costumes by the distinguished Russian Georges Wakhévitch, a frequent designer at Covent Garden; Broadway had seen sets and lighting by Jo Mielziner – London's lighting was by Michael Northen – and costumes by Alvin Colt. Wakhévitch's work was appreciated as an invaluable component of the play's atmosphere, but the Gallic authenticity for the eye was not carried through the casting. Broadway had a major figure in the César of Ezio Pinza, a name at the New York Metropolitan Opera, who already had the public affection from five years of playing the lead in *South Pacific* at his back; London had the opera singer Ian Wallace, a man mostly known for singing a song about a hippopotamus.[16] In the place of Walter Slezak's Panisse, London chose the elephantine and delightful Robert Morley, a stranger to St Cecilia.

Plays and Players may have had its tongue in the cheek when it announced that Morley was to be a 'singing star' in the forthcoming Drury Lane spectacular. The lack of a British recording has robbed us of the chance of discovering how he coped with his numbers, but Morley was an interesting choice; one wonders how he coped with such moments as 'Panisse and Son' in which Panisse describes, with infinite taste, his unsuccessful attempts to give his wife a child. How did Morley deal with the decidedly gloopy lyrics, and keeping in time with the music? His co-star had all the qualifications for starring in a musical except charisma. Astoundingly, Wallace was only thirty-seven years old when he took the role, but came over as a much older man before the Leichner[17] had a chance to do its work. Beaming *bonhomie* he may have had in plenty, but Wallace had the stage presence of a hat-stand. Faced with scenes opposite the supremely experienced Morley, one wonders how he fared. Two young Americans were brought to London to play Marius and Fanny: Kevin Scott, who had already played Broadway in two flops, *Carnival in Flanders* and the revue *Almost Crazy*, and Janet Pavek. After *Fanny* Scott pursued his British career, but at the end of her contract Pavek returned to New York, playing a featured role in the floppy *Christine* and singing small roles in some Gilbert and Sullivan operas. Doreen Duke played Fanny from June 1957 and 'with her English approach takes some of the Amercanism away from the play, which seems all to the good'.[18] When Duke fell ill for a time shortly after assuming the role she was replaced by chorus member Sheelagh Aldrich.

Scott and Pavek got by far the best of the songs, written when Rome's emotional gander was up. The title song, with its reiterated cry of 'Fanny, Fanny, Fanny' rushes into life with magnificent urgency, surely one of the great love songs of American musical theatre, with its aching reminder that Marius is 'a boy with no heart to give' because it is given already to the all-demanding sea. The melody has already begun and permeated the overture, and after Marius has cast off its passion it continues to haunt the second half of the play. Marius' other hymn to love, 'Restless Heart', has the same ring of yearning, and on the distaff side Fanny has the halting 'I Have to Tell You'. Elsewhere, the numbers fall to César and Panisse, and while one wonders what degrees of delicacy Morley may have brought to 'Never Too Late for Love' and the touching 'To My Wife', one knows that Wallace would have been in his element with César's declamatory hymn to domesticity 'Welcome Home', with its bell-like celebration of the slippers and pipe life. At this central most domestic point of the play and score, Wallace must have seemed perfect casting.

Truthfully, much of *Fanny* is told in the plainest of music, but Rome's way with a song is very different from, say, Rodgers and Hammerstein. When needed, Rodgers and Hammerstein deliver a whole plum, perfectly shaped, which does the job in its context and will also work as well out of it. Character is often firmly at the back of a Rodgers and Hammerstein song, but not detrimental to its wider possibilities. Rome doesn't work like this, and *Fanny* really has no songs of this type; they are all more purposeful. In *Fanny*, Rome's faithfulness to story and tone is subtle, a skill he shares with Loesser. In fact, there are several moments in *Fanny* when we have to pinch ourselves that this isn't a Loesser score. 'Why Be Afraid To Dance?' collides in feeling with *The Most Happy Fella*'s 'Ole People Gotta Sit Dere An' Die'; Fanny's 'I Have to Tell You' might as well have been written for *The Most Happy Fella*'s Rosabella. And Marius's aria to Fanny is a sort of cousin to 'Joey, Joey', Joey's Act One song in *The Most Happy Fella*, with its constant repetition of 'Joey'. Of course, the two shows are anyway essentially linked by their central story of an older man marrying a much younger woman whose heart, or emotions, may lie elsewhere. Most British critics demoted *Fanny* to the second-class department. 'What,' asked the *Sunday Times* reviewer, 'can I possibly find to praise in this dreadful musical?' 'Let me put it to the reader,' proposed Caryl Brahms.

> Could you believe in a Marseilles so neat, so genteel, so coy and well-disciplined that it seems to have been transplanted not even to Grimsby – that sober, self-respecting kipper-catching city where every wind blows in from the arctic North and the sea mist lingers – but to some coastal Streatham-on-Sea?
>
> Here, then, we have Marcel Pagnol's trilogy of love, pride and pig-headedness forsaking the sun-baked, fish-laden, garlic-breathing Midi of France for that mad breeze that blows off Tooting Bec.
>
> No garlic for Mr Robert Morley. His Panisse might pass for an elderly Peter Pan, cutting elderly English capers with all the aplomb of an elderly Englishman slumming it abroad.
>
> No medals for Mr Ian Wallace's César, either, at war, as he is, with the medium. Do you remember laughing and weeping and believing in Raimu's[19] performance as the crusty, wilful old lamb of a lion on the screen? Mr Wallace demonstrates that kind hearts are more than French accents but less than the ebb and flow between actor and actor. This César remains an island, vocally isolated, while the cast washes and breaks around him.[20]

The illusion that Wallace or Morley might be French was no more apparent to the *Observer* critic, for 'Ian Wallace in a beard and Robert Morley in a beret are so resolutely, unmistakably British. They reek of toothpaste. They have no garlic on their breath.'[21] More generally, 'Are we, I wonder, in at the death of the American musical?' asked Derek Monsey in the *Sunday Express*. 'It is beginning to have a quaint, old-fashioned, uninspired, often tasteless and amateurish quality rather like English pantomime has [...] it is a highly organised commercial venture. It is designed for dividends.'[22] Likewise, Anthony Cookman in the *Tatler* lamented the apparent drying up of the Rodgers – Hammerstein works: 'we aged but they did not. They ran and ran.' Cookman paused to consider Rome 'a composer who seems to turn with a shudder from the waterfront stinking of fish towards the Vienna of the Strauss waltzes, and waltzes on the quayside of Marseilles have a most inept smack of incongruity'.[23] J. C. Trewin considered it 'calamitous' that such a piece should be welcomed by a theatre as distinguished as the Lane.[24] For the *Stage* R. B. Marriott was similarly unimpressed, complaining of long-winded dialogue, dances that didn't lift, the lack of melodramatic attack essential to Pagnol's story and a weakness in performance and direction, with the 'interminable' death scene that was 'inherently boring'. He considered 'Love Is a Very Light Thing' 'one of the most repellently sentimental chants to boyhood ever heard in a modern musical'.[25]

There were four home-grown musicals. Allon Bacon's adaptation of T. W. Robertson's Victorian comedy *Caste*, **She Smiled at Me**, had Jean Kent for its leading lady, but she was detained for only four performances. **Summer Song** took a leaf from the works of Robert Wright and George Forrest by plundering Dvořák's music to decorate a bio-musical of the composer, but the public seemed uninterested. Impresario Jack Waller plundered the trunk of his dead composer-collaborator Joseph Tunbridge to concoct **Wild Grows the Heather**, but this version of J. M. Barrie's *The Little Minister* proved a museum piece. The success of the year was **Grab Me a Gondola**, a satire on the antics of a film star of the time, Diana Dors. A personal success for its star, Joan Heal, it was depressing to find a successful show setting the bar so low, with a score that would never have found a foothold in America.

1956 Broadway Exports

My Fair Lady (2,717), *The Most Happy Fella* (678), *Bells Are Ringing* (924) and *Candide* (73).

1956 Broadway Only

The three substantial successes were **Happy Hunting** (413), the appealing **Li'l Abner** (693) based on a famous American comic strip, and Sammy Davis Jr. in **Mr Wonderful** (383). **Shangri-La** (21) was a disastrous adaptation of James Hilton's novel, *Lost Horizon*.

18 The airborne Gladys Cooper takes flight at the age of seventy in the strangely original *The Crystal Heart*, probably the most misunderstood 'American' musical of the 1950s

1957

The Crystal Heart
Damn Yankees
Bells Are Ringing

I N A YEAR when some British critics suspected the fuel in the tank of American musicals was running low, the first arrival strengthened the belief. *The Crystal Heart* (Saville Theatre, 19 February 1957; 7) didn't come across as an American show, but it *had* come across. For all the British cared, it was just another of their home-grown failures, except the word didn't really suffice in this case. *The Crystal Heart* has its place in West End history as fiasco. The London run was described as pre-Broadway by its American producers Lyn Austin and Thomas Noyes, who announced its opening with two star players, Gladys Cooper and Roddy McDowell. By the time it premiered at the Lyceum, Edinburgh, in January 1957, Toby Rowland had moved in as main producer, McDowell's name was nowhere to be found, and the show was in disarray. The trouble magnified a few days after the Edinburgh opening, when during an energetic routine which involved the septuagenarian star being lifted on high by the boy dancers, she was dropped and injured. For much of the pre-London run Cooper was off, and when she returned in time for the London opening the ballet was cut.

There was still reason enough to take note of what was on offer. R. B. Marriott pinned the show's style: 'the treatment is meant to be a mixture of poetry, gentle cynicism, subtle wit and down-to-earth sensuality'.[1] In the company of other American musicals of its time, *The Crystal Heart* did indeed attempt something new, Pirandello out of Ionesco by way of N. F. Simpson, with the tang of melodrama and the spray of the sea and an inconsequent frivolity with its leading character a sort of desert island Lady of Chaillot. In the 1830s Mistress Phoebe Ricketts is an elderly brandy-drinking widow obliged by the terms of her dead husband's will to live on an island peopled only by her female companions, including her young niece. When a boat disgorges a group of men onto the island, romantic complications unfold. The original book and lyrics were the work of William Archibald, probably best remembered for making successful plays from the works of Henry James (*The Innocents* from *The Turn of the Screw*, and *The Portrait of a Lady*) but also the collaborator with *The Crystal Heart*'s composer Baldwin Bergersen on the 1945 Broadway *Carib Song*.

On the Saville's opening night restlessness broke out in the theatre, not least when Cooper trilled a song called 'Pretty Little Bluebird', and got 'the bird'. At final curtain she took a deep and graceful bow to the accompaniment of jeering and booing. The distinguished actress had done her best with a part that required her to make her entrance dressed in a fantastic costume, dripping with jewellery and sporting a vividly coloured wig, the first of many she popped on through the evening. 'She sings, but might be better advised to speak her songs,'[2] reported the *Stage* critic from Manchester, while Marriott declared her performance 'a gallant attempt to turn a weak yet rather repellent part into something worthwhile'.[3] Lisa Gordon Smith in *Plays and Players* thought its 'potential qualities were well hidden in its actual presentation [...] The music, for instance, was excellent, even though buried under "clever-clever" orchestrations [by Ted Royal]'.[4] *Plays and Players* was moved to editorial comment, for the catastrophe proved that

> A show which meets with such complete disaster on its provincial opening simply cannot be brought into the West End without some drastic improvements being made [...] In the case of *The Crystal Heart*, it should have been apparent to the management that, although the authors of this musical were to be commended on trying to break new ground, their work stood no chance of success without immediate revision. [...]
>
> It was surely the authors of *The Crystal Heart* against whom the audience were venting their spleen, and it was both thoughtless and cruel to submit Gladys Cooper to such a frightening ordeal [...] it is monstrously unfair that she should have been treated like a criminal in the pillory.[5]

For all this, something lurks in Bergersen and Archibald's fantasy, not least its strange way of talking, and its haunting songs. 'I Wanted to See the World' is one of the most telling, straightforward love songs of its period; no matter, for it is never heard. Total failure all but obliterates any qualities that might be found in musicals. On the second night the upper gallery was closed, the closing notice was posted and Cooper took four curtain calls. She was 'angry, very angry. I think that if people disapprove they should shut up and walk out as they do in America. It made me fighting mad. I went down with every flag flying.' Asked about her injury, Cooper replied, 'I take a pill to deaden the pain. I play on a pill.'[6] There was no booing on the second night, although several made a discreet exit at the end of the first act. Someone pointedly read a newspaper and another snored. *The Crystal Heart* was off at the end of the week, an achievement repeated when the show was presented the following year off-Broadway with Mildred Dunnock as Mistress Phoebe. It should be remembered that Harold Hobson, who was at the forefront of critics (and often almost alone) in welcoming the new wave of serious drama of the period, considered *The Crystal Heart* 'more ambitious than the smug conventionalities of ordinary musicals [...] For myself, money aside, I would rather have written this failure than successes like *The King and I* and *South Pacific*'.

A month later it was back to the mainstream Broadway musical. To see a British cast struggling through a *peculiarly* American musical was not unusual, but **Damn Yankees** (Coliseum, 28 March 1957; 258) compounded the difficulty with its subject matter: baseball. *Reynolds News* decided that

The British cast can only make a second-hand try at situations totally foreign to them. It is not surprising that they are unconvincing and only emphasise the weaknesses [...] It should by now have dawned on our theatrical impresarios that the undisputed reign of the Broadway musical, which began so gloriously with *Oklahoma!*, is over. The fizzle-out, which began in earnest with *Plain and Fancy* and *Fanny*, continues here.[7]

(Spoken too soon; the following year would bring *West Side Story* and *My Fair Lady*.) Derek Granger thought, 'The final effect is of a rather pale, routine-made copy of a show from which the vital energy seems to have been mislaid.'[8] London staged a replication of the Broadway original: Bob Fosse's choreography redone by Zoya Leporska, and George Abbott's direction warmed through by James Hammerstein, with the whole affair overseen by the ubiquitous reproduction expert Jerome Whyte.

Publicists were kept busy, not least with photographs of its star performer, Belita (Maria Belita Gladys Olive Lyne Jepson-Turner), best known, after a career in classical ballet, for her ice skating. In the early 1950s she starred in the then fashionable ice-shows at London's Empress Hall, and appeared in a few films, including *Silk Stockings* with Fred Astaire, although she was unbilled. Casting her as *Damn Yankee*'s Lola was a mysterious move, and proved a mistake from which her career did not recover. After three months she was replaced on 25 June by Elizabeth Seal. The public's attention was drawn to this when a week before taking over Seal was photographed at Chessington Zoo, naming a seal. Meanwhile, Betty Paul,[9] in the thankless role of the dutiful Meg, made little impression in her only American musical in London, although there was mass press coverage for a hat that had been especially created for her by Madge Chard (a stitched broad navy and white cotton stripe with waffle pique peak and grosgrain bow in red). One wonders what effect such revelations had on the box office. After the first night His Highness Prince Chula Chakra-Bongse of Siam offered to write a play for Paul.

A common criticism of *Damn Yankees* was that baseball was a wholly American pastime and a step too far for the British taste, underlining Milton Shulman's *Evening Standard* review headline, 'Let's retaliate with cricket on Broadway'. This was a little disingenuous. American musicals in London had long been about subjects that the British knew little of, and baseball was only the peg on which George Abbott hung his version of the Faust story, collaborating with Douglass Wallop on the adaptation of his book *The Year the Yankees Lost the Pennant*. It was not beyond the British imagination to understand the American obsession with the game. A musical about cricket would hardly have had the virility of *Damn Yankees*, most evident in the team players' anthem 'Heart' – a popular song outside the show – and 'The Game'. The sporting motif was merely a handle to exemplify American aspiration and mores; audiences didn't need to know the rules of the game, any more than they needed to understand the clothing industry for *The Pajama Game*.

Audiences may have been more alarmed by the links to Goethe, surely the sort of territory a British audience in search of undemanding diversion would have avoided? The Faust connection was obvious. When staid middle-aged Joe Boyd, who lives mainly to support his beloved baseball team the Senators, voices his willingness to sell his soul to the Devil if he could only save them from defeat, the Devil offers him a contract. His paunchy physique reduced to a six-pack, Joe (Phil Vickers), happily married to wife Meg (Betty Paul), becomes handsome young Joe Hardy (Ivor Emmanuel), who amazes as 'Shoeless Joe from Hannibal, Mo' (as reported by the reporter Gloria, played by Judy Bruce in her first West End lead). The Devil, in the guise of the svelte Mr Applegate (Bill Kerr), brings in reinforcements in the form of seductive Lola (Belita / Elizabeth Seal) to keep his plan on course, but 'old' Joe's love for his wife wins the day, and he plays the escape clause he has arranged with Applegate, returning to his former self and his comfortable downtown American life. Contentment is reached, but Joe then has to accept that the Senators will go on losing. There was nothing here, despite the complicated rules of baseball, that anyone vaguely aware of the allures of sport could not understand.

Damn Yankees was the last Adler–Ross collaboration, for Ross died of bronchiectasis at the age of twenty-nine, a few months following its Broadway premiere. Adler would go on to write the songs for the New York *Kwamina* (1961) and *Music Is*, an adaptation of *Twelfth Night*. Both flopped; neither had the brash confidence of the team's *The Pajama Game*. That score exemplified the high-energy Broadway that Britain looked to in the mid-1950s, with its list of extractable hits, but *Damn Yankees* was less rich, and only 'Heart' and 'Whatever Lola Wants' worked their way out of the theatre. Much of the time was spent on numbers that remained average Broadway, with a peppy opener that worked effectively in the theatre, 'Six Months Out of Every Year'. The lack of a ballad marked it out, too, although 'Goodbye, Old Girl', signalling the moment when young Joe arrives to 'take over' the body of middle-aged Joe, provided the most effective theatrical moment. It was a rare opportunity for Adler and Ross to show sensitivity, but the secret at the centre of *Damn Yankees* was ready for its final curtain, with the Devil berating Joe for having escaped his clutches. Joe and Meg blank out his presence with a reprise of 'A Man Doesn't Know' (*Damn Yankee*'s other sensitive moment), capped by an orchestral climax of the title notes of 'Heart'. Ultimately *Damn Yankees* has really been about ordinary human emotions, but its appeal in Britain was limited, and the production closed with a loss of £23,000. Jerry Lewis played Applegate in an American touring production that played a season at the Adelphi in 1997. At last the show had a star performance at its centre, although interpolating a 'spot' for Lewis unbalanced the work and diminished the other already insubstantial characters.

The British-born Jule Styne was back in his birth-place London for the first time in fifty-two years for the opening of **Bells Are Ringing** (Coliseum, 14 November 1957; 292). His biographer explains that 'although he anticipated the return with some excitement he dreaded it emotionally. Whatever his state of mind, the London cast of *Bells* was appalling. Without Judy Holliday, Ella Peterson was caricature; the play was entirely lifeless, quickly sentenced to a short, unhappy run.'[10]

Holliday and the show's librettists, Betty Comden and Adolph Green, had long worked together in their early careers, in consort with Leonard Bernstein and their cabaret turn The Revuers. *Bells Are Ringing* was one of the summations of those relationships, with Holliday as the essential component. Without its star, the show was less willing to ignite on stage, and even in Vincente Minnelli's 1960 film Holliday seemed ill at ease, and complained during its making that she wasn't being funny enough. *Bells* was a bespoke work, and on stage it suited nobody *but* Holliday; pity anyone else who had to shuffle on a pretence of the role of the unassuming Ella Peterson working at the switchboard at the run-down telephone answering service 'Susanswerphone', where she becomes an unseen friend to the many and varied callers who come to depend on her invisible caring. It is, of course, inevitable that she should fall for one of them, the disillusioned playwright Jeff Moss, who believes he is speaking to a kind old lady. Only after they meet and fall in love does Ella reveal her identity. There was nothing original about the story, but around it Comden and Green introduced diverting subplots involving a dentist obsessed with song-writing, and a bookie illegally using 'Susanswerphone' as a front for his betting customers and simultaneously making eyes at Ella's boss Sue. At times *Bells* seemed as much a revue as a musical, inspired by the telephone directory.

The transforming of the material was in the talents of Holliday and the Styne–Comden–Green score which served her well. There were three ballads that became genuinely popular; two have remained standards long after their origins have been forgotten: 'Just in Time' and 'The Party's Over'. Holliday also got the opening number that established her plight, 'It's a Perfect Relationship' (the perfection being that she 'knew' so many people who had no idea who she was), and two comedy turns, 'It's a Crime' and the eleven o'clock 'I'm Going Back'. (Holliday had threatened that unless the writers came up with such a song she wouldn't open.) The rest of the cast had less distinguished material, but everything was effective, contributing to another in the life of Comden and Green's New York fairy tale fantasies in which the city was shrunk to a cosy village. The tastiness of *Bells* resided in the collision of Ella's downtown life with the hedonism of Moss's world, as evidenced in 'Drop That Name'.

The skills of Holliday were not easily replicated. The London signing was Janet Blair, whose earlier brushes with musicals had included a three-year stint touring America as Nellie in *South Pacific*. Blair's difficulty was not only that she had the spectre of Holliday at her back but that in London *Bells Are Ringing* had absurdly been touted in some quarters as the best American import since *Oklahoma!* Nevertheless, the *Manchester Evening Chronicle* reported a 'tumultuous' first night reception,[11] with Blair taking ten curtain calls. The *Stage*'s local reviewer thought her 'the show's best attribute',[12] while the *Manchester Guardian* decided 'it needs a good deal of pulling together in the present version and also falls away rather badly in the second half. But it has the essential virtues ...'[13]

At the Coliseum, Blair's opening night performance was hailed by a voice from the gallery calling, 'You made the show.'[14] The London reviews were not unreasonable. The *Manchester Guardian* continued its provincial argument, recognising that a good musical comedy

> must be more than gay and talented: its gaiety must be infectious. The new piece is too painstakingly contrived for this to be possible. There is too much plot, and so too little room for extravagance. Then for most of the time the music lacks the verve which can provide momentum to keep a show going for a whole evening.[15]

Harold Hobson's Sunday verdict was that the show was 'dead at the centre [...] a kicking corpse'.[16] *The Times* thought the plot 'put across with busy purposefulness in an immensely long [first] act. Afterwards the story runs into the sands, and the rest of the play consists largely of little skits and revue tunes which are nothing out of the way'.[17] The *Observer* thought rather more highly of the score, giving it '14 out of 15, though it has to pant a little at times to keep up with the sly penthouse fun of the lyrics'.[18] As for the show's star, 'What if she is not a Judy Holliday? Imagine an American blend of Jean Carson and Petula Clark with the vocal attack of a modified Ethel Merman and you have a fair answer.'[19] For Milton Shulman, Blair aimed 'more at warmth than comedy [...] one suspected and regretted the missed laughs'.[20]

When Blair's contract ended in May 1958 she was replaced by the equally unsuitable Julie Wilson, who had come to London to appear in a Mayfair cabaret, not to take-over in *Bells Are Ringing*. Both were understudied by the unsuitable Shirley Sands. It was hoped that Wilson might rejuvenate the show, but it wasn't to be. In *Plays and Players* the gossip columnist 'Davy Garrick' in 'Green Room' wrote

> It has been one of the biggest theatrical mysteries of the West End why *Bells Are Ringing* has not become an outstanding hit. It has an unusual story; many tuneful numbers, especially that charming 'Long Before I Knew You',[21] and enormous pace and verve. Maybe *this* is the answer? It is certainly the only one I can think of. *Bells Are Ringing* was preceded at the Coliseum by two American shows that left audiences limp and flat, especially the disastrous *Damn Yankees*. In my opinion these productions very nearly killed American musicals over here.[22]

Holliday had been happy with her leading man, Sydney Chaplin, but London got George Gaynes in his only West End role. His wife, Allyn McLerie, who had divorced Adolph Green in 1953 and played in the Broadway production, was pushed up the British cast list although she took the minor role of Gwynne. Jerome Robbins' New York original was reproduced by Gerald Freedman, whose later credits included directing *The Gay Life*, *The Robber Bridegroom* and Jerry Herman's *The Grand Tour* on Broadway. For some reason the Coliseum had different costumes, and a different set designer in Henry Graveney, who provided décor on the broadest of lines. In Britain the show never sat comfortably in its theatre, and the fuse remained unlit. It was Blair's only London booking.

None of the British musicals of 1957 managed to establish themselves as solid hits. A cloud of academia hung over **Zuleika**, taken from Max Beerbohm's 'Oxford' novel, as well as too many changes of leading lady before reaching London. **Harmony Close** promised to be rather more relevant to life as lived: a show about a disparate group of contemporary Londoners, but the show didn't reach beyond Hammersmith. Julian Slade and Dorothy Reynolds's successor to *Salad Days*, **Free as Air**, had a carefree nature and one of their best scores, and ran a year. The originally Swiss **Oh! My Papa!**'s strong cast headed by Peter O'Toole and Rachel Roberts did not prevent its quick rejection, despite its popular title song.

1957 Broadway Exports

Simply Heavenly (169), **West Side Story** (732) and **The Music Man** (1,375).

1957 Broadway Only

Shinbone Alley (49) was based on Don Marquis's stories of 'Archy and Mehitabel'[23] and starred Eartha Kitt and Eddie Bracken. **Copper and Brass** (36) had Nancy Walker as a policewoman in love with a jazz musician, with Benay Ventura in support. Another flop was **Rumple** (45) about two American comic strip characters, Rumple (Eddie Foy Jnr) and Anna, who come to life to get their creator drawing again. One of the year's successes was the sultry **Jamaica** (558) with Lena Horne delivering Yip Harburg and Harold Arlen's songs, but the most interesting possibility for London was **New Girl in Town** (432), from Eugene O'Neill's play *Anna Christie*. Noteworthy not least because of its 'serious' source (and its composer Bob Merrill would go back to O'Neill for another musical, *Take Me Along*), its choreography by Bob Fosse, and its cast headed by Gwen Verdon as the child-abused Anna, Thelma Ritter and Cameron Prud'homme. Disappointingly, neither of Merrill's O'Neill musicals transferred to London.

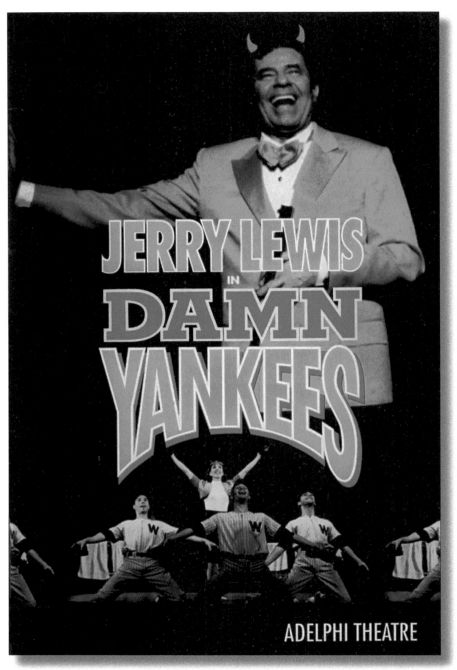

19 An ideal opportunity to do your cabaret act: Jerry Lewis as a Satanic star in the West End presentation of an American road company revival of *Damn Yankees* in 1997

1958

Where's Charley?
My Fair Lady
Simply Heavenly
West Side Story
Cinderella

1958 WAS A GOOD YEAR for the American musical in London: five productions, two of which were landmarks. *Where's Charley?* (Palace Theatre, 20 February 1958; 404) made it to London ten years after its Broadway premiere. Based on Brandon Thomas's 1892 British farce *Charley's Aunt*, the adaptation was by George Abbott and the songs by Frank Loesser. In New York Ray Bolger, best known in Britain for his scarecrow role in the film *The Wizard of Oz*, had played the title role of Charley Wykeham, making a hit of 'Once in Love with Amy', in which Bolger did a soft-shoe shuffle and invited the audience to join him in singing the chorus. The British production from H. M. Tennent, generally regarded as the 'establishment' management of the West End, who had previously presented mostly plays and intimate revues, had an all-British cast headed by Norman Wisdom, already famous for his variety and comedy film appearances and with his signature song 'Don't Laugh At Me 'Cos I'm a Fool'.[1] By 1958 Wisdom was not averse to female impersonation in the cinema, and his talent for pratfalls, alongside a strong singing voice, made him the ideal British contender for the hero. Loesser approved the choice, and cannot have demurred at pert Pip Hinton as Amy Spettigue, the sumptuously sopranoed Marion Grimaldi as the *real* Charley's aunt, and the constipated blunder of Felix Felton as the scheming Mr Spettigue, especially potent in his spluttering 'Serenade With Asides'.

Ethan Mordden has written that Loesser's contribution was 'not a distinctive score in general. Not till *Guys and Dolls* in 1950 did Loesser discover − and then vary − his voice, shifting style from work to work to give each a unique *tinta*. In *Where's Charley?*, he constructed a conventional late-forties musical-comedy score ...'[2] Mordden makes a perfectly understandable point about the work *as a Broadway musical*. Perhaps this slightly misses the point of *Where's Charley?*, which is essentially a *British* musical, in its source material, its tone, its tunes, its manner, and as such an exceptional example. Thomas's play was a war-horse of a comedy, part of the repertory landscape, and now in its straight version seems overlong and not over-funny. Two years before Wisdom took on the role of Charley Wykeham, Frankie Howerd had headed a three-month season of the straight play at the Globe Theatre. The fact that the musical is American is irrelevant: if anything the necessary dialogue cuts are an improvement, and the songs remain with the story and characters. The Americans were showing the

British how to write a perfectly shaped British musical, although much of the lesson remained unlearned.

Mordden recognises in one of the main love songs, 'My Darling', too much of the Hit Parade, but if that straining for commercial success is evident it is achieved with no loss of taste or period feel or integrity. Rather, the score unfolds as a string of skilful character-led numbers: 'Better Get Out of Here' displaying the social/sexual etiquette of the day as it affected the young; 'Make a Miracle' with its kaleidoscope of period detail, underpinning the relationship of Charley and Amy; 'The Woman in His Room', a perfect period vignette for a petulant heroine; 'The Gossips' moving the story on with bitchy assurance. Then, there is the Second Empire grandeur of 'At the Red Rose Cotillion' and the brio of 'The New Ashmolean Marching Society and Student Conservatory Band', which may have been in Alan Jay Lerner or Leonard Bernstein's minds when they wrote 'The President Jefferson Sunday Luncheon Party March' for their 1976 *1600 Pennsylvania Avenue*. The most lushly romantic song is reserved for the elders, 'Lovelier Than Ever', with its cascading rhyme ('Springtime, you're being devastatingly *clever* / And lovelier than *ever* before').

Mordden is misguided when he says that by the time of *Where's Charley?* Loesser had not discovered his distinctive voice. Surely what we are hearing is Loesser's *first* distinctive voice, one that would retain its individual character but vary from work to work. If the show sounds like a *generalised* American musical (and perhaps it is), it sounds like a *particularised* British one. Loesser's achievement is the greater because it transcends the transatlantic genres. There is not a trace of brashness or New York smartness about it, and it resists the cute and coy. The original London cast recording reminds us that the show had a cast worthy of its felicities. Caryl Brahms understood something of the measure of Loesser's achievement when it came to the songs.

> We know them all, of course, or most of them – musicianly popular songs, that extend our understanding of the singer or the situation. Songs with feeling and with thought at the back of them. Songs that make no twinkle-twee concessions to the Victorian manner but belong wholly to our own day. We learned to hum them from the film *Where's Charley?* and the smash hit 'My Darling, My Darling' is currently receiving the full treatment from the song pluggers. And the amazing thing is that the lack of compromise in the lyrics and music works in the same way that good furniture of different periods can sometimes make a satisfactory whole. It is to good furniture that I would liken this production of *Charley's Aunt* – shapely, commodious, durable and a joy.[3]

Of course, the story of Charley Wykeham and his Aunt (from Brazil, where the nuts come from) is a minnow compared to the classic dimensions of the next musical to open in London. *My Fair Lady* (Theatre Royal, Drury Lane, 30 April 1958; 2,281) has elemental qualities, trailing its theatrical antecedents.

Over its shoulder stood George Bernard Shaw's great 1912 romance in five acts, *Pygmalion*; over *Pygmalion*'s shoulder stood W. S. Gilbert's 1871 comedy *Pygmalion and Galatea*, over *Pygmalion and Galatea*'s shoulder stood Ovid's monologue *Pigmalion*; in the wings stood the 1943 Broadway musical *One Touch of Venus*. These were merely some of the notions and struts upon which the phenomenal success of *My Fair Lady* was built. Never mind that in New York the garlands had never been so plentiful; the British edition of Loewe and Lerner's (and Shaw's) work was the most heralded, most welcomed, most appreciated, most revered of the period. Laurence Olivier had tried to get the British rights to the musical, but these had been acquired by H. M. Tennent. Rex Harrison had been playing in Tennent's London production of *Bell, Book and Candle*⁴ when they were asked to release Harrison to play Professor Higgins in the New York *My Fair Lady*. Tennent agreed on condition that they would eventually produce the West End production.

The probably apocryphal story of the woman who sat in the stalls at Drury Lane next to an empty seat helps us appreciate the legendary status of *My Fair Lady*. When the woman explained to an attendant that she had bought two tickets, one for her husband and one for herself, the attendant berated her for not having offered the other ticket intended for her husband to a friend. 'I would have brought a friend,' the woman explained, 'but they are all at my husband's funeral.' Somehow, this caught the measure of the public enthusiasm, its *determination* to capture the *My Fair Lady* experience. Lerner's wisest decision was not to meddle with Shaw more than was necessary; Loewe's job was to interrupt Shaw without losing the momentum of that peerless dialogue. The pair had done some ground-work, too, staying in London at the Westbury Hotel off Bond Street and venturing to Limehouse, eavesdropping, rather in the manner of Higgins himself, to Cockney as it was spoken.

Rather in the manner of *Where's Charley?*, *My Fair Lady* was never ostentatiously an American musical, not in the way that the next one coming along, *West Side Story*, would be. *My Fair Lady* might have been conceived in Stroud or Pimlico. Although New York-born, it seemed in its Broadway birth to have been sent over from another culture, another country. It had been, for its story was British, its author Irish, its stars imported. All this was so obvious that when the show was welcomed in London it was with profound celebration. This was most personified by Julie Andrews, who had been a child favourite on British radio and the variety stage. She had gone on to play Polly Browne in Sandy Wilson's 1920s pastiche *The Boy Friend* in New York, and then became the definitive musical Eliza Doolittle. Hers was an almost triumphant return to Britain, and she at last felt free to let her Cockney impersonation free of the strictures she had exercised for Broadway.

For Rex Harrison as Professor Henry Higgins, who takes up the caterwauling flower girl and the challenge to turn her into a sophisticated social success, it was a different sort of triumph, not least over the much-publicised fact that he could not 'sing'. Is there another case in American/British musicals where this became such an issue, one that seems to have obsessed the press and been a dinner table topic in the smartest circles? There was the suspicion abroad that Harrison had *invented* a whole new way of putting over a song. This was grist to the publicist's mill, as were the rumours (probably true) of frictions between Harrison and Stanley Holloway (Alfred Doolittle), for whom the show was the summation of a long career. Whatever dissensions existed, it seems never to have been contemplated that any but the original stars would open in the London production. Coming home, and at last Shaw's story was to find its proper place, with the real Covent Garden just beyond the doors of Drury Lane's theatre. On Broadway, London had been merely a fantasy; in London, the fantasy became real.

Most of Lerner and Loewe's brilliant (in the sense of shimmering) score had already permeated the British consciousness long before the London opening. This was the golden youth of the long-playing record, and there had never been an original cast recording that generated such British passion. Copies of the mono Broadway LP seem to have been among the most smuggled items of the time, as for some reason its sale had been prohibited in the United Kingdom. More excitement was generated when the West End cast recorded the songs all over again, this time in stereo. It seemed for once that London had all the advantages over New York.

Then there was the Cecil Beaton connection, most renowned in the 'Ascot Gavotte' scene, when the designer got what was in effect a mannequin parade of his black and white dresses. In a decade when Technicolor ruled, it was a clever trick to transfix the public. This was one of the show's greatest *coups*, a set piece with which none of the principals had any connection, truly a *coup de théâtre*. In how many American musicals were the public aware of who had designed the décor or the costumes? There was something about *My Fair Lady* that had people taking an interest in such things. And come to that, how many 'logos' of shows showed the author from whose work the musical had been worked up manipulating his characters as if they were marionettes? *My Fair Lady* did, thus letting the world know what Shaw had looked like, and how vital he had been to the whole process that was *My Fair Lady*. Even that image, Shaw the controller, stood as a component of the special qualities of the piece, a reminder that as much as anything *My Fair Lady* was in homage to GBS.

Reviewing the plays of 1958, J. W. Lambert noted

> the most bruited entertainment of all – *My Fair Lady*. Once more we are back in company with a living legend. Once more before we scrutinise it we must respect it, must bow to the power which has set the Western world in a ferment, caused a lively trade in semi-smuggled gramophone records and, even in London, a brisk black-market in tickets. Somehow the thing has become a sort of middle-brow Mecca; those who have been

should surely be allowed to dye their beards, or wear a specially designed beauty-spot. So great was the excitement in April that, in scrutinising the cause of the legend, it was difficult not to react against it.[5]

'Let me say at once,' wrote Caryl Brahms for *Plays and Players*, 'that the evening is Shaw's. His words wing home. His situations hold. His wit is keen and shows no sign of blunting. His play lives on in the songs of Lerner and perhaps more particularly in the music of Loewe.' She noted 'the magic of the songs. Never have numbers been more skilfully used to light up and lift a scene, so that the old text, like spring, comes round again, and flowers, like the prunus, in the most natural, disarming and refreshing way.'[6]

This was a rare case of the Broadway stars (all three of them) being sent to London for the London production – particularly appropriate as all three were British. Harrison stayed for a year, and was followed by Alec Clunes who stayed for two years, and Charles Stapley, who had stood in for Clunes throughout his tenure. Anne Rogers took over when Andrews left the company after eighteen months and was succeeded in 1961 by Tonia Lee, who had been the Eliza understudy and already played the role 239 times. After an accident during a performance Lee left the cast in 1962. She may have wished she had taken up the offer of the King of Burundi, who, after seeing her Eliza, assumed that she would become his wife. She was replaced by Jean Scott, who subsequently claimed to have played the part for 154 and a half performances.

After eighteen months Holloway's role was taken over by James Hayter, and Robert Coote's Colonel Pickering by Hugh Paddick. Although Peter Gilmore was originally cast as the unlucky Freddy Eynsford-Hill, he was replaced before opening night by Leonard Weir. Touring versions, replicating Herman Levin's production, proved highly successful in the provinces, with Elizas such as Wendy Bowman and Jill Martin, and Higginses such as Tony Britton and Myles Eason. Britton headed the London revival of 1979, when his Eliza was Liz Robertson. A 2001 revival at the National Theatre and Adelphi was headed by Jonathan Pryce and Martine McCutcheon, whose troubled engagement as Eliza attracted much press coverage. She was succeeded by Joanna Riding. One suspects that, good as any revivals may be, they will never recapture the authenticity of the original. As a song in one of the most interesting American musicals unseen in Britain, *The Golden Apple*, explained: 'It's the Going Home Together'.

The next American musical reached London because the actor Laurence Harvey saw it in New York, enthused to impresario Jack Hylton, and ended up co-presenting and directing the British edition. *Simply Heavenly* (Adelphi Theatre, 20 May 1958; 16) was the work of writer Langston Hughes and composer David Martin. Artistically betrothed to Harlem, Hughes had been librettist for Kurt Weill's great 1947 opera of American tenement life *Street Scene*. His words for *Simply Heavenly*, adapted from his 'Harlem' novel *Simple Takes a Wife*, had none of the gravitas or emotional grandeur of the former work, content instead to chart the emotional complications of Jess Simple. Matters were not much helped by Martin's insufficient music and the pretty dull songs. The reviews were discouraging, with Lisa Gordon Smith in *Plays and Players* exclaiming 'They called it *Simply Heavenly* – but it simply wasn't! [...] I felt as though I had been exiled in Harlem for years.'[7] For *Theatre World* 'somehow the whole show did not hang together. Perhaps it needed a firmer hand than Laurence Harvey's to direct. It certainly needed some more inspiring music than that provided by David Martin which at times was merely loud to the point of being unendurable.'[8] *Simply Heavenly* was quickly shut up. When almost fifty years later it was resurrected in London, the critics seemed much happier with it.

Broadway décor had been by Raymond Sovey, but London's designer was altogether more appropriate. In 1931 the painter Edward Burra designed the sets for the ballet *A Day in a Southern Port*, also known as *Rio Grande*, with a score by Constant Lambert that (attractive to Burra) favoured 'black' rhythms. In 1936 Burra signed on as a British surrealist, and in the 1940s designed sets and costumes for the Sadler's Wells ballet *Miracle in the Gorbals*, and a Covent Garden *Carmen*.[9] It is to Hylton's credit that Burra was commissioned to design *Simply Heavenly*. Anyone familiar with Burra's luminous paintings of Harlem life such as 'Savoy Ballroom, Harlem' (1934) and 'Harlem Scene' (1934–5) will know his fascination with the place. One reason to celebrate *Simply Heavenly* was the lively cast; this included Bertice Reading, who three years before had been a passenger on *The Jazz Train*, a 'musical [in fact a revue] dedicated to the negro people'.[10] However, what marked *Simply Heavenly* above average was the contribution of Burra, whose passion for jazz music, intimate knowledge at first hand of Harlem street life, equal obsession with high (ballet, opera) and low (B-films, strip-joints, brothels and musical comedies) art signalled his perfect suitability: where could a better designer for *Simply Heavenly* have been found? It was his only musical. What opportunities in the use of major British painters of the period were lost! Imagine if Burra had been persuaded to provide the décor for London's *West Side Story*. How very differently, if that example were taken up and made popular, we might now perceive those replications of New York's musicals, made the more remarkable because of Keith Vaughan's designs for *Golden Boy*, Francis Bacon's designs for *Hair*, instead of the standard design corsetry that too often wrapped itself around American musicals. Let us dream of John Minton's allegorical take on *Carousel*, Paul Nash turning up at Drury Lane with his designs for *Oklahoma!*, and Prunella Clough enabling us to appreciate a revival of *The Desert Song* with fresh, abstracted, eyes.

The commercial disappointment of *Simply Heavenly* did nothing to deter Hylton from promoting more black material. Three years later he had a reasonable run with the all-black *King Kong*, 'an all-African jazz musical' that had never approached New York but been a great 1959 success in South Africa. The *White Star* newspaper declared it 'the greatest thrill in twenty years of South

20 When is a star not a star? So far as the West End *Bells Are Ringing* (1957) was concerned, when Judy Holliday's name wasn't above the marquee

African theatre-going'.[11] The achievement was remarkable not least because its cast was amateur. Caryl Brahms 'found the colour and the friendliness refreshing but then the liveliness and hopefulness of amateurs, the orphans of the arts, revives this jaded palate when met with in the mass'.[12] Most muscular was Nathan Mdledle as the doomed township boxer King Kong, 'bigger than Capetown, King Kong, harder than gold', based on the real-life Zulu boxer Ezekiel Dhlamini. Amateur it may have been, but *King Kong* had a heart and style of its own, a strong score, a tenderness (as in the beautiful 'The Earth Turns Over'), charm (personified in the penny whistling of young Lemmy "Special" Mabaso) and dramatic force that evaded the workmanlike *Simply Heavenly*, which has nevertheless enjoyed West End revival and a much more enthusiastic critical reception than it enjoyed in 1958.

Black entertainments became a feature of London theatre in the 1960s. Another Langston Hughes entertainment, the non-Broadway *Black Nativity*, first played London in 1962 and persisted in cropping up all over the West End for a few years.[13] A black account of Christ's birth, it was presented as a 'Gospel Song-Play', with its second half devoted to a procession of gospel numbers. Its success seemed a mystery to *Theatre World*, for which 'Making a joyful noise unto the Lord sounds hardly the formula for a West End success.'[14] 1962 also saw the debut of the delightful miniature *Cindy-Ella*, a musical retelling of the Cinderella story by four black performers.[15] In 1965 black was once again at the fore in the revue *Nymphs and Satires*, co-written, presented and directed by Leon Gluckman, who had previously directed *King Kong*. The 50/50 black/white cast (including the West End's King Kong, Nathan Mdledle) performed what *Theatre World* described as 'more a concert than a revue'.[16] How many black faces were seen nightly in the stalls and circles of the theatres presenting these black entertainments?

The third American musical of the year based on British material possibly brought home the Bacon, although it is likely that many who saw **West Side Story** (Her Majesty's Theatre, 12 December 1958; 1,039) during its long London run had no inkling that they were attending a musical version of Shakespeare's *Romeo and Juliet*. As with *My Fair Lady*, expectation was high (although the box office advance was poor) and rewarded with a run that exceeded the Broadway production by 300 performances. For the first time since *Oklahoma!* an entirely American company (but not the Broadway original cast) was shipped to Britain, arriving a few days before the Manchester premiere. A month after the London opening Tennent were looking at a production cost of £37,490 9s 10d. Unlike *My Fair Lady* and almost everything else that had gone before, *West Side Story* broke the mould. Curiously, the effect on American musicals (and certainly on those that followed to the West End in its wake) was limited, but its effect on the British may have been considerable. This marked the point at which the British saw the Broadway musical take to the streets. The British buzz was that here was a piece that worked on the fusion of its elements: the book by Arthur Laurents, the music by Leonard Bernstein, the choreography by Jerome Robbins; acting, singing and dancing from its players. The creators had essentially, and perhaps subconsciously, written the first truly ensemble musical play of the twentieth century, an ensemble not only of performers but of dramatic skills. Now, ballet was not segregated. When ballet discarded the words, a substitute dancer did not suddenly take over as had happened to Curly and Laurey in *Oklahoma!*

This ensemble aspect may have been overdone. Put it this way: *West Side Story* was probably the first almost guaranteed star-resistant musical of our time, and has remained in the repertoire as such. The demands of its libretto, dances and vocal numbers makes it star resistant: how many stars can act, sing and dance at the same time? That takes a trouper, and *West Side Story* is made for them. The material is all, but hopes were high that whatever shows followed would refresh musical theatre. Agnes de Mille said, '*West Side Story* is a point of departure. After this we shall move into a more fluid, mobile theatre.'[17] The reverberations bouncing alongside the show were said to be felt in the world of ballet. *The Times* assured its readers that '*West Side Story* not only changes the musical theatre; it increases enormously the pressure on classical ballet, pinnacle of the dance world, to abandon the supernatural [how about *Giselle* or *Swan Lake*?] and to confront life as it is lived in the middle of the twentieth century.'[18] Had the writer forgotten such 'street-wise' ballets as the 1944 Arthur Bliss – Robert Helpmann *Miracle in the Gorbals*? Ballet had been confronting real life long before *West Side Story* apparently shuddered its foundations.

Was this prophecy to be fulfilled? Ground-breaking, perhaps, but *West Side Story* proved in its way an isolated event. In their future projects neither Bernstein or Sondheim took the musical back to the tenements. So far as London's view of the Broadway musical was concerned, the tidal wave of *West Side Story* swept over all and receded, and life went on much as before. The following year Bernstein's score for *Candide* was for a world away from the streets of New York, and in 1960 the American musical showed up as old-fashioned as ever with *Flower Drum Song*, *The Most Happy Fella*, *Once Upon a Mattress* and (if we must) a *Rose-Marie* revival. So perhaps the coruscating effect on Broadway shows would be felt the following year? As it happened, in 1961 London received *The Music Man*, *The Sound of Music*, *Bye Bye Birdie*, *The Fantasticks*, *Do Re Mi*, all offering various degrees of cosiness. The fact is that Broadway's substantial contribution to the street musical (at least during the period of this book) resides in 1958.

Diverting for a moment to the British musical, we see that for that moment it was, in its modest way, of considerably *more* interest than the American product finding its way into the West End, for here the British musical took to the streets in a big way. Consider the list of street-wise shows that filed into Shaftesbury Avenue, riding the tsunami of *West Side Story*, among these *Fings Ain't Wot They Used T'Be*, *The Crooked Mile*, *The Lily White Boys* and, last if not least, *Johnny the Priest*. Absurd to suggest that any of these home-grown shows came close to the quality of the Bernstein-Laurents-Sondheim work, but they were cousin to it. It is as if a wayward breeze had blown the seeds of *West Side Story* across the Atlantic, and they had not fallen on fallow ground. Perhaps it is mere coincidence that at the point when the American musical in London seemed at last to be getting *seriously* serious (stepping up from the 'seriousness' of *Oklahoma!*), the British musical for one shining hour had its 'Camelot' moment of seriousness which lasted roughly between 1958 and 1960, before turning its back on theatre *verité*. After what was for some the primal shock of *West Side Story*, the Broadway musical went on glancing back; the British musical tried to look at the world around it.

In London *West Side Story* had luscious praise from many. 'How does it compare with *My Fair Lady*?' asked the *Star*. 'But you can't compare brandy with champagne. And this is liqueur brandy, powerful, heart-warming, inspiriting [...] this is the first really serious musical, illuminating, as it does, a burning problem of more than parochial importance [...] a work of art – at once cruel, compassionate, ugly, beautiful and supremely moving.'[19] *The Times* noted that the characters were mostly 'morons' and 'self-pitying teenagers [...] In colour sombre, in tone harsh, and in language and social content elusively alien, *West Side Story* [...] makes an inevitably difficult approach to English sympathies.'[20] Elements of the press showed a reactionary concern about the effect the musical would have on the British. For the *Daily Mail* Edward Goring suggested that 'Many people, I suspect, will recoil from the knuckle-duster impact of this Teddy Boy musical.' The piece was 'violent. Race hatred and teenage warfare end in tragedy. The music of Leonard Bernstein is modern and magnificent, but it will displease ears attuned only to the old-fashioned charm of *My Fair Lady*.'[21] These warnings were drowned out by such recommendations as that of T. C. Worsley. '*West Side Story* really *is* fabulous. It really is worth queuing in the rain for. It really *is* worth the black market price [...] so powerfully and immensely effective that you don't even notice whether it is sung, acted or danced.'[22]

The British critic most ill at ease with *West Side Story* at its first night was Harold Hobson. Meeting Hobson on the way out, Noel Coward enthused 'That was great theatre we've had tonight, wasn't it?' 'No,' replied Hobson. Coward fixed him with a stare. 'Harold,' he said, 'do be careful; please, please be careful.' Whether Coward's concern was for the damage a bad Hobson review would do to *West Side Story* or to Hobson's reputation is unclear. Hobson seems not to have heeded Coward's plea; for him, the piece didn't cut the mustard.

> I would rather have one single touch of genius [perhaps this was what Hobson had perceived in *The Crystal Heart*], however casual, chancy or uneducated, than a sackful of intellectual lubrication. This touch of genius never comes. *West Side Story* remains a staggering *tour de force*, like *War and Peace* translated into Zulu. It is Shakespeare pillaged in pidgin-English. As for the integration of acting, singing and dancing, 'The voice of a Patti has never combined with the ankle of a Pavlova'.[23]

Hobson had a point. Meanwhile, Angus Wilson (surely an unlikely candidate to review musicals) bemoaned 'the genteel, smarty-arty bits of self-conscious "beauty" that make the first half, despite two superb ensemble scenes, drag at 50 miles an hour'.[24]

There is little reason to suppose that the London production was less effective than the Broadway original, although the effectiveness may have dissipated as the American players departed and made way for British take-overs. The intervention of the Lord Chamberlain's Office was modest. Veering on the side of caution, the Lord Chamberlain insisted that the word 'buggin' should be changed to 'lovin'; 'Sperm to worm' to 'Germ to worm!', 'brass-ass' to 'brass-pants', and 'You came with your pants open' to 'You came with your zipper open'. Maria was to be adequately covered at all times. As for when Maria and Tony, according to the stage direction, 'sink back together on the bed', this was to be made 'in no way objectionable'.[25] Such tinkering in no way hampered the emotional progress of the goliath that was *West Side Story*, but, viewed through a glass darkly, perhaps *West Side Story* ploughed the lonely furrow, separated from the other Bernstein works that played in London. Part of its cleverness was to marry the rhythmic savagery of its music with numbers that wound back to operetta (this is surely the category for 'I Feel Pretty', 'Maria' and 'Tonight'), bringing forth sounds that would not have sounded foreign to Vincent Youmans or Sigmund Romberg. The fusion that infused *West Side Story* was a commixture of style as much as of its much trumpeted integration of drama, music and dance. The apple cart of the American musical, at least so far as London would see, had barely been shaken.

Harold Fielding's debut as a London impresario of American musicals was with Rodgers and Hammerstein's **Cinderella** (Coliseum, 18 December 1958; 168), the first 'pantomime' seen at Frank Matcham's most metropolitan theatre since 1944. The work had been written for Julie Andrews and screened on American television in 1957, but was far from being Rodgers and Hammerstein's finest work. Fielding's production, the work's first appearance on stage, tweaked Hammerstein's script in its effort to turn the piece into a convincing British panto, with 'additional pantomime material' by Ronnie Wolfe. The most obvious alteration to the original was to add the role of Buttons for pop-singer-turning-actor Tommy Steele (understudied by Ted Rogers), who shared top billing with the gruff comedian Jimmy Edwards and the television 'personality' Yana. Matters were not helped by the introduction of some material by Mr Steele, notably a duet for himself and Edwards, 'You and Me', surely a nadir in British musical history. The British pantomime tradition dictated that America's female Ugly Sisters were now played by men: Kenneth Williams and Ted Durante. British tradition was broken by offering a male Prince, the Tupperware-stolid Bruce Trent, given the show's main ballad 'No Other Love' reused from Rodgers and Hammerstein's 1953 *Me and Juliet*. Fielding's team included Freddie Carpenter as director, Loudon Sainthill for sets and costumes, and Ronnie Hanmer 'augmenting' the original orchestrations of Robert Russell Bennett.

Philip Hope-Wallace in the *Guardian* thought it was 'snappy and splendid to look at but rather lacks heart, warmth, and – strangely enough – humour' with microphones 'as thick as parking meters in Mayfair'.[26] *The Times* verdict was that 'The spectacle seems to have a daunting effect on the funny men',[27] and Edwards was heard to say 'bloody' twice, while the *Observer* reported Yana's 'hard icing-sugar sweetness' as 'most unsuitable'.[28] Fielding announced that the salaries paid to its stars topped those paid to the leads of *My Fair Lady*.[29] As Fielding's salaries were reputed to be miserly, one can only shudder at what they were taking home at Drury Lane. No opportunity to broadcast the show's wonders was missed. The *Slough Observer* arranged for a nineteen-year-old machine operator at the Slough Horlicks factory, Rita Byfield, to travel to London to see the show and meet Steele. As she chatted with the 'Bermondsey wonder boy' Rita's married sister told the reporter 'We never thought we'd get this close to him'. Steele 'lit a fag. "Wanna drag?" he asked Rita. "She did."' According to the newspaper, the show 'featured a forty-minute act of singing punctuated by clowning and comedy'.[30] The critical plaudits were mostly for Betty Marsden as the Fairy Godmother. Fielding's flair for publicity and sometimes quirky casting marked his long career, among which were many noted successes. Still to come were some major American shows: Cole Porter's panto *Aladdin* (1959), *The Music Man* (1961), *Sail Away* (1962), *Sweet Charity* (1967), *You're a Good Man, Charlie Brown* (1968), *Mame* (1969) and in 1970 *The Great Waltz* and a revival of *Show Boat*.

The British musical showed signs of sitting up and taking notice of its surroundings. That could scarcely be said of **School**, with its music by Christopher Whelen, another adaptation from T. W. Robertson; his *Caste* had been turned into *She Smiled at Me* in 1956. **Lady at the Wheel** had the advantage of two spiky leading ladies, Lucille Mapp and Maggie Fitzgibbon, but didn't long survive its transfer from Hammersmith into the West End. John Cranko and John Addison came up with **Keep Your Hair On**, one of the most surreal of British offerings. It got bad notices, as did **Mister Venus**, a clumsy vehicle for Frankie Howerd. **Expresso Bongo** was at the forefront of a new wave of British works that rooted themselves in contemporary Britain (well, contemporary Soho). By luring a respected 'straight' actor Paul Scofield into the leading role, it suggested itself as a quality product, and – compared to several of the year's other offerings – it was. The same team came up with the successful **Irma La Douce**, a work adapted from the French, and British by default. Sandy Wilson's **The Buccaneer** was a miniature about the attempted American takeover of a traditional British boys' comic. **Valmouth**, a musicalisation of Ronald Firbank's novella, seemed to mark Wilson's removal to the esoteric margins of musical theatre.

1958 Broadway Exports

Flower Drum Song (600).

1958 Broadway Only

The Body Beautiful (60) was the first collaboration of Jerry Bock and Sheldon Harnick. *Oh Captain!* (192) had Tony Randall playing the role originated by Alec Guinness in the British movie *The Captain's Paradise*. Two decisive flops were *Portofino* (3), delivered a quick death despite having Georges Guétary and Helen Gallagher as its leads, and *Whoop-Up* (56), set on an Indian reservation. Of more interest was *Goldilocks* (161), with its happy Leroy Anderson music, some of it involving Elaine Stritch, and the unusually inspired *Say, Darling* (332), a musical about the making of a musical, *The Pajama Game*.

1959

Candide
The Love Doctor
Aladdin

C *andide* (Saville Theatre, 30 April 1959; 60) crept almost modestly into London: 'a new musical based on Voltaire's Satire' according to its programme, with book by Lillian Hellman assisted by Michael Stewart, lyrics by Richard Wilbur, John Latouche (who died just before the Broadway premiere) and Dorothy Parker, and music by Leonard Bernstein. *Theatre World* had its doubts.

> ... one cannot help wondering what audiences unacquainted with the work will make of this show, the story line of which is very disjointed. Pangloss and Cunegonde especially escape so many times from incredible fates, with never an explanation given, that it becomes quite confusing. Indeed an exasperated member of the audience was heard to exclaim peevishly 'but how *did* they get out of that coffin flung into the sea?'
>
> We have come to take for granted musical comedies with a more serious theme and certainly a great deal of what is stated in *Candide* is no laughing matter. Lillian Hellman, who wrote the book [...] seems unable to make up her mind which line to take. The show is divided into two halves, the first being like an uproariously funny comic strip while the second is suddenly serious and sentimental. Candide's ultimate disillusion is saddening and if Miss Hellman could have kept some of Voltaire's irony in her adaptation the whole would have been more satisfying than it is. As it now stands the two halves do not seem to fit and the sentimentality of the end is unhappy.[1]

It was a minor miracle that the show arrived in London at all. The Broadway production had opened two and a half years earlier and closed after seventy-three performances. After the New York failure it was unlikely that Britain would see the work, but the daring of the management of Linnit & Dunfee made it possible, in a version decorated by Osbert Lancaster's settings and costumes (Broadway had used Oliver Smith's settings and Irene Sharaff's costumes). At the Saville the original Bernstein and Hershy Kay orchestrations were available (the orchestration went uncredited in the London programme) but in New York these had necessitated fifty-five musical instruments; for Linnit & Dunfee the musical director Alexander Faris had to manage with twenty-seven. The cast was headed by the American opera singer Mary Costa, already known for her roles at the Royal Opera Covent Garden, in her only musical play appearance as Cunegonde. Denis Quilley took the title role in his first American musical,

Laurence Naismith as Dr Pangloss enumerated his belief in 'The Best Of All Possible Worlds', and Ron Moody was much praised as the Governor of Buenos Aires. Edith Coates, a veteran British opera singer, played the Old Lady.

One wonders if the show had at last been picked up by the West End to maximise on Bernstein's reputation. It had yet to see his 1944 *On the Town* or his 1950 *Peter Pan*, and hadn't been especially excited by *Wonderful Town*,[2] but with the success of *West Side Story*, a show that Broadway had already acclaimed, his profile was high. *Candide* was a fish of another colour, a musical comedy apocalyptic in its moral diversity, its liberal irony, its air of desperation, its irreligious slant at the Catholic church and religion in all guises, its air of fantasy and sardonic emotion, its refusal to balk at sexual fact, its adhesion to operetta and its lunges at opera. Was this one to appeal to the West End coach trade? The British were having enough trouble with their own musicals trying to present a grim reflection of modern life, and now from Broadway came something so out of line with what was expected of the genre that it had to be repelled. Putting it into the Saville Theatre, just off the main stem of the West End, was almost a death blow in itself, and the subject, a French satire of 1759, condemned by the Vatican, was bound to alarm. Before the Broadway opening several numbers were cut, including two on a subject that no British musical had even dreamt of approaching. Voltaire wrote:

If he [man] enjoys delights of which [the animals] are ignorant, how many vexations and disgusts, on the other hand, is he exposed to, from which they are free! The most dreadful of these is occasioned by nature's having poisoned the pleasures of love and sources of life over three-quarters of the world by a terrible disease, to which man alone is subject.[3]

At one stage Bernstein had approached the British composer Julian Slade to write lyrics for the show, and discussed the 'venereal' numbers; ultimately, the two 'syphilis' songs in the original score were dropped before opening night. They were among other casualties which included a song for Candide 'Was It for This?' (Bernstein intended it as a Puccini pastiche), and 'One Hand, One Heart' which would find its way into *West Side Story*. How many changes Hellman and Bernstein made before London is unknown, but the London listing of musical numbers differs from the Broadway original.

In London, Act One included 'Oh What a Day For a Holiday' unlisted on Broadway; on Broadway there was the 'Lisbon Sequence' and 'My Love', unlisted in London. London's Act Two lacked the Broadway's opening trio 'Quiet' and the 'Gavotte'; Broadway does not list Cunegonde and the Old Lady's duet 'We Are Women' or the Old Lady and Candide's duet 'I've Got Troubles'. For the Broadway revival of 1997, numbers unknown to the original New York or London productions were introduced, among them a 'Ballad of the New World' and 'Auto-da-fé'. With the National Theatre's 1999 production, bewilderment continues as more song titles appear, among them 'Universal Good', 'Paris Waltz',

21 Judith Bruce swinging to the Liberals:
a postcard issued by the Liberal Party during the 1959 General Election

'Words, Words, Words', 'Money, Money, Money', 'Nothing More Than This' and 'King's Barcarolle'. The restlessness that is *Candide* could not be more obvious. Sacrosanct in its shifting character are Cunegonde's waltz 'Glitter and Be Gay' and the final anthem 'Make Our Garden Grow', in which after adventures simple contentment is found in the chopping of wood and the cultivation of a little plot of earth.

Of all American musicals of the twentieth century, *Candide* alone is seemingly doomed to wander the world endlessly in search of itself. Despite the several successes of its revivals it has failed to escape cult status, and has often found refuge in the opera house. The list of musical numbers for the 1999 National Theatre production is unrecognisable from the original London production listing. By 1999, writers unknown to the Saville Theatre programme had crept into the credits: now the book had been adapted by Hugh Wheeler in a new version by John Caird (whatever that meant), and Sondheim and Bernstein had been added to the list of 'other lyricists', a list to which Hellman had now been relegated. Rather in the way of a London bus, there would be another *Candide* along in a minute. Meanwhile the first-night audience at the Saville were in two minds; the curtain descended to cheers and booing. At the show's closure Moody wrote 'if ever a show went rotten from the top, this one did. Mismanaged, misproduced and miscast.'[4]

The next entry had toured in America *en route* to Broadway as *The Carefree Heart* but had closed on the road. Redressed and revised and equipped with a completely British cast, the piece surfaced in London as **The Love Doctor** (Piccadilly Theatre, 12 October 1959; 16). Concocted from three comedies of Molière, it came with credentials. The score was by the successful Robert Wright and George Forrest, whose *Song of Norway* and *Kismet* had enjoyed spectacular British success, and the new piece was to be one of their rare wholly original scores, not based on the compositions of classical composers. From America came the distinguished director Albert Marre, who had overseen Wright and Forrest's *Kismet*, and choreographer Todd Bolender, while France provided the pretty cut-out décor of Bernard Daydé. The cast was headed by Ian Carmichael as a tramp posing as a learned physician, and Joan Heal as Toinette. Their first reaction on hearing the songs performed by the composers was distinctly reserved, but they signed up.

After a halting tryout at Manchester during which Michael Stewart was flown into London as a show doctor, *The Love Doctor* moved on to Oxford amidst a chaos of constant revision which involved the arrival of two new directors, Wendy Toye and Robert Morley. Sensing disaster, Carmichael on behalf of the exhausted company begged the management to cancel the West End booking. This was not possible, and the show opened in London to noisy disapproval from the audience and disastrous notices, with such headlines as 'Pass Me the Morphia',[5] 'I Was Fortunate – I Fell Asleep'[6] and 'Musical With a Note Missing'.[7] At its Manchester opening the *Stage* critic singled out a 'sparkling and risqué'[8] duet for Carmichael and Heal, 'Anatomy'. In London R. B. Marriott offered 'very little praise. The orchestra bangs out the tunes with plenty of gusto and the company sing as if for dear life. Yet, somehow, nothing comes to life. The comedy falls flat and the romance never takes wing. Daydé's colours never shine and one grows tired of the cut-out scenery.'[9] W. A. Darlington for the *Daily Telegraph* found

> a very peculiar dish indeed. The recipe employed has been to mash together the medical plays of Molière, throw in a pinch of *The Man Who Married a Dumb Wife*, drain off the essential juices and serve up the remainder as a musical of the customary type [...] It has a great air of enjoyment, but something is missing at its heart.[10]

According to the *Manchester Guardian*, the second act fell catastrophically apart, with the performers colliding with stage hands and scenery: 'it is overblown, over-sexed, over-played and over here.'[11]

Milton Shulman's review was positive in its negativity.

> Not since the first night of *Salad Days* have I seen such a concentration
> of simpering archness, relentless coyness and desperate whimsy heaped
> together on one stage. Being drowned in a vat of perfume glucose could
> have little on this [...] The décor and costumes [...] with their insistence on
> glaring stripes and pugnacious polka dots, gave me at times the sensation
> of having a bilious attack with Noddy in Toyland.[12]

The cast harboured many performers who laboured hard and long in West
End musicals, including Patricia Routledge, Eleanor Drew, Peter Gilmore and
Anna Sharkey, but all were soon out of work, and *The Love Doctor* slipped into
a coma from which it has not awoken, weighed down by a £35,000 loss. One
of its many problems had been H. M. Tennent's curious casting, not least Joan
Heal. Tennent went on to cast her as the leading lady of *Joie de Vivre*, a musical
débâcle based on Terence Rattigan's play *French Without Tears*, and the intimate
revue *One to Another*. Together, this trio of misfortunes did nothing to help
Heal's career.

Many musical theatre enthusiasts would have made the effort to sit through
Aladdin (Coliseum, 17 December 1959; 154), a Cole Porter pantomime-musical
and his final score, originally written for American television where it aired
in February 1958. Now it was sumptuously mounted for the London stage by
Harold Fielding, whose *Cinderella* of the previous year had been a conspicuous
commercial, if not artistic, hit. In the London theatre programme Fielding
seems to suggest that Porter wrote the score to Fielding's commission, and –
strangely – there is no allusion to the television version. No lavishment was
spared in the £90,000 production, with Loudon Sainthill creating 'a perfect orgy
of good taste [...] a feast of Chinese magnificence in both settings and dresses
such as the eye of man has hardly beheld till now'; nevertheless, the *Daily
Telegraph* headline ran 'Gone Was the Spirit of Pantomime'.[13] Sumptuousness
was ensured by Robert Helpmann's direction and choreography, and Michael
Northen's lighting was much praised. Although Fielding reported that the
show would be transferring to Broadway the following year, no New York run
transpired.

There could be little disguising the poor songs, with such dispiriting titles
as 'Come to the Supermarket in Old Pekin', although Fielding's production
incorporated a few numbers from earlier Porter works. The combination of
pedestrian music and insipid lyrics, all too obvious in the London cast recording,
created an atmosphere of nightclub scenes in bad British B movies. *The Times*
charitably suggested the music was 'not very Chinese, but seems to belong in
spirit to a smart revue in the middle thirties'.[14] The book, 'feeble' according to
the *Observer*, and 'the deadening weight of a text with no spark of fancy or wit',[15]
had for some reason been rewritten for London by Peter Coke;[16] the original
book by S. J. Perelman was forgotten. Penelope Gilliatt considered the show

'runs about as long as the uncut *Hamlet*' and that although a feast for the eye it had 'about as much action as a vicarage tableau' and that in its non-pantomimic moments 'the house was sunk in stupor, as though watching some night-marish three hour commercial on the telly'.[17] Enough were willing to submit to the ordeal to carry the show through until the early Spring. For one critic the most magical moment came when Aladdin (Bob Monkhouse) asked the audience to light matches to assist in the making of a Palace of Light, and the auditorium became aglow, with rows of elderly gentlemen revealed behind their Swan Vestas. What so very many elderly gentlemen were doing at a pantomime in the first place remains a mystery.

As an antidote to the American imports, Joan Littlewood's groundbreaking production of ***Fings Ain't Wot They Used T'Be*** rocked the foundations of the British musical. Ten years after Novello's *King's Rhapsody*, audiences welcomed not Ruritanian kings and their mistresses but prostitutes and their pimps in a piece that went further than the previous year's *Expresso Bongo* in establishing a kitchen-sink British musical. Another Soho piece, ***The Crooked Mile***, was in every way bigger; the ambition was evident in the score by the two Peters (Wildeblood and Greenwell). There was also the interesting ***Make Me an Offer***, a sort of hymn to the Portobello Road. Trying to hold back the tide of progress, with decorous music, delightful costumes and plenty of tartan swirling, Alan Melville and Charles Zwar's ***Marigold*** offered a riposte to the Broadway invasion. ***Kookaburra*** was a small-scale Australian romance with music by Eric Spear, and ***When in Rome*** (adapted from the Italian) a brash piece that seemed aimed at the coach-party. The Mermaid Theatre had a very substantial hit with ***Lock Up Your Daughters***, taken from Henry Fielding's *Rape Upon Rape*. John Osborne's ***The World of Paul Slickey***, a slack and tuneless muddle with music by Christopher Whelen, attacked everything its author disliked about Britain. It was reviled and has never been revisited.

1959 Broadway Exports

First Impressions (84), ***Destry Rides Again*** (473), ***Gypsy*** (702), ***The Sound of Music*** (1,443), ***Fiorello!*** (795) and ***Once Upon a Mattress*** (460).

1959 Broadway Only

The major flops of the year were ***Happy Town*** (5), which left New York anything but, and ***Juno*** (16), based on Sean O'Casey's *Juno and the Paycock*, directed by José Ferrer and choreographed by Agnes de Mille. In 1921 Dublin the Irish Republican Army's fight against the British is reaching its climax as the people defiantly insist 'We're Alive'. The Boyle family, led by the long-suffering mother Juno and wastrel father, provide the focus of Marc Blitzstein's intermittently brilliant songs. This was a 'serious' musical that stood no chance of being seen in London in the political climate of the 1950s. The underground IRA was responsible for bombings on the mainland through the decade, as well as violent attacks on the country's borders between 1956 and the early 1960s. Irishness in musicals might be acceptable in such nonsenses as *Finian's Rainbow*, but the humanising of IRA sympathisers in *Juno*, especially if they *sang*, would have been quite unacceptable in Shaftesbury Avenue. Only so much seriousness in musicals could be tolerated. Nevertheless, Brendan Behan's play *The Hostage*, with its rowdy and touching songs, enjoyed a *succès d'estime* in London at Stratford East in 1958 and 1959, before transferring to the West End. *The Nervous Set* (23) dealt with the problematic marriage between a beatnik wife and her husband. *Saratoga* (80) was second-drawer material burdened with substantial names: Howard Keel its star, music by Harold Arlen, lyrics by Johnny Mercer and sets and costumes by Cecil Beaton, but nothing of note emerged. A likely candidate for London was the diverting *Redhead* (455), worked around the Jack the Ripper murders in Victorian London and centred on the Simpson Sisters' Waxworks. A vehicle for Gwen Verdon, outstanding among Bob Fosse's direction and choreography, the music by Albert Hague (*Plain and Fancy*) and lyrics by Dorothy Fields were more characterful than memorable. Bob Merrill wrote the songs for *Take Me Along* (448), another unlikely adaptation from Eugene O'Neill, starring the comic Jackie Gleason and the British actress Eileen Herlie, the Gertrude in Laurence Olivier's film of *Hamlet*. Her singing of 'We're Home' was a little gem in a patchy score.

1960

The Dancing Heiress
Flower Drum Song
The Most Happy Fella
Rose-Marie
Once Upon a Mattress

B ELONGING TO THAT RARE BREED of American shows that showed up in not quite the West End rather than on Broadway, *The Dancing Heiress* (Lyric Opera House, Hammersmith, 15 March 1960; 15) had been conceived by actor Jack Fletcher as a straight play, but metamorphosed into a musical after his meeting with the composer Murray Grand at the Upstairs-Downstairs Club in New York. Here was a pastiche of Hollywood film musicals of the 1930s set in New York in 1933, which Lisa Gordon Smith for *Plays and Players* pronounced 'well observed; but a take-off must be rather a comment rather than a reproduction. This show reversed the process.'[1] Here was another opportunity for Millicent Martin, whose stardom had already been claimed for her work in *Expresso Bongo* and *The Crooked Mile*, but *The Dancing Heiress* was years away from their kitchen sink milieu. *The Dancing Heiress* had its share of take-offs of songs of the period it was celebrating (or sending up?): 'Tip Toe Through the Tulips' became 'Zig Zag Through the Raindrops', 'Life is Just a Bowl of Cherries' turned into 'Life is Peaches and Cream', and 'The Continental' into 'The Internashnal [*sic*]'. Grand and Fletcher's burlesque of Astaire–Rogers movies 'burlesques itself at the same time, causing much muddle'.[2]

The American Fred Sadoff was named as director when the show opened at the Shakespeare Memorial Theatre in Stratford-upon-Avon, but by the time it arrived at Hammersmith Sadoff had gone, replaced by the show's choreographer John Heawood. *The Dancing Heiress* provided rare leading roles for the dancer Irving Davies, Lally Bowers (duetting with Davies for the show's one memorable number 'Life is Peaches and Cream') and film actress Jill Ireland carrying the only two solos of the night 'Under-Tow of Love' and 'That Same Old Sensation'. Supposedly the star, but having fewer numbers than Ireland and not a solo to her name, Martin may have felt let down. For Smith 'The larger part leaves one with the impression [...] that [the authors] were filling in time with padding in order to turn a promising nucleus into something long enough by the clock to be considered a full-length show.'[3] After its prescribed spell at Hammersmith, *The Dancing Heiress* shut up shop. A smaller and more artistically successful show set around Hollywood, *The Great American Backstage Musical*, played London in 1978.

The second of the 1960 entries was a Rodgers and Hammerstein work that stands at the sidelines of their best products. *Flower Drum Song* (Palace Theatre,

22 An American product by default, *The Dancing Heiress* (1960) applied for British citizenship with a satirical swipe at Hollywood musicals of an earlier age

24 March 1960; 464) followed on the heels of the themes of racial clashing that had been essential to *South Pacific* and *The King and I*. By 1960, however, Rodgers and Hammerstein themselves were not as resplendently successful as they had once been. Their Broadway success of *The King and I* in 1951 had been followed by two flops, *Me and Juliet* (1953) and *Pipe Dream* (1955), neither of which made it to London. The seven-year gap between *The King and I* and *Flower Drum Song* was marked in the West End by the fact that never again would there be a premiere of a Rodgers and Hammerstein musical at Drury Lane.

In some ways *Flower Drum Song* was a brave choice of subject, but there were things about Chin Y. Lee's novel that were reminiscent of some earlier Rodgers and Hammerstein successes. Once again, racial conflict played a part as in *South Pacific* and *The King and I*. Now the tensions were between contemporary Chinese and Americans living in America, and the hinterland inhabited by Chinese-Americans; old values, authentic oriental tradition versus American influences. Gene Kelly's New York direction was replicated for London, with Carol Haney's dances recreated by Deirdre Vivian, the whole reconstituted by Jerome Whyte, who was faced with the almost insuperable task of finding Chinese actors in Britain who could play leading roles (or chorus) in a major musical. This had already proved a problem for the New York production. In London many possible candidates had already been taken up for the large cast of *The World of Suzie Wong*.[4] The British auditions didn't reveal many talents, and the net had to be cast wider. Meanwhile, advance bookings, lured by the Rodgers and Hammerstein brand, broke all records at the Palace.

On Broadway the show was a career-changer for its two female stars, Miyoshi Umeki as demure Mei Li, and Pat Suzuki as the Chinese-American Linda Low, who has absorbed everything she loves about Uncle Sam. *Flower Drum Song* established both as Broadway names; Umeki also made it to the film version, but Suzuki was replaced by the more cinematically acceptable Nancy Kwan. The London Mei Li was Yau Shan Tung, a Chinese-Parisian whom Whyte discovered in France. With no stage experience to speak of, she was taken to New York for five weeks, and watched the Broadway performance every night. The new Linda Low was a Hawaiian, Yama Saki, helped to a musical career by missionaries who financed her voice-training. Saki (her name meant Miss Mountain Top) was grateful that her employment meant she could repay the debt she owed them. Both she and Shan Tung seemed to vanish from mainstream theatre after Rodgers and Hammerstein had done with them.

London was a lucrative stopping-off-point for any Rodgers and Hammerstein show, although it is doubtful that they ever took much interest in their British editions. It was unthinkable that their works might be squeezed into a smaller theatre, but *Flower Drum Song* didn't benefit from the wide open spaces demanded by *Oklahoma!* or *South Pacific* and might have been more comfortable in a smaller house than the Palace. In London the latest Rodgers and Hammerstein faced very different criticism to that received by the Broadway

TEATRE *World*

JUNE 1960

2/-

Scenes from :
"The Most Happy Fella"
"A Passage to India"
"The Gazebo"
"Rhinoceros"
Pitlochry Festival

23 Art Lund recreating his Broadway role of Joe, with Helena Scott as Rosabella
in an emotional crisis at the end of Act I of Frank Loesser's Frankenstein
of a musical, *The Most Happy Fella*, in 1960

production, where none had been unfavourable. The British critics were unimpressed: Alan Pryce-Jones in the *Observer* described 'this dim, hideous musical', while *The Times*[5] deemed it 'surely the least enchanting' of their shows. Nevertheless, extracts shown on television during Bernard Delfont's Sunday Show in July 1960, the writers' reputation and some popular songs ('I Enjoy Being a Girl', 'Sunday', 'You Are Beautiful') helped the piece to a creditable run.

The charmless London cast recording is documentary evidence of how far from its original conception a West End reconstitution of a Broadway musical could slide. In the plaintive 'Love Look Away', Broadway's Arabella Hong sings simply but validates the number as one of Rodgers and Hammerstein's most crafted; London's Joan Pethers just gets it over and done with. This may have been one of the most thrown together recreations of Broadway to reach London. In New York the only name it could pin to itself was that of its director, otherwise its leading performers meant nothing to the average American playgoer, but it *made* stars of Suzuki and Umeki. That process didn't repeat in London, where the stars remained Rodgers and Hammerstein. *Flower Drum Song* appeared as a film in 1961, so dull that one wonders if anyone has ever reached the final credits. In the theatre the show has had no afterlife in Britain, although a few of its songs occasionally resurface.

The penultimate Frank Loesser show to reach London was **The Most Happy Fella** (Coliseum, 21 April 1960; 288), four years after its Broadway debut. Don Walker's orchestrations were about the only thing to survive from Broadway, for London had a different director, Jerome Eskow, new décor by Tony Walton and choreography by Ralph Beaumont. Above all, the work was testament to Loesser's versatility, or more accurately his unwillingness to write to a pattern, as did Rodgers and Hammerstein. A Loesser show was always to some extent unidentifiable; try connecting the scores of *Where's Charley?* with *Guys and Dolls* or *The Most Happy Fella* with *How To Succeed in Business Without Really Trying* or the composer's *Greenwillow* which opened in New York around the time of the London opening of *The Most Happy Fella*. There *are* links, and Loesser's voice is present throughout, but it was in the matter of the material he harnessed that his distinctive contribution is made. *The Most Happy Fella* is one of the most distinctive Broadway musicals of the twentieth century in what it attempts. In melding sounds of the Great White Way with the opera house Loesser offers a smorgasbord of theatrical music.

The Most Happy Fella, based on Sidney Howard's play *They Knew What They Wanted*, was his first and only solo effort: book, music and lyrics. The achievement was considerable. This is a thoroughly domestic affair, of little significance except to the two main protagonists: Tony, the ill-educated, ageing wine grower from California, and the waitress Rosabella with whom he falls in love. After noticing her in a restaurant, Tony writes to Rosabella inviting her to marry him, but sending a photograph of his handsome young farm-hand Joe. When she arrives at Tony's home in Napa Valley she feels cheated, and in

24 Bill Kerr as the Wizard, Patricia Michael as Princess Number Twelve and Thelma Ruby as the Queen in the endearing but troubled West End *Once Upon a Mattress* at the Adelphi Theatre in 1960

her emotional disappointment succumbs to the advances of Joe and becomes pregnant by him. Meanwhile she and Tony begin to fall in love, but when Tony learns the truth she heads off. Tony is furious, but realising his intense love for her he brings her back. It is only now, when he tells her they will begin anew that he asks her name, which is 'Amy'. This is one of the show's most poignant moments; only when the audience is about to go out into the night do they learn the heroine's name; for Tony and Amy, their relationship has a new reality. The story is a simplicity, the account of a mail-order marriage that goes right, but it is probably a simplicity that modern audiences would find difficult to accept. The story recalls a little-known but effective song by Forman Brown, 'Catalog Woman', in which a woman is sent as a mail order bride to a farm where she works and slaves and brings up children, but admits, as she sits on the porch, that she is ecstatically happy. Sidney Howard's story and its direct appeal to the senses somehow suited Loesser's needs; in such domesticity he discerned the anguish he wished to express.

The London production was well received. Eskow's direction was 'a miracle of precision';[6] all, according to *The Times*, was 'Arcadian lightness, grace, and gaiety'[7] but there were reservations. Anthony Cookman decided that

> The trouble is that Mr. Loesser's lyrics are with one or two exceptions rather dull, and the tunes, again with happy exceptions, are simply not gripping or melodious enough to carry through his ambitious plan. When they are signally good, as 'Standing on the Corner', for example, they are not markedly operatic, and when they come closest to a good operatic effect they just fail to strike the popular note.[8]

Cookman's verdict contrasts with the welcome the show had received on Broadway. J. C. Trewin, too, had doubts: 'It is a touching little narrative, but at the Coliseum it suffers from being thinned out across the immense stage and interrupted by more than forty musical numbers, some of which are fragments and few of which dance in the memory.'[9]

The cast could not have been bettered, with a strong American presence in Broadway's original Joe, Art Lund, who would return to London in 1963 for *No Strings*. Libi Staiger, with a voice to cut through sheet metal, was the open-hearted Cleo and chubby Jack De Lon (visually reminiscent of Stubby Kaye) was Herman, given the show's only stand-out number 'Standing on the Corner', already a hit by the time the show premiered at the Coliseum. Staiger and De Lon had already played their roles in the 1959 Broadway revival; De Lon would play Herman for the last time in New York in 1966. Helena Scott, who came from Broadway having played Natalie in *The Merry Widow* in three New York revivals and Rose Maurrant in *Street Scene*, was the British Rosabella. The Maori singer Inia Te Wiata was a fine choice as Tony, bringing conviction to his only musical. Because of the role's vocal demands Edwin Steffe, fresh from a disaster of a Broadway musical *Happy Town*, was brought in to play Tony at certain performances, and unusually shared top billing with Wiata. The London cast recording, although lacking the breadth of the Broadway original recording (which had the entire show on three LPs), immortalises performances that suggest this was not a tired attempt at repeating a New York hit. Subsequently Steffe and Stella Moray, who took over the role of Cleo from Staiger during the run, recorded their songs for a cover version of the score with World Record Club.

In America *The Most Happy Fella* has the status of a masterwork, an eminence it has never achieved in Britain, where the stretch of opera with musical was regarded with suspicion. Another full studio recording of the score and two New York revivals have helped solidify its reputation. Ultimately it is Loesser's abundant gift that enhances the work: the blissful casualness of 'Happy to Make Your Acquaintance', the tearing desire of 'My Heart Is So Full of You', the yearning 'Somebody Somewhere'. Broadway had seen 676 performances, but the Coliseum run of nine months could hardly be counted a crowd-pleaser.

In 1960 the popular singer David Whitfield's recording career was drawing to its close, hastened by the interest in rock and roll and the declining taste for throaty tenors. His stage appearances were mostly in variety, but he chanced his luck with two operettas, *The Desert Song*, in which he toured and rivalled John Hanson's better-known but more mature Red Shadow, and **Rose-Marie** (Victoria Palace Theatre, 22 August 1960; 135). The work had been the first of the big American imports to reach Drury Lane in 1925, with Derek Oldham and Edith Day taking the production to 851 performances, whereas the Broadway run had closed on 557. Day repeated her role in a revival at the Lane four years later for 100 performances, and there had been another short-lived production at the Stoll in 1942 with Raymond Newell and Marjorie Brown. The production values for the 1960 edition were sound enough: direction by Freddie Carpenter, décor by Peter Rice, choreography by Ross Taylor and a strong cast that included Stephanie Voss as the titular heroine, Maggie Fitzgibbon in another wide-mouthed role as Lady Jane playing opposite the revue artist Ronnie Stevens as Hard-Boiled Herman, and Gillian Lynne as the Indian Wanda. Its impresario, the controller of the Moss Empires circuit Leslie MacDonnell, said 'We have enough faith in the show's impact on a modern audience to give it an entirely new production – new scenery and dresses, a complete re-orchestration of the score, and a bigger chorus'.[10] This 'entirely new production' did not seem to involve any rethinking of the now antique piece. Robert Muller in the *Daily Mail* witnessed 'a complete absence of vitality and sparkle, a total disregard for the sophisticated tastes of modern audiences, and a kind of aesthetic numbness' in a 'prehistoric production' which involved wobbling sets, rudimentary acting, 'inexcusably bad' dancing, and the star name's 'feeble' stage presence.[11] It was no surprise that the *Daily Telegraph* reported blunt comedy and 'shatteringly unoriginal' staging,[12] and *The Times* longed for 'more full-blooded masculinity' from the show's star. In the event, Whitfield proved less of a draw than John Hanson who subsequently regurgitated *The Desert Song* and *The Student Prince* in the West End. Whitfield's *Rose-Marie* played out four months, after which he was bundled off on tour with Julia McKenzie as the girl of his dreams.

It seemed as if Broadway was not sending over vintage products. Perhaps it had fewer of them to send. New York had welcomed Mary Rodgers' score for her debut musical – could it be that Richard Rodgers' daughter would strike out a career of her own? There were distinctive things in her first effort, **Once Upon a Mattress** (Adelphi Theatre, 20 September 1960; 38) but it seemed a strange time of year for a show with an identity crisis: was it a musical or a pantomime? The authors insisted on the former, worked up from the fairy story of the Princess and the Pea – how a true member of the aristocracy could not sleep if a pea were placed below her mattress. Musicals had been based on slenderer ideas, if not smaller vegetables. Mary Rodgers' music, lyrics by Marshall Barer and book by Barer, Jay Thompson and Dean Fuller had been welcomed with open arms in

25 Jeremy Brett and company from the British musical *Johnny the Priest*, music by Antony Hopkins, book by Peter Powell, partly inspired by *West Side Story*, at the Princes Theatre in 1960

New York, but in London Jerome Whyte's recreation of the Broadway original, despite an avalanche of advance publicity, was critically dismissed.

There was little sympathy offered in London. Milton Shulman complained that the writers 'never produce anything more amusing than some contemporary wisecracks about mediaeval sex. Or perhaps I should say some mediaeval wisecracks about contemporary sex.'[13] Philip Hope-Wallace feared it might be 'the kind of flaccid entertainment at which a critic might well die [...] in his sleep'. He found the costumes 'hideous', the music 'dreadfully unappealing', the lyrics 'pitiful'.[14] The *Sunday Times* denounced it as 'a pitiful, piteous and pitiable musical which tries all the oldest jokes in the world'.[15] The *Illustrated London News* had a few good words for London's Winifred Jane Connell, who 'has moments of Beatrice Lillie and others of Beryl Reid, and who in her own right is an utterly delightful zany'.[16] Robert Muller spoke for many when he decided that 'I have no doubt that *Once Upon a Mattress* will find favour with what's left of the panto trade. [Was anything left of it by September?] As for me, Hey-Nonny-No, Hey-Nonny-No, Hey-Nonny-Nonny-NO!'[17]

Once again, the failure of the management to lure the original American performers to Britain may have affected the show's fate. Had Carol Burnett taken to the Adelphi stage, much might have been forgiven and all may have been well, but in 1960 Connell was no star and had no reputation in Britain (but neither had Burnett); that would have to wait until the London *Mame* six years later. Patricia Michael remembers

> Jane Connell was the most wonderful person. On the Friday of the first week of rehearsals the management didn't get around to paying us chorines in the morning so none of us had enough money to go out to lunch. Jane came by and asked if anyone was going to lunch and we rather embarrassedly said we didn't have any money. Without a second's pause she handed around pound notes saying 'I don't know what these things are anyway!' I gather that on the opening night she rather went over the top with her mugging and the London critics savaged her. Her (I think eleven year old) daughter wrote a letter to the critics which Jane discovered before it was mailed and posted on the theatre notice board for us all to see. I don't remember the letter other than that it wasn't angry, just very upset with what the critics had said about her mother.[18]

The rest of the cast list revealed a string of able players in need of stronger stuff, not least Max Wall, whose career had hit the buffers. He had last appeared at the Adelphi in *Panama Hattie* in 1944, and after enduring public scorn during the run of *The Pajama Game* had suffered a breakdown in 1957. Any expectation that *Once Upon a Mattress* would revive his fortunes was misplaced: that came with the revue *Cockie!* in 1973. Patricia Lambert brought style to the role of the pregnant and unmarried Lady Larken, a plot development too far for the female editor of *Theatre World* who pronounced it 'rather tasteless'. Others battling against the odds were Thelma Ruby as the Queen, Milo O'Shea as the King, and Bill Kerr as the Wizard.

London was not in the mood for fairy-tale, no more than it was for Julian Slade and Dorothy Reynolds' *Follow That Girl*. Musical theatre in Britain was emerging from a protracted dose of earthy musicals set in the back streets of contemporary London, making worlds inhabited by mermaids (*Follow That Girl*) or insomniac princesses (*Once Upon a Mattress*) seem infantile. The *Mattress* may basically have had one joke, but it was cleverly exploited; *Flower Drum Song* hadn't managed even one. The reasons for the speedy collapse of the British *Mattress* were many, but on the cast recording the songs emerge with dignity, and the score has barely a glimmer of the sentimentality that pervaded so much of Richard Rodgers' work. Connell sounds competent and Burnett is hardly missed. There are two interestingly shaped duets for Larken and her lover Sir Harry (Bill Newman), 'In a Little While' and 'Yesterday I Loved You', for which Lambert captures the necessary style. The several comedy numbers have real charm, too, even when Connell is at her most raucous in her introductory 'Shy'. Best of all, Wall gets to give at least a suggestion of what his Act Two 'Very Soft Shoes' must have been like in the theatre; a breeze of greatness.

An advertisement in the theatre programme by Eventide (Bedding) Ltd informs us that 'Eventide mattresses are used night after night in the new musical *Once Upon a Mattress*.' Hopefully they were on sale or return.

The British critics had deceived their readers into believing that here was a valueless enterprise, but this is a nimble score. There is almost a wealth of invention in melody, in shape, in the very ideas that give rise to the songs. After the Minstrel has beckoned us into the fairy tale via 'Many Moons Ago' the company go into 'An Opening for a Princess', at once an 'opening' chorus number and a statement of the plot: the search for a suitably aristocratic bride for the Prince. 'In a Little While' is layered by the fact that Lady Larken and her lover need to press on with a shotgun wedding. Most mischievous is 'Man to Man Talk' in which the young Prince is told the facts of life by his father, the mute King.

It was a depressing year for producers of British musicals, most of which were finished before ink had dried on the posters. Two shows insisted on taking the British musical back to the kitchen sink: *The Lily White Boys*, perhaps the only socialist polemical British musical, and *Johnny the Priest*, an unconvincing, curious but fascinating piece based on a R. C. Sherriff play about a well-intentioned vicar who tries to help a juvenile delinquent. It was speedily removed from the scene, although no one realised it marked the end of the line for the low-life British musical. *The Golden Touch*, another work from the authors of *Grab Me a Gondola*, hardly touched down before taking off, as did *Call it Love*, in fact a play to which *The Boy Friend*'s composer Sandy Wilson contributed a handful of milk-and-water songs. *Joie de Vivre*, Terence Rattigan's attempt to break into musical theatre with an adaptation of his play *French Without Tears*, was an immediate disaster, and Julian Slade and Dorothy Reynolds's Christmas musical *Hooray for Daisy!* won few admirers. Rather more success awaited their *Follow That Girl*. A play with songs, *Innocent as Hell* met with no interest. As much might have been said of Lionel Bart's *Oliver!* pre-London tour, so listless that it almost closed on the road. Its West End opening seemed to rejuvenate hope in the British musical. Such hope was misplaced, but *Oliver!* was to become one of the only international British musicals of the period, with Broadway and film success.

1960 Broadway Exports

Bye Bye Birdie (607), *Camelot* (873) and *Do Re Mi* (400).

1960 Broadway Only

Those least likely to travel to London were the obvious flops: *Christine* (12), Maureen O'Hara's brief tenure as a Broadway singing star in the story of an Irish woman in love with an Indian doctor, and *Beg, Borrow or Steal* (5).

Wildcat (171), a vehicle for Lucille Ball, had a troubled production history and songs by Cy Coleman and Carolyn Leigh, and the fate of the *Titanic* was recalled by Meredith Willson's ***The Unsinkable Molly Brown*** (532). Britain would eventually be denied the chance to see another Broadway success around the same subject, *Titanic*. The two works probably most deserving of a transfer were Frank Loesser's gentle ***Greenwillow*** (95) with Anthony Perkins, and ***Tenderloin*** (216), a tale of Victorian corruption in New York with a fine Jerry Bock and Sheldon Harnick score. In the nineteenth century, amongst the birth pangs of the American musical, *Tenderloin* might have been shipped off to Britain with its songs and libretto intact but its location changed to Victorian London. Indeed, London never saw so rich a musical play about its own unsalubrious past.

1961

The Music Man
The Sound of Music
Bye Bye Birdie
The Fantasticks
Do Re Mi

M EREDITH WILLSON? It's a one-show name so far as Britain is concerned, and linked to one of the most persistent show tunes of the period. *The Music Man* (Adelphi Theatre, 16 March 1961; 395) had played for 1,375 performances in New York from 1957, and Willson's other Broadway offerings did well too. 1960 brought the *The Unsinkable Molly Brown* and 1963 a dollop of Christmas charm with *Here's Love*, based on the movie *Miracle on 34th Street*. In 1969 there was a show about Christopher Columbus, *1491*, that tried and failed to reach Broadway, and then silence. 'Ya Got Trouble' went one of the big numbers in *The Music Man*, and it was true of Willson when faced with the problem of providing a follow-up to this dynamic, witty, delightful piece, the only one of his works to play London.

The story is fixed in the history of America at its most provincial: the small community clinging to its hometown beliefs, the allegiance to straight-thinking and small-minded contentedness unexpectedly confounded by the arrival of a charlatan stranger. The province is 1912 Iowa, where cussed stubbornness abounds. The catalyst for change is Professor Harry Hill, a travelling salesman who trades boys' bands and musical instruments to gullible parents. The Emperor's New Clothes are a set of band instruments and costumes to turn the youngsters of Iowa into a marching troupe that will fill their elders with pride, except that Hill's technique is to pocket the parents' money and vanish.

The score has characteristics that distinguish it from many others. The opening 'Rock Island' enacts on a train, on which Hill's fellow-salesmen talk in rhythm with the locomotive. It's a quirky start, and other inventive ideas crowd in. We meet the heroine, Marian Paroo the respected local librarian, over a 'Piano Lesson' for her baby sister Amaryllis, its halting progress providing the music for a duet between Marian and her mother, always on the look-out for a man who will take her daughter off her hands. Marian may not be as disinterested as Mrs Paroo imagines, for she has hopes of finding a special person: 'Goodnight My Someone'. This is swiftly followed by the show's, and Hill's, signature song 'Seventy-Six Trombones', with the so-called Professor whipping up enthusiasm for the promised band. How many of the audience realised that the refrains for 'Goodnight My Someone' and 'Seventy-Six Trombones' are the same? Anyway, that trick is revealed towards the end of the show when Willson runs both songs alongside.

PALACE THEATRE

SHAFTESBURY AVENUE - W.1   GERRARD 6834
Licensed by the Lord Chamberlain to and under the direction of Emile Littler

Originally
Presented in New York
By LELAND HAYWARD,
RICHARD HALLIDAY,
RICHARD RODGERS & OSCAR HAMMERSTEIN 2nd

WILLIAMSON MUSIC LIMITED
presents

THE SOUND OF MUSIC

MUSIC BY
RICHARD RODGERS

LYRICS BY
OSCAR HAMMERSTEIN 2nd

BOOK BY
HOWARD LINDSAY & RUSSEL CROUSE

A true story
adapted from " The Trapp Family Singers " by MARIA AUGUSTA TRAPP

Starring

JEAN BAYLESS   ROGER DANN
and
CONSTANCE SHACKLOCK

EUNICE GAYSON   HAROLD KASKET   OLIVE GILBERT
BARBARA BROWN   NICHOLAS BENNETT   DIANA BEAUMONT
JAY DENYER   LYNN KENNINGTON   SILVIA BEAMISH
PETER SWANWICK   HILARY WONTNER

Scenic Production by   Costumes by
OLIVER SMITH   LUCINDA BALLARD

Orchestrations by   Music Director   Choral Arrangements by
ROBERT RUSSELL BENNETT   ROBERT LOWE   TRUDE RITTMAN

American Production Directed by
VINCENT J. DONEHUE

Musical Numbers Staged by
JOE LAYTON

London Production Supervised and Directed by
JEROME WHYTE

FOR LONDON PALACE LTD.

THEATRE MANAGER	...	...	...	...	...	...	...	...	...	...	HARRY W. BRIDEN
ASSISTANT MANAGER	...	...	...	...	...	...	...	...	...	...	W. TAYLOR
BOX OFFICE	...	...	...	...	...	...	...	...	...	...	J. W. HAYES
CHIEF ENGINEER	...	...	...	...	...	...	...	...	...	...	ERIC B. WILLETT
PUBLIC RELATIONS	...	...	...	...	...	...	...	...	...	...	PATRICK SELBY

Scene photography in this Souvenir by TOM HUSTLER, London, W.1

26 No star nonsense about the 1961 London production of *The Sound of Music*,
with the cast's names in smaller type and well below those of the show's creators

Another characterful trick is to make a male quartet of supporting characters (Olin, Oliver, Ewart and Jacey, the stalwart city fathers who are encouraged by Hill to break into song every time they ask him for some credentials). This is an admirable excuse for several items: 'Sincere', 'Goodnight Ladies' which has the quartet competing with the poultry chattering of the ladies in 'Pickalittle', 'It's You' and 'Lida Rose'. Barbershop harmony becomes one of *The Music Man*'s happiest conceits. Thereon in, the score is mainly conventional Broadway, but the quality is manifest: Harold's whispered serenade to Marian inside the sacred confines of her library ('Marian the Librarian'), her literary hymn to her imagined lover ('My White Knight'), the rousing 'Wells Fargo Wagon' which might have come out of *Paint Your Wagon*, the skirt-lifting happiness of 'Shipoopi'. Ultimately the inevitability of the love between Hill and Marian is announced by 'Till There Was You', one of the best love songs of the period, and one that achieved great popularity in Britain, where it was recorded by the Beatles.

Harold Fielding presented this Broadway restaging, now directed by Robert Merriman from the original of Morton Da Costa, with Onna White's choreography recreated by James Barron. On Broadway, Robert Preston's performance as Hill was so impressive that there could have been no other choice for the excellent film version of 1962. For London, America sent Van Johnson (understudied by British Gordon Boyd who in 1962 would burst forth as the romantic leading man of Julian Slade's *Vanity Fair*). Johnson had competence but none of the bravura that Preston brought to the role. For *Theatre World* he 'has all the required charm, but perhaps not enough brazen impudence for the part'.[1] Broadway had one of its finest leading ladies, Barbara Cook, as Marian; London had Patricia Lambert. Graduating from the Fol De Rols Concert Party, Lambert had joined a Palladium pantomime before being cast as Lady Larken in *Once Upon a Mattress*. *The Music Man* was her main chance of West End stardom, but despite good notices and a reputation for soundness, the best that followed would be a supporting role in a British musical from J. M. Barrie, *Our Man Crichton*. The original London cast recording of *The Music Man* shows Lambert more centred and dramatic than Cook, notably in 'My White Knight'. *Theatre World*'s Roy Plomley considered that Lambert 'knocks spots off New York's Barbara Cook'.[2] There is something thrilling, too, about the British 'Till There Was You', even if Johnson lacks passion. The British dependables making up the rest of the cast knew how to deal with this material, with Bernard Spear as a nippy Marcellus Washburn.

The next arrival marked the end of a collaboration that had dominated London's musical theatre since April 1947, when *Oklahoma!* had opened at Drury Lane. When Hammerstein died in August 1960, a few months after the Broadway premiere of his last musical written with Richard Rodgers, a line was drawn under one of the most successful partnerships in musical theatre. Their final piece had been commissioned by its Broadway star, Mary Martin, who had originally envisaged this adaptation of Maria Augusta Trapp's memoir as a straight play, with perhaps a single song from Rodgers and Hammerstein. That was until they realised the potential of the property. They eventually provided a musical play which was if not the peak of their collaboration, the culmination and the commercial superlative, reaping 1,443 performances in New York. In London *The Sound of Music* (Palace Theatre, 18 May 1961; 2,385) yielded even more popular reward, becoming in its time the longest running West End musical to be imported from America, closing shop in January 1967.

For the first time in his collaboration with Rodgers, Hammerstein wrote only the lyrics, the book now the responsibility of the veteran Howard Lindsay and Russel Crouse, who had already written librettos for *Anything Goes* and *Call Me Madam*, but the theme of the piece essentially subscribed to Hammerstein's previous work. As in *South Pacific*, *The King and I* and *Flower Drum Song*, there was the sound of clashing cultures, represented in *The Sound of Music* by good and evil, the sanctuary of the convent against the Nazi boot, the innocence of childhood against the mindless savagery of Hitler. The moral values could scarcely have been more black and white. According to the legend below the show's title, here was 'a true story' told of the Trapp Family Singers in 1938 Austria. Maria Rainer, a spirited young postulant at Nonnberg Abbey, is a problem to her fellow nuns and seems unsuited to the strictures of convent life. The Mother Abbess sends her into the outside world, to the Von Trapp Villa where the widowed Captain Georg Von Trapp runs his childrens' lives with military precision. The shadow of the *Anschluss* is upon Austria, but Maria brings happiness to the children and is attracted to the Captain, whose eldest daughter Liesl is in love with a seventeen year-old Austrian, Rolf. The Captain breaks off his attachment to the worldly Elsa Schraeder, and marries Maria, but the power of the Nazis is growing. They demand that the Captain becomes one of their number. Maria uses the family's appearance at a singing festival to manage their escape, and assisted by the nuns she, the Captain and his children make their way over the mountains to freedom. This retelling of the Trapp story overlooked the fact that Maria was in reality a rather plain woman not renowned for her sense of fun, and in truth the disappearance of the family had been rather more prosaically achieved.

For some critics the main sticking-point was that the whole thing assumed that audiences had a very sweet tooth, an assumption that was proved correct when its huge commercial success made critical objection obsolete. Of course *The King and I* had been about a governess, who, like Maria, was sent into a 'foreign' environment where she was surrounded by tiny tots to whom she sang encouraging songs. Perhaps by the time of *The Sound of Music* the tots were getting a little out of hand, popping up all over the show, for 'Do Re Mi', 'The Lonely Goatherd', 'Edelweiss' and most cloyingly for their very own cabaret number 'So Long, Farewell'. One can imagine the ranks of stage mothers pinning their hopes on their little charges getting into the Von Trapp line-up at the

Palace Theatre. Children had always been part of the Rodgers and Hammerstein musical theatre landscape: think of them warbling 'Dites-Moi' in *South Pacific*, marching their way through *The King and I* and forming an orderly crocodile for Mr Snow in *Carousel* or complaining about 'The Other Generation' in *Flower Drum Song*, but by *The Sound of Music* they were spending much less time in their dressing rooms. And in this show, if it wasn't the children, it was the gathering of nuns shaking their heads in genteel confusion over a problem called Maria, or making their way through the abbey to the strains of Rodgers' idea of what nuns' music should sound like on Broadway. At a high-point in its popularity, the 'Processional' threatened to eclipse Mendelssohn's 'Wedding March' as an accompaniment to brides walking down the aisle in British churches – presumably without the 'Maria' descant, another curious moment in the show's score. Are the nuns thinking out loud? Chattering among themselves? Or getting in a crafty reprise of a song heard long before in Act One?

The clarity of Hammerstein's lyrics was as encouragingly optimistic as in *Carousel*, but any dash of vinegar was missing, despite the Nazi's involvement. Those Nazis are nowhere musicalised in *The Sound of Music*. Ever since and most noticeably during *Carousel*, Rodgers' music had assumed church-like qualities, but in *The Sound of Music* the hymnal predominates. The *Sunday Times* accurately described Rodgers' music (which it thought the best thing of the evening) 'like Moody and Sankey soused in sugar'.[3] It is there in the obviously preposterous opening 'Preludium', there in 'The Sound of Music', in skittish disguise throughout 'Maria', resplendent in 'Climb Every Mountain', evocatively recalled in 'Processional', and – distilled into the least florid hymn of the evening – in 'Edelweiss'. There is little bite about this score; what there is resides in the character songs 'How Can Love Survive?' and 'No Way to Stop It', sung by hard-headed Elsa Schraeder and Max Detweiler, but even here the bite is pretty toothless. These are the numbers the Rodgers and Hammerstein audience would have forgotten by the time they left the theatre; had the words been by Hart, they would have had edge, but then we realise that Hart would never have contemplated *The Sound of Music*.

By this time in their collaboration the distillation of simplicity is all, unless it is matched by Hammerstein's (and subsequently Rodgers') distillation of virtue. For the first time in their work, the score is itself *about* music (their *Allegro*, despite its title and title song, isn't), and to that extent the songs are organic. The nuns have it through their opening harmonies, their skipping allusions to their problematic novice. The children have a propensity for singing, and Maria obliges with songs that describe music and musical activity, 'Do-Re-Mi' or 'The Lonely Goatherd' or, explaining her philosophy, 'The Sound of Music'. The only reason for 'So Long, Farewell' is to display how the children have fashioned music into their personalised cabaret.

What Rodgers and Hammerstein seem to be clear about is that if music is a balm, the sweeter the better. Every other Rodgers and Hammerstein work

27 Lithe and youthfully zestful, *Bye Bye Birdie* (1961) had the happiest of scores,
and a genuine British pop-star as its Conrad Birdie

has its share of extractable songs, but many of those also attach closely to their originators: there is reason for Emile in *South Pacific* to sing 'Some Enchanted Evening' or 'This Nearly Was Mine', reason for Anna in *The King and I* to sing 'Shall I Tell You What I Think Of You?' or for Billy in *Carousel* to rhapsodise on 'My Boy Bill'. The songs in *The Sound of Music* serve less purpose, except for 'Maria', 'You Are Sixteen' and the two obviously character numbers that have been overlooked, 'No Way To Stop It' and 'How Can Love Survive?'. These were the two numbers mentioned in Robert Muller's comments on Eunice Gayson who 'miscast as a white telephone Other Woman [has] the worst scenes and the worst numbers'.[4] Those numbers are not *worse* but *different* (and for some perhaps preferable to much else in the score) but even here the lyrics lack edge. (Note the lame repeat of 'Trapped by our capital gains are we' that rounds off 'How Can Love Survive?'.) Muller spoke of 'the final fruit' of the Rodgers and Hammerstein collaboration as 'an over-ripe, not to say, soggy, old plum', in which Hammerstein's words 'simper and languish, emphasising the material's dramatic poverty and gross sentimental excesses'.[5]

If there was blame for the sweetness of the piece it was mostly directed at the words. Harold Conway thought it 'a prosaically told story' with songs that were 'totally captivating'.[6] The *Sunday Times* suggested that 'Hammerstein's genial nature led him in his later years to be too unexacting in his demands on human nature. In *The Sound of Music* he lowers the standard of admiration by bestowing it too easily. It is a mistake to treat the von Trapps as heroes'.[7] The whole point of the piece is that the von Trapps were heroic; we are meant to be profoundly stirred as they escape the Nazi oppression, but, as has been pointed out, shouldn't our sympathies be as much with those abandoned nuns? As the curtain falls on Act Two, with the Mother Abbess intoning a biblical farewell to the escapees, we might recall the nuns at the centre of Poulenc's opera *Dialogues des Carmélites*, facing death during the French Revolution.[8] In comparison to this, or the shadows that fall from the Nazi regime over *Cabaret*, the tone of *The Sound of Music* is cosy. The *Times* description of the play 'as pretty and as sentimental as an Ivor Novello romance'[9] refers us back to *The Dancing Years*, in which Novello made use of the Nazi shadow without detracting from his confectionery.

A novelettish quality is more pronounced in *The Sound of Music* than in any of Rodgers and Hammerstein's works, and may have inspired Anthony Cookman to call it a 'betrayal of the American musical [...] What a falling away.'[10] The falling away is by inference principally the responsibility of the two men who had elevated the American musical to a more integrated art form, or attracted a reputation for having done so. The generality (and geniality) of Hammerstein's lyrics is probably more pronounced than ever before, and partly because in this play there is no musical expression of the leading man's character beyond the milk and water 'Edelweiss'; compare the clear statement of personality in 'Por Jud is Dead' in *Oklahoma!* or Bigelow's 'Soliloquy' in *Carousel* or the Siamese

King's 'Puzzlement' in *The King and I*. The Captain doesn't even get the chance to put into his own words the feeling he has for Maria in 'An Ordinary Couple', where he repeats the words that she has already sung to him.

Something odd happens during 'My Favourite Things' too, when Maria and the Abbess discuss Maria's future. Maria tells the Abbess about her favourite things, a long list with generous helpings of adjectives. The Abbess is all interest, and probably of high IQ, because when Maria pauses for breath the Abbess repeats verbatim the list Maria has recited. It's a prodigious feat of memory, rattling off those verses and that chorus, but would the Abbess have the *same* list of favourite things as her young student? Why didn't Hammerstein see that, to make it real, he needed to supply her with a whole new list? As it is, 'My Favourite Things', another 'cheer up' song in the line of *The King and I*'s 'I Whistle a Happy Tune' and indeed like *The Sound of Music*'s own 'Do-Re-Mi' and 'The Lonely Goatherd', is the more generalised because Hammerstein hands out the same slab of lyrics to both characters. It's a deceit that goes unnoticed except by those who attend the present-day sing-a-long showings of the film in appropriate costume. If Hammerstein had allowed the Mother Abbess her own list of favourites, it would have widened the choice, forcing fewer people to go dressed as a brown paper parcel tied up with string.

For his reincarnation from Vincent J. Donehue's original direction and Joe Layton's choreography, Jerome Whyte chose an all-British cast. Martin's name had been above the title, but the twenty-five-year-old Hackney actress Jean Bayless was below it. Had an established British star been considered for the part? In 1955 Bayless (then Jo Ann Bayless) had taken over from Julie Andrews in the Broadway *The Boy Friend*, but back in Britain had struggled through the home-grown musicals *School* and *Harmony Close*. Bayless's Maria lacked the starry impact of Martin's performance but was not without its admirers. Sadly, without a name above the marquee, it was always the show, not the domestic players, that the British flocked to see. When Bayless left, her understudy Sonia Rees kept the curtain up, which was all the management cared about. The London Captains were unexciting: originally the French actor Roger Dann, whose only previous West End musical was the British *Romance in Candelight*, and subsequently Donald Scott, a refugee from one or two unsuccessful British musicals who had been Dann's stand-in before being sent to New York to take over from Broadway's original Captain, Theodore Bikel.

As Max, Harold Kasket was followed by the jobbing John Blythe, the original Liesl Barbara Brown – said in the London programme to have turned down a £100,000 Hollywood contract because she preferred to stay at home – by Susan Passmore and the original Rolf, Nicholas Bennett, by Richard Loaring. Eunice Gayson was a perky Elsa despite some flat singing, and Olive Gilbert, with the distinction of having appeared in every Ivor Novello musical from *Glamorous Night* on, had the longest run of her career as Sister Margaretta, staying until the show's closure, and getting her name, despite the smallness of her role, amongst those of the billed principals. The irony of this situation may not have been known to Gilbert, of whom Hammerstein had written disparagingly. Those watching Gilbert's substantial and mature figure may have wondered at the programme note explaining that she had recently 'toured England in *The Dancing Years On Ice*'.[11]

For third-billed Constance Shacklock, the role of Mother Abbess signalled a turning away from her career in opera and the concert platform. For the cast recording Shacklock's 'Climb Every Mountain' provides a thrilling centrepiece. The role was in the line of Gilbert and Sullivan's elderly women; the Mother Abbess, kindly and sweet-faced as she may be, is directly descended from the Katishas, the Duchesses of Plaza-Toro, the Lady Janes, the Little Buttercups of the Savoy Operas. She is also the last and most religious in the line of the mature ladies of Rodgers and Hammerstein musicals, among her antecedents Eller Murphy from *Oklahoma!*, Bloody Mary from *South Pacific*, Lady Thiang from *The King and I*, and Madam Liang from *Flower Drum Song*.

More than any other collaborators since Gilbert and Sullivan, Rodgers and Hammerstein may be said to have worked to a template. The shapes of its pattern, its subjects, may have changed, shifted, been adjusted from show to show, but the shaping was theirs alone and maintained throughout their writing life together. Beyond all the particulars that belong to their works, this is what binds them together and gives them such a specific identity in American musical theatre, and in the British perception of American musical theatre. And then there is that particular tidiness of their work, so easily digestible. British theatregoers could not have cared less for such niceties, and kept returning to the Palace to see either Bayless or Rees wheeled on stage on a papier mâché rock until the release of the 1965 film version made people notice a difference between the shuddering backcloths and ply-wood Austria on offer at the Palace and the Todd-AO version on screen.

Petula Clark played Maria for the 1981 London revival at the Victoria Palace, with Michael Jayston as Captain, June Bronhill as Mother Abbess and Honor Blackman as Elsa. Clark's success outstripped that of the original British Marias, playing throughout to sold-out houses. For the occasion, two songs written for the film, 'Something Good' and 'I Have Confidence', were drafted into the production. Connie Fisher, followed by Summer Strallen, starred in the November 2006 revival at the London Palladium. Simon Shepherd was cast as Captain, but was removed after a few performances and replaced by Alexander Hanson. In Shacklock-like tradition, the 'classical' singer Lesley Garrett was the Mother Abbess. The production, greatly boosted by a television 'search for a star' campaign mounted by the producers for the BBC, ran through February 2009.

Of all the Broadway musicals that landed in London in the 1960s, *The Sound of Music* will almost certainly endure. The reasons are not difficult to find; they are there in its simplicity, its distillation, its elemental concerns, its reduction of emotion, its songs. As the last of Rodgers and Hammerstein it is not the weakest, and the patterns established by *Oklahoma!* may still be found. The template was used again in *Carousel*, but for their next work was largely discarded. Only Broadway had the opportunity to see that very different piece, *Allegro*, and rejected it in 1947. It would have failed miserably in London. In its way this was Hammerstein at his most regressive, for what is *Allegro* but a little musical about a bonny all-American baby boy who grows up to be a doctor, is offered a successful cosmopolitan career pandering to hypochondriacal socialites but rejects it in favour of returning to his hometown to practise medicine among the people he grew up among? *Allegro* disclosed much about Hammerstein's essential homeliness, domestic fascination, the turning away from commercially and financially recognised success. Its theme song is one of the most basic he and Rodgers wrote: 'One Foot, Other Foot', marking as it does the fundamental progress of a man's life – putting one foot in front of the other. But *Allegro* was daring in its techniques, in its tone, in its refusal to conform to what was in 1947 expected of a musical comedy, and anathema to those who turned to Rodgers and Hammerstein for a certain type of neat entertainment. Characters lived and died on stage, and spoke after death; songs were suggested before they reappeared in fuller form later in the show; the chorus was Greek, commenting on what was happening on stage.

In *Allegro* something happened to Rodgers' music, whether of his own volition or whether as a response to Hammerstein's manifesto we cannot tell. There are moments in *Allegro* that are in the manner of early Gershwin, something that we feel we must have heard in *Of Thee I Sing*, and there are long stretches when, if we didn't know the provenance, we would think we had just discovered some new stuff by Kurt Weill, with passages that seem to have escaped *Lady in the Dark*. The general consensus was that *Allegro* wouldn't do; it didn't work. And so the progress of Rodgers and Hammerstein was sent back to the templates of *Oklahoma!* and *Carousel*. *The Sound of Music* is at the end of the line, and much had happened to Rodgers' music and Hammerstein's books and lyrics since their first working together. In the shows that Rodgers went on to compose with new collaborators the distillation and simplicity were often accentuated.

Hammerstein's death in August 1960 made Rodgers professionally a widower for the second time, Lorenz Hart having died in 1943. So far as Britain was concerned, *The Sound of Music* was almost the last brush it had with the composer who had alerted it to a challenging shift in musical theatre with *Oklahoma!* There would be *No Strings* (London, 1963) for which Rodgers wrote both lyrics and music – as a wordsmith Rodgers proved to be a strange blend of the qualities of both Hart and Hammerstein, if predominantly the latter – but the British public didn't take to it. Without the additional 'and Hammerstein' above the marquee the box office twiddled its thumbs. The reputation of the partnership was enhanced because in London only the best, or at least the most commercially successful, of their work had been presented. The British were unaware of their *Allegro* (1947), *Me and Juliet* (1953) and *Pipe Dream* (1955). After *No Strings* Britain remained in ignorance of the last Rodgers scores: *Do I Hear a Waltz?* (1965), with Sondheim's lyrics; *Two by Two* (1970), inevitably a musical about Noah starring Danny Kaye, and *Rex* (1976), an attempt at a Henry VIII musical with lyricist Sheldon Harnick and a clutch of sinuous Rodgers ballads. As cloying as anything that had come before, *I Remember Mama* also stayed in New York.

In March 1960 the editorial of *Plays and Players* declared

> what dear, old-fashioned things American musicals now seem to be. True, there is *West Side Story*, but this is the exception that proves the rule. [The other imports playing in London that month were *My Fair Lady* and *Flower Drum Song*. The home-growns were *Fings Ain't Wot They Used T'Be*, *Make Me an Offer* and, via its French origins, *Irma La Douce*. The Julian Slade and Dorothy Reynolds' *Follow That Girl*, repudiating sordidity, opened on the 17th.] American musicals are large-scale spectacular, tuneful; British musicals today are small-scale, less colourful, but dramatically vital. No longer are pretty tunes and colourful dances the order of the day; the new British musical has become a vehicle of forthright, sometimes downright savage, social comment.

This bold statement about the state of the British musical comes at almost the exact moment when it was about to undergo another shift. Within a few months the kitchen-sink musical, the *verismo*, the music not of the spheres but of ponces and tarts, was swept away, and social comment was unwanted. What *Plays and Players* didn't contemplate was that such works were largely unexportable. So far as the culture of musical theatre was concerned, Broadway to London remained a one-way street.

The editorial knew that in New York, for financial reasons, 'no management will consider a production unless they think it will run for years' whereas

> In London it is still possible to put on a show for a narrower public which will clear expenses in a matter of months. We can therefore experiment in ways that are not possible in America. Even so, however, it seems that our writers have shown more initiative than their opposite numbers in America, and that they have realised that the musical need not be merely escapist. In doing so, they have at last put the British musical ahead of the American.[12]

However, the British experiment was beginning to sicken and fade, oddly at a time when social and sexual attitudes in Britain were increasingly liberal. The British musical was a victim of its own introspection. Broadway was much the more resourceful, for it too, in its way, had done with Rodgers and Hammerstein. Reinvention and regeneration was in the air, and much of that air blew over the Atlantic.

A month after Jean Bayless had first been pulled on stage at the Palace on 18 May 1961 balanced on that papier mâché rock, came the first of several works that showed a refreshed Broadway product's superiority over its British counterpart. *Bye Bye Birdie* (Her Majesty's Theatre, 15 June 1961; 268) turned its face away from the conformity of the Rodgers and Hammerstein school. Youthful, vital, tuneful and funny, it brought a breath of fresh airs, especially in its quality score by composer Charles Strouse and lyricist Lee Adams, whose subsequent works included several seen in London, *Golden Boy*, *Applause*, *Annie* and (a London original) *I and Albert*. Strouse and Adams brought a modernity to the beginning of the decade, eschewing the operetta elements that had threaded many of the recent imports such as *Candide, The Most Happy Fella* and *The Sound of Music.*

Michael Stewart's original book told of theatrical agent Albert Peterson who faces financial ruin when his protégé pop-singer Conrad Birdie is called up for the US Army, as happened to Elvis Presley in 1958; it means that Albert may not be able to marry his sweetheart Rose Grant, whose great hope is that he will become a respectable English teacher. Rose's plans to exploit the situation have Conrad colliding with a stereotypical happy American family, the MacAfees. As always with H. M. Tennent's management, the casting was interesting. The ace in the pack was the Broadway Rose, Chita Rivera, already known in London from *West Side Story*, and now inspiring Caryl Brahms to decide that 'The play does have a wit and liveliness, if not a life, and a noisiness of its own which is souped up into a sweetish-sour flavouring, to which Miss Rivera is the red-pepper and lemon juice, the lift, the kick, the vodka before the repast and the urbane brandy after it.'[13] Two months before the London opening, Dick Van Dyke left the Broadway cast, but wasn't signed for the West End, where Albert was played by the less stellar Peter Marshall, a stronger singer than Van Dyke. Tennent had (eccentrically) originally cast the British actor Brian Reece as Albert, but he withdrew because of illness.[14]

A clever move by Tennent was to hire a top-lining British pop-star as Birdie. Unlike Broadway's Dick Gautier, Marty Wilde had the style and ability to make the switch to Conrad Birdie plausibly. Here was the genuine article: Wilde's most recent single, 'Rubber Ball', reached Number 9 in the British charts in 1961. In the British stage musical *Expresso Bongo* (1958) the young hopeful pop-singer Bongo had sung a ludicrous hymn 'The Shrine on the Second Floor', an effect negated by Cliff Richard's 'straight' version in the subsequent film. Four months after the opening of *Bye Bye Birdie* there was a 'pop' title song for the Julian Slade–Dorothy Reynolds British musical *Wildest Dreams*. Around this time there was a rush of pop-singers breaking into film-acting, as in *Serious Charge* (Cliff Richard), *Rag Doll* (Jess Conrad), *The Painted Smile* (Craig Douglas) and *Beat Girl* (Adam Faith); never mind that their contributions ranged through several degrees of awfulness. Did Tennent hope that Wilde's name on the bills might attract his army of teenage fans to the West End? On the other hand, his reputation as a teeny-bopper's idol may have kept the middle-aged away.

As it was, Wilde's presence handed Tennent miles of coverage in the popular press. The Canadian Sylvia Tysick, the 'Anybodys' of the London *West Side Story*, was well cast as Kim MacAfee, a lesser singer than Broadway's Susan Watson, but more personable. The underused Tysick would only play one more musical, the British *Passion Flower Hotel*.

Strouse and Adams's confident score was a stream of character-infused numbers, the most prominent 'Put on a Happy Face', sung by Albert to one of the MacAfee race; this, 'Kids' and Conrad's determination that there was 'A Lot of Livin' to Do' earned a popularity outside the production. The pubescent teenagers of *Bye Bye Birdie* had 'The Telephone Hour', a welcome antidote to the overweening sweetness of the children in *The Sound of Music*. Here was America laughing at its own cultural values, not least the obeisance paid to the Ed Sullivan TV show, on which the MacAfee family get to appear, celebrated by an ecstatic Mr MacAfee in his 'Hymn for a Sunday Evening'. Charm kept the balance in 'How Lovely to be a Woman' and 'One Boy'. For many, Rivera provided the highlights in her dance items 'How to Kill a Man' and 'Shriners' Ballet'. The critics' response was friendly enough. The *Guardian* noted

> The plot is unashamedly sentimental, the satire gentle [it compared the story to the 'savage, bitter *Expresso Bongo*'] and the tunes are of an uncomplicated niceness which will keep *Housewives' Choice*[15] going for a year or so. Why then is it so successful? How is it that competence is somehow transmuted into brilliance? The most obvious explanation is the presence of Chita Rivera.[16]

A sequel, *Bring Back Birdie*, with Rivera once again playing Rose, was a four performance Broadway disaster in 1981, but fifty years on the original retains its affectionate ebullience. Any revival would necessarily be something of a period piece, but how much of its time was *Bye Bye Birdie*? It comes on as youthful, but it isn't really. 'The Telephone Hour' lampoons adolescence, 'Kids' berates it. Conrad may be a contemporary 'pop' singer with hip attachments, and he does seem to dabble in rock 'n' roll, but it isn't long before he's singing pop stuff ('One Last Kiss') that might have been sung by Dickie Valentine or Frankie Vaughan to auditoria full of housewives, and ultimately getting down to a standard show number in 'A Lot of Livin''. Aspects of *Bye Bye Birdie* may lead us to think this was a piece that might swing young people into queuing up to see musicals, but it lags behind its own recognition of popular culture. By the time Strouse and Adams' dimly talented hero was taking stage, Elvis Presley and Bill Haley had already worked their way into encyclopaedias.

A feyness calculated to bewitch the most dewy-eyed of theatregoers infected **The Fantasticks** (Apollo Theatre, 7 September 1961; 44), the first of three shows by composer Harvey Schmidt and his librettist-lyricist Tom Jones to reach London. None would achieve the success they enjoyed in New York. There, *The Fantasticks* ran for an astounding forty-two years, all of 17,162 performances at the tiny off-Broadway Sullivan Street Playhouse. The show's dwarfish proportions made it ideal off-Broadway fodder, for all it demanded was eight actors, two pianos, a backcloth and a few props. Throughout its history *The Fantasticks* has been a lily that needs no gilding. Edmund Rostand's play *Les Romanesques* provided the story of two young lovers, played in London by Peter Gilmore and Stephanie Voss, kept apart by fathers who build a wall to separate them.

The appeal of *The Fantasticks* came as much from primal drama as from American musical theatre, with its eternal themes boiling down the usual boy-girl romances of most musicals into something organically symbolic. The songs caught the whimsical mood, most especially 'Try to Remember', a melancholy recall of young life gone by, and the down-beat 'Soon it's Gonna Rain'. The music, newly orchestrated for London for two pianos, harp and percussion by Julian Stein and Raymond Holder, failed to impress the British press. The *Sunday Telegraph* thought that 'At its best Harvey Schmidt's score sounds as if it were failing to adapt Gems from Bernstein for drums, harp and two pianos. At its worst, it sounds as if it were producing Family Favourites from Slade and Reynolds.'[17] The point had already been made by Robert Muller, who considered the score the sort of stuff Slade and Reynolds would have written after a brief visit to Greenwich Village.[18] Milton Shulman reported 'one feels one has been kicked in the face for hours by an army of amiable pixies' during a 'suffocatingly arch' entertainment.[19]

The West End wasn't the right place for this show; it needed an off-West End to make it feel at home. Producers and managements should have been paying attention, for *The Fantasticks* was another harbinger (after *The Threepenny Opera* of 1956) of a new phenomenon in the West End: the importation of shows that had only played off-Broadway – 'fringe' before the term was in popular use in Britain. The main appeal of such shows to British managements was obvious: off-Broadway meant smaller productions than the usually mammoth Broadway beasts that demanded to be brought over the Atlantic. They were cheaper, too – always a recommendation to a management. The costumes would not break the bank, and audiences would make do with something that stood in for a decent set. Usually, the off-Broadway shows managed without stars, even eschewed the idea of them. Even cheaper. The fact that London did not have an off-West End seemed not to bother the managements, who throughout the 1960s began to shoe-horn off-Broadway productions into the West End. In that decade alone, theatregoers had the opportunity to see many off-Broadway imports: *Little Mary Sunshine, All in Love, You're a Good Man, Charlie Brown, Man with a Load of Mischief, Your Own Thing* and *Dames at Sea*. None was conspicuously successful.

At least for *The Fantasticks*, the negligible production demands and attractive songs have helped it to a reasonable after-life, mostly in repertory. A West End revival at the Duchess Theatre in June 2010 emphasised the work's most irritating characteristics, when what was needed was to slice through the sentimentality. The smallness of the piece had been a problem in 1961; forty-three years later the times were even more inhospitable. The director's programme note informed audiences that

> The setting is nowhere, just a bare stage. As Peter Brook noted in *The Empty Space*, the essence of theatre can be reduced to walking across an empty room which another man watches; but *The Fantasticks* manages to make magic of its rudimentary set. Through its simplicity, and by spurning any description of the specific time and place, the musical offers the audience a magical experience which is only attainable in the theatre, encouraging them to use their own imagination to be part of – and complete the world of – the show.

How brilliant for managements – let the audience *think* they can see a fabulous set!

After a preview the 'West End Whingers' reported:

> What we hadn't been prepared for was the style of the performances which Japanese director Amon Miyamoto of the 2000 Sunrio Puro Land, Tokyo production of *Hello Kitty Dream Revue (One)* had plumped for, which turned out to be *Play Away*[20] circa 1972, an interesting directorial choice which principally involves people bouncing up and down excitedly and generally being very perky. What a way to treat London Musical Comedy.[21]

The opening night's critics derided this rethink of Word Baker's original production. Michael Billington noted the 'dimpled, ingratiating cuteness [...] whatever New York might think, I can't help feeling that the time for this kind of faux-naïf, sub Commedia dell'Arte diversion has passed.'[22] Charles Spencer thought that 'The British know a great pile of steaming phoney baloney when they see one [...] no amount of talent can redeem this terrible show.'[23] By 2010 criticism was also in the hands of theatregoers via the internet, with postings from those who had *paid* for their ticket. Their views of the revamped *Fantasticks* were not encouraging: 'A group of eight mature ladies saw this in May and thought it a load of rubbish' (Pam O'Shea); 'Pure cheese' (Lisa Reeves); 'zero entertainment. Waste of time and money' (Caroline). Achieving the distinction of having done a revival of a flop that ran even less than its original month's run, the management put up the closing notices on the second night. In 1969 the authors had tried to repeat the magic of *The Fantasticks* on Broadway with a new piece in the same vein, *Celebration*, but this time New York resisted the invitation, and Britain never heard of it

Two days before the original British *The Fantasticks* closed, the final import of the year arrived, but **Do Re Mi** (Prince of Wales Theatre, 12 October 1961; 169) might have done better to stay home. *Say, Darling* and *Gypsy*, the Jule Styne shows following on from *Bells Are Ringing*, had not travelled. (*Gypsy* would have

28 The unquestionably miscast Max Bygraves obliged to play a role originally created on
Broadway by Phil Silvers in the brash Styne–Comden–Green *Do Re Mi* (London, 1961)

to wait until 1973.) *Do Re Mi* was a year-long runner in New York, in considerable part because of its star Phil Silvers, best known in Britain for his role of Sgt. Ernest G. Bilko in a 1950s television comedy series. In *Do Re Mi* Silvers brought intense energy and charisma to his role of Hubert Cram, a chancer constantly on the look-out for easy money, and an unsatisfactory husband to Kay (on Broadway, Nancy Walker). Now it is the juke-box business that inspires him, and he takes up a young waitress-singer Tilda Mullen to make his dream come true.

The juke-box was indeed fashionable when *Do Re Mi* premiered. It had already featured in several British films such as the 1958 *The Golden Disc*, and BBC TV produced *Juke Box Jury* which ran from June 1959 through 1967. Garson Kanin's book for *Do Re Mi* had some of the atmosphere of the British *Expresso Bongo*, where the treatment of Tin Pan Alley characters was rather more sophisticated, helped by dashes of unpleasantness and bitterness. In *Do Re Mi* the grapes never turned sour but clung to the Broadway vine. Styne's score was particularly brassy, and the authors seemed to have an eye on the sort of atmosphere that had been created in *Guys and Dolls*, except that *Do Re Mi* had none of that show's wit, invention or charm. Here was another in the line of Comden and Green's New York fairytales, encased on stage in giant proscenium-arched juke-box designs by Boris Aronson, singled out by some British critics as particularly garish.

Opening in Manchester, the British edition replicated the production which was still running in New York, but without the skill of Silvers and Walker its weakness was more exposed. Even when well done, *Do Re Mi* was second division. In place of Silvers, audiences got Max Bygraves, a variety comic and singer of comedy songs such as 'I'm a Pink Toothbrush' and 'Gilly Gilly Ossenfeffer Katzenellenbogen by the Sea'. The popular Bygraves had no technique in his armoury to equip him for the barnstorming numbers. Director Bernard Gersten was quoted in *Show Pictorial* as pronouncing that 'It's the end of Max Bygraves as a solo personality artiste. After *Do Re Mi* people will be falling over themselves writing shows specially for Max.'[24] Sensibly, they did not. Styne was reported as being thrilled with the casting, but Silvers was the absent spectre at the feast of the British *Do Re Mi*. When, a little way into the run, Bygraves insisted on interpolating 'Hey, Look Me Over' from the Cy Coleman – Carolyn Leigh 1960 *Wildcat* as an extra solo, Styne's reaction may be imagined.

Caryl Brahms thought the show

> a strident American musical, laconically strung together, suitable for coach parties up for the Motor Show [...] In it are Max Bygraves (Mr Un-funny) and Maggie Fitzgibbon (Miss Friendly – even in the frenzy of her big number 'Adventure').[25]

Welcome as Fitzgibbon was on any stage, the low-key British cast recording finds her working too hard. Among the many faint-hearted reviews, the *Spectator* decided that '*Do Re Mi* contains everything that has almost ruined several other American musicals, and nothing else.'[26]

As the secondary lovers Jan Waters and Steve Arlen were more than satisfactory, but the excitement quota was low. The company bellowed a choral reprise of 'Fireworks' at finale time, but what came to mind was damp squibs. At least the big romantic song given to Arlen, 'Make Someone Happy', was quality Styne/Comden/Green, more melancholy than cheering, but elsewhere the score was serviceable for Silvers if not for Bygraves. The 'pop music' items, which presumably fed the juke-box, sounded middle-aged, lacking the pep of similar items in *Bye Bye Birdie*, written by a younger team. 'What's New at the Zoo', Waters' quirky number with the chorines, was cousin to every nightclub number that had ever been staged on Broadway, a sort of left-over from *Pal Joey*. Comden and Green had written much the same sort of material in *On the Town* in 1944.

Bygraves had little regard for the show's integrity. A little way into the run, when the American producers had gone home, he had tricks up his sleeve. At the end of each performance, after he had taken his call and surrounded by the rest of the company, he started singing his 'hits', 'I'm a Pink Toothbrush' and 'Tulips from Amsterdam', accompanied by his pianist in the pit. Jan Waters recalls that 'Eventually, Maggie Fitzgibbon said "I'm not putting up with this any longer. When he's taken his call, why don't we all just divide in the middle and walk off and leave him to it?" Which we did. I don't suppose he even noticed!'[27]

There were two works with daring among the British musicals. One was Anthony Newley and Leslie Bricusse's **Stop the World – I Want to Get Off**. It seemed a new concept, with only two principals, a Greek-like chorus of girls and Everyman pretensions. Several of its songs were popular. **Belle** was in its way more brave: a musical about Dr Crippen's murder of his music-hall wife, Belle Elmore. The intention was admirable, and much fun was had along the way in Monty Norman's pastiche score. The critics were unimpressed by **Wildest Dreams**, the final Slade–Reynolds collaboration.

1961 Broadway Exports

Carnival (719), *Sail Away* (167) and *How to Succeed in Business Without Really Trying* (1,417).

1961 Broadway Only

Two of the year's musicals were based on movies: **The Conquering Hero** (8) on Preston Sturges' 1944 film, and **Donnybrook!** (68) on John Ford's *The Quiet Man* of 1952. **The Happiest Girl in the World** (97) had a fund of melodies, but they had been written long before by Offenbach. The Styne-Comden-Green **Subways Are for Sleeping** (205) was not considered top-notch. More successfully, Jerry Herman's first Broadway musical **Milk and Honey** (543), centred on a story about middle-aged love in Israel, marked the start of a major career. **Kwamina**

(32) was Richard Adler's first musical following the death of his collaborator Jerry Ross. Set in Africa, it starred Adler's wife Sally Ann Howes, but despite its interesting score built around the tale of inter-racial romance it didn't succeed. *The Gay Life* (113), based on Arthur Schnitzler's play *The Affairs of Anatol*, had music by Arthur Schwartz, but, like **Let It Ride!** (68) and **Young Abe Lincoln** (93), was a commercial failure. **Kean** (92) was an intelligent attempt at musicalising the life of the nineteenth-century actor Edmund Kean, star of Drury Lane. With Robert Wright and George Forrest writing a rare (for them) original score, the piece was dominated by Alfred Drake's central performance. Less desirable was a 'Hawaiian' musical, **13 Daughters** (28), whose cast included Don Ameche and John Battles.

29 Although much improved from its American origins, the British edition of that modest pastiche of American operetta *Little Mary Sunshine* (1962) made no impression on the West End

1962

Little Mary Sunshine
Sail Away
Gentlemen Prefer Blondes
Fiorello!

ittle Mary Sunshine (Comedy Theatre, 17 May 1962; 44) was a rare
thing, a gentle American parody of the style of Friml and Romberg operettas
of an earlier age. The sole work of Rick Besoyan, it struck chords nostalgic and
ridiculous: in the *Herald Tribune* Walter Kerr wrote 'I felt pain: pain that I almost
never see anything so easy and foolish and delightful on Broadway any more.' It
was the first off-Broadway musical to be recorded by Capitol Records, who for
the occasion upgraded the two-piano accompaniment heard in the theatre to
a small orchestra. New York's affection for Sandy Wilson's *The Boy Friend*, in
effect a 'new' 1920s musical comedy with its cloche hats, affected gestures, stock
responses and insistence on period feel, had revealed an American susceptibility
for theatrical pastiche.

Early twentieth-century stout-hearted mounties ('The Forest Rangers')
introduce the audience to the Colorado Inn in the Rocky Mountains, the home
of virtuous Little Mary Sunshine, whose heart is lost to manly Captain 'Big Jim'
Warrington. As the foster child of Chief Brown Bear of the threatened Kadota
tribe of Indians, Little Mary is drawn into a land dispute, and the difficulties
caused by the troublesome Yellow Feather. The principal characters (innocent
heroine, clean-minded hero, male comedy actor and his naughty female
soubrette, a romance between an elderly army officer and a one-time star of
opera, supported by a small cast that includes six boys and six girls who make
up the parted chorus) play out to the predictable happy ending. The songs
vividly reflect originals from the type of productions that Besoyan was guying:
Little Mary's plea for happiness 'Look for a Sky of Blue' mirrored 'Look for the
Silver Lining' (lyric by B. G. DeSylva, music by Jerome Kern) from *Sally*; 'Tell
a Handsome Stranger' recalled Leslie Stuart's 'Tell Me, Pretty Maiden' from
Floradora; Little Mary and Captain Jim's prolonged attempt at saying goodbye
to one another, the 'Colorado Love Call' was in clear imitation of *Rose-Marie*'s
'Indian Love Call'. Sometimes the pastiche was of mood rather than any specific
item.

Despite, or because of, its homemade feel, the American production went
on for 1,143 performances, and was still running when Besoyan travelled to
Britain for the provincial premiere of the all-new British production at the
Theatre Royal, Norwich on 20 March 1962. The local critic reported 'Judging
by the enthusiastic send-off this British production should stand a good chance
of rivalling the trans-Atlantic success, although it was a little time before the

audience was drawn into its mood. Once they were won over, the waves of laughter showed their enjoyment.' In London there was even less enthusiasm, as the headlines following its first night failed to disguise: 'Dine Well Before You Attempt to Stomach This' (*Daily Mail*); 'Gone – And Best Forgotten' (*Evening News*); 'A Superficial Spoof Fails to Catch On' (*Daily Telegraph*). Eric Shorter found it 'sails too often and too near to the worst excesses of the past: without its music and without its voices, not to speak of charm'.[1] Herbert Kretzmer found that

> Once you have absorbed the idea that you are watching a send-up of early U. S. operetta, you are left with about fifteen ricky-tick songs and lyrics that are deliberately derivative and a plot altogether too tiresome to recall [...] In the background the cardboard valleys yawn. In the auditorium the audience yawns too. What makes the evening something less than compulsive entertainment is that the tradition *Little Mary Sunshine* sets out to parody cannot be parodied at all.[2]

The same might have been said of *The Boy Friend*; perhaps, somewhere, it *was* said. Like the Kadotas, *The Times* had reservations, aimed not at the production but at Mr Besoyan:

> The book and lyrics are accurate pastiche, but the music itself pays the price of trying to send up originals which, for all their shortcomings, have an obstinate habit of sticking in the public mind. Although nothing could be squarer than Romberg and Friml, Mr Rick Besoyan's tunes lack the homely conviction one senses about a hit [...] they just about succeed in holding the show together.

Allowing that the show might well become a cult, the critic considered 'The book is too explicitly condescending to admit of any delicacy of satire; sometimes a residue of genuine sentimentality works better in this kind of thing.'[3] It certainly had in *The Boy Friend*. Perhaps affected by the hot summer night, Milton Shulman predicted a long run.

The British reinvention of the show was the work of Paddy Stone. The casting was superb, with Britain's most underrated musical actress Patricia Routledge in the title role, relishing every nuance and inflection. At this time Routledge had not yet begun her American career: starring roles on Broadway in *Darling of the Day* for which she won a Tony, and as all the President's wives in *1600 Pennsylvania Avenue*, as well as two shows intended for Broadway which collapsed *en route*, *Love Match* in which she played Queen Victoria and *Hello Harvey*. Her Captain Jim was the bluff-voiced Terence Cooper, with all the stolidity of Nelson Eddy. The comedy partnership of Bernard Cribbins, then in the British Hit Parade with one of several frisky songs he made popular, and Joyce Blair, was all brightness. This partnership was replaced by John Quayle and Patricia Michael for one week only on the pre-London tour in Wolverhampton, when both Cribbins and Blair fell ill. Other sources of delight were the aged Erik Chitty in long fur coat and goggles as General Oscar Fairfax, and the spreadingly elegant Gita Denise as the one-time opera star Mme Ernestine von Liebedich, duetting in 'Do You Ever Dream of Vienna?' The rest of the small company had its surprises, too: the six girls included several who went on to substantial careers – Anna Dawson (who had just emerged from the female lead of Julian Slade's *Wildest Dreams*), Patricia Michael (who would go directly, after leading the cast of a Dublin production of the British *Grab Me a Gondola*, into a featured lead in *Fiorello!* and later star in *How to Succeed in Business Without Really Trying*), Hilary Tindall and Judy Nash, with Edward (Ed) Bishop, soon to sign up for the TV series *UFO*, as Chief Brown Bear.

More sprightly than its American cousin, *Little Mary Sunshine* was pretty and diverting but tickets went unsold. The weather was warm. After a handful of performances for which the perspiring public could not be inveigled into the stultifying heat of a London theatre, the press was invited to Routledge's dressing room to see her present a cheque from the cast to the management, basically refunding their salaries to keep the curtain up (around £17 a head). The gravitas of the situation cannot have been helped by some of the headlines: the *Evening Standard* reported the handover with '£300 Whip-Round for Little Mary Sunshine'. The gesture did not save this pleasing diversion, another proof that London could not offer safe haven to off-Broadway shows. The gentle happiness it instilled in the stalls owed much to the vision of Paddy Stone, described by Patricia Michael as

> wonderful and talented but highly incendiary [...] He could lose his rag on the turn of a dime and rage at an actor with truly inventive vitriol. I came to realize that when this happened you had to be aware that all he was trying to say was something like 'No love, you're on the wrong foot there.' I also realized that he never spoke to anyone in that way unless he felt that they could do better. His rages were true compliments.[4]

None of the other imported musicals flourished. The only Noel Coward musical to show on Broadway before moving to the West End, **Sail Away** (Savoy Theatre, 21 June 1962; 252) remained essentially a British work, although it passed itself off as transatlantic. It probably deserved better than its seven-month run. At last, after a career in musical theatre dominated by his dalliance with operetta, with which he had enjoyed his only popular success *Bitter Sweet*, Coward in *Sail Away* distanced himself in a work that genuinely attempted to be a musical play, even when some of it was essentially revue. The plot forsaken, everything stopped for such items as 'Why Do the Wrong People Travel?' and 'Useless Useful Phrases'. In the geriatric love-hate song 'Bronxville Darby and Joan', not heard in the New York production, there was a lurid attraction in seeing Edith Day, the British Rose-Marie and Rio Rita of the 1920s, pouring sweet venom on her long-suffering husband played by Sydney Arnold. There was bitter-sweetness in the love story of a middle-aged hostess of a cruise-ship and a much younger man.

It was London's good fortune that Elaine Stritch repeated her Broadway role of Mimi Paragon (the Australian production got its own Aussie Maggie Fitzgibbon, and sometimes in London audiences were treated to Stritch's substitute, Stella Moray). The score had some fine romantic numbers, the best of them – 'Later than Spring' and 'Something Very Strange' – autumnal in tone. Leading man David Holliday, one of the best of this period, impacted with the title song already heard in Coward's 1950 *Ace of Clubs*, 'Don't Turn Away from Love' and 'Go Slow Johnny'. Stowed away in the supporting cast was Dorothy Reynolds, Julian Slade's fellow-librettist and lyricist, as a difficult romantic novelist. Reynolds was only required to show her assured comedy skills, not sing. Furnished with what was renowned at the time as the handsomest line-up of chorus boys in London, *Sail Away* went west after the Christmas business tailed off, observing the usual trajectory of Coward's musicals.

Getting Anita Loos's famous peroxide heroine to London for **Gentlemen Prefer Blondes** (Princes Theatre, 20 August 1962, then Strand Theatre; 220) took twelve years. The lady had, naturally, aged. Broadway's blonde had been Carol Channing, but neither she nor any other American star was cast for the West End. Dora Bryan had spent the 1950s in and out of West End revues and films, making time for a personal success in Vivian Ellis and A. P. Herbert's romance of the canals *The Water Gipsies*. By 1962 Bryan may have seemed like the best bet for a British Lorelei, but there was a lack of authenticity about the performance: too much Oldham, too little Little Rock. It was, after all, her innate Britishness that made Bryan so appealingly effective. The show was newly directed and redressed for London, but *Theatre World* noted that 'the early performances gave evidence of a lack of cohesion' and that 'the cast, doing their utmost to recapture the spirit of the 1920s, are not always successful, nor are they helped by the production, which, in the opening sequences on board particularly, remind us that by comparison *Sail Away* is a very slick effort.'[5]

It was London's fourth exposure to a Jule Styne score, after the first, *High Button Shoes*, with which it shared a trademark brashness. Styne's work would always be associated with shows that were unmistakably American in tone (compare them to say, *Carousel* or *The King and I*, where the 'Americanness' can seem almost incidental, enabling them to pass almost as home-grown), and in such a circumstance it was not enough for a British production to chance an impersonation. The British cast recording is unconvincing, and the supporting cast is frankly nothing to write to New York, let alone home, about, even during the main numbers, 'Bye Bye Baby', 'A Little Girl from Little Rock' and, crucially, 'Diamonds Are a Girl's Best Friend'. Wherever Bryan takes us, it isn't within miles of Broadway. *Gentlemen Prefer Blondes* survived an early transfer to the Strand Theatre but was packed off after a total of six months. Bryan would be more successful three years later with *Hello, Dolly!*

In September 1962 a letter to the *Stage* suggested some of the problems facing American musicals transposed to London.

I wonder [wrote Antony Howard] if the failure as a production of *Gentlemen Prefer Blondes* has at last convinced West End managements of the futility of casting home-grown stars in American musical leads. It just does not work, this fobbing-off English audiences with sub-standard copies of Broadway originals [...] the leading parts, be they male or female, in American musicals are with negligible exceptions 100% American 'types', something which we just do not produce in this country and cannot hope to imitate.

Howard denounced the casting of Bygraves in *Do Re Mi* and Bryan in *Gentlemen Prefer Blondes* as 'so glaringly wrong that one wonders if managements have any feeling at all for the artistic effect of a production and the intentions of the author' and declared *Gentlemen Prefer Blondes* as 'the most abortive travesty of a good Broadway musical seen in the West End since the war'. Surely, Howard asked, if Styne had attended the show's rehearsals he would have insisted that Don Walker's original orchestrations were not tampered with? 'Having listened to the Broadway cast recording time and again, my heart sank at the Princes Theatre at the beginning of the overture and hardly revived before the final curtain as one liberty after another was taken'.[6]

Howard's complaint is reinforced by the British casting of many American musicals of this period, and the effect was often calamitous. The next 1962 entry, *Fiorello!*, made Howard's point for him, in a show so American that it seemed utterly foreign in British hands, and although the following year there was sometimes a token American cast member or two to bring a dash of Broadway reality to the proceedings (James Mitchell in *Carnival*, Art Lund and Beverly Todd in *No Strings*, Pat Turner in *The Boys from Syracuse* to name some of the few) the imposed Britishness remained dominant.

Never mind that in New York **Fiorello!** (Piccadilly Theatre, 8 October 1962; 56) had won the Pulitzer Prize for Drama, it was rank folly to transfer it to London – a bio-musical about the New York Mayor Fiorello LaGuardia, a man about whom the British knew nothing and cared less. In fact the British production had probably never been intended for the West End, but was newly directed by Val May for the resident repertory company at the Bristol Old Vic in September 1962, with new costumes and designs and, perhaps less wisely, new orchestrations (the originals, after all, had been by Irwin Kostal). At Bristol the show played to 90% capacity, but audiences there were supporting their local team.

There must have been doubts as to what London would think of it. What was this? Who or what *was* Fiorello? May's production seemed to acknowledge the fact that a British audience would sit mystified throughout by having key events announced by a man standing at a lectern. This hampered the ensuing drama from achieving its full force. On Broadway the title role had helped make Tom Bosley's name, but in London Derek Smith failed to attract interest. There was compensation in the female leads, each of whom had strong numbers: 'I Love a Cop' for Bridget Armstrong, 'When Did I Fall in Love?' for Marion Grimaldi, 'Gentleman Jimmy' for Patricia Michael, and most enjoyably 'The Very Next Man' for Nicolette Roeg as Fiorello's long-suffering and doting secretary. For some reason, the cabaret comedy team of Peter Reeves and Bryan Blackburn featured in the cast list, to little effect. For the end of Act One a film of World War I aeroplanes in flight was back-projected onto a screen, but on the first night the film was played backwards. Backward-flying planes added a note of fiasco to an enterprise that failed to take wing.

The contrast between New York and London critics could not have been starker. With no name to lure customers in, the notices spelt doom. The *Daily Mail* review was headed 'Un-American, Unoriginal, Unmemorable and Un-Good'; below, Bernard Levin announced 'The cast is ruthlessly un-American, and ruthlessly un-good' and that 'whoever designed the sets [Graham Barlow] has a good deal of nerve'.[7] In the *Western Mail* under 'Undesirable Imports' the critic was astonished 'that this brash and inartistic mélange of noise and sentiment could once have been voted New York's musical of the year by United States critics. But that was back in the fifties, and absolutely nothing in the theatre dates like an American musical'.[8] Harold Hobson's Sunday verdict was that 'Mr. Smith never suggests that La Guardia is anything more than a petty man in a perpetual peripatetic pet. Some of the female singing sounds like Dr. Beeching's railway engines lined up with their whistles blowing.'[9] *The Times* was in the minority, declaring 'a musical in the best American tradition [...] an excellent piece of ensemble work', although it thought Grimaldi 'pallid' against Roeg's 'genuinely affecting' performance.[10] Perhaps summing it up, W. A. Darlington in the *Daily Telegraph* asked 'Do American political campaigns thrill you? If so, *Fiorello!* at the Piccadilly is just your musical.'[11]

No blame could be attached to Jerome Weidman and George Abbott's muscular book or the score, the first by the team of composer Jerry Bock and lyricist Sheldon Harnick to reach London. Bock and Harnick would have to wait until their *Fiddler on the Roof* to establish a British reputation. Even then it is doubtful if their names ever meant a fig in the West End, although their work was consistently intelligent and appealing. *Fiorello!* had a wry attitude to New York political chicanery, exemplified in two stand-out numbers, 'Politics and Poker' and the 'Jack-in-the-box' number 'Little Tin Box', and – as always with these writers – character was at the forefront of the songs. Their next Broadway work, *Tenderloin*, a story of moral and political corruption in the red-light district of New York in the nineteenth century, was a sort of prequel to *Fiorello!* *Tenderloin* had a fine score, probably better than that for *Fiorello!*, but London wasn't offered it.

In British musicals, Hugh Hastings' adaptation of his successful play *Seagulls Over Sorrento* flooded the stage with sailors, but the ship went down with all hands, and **Scapa!** was hustled out of the Adelphi Theatre to make way for Lionel Bart's tribute to the London blitz, **Blitz!**, a substantial success. Julian Slade returned to London with his music for **Vanity Fair**, an adaptation of William Makepeace Thackeray's novel, but the intractable source and the weakness of the score did for it.

1962 Broadway Exports

No Strings (580), **A Funny Thing Happened on the Way to the Forum** (964) and **Little Me** (257).

1962 Broadway Only

A very American batch of musicals included **All American** (80) and **Mr President** (265). Two works inhabited the world of small business: **I Can Get It for You Wholesale** (300) was set in New York's rag-trade with Harold Rome songs and featured player Barbra Streisand stealing many of the notices; and **Bravo, Giovanni** (76) headlined Cesare Siepi as a restaurant owner whose livelihood is threatened by a chain of eateries. **Nowhere to Go But Up** (9) was a one-week runner about Prohibition agents, and **A Family Affair** (65) marked the debut of John Kander as a Broadway composer.

1963

Carnival
How to Succeed in Business Without Really Trying
On the Town
A Funny Thing Happened on the Way to the Forum
The Boys from Syracuse
Pocahontas
No Strings

B OB MERRILL had already attracted attention on Broadway as composer-lyricist for two adaptations from the plays of Eugene O'Neill, *New Girl in Town* (1957) from *Anna Christie*, and *Take Me Along* (1959) from *Ah, Wilderness!*, neither of which reached the West End. Britain's first awareness of Merrill came with **Carnival** (Lyric Theatre, 8 February 1963; 34) in Michael Stewart's adaptation of Helen Deutsch's *Lili*, a film based on a winsome story by Paul Gallico. On Broadway praise was lavished on Anna Maria Alberghetti's interpretation of Lili, the naive mop-headed diminutive who arrives at the tent-flap of Schlegel's rundown travelling circus from her blissfully uneventful hometown of Mira. Lili is drawn to the glitter and romance of the womanising Marco the Magnificent, but is befriended by the puppets worked by the embittered, love-lost puppeteer Paul. Only when she realises the affections expressed by the puppets are really those of Paul, does the curtain fall on Lili's happiness. In New York, Alberghetti was succeeded by her sister Carla, but neither was invited to play in London, the producers perhaps concerned that British audiences might confuse them with a type of pasta. They didn't ask Anita Gillette either, who had substituted for both Alberghettis during the Broadway run, but a few months after the London *Carnival* Gillette had her own memorable flop on Shaftesbury Avenue with *Pocahontas*. No matter: London's Lili was an enchantment.

H. M. Tennent's choice for Lili was the twenty-two-year-old Sally Logan, who, according to the show's souvenir brochure, 'was singing and dancing in the parks of her native Glasgow, in a double act with her father, when she was thirteen'. The five-foot tall singer had already been signed to play Goldilocks at Newcastle for Christmas 1962 when Tennent, who were used to recognising talent when they saw it, offered her the role. The West End reviews for the show were far from encouraging, despite Gower Champion's original direction, warmed through for London. Caryl Brahms wanted to know

> Why bring us this when there is so much that we want to see on Broadway? [...] The playgoer on Broadway is no fool. He has seen the best and the worst of musicals. It is his particular art-form. And he has kept this trite

little lollipop and all who take part in it alive for a year – possibly longer. So something must have happened to it in transit.[1]

In a letter to the *Stage* Peter W. Burton suggested what this might have been. For him it was 'ruined by a hideous British production. Bad sets, costumes, lighting, orchestration [...] and too small a cast combine to spoil the show. Owing to there being too few people on stage two big production numbers were unrecognisable as such.'[2] *Theatre World* reported 'the magic does not work. The Southern European setting made phrases such as "some place else" sound – at least to English ears – ludicrously out of place, and the mid-Atlantic accents of some of the cast further destroyed illusion.'[3]

The Broadway Marco was the only American player sent to London, but few would have recognised in James Mitchell the 'dream sequence Curly' of the *Oklahoma!* movie. As the psychologically scarred puppeteer the opera singer Michael Maurel brought a sonority that had been missing in Broadway's Jerry Orbach. Another newcomer, Shirley Sands – principally a band singer, although she had played in the London *Bells Are Ringing* in which she understudied Julie Wilson – was a striking Rosalie, the worldy antithesis to the dewy-eyed Lili. Her way with Rosalie's torch song 'It Was Always You' singled her out as someone to be noticed. Another incidental pleasure was a rare opportunity to see Bob Harris, who for the entire run of *Salad Days* had played the mute Troppo, in a featured part that showed him to be a fine actor. The British cast recording captures some of his dialogue, and shows he had the measure of this piece. It has the advantage, too, that Logan's performance strips away the sentimentality of her Broadway progenitor. Roy Plomley, reviewing the London album, thought it immensely preferable to the Broadway version, partly because 'Sally Logan lacks the coy mannerisms of New York's Anna Maria Alberghetti'.[4] It was, however, the puppets and Harris's 'performance of wistful delight' that possibly won the day.[5] British critics thought little of Merrill's score. R. B. Marriott in The *Stage* was unequivocal.

> The story is very thin, even for a musical; there are no memorable songs; puppets are all very well and charming, but one expects something more as the highlight of a big musical show. The leading part of Lili [...] is without interest: negative, unchanging, tedious. And the sentiment is so mushy and messy that it makes you feel sick. [...] It does not add up to a worthwhile evening's entertainment for grown-ups, no matter how easy-going and light-hearted a mood they may be in.[6]

Marriott's bilious reaction was shared by the majority of his colleagues, as the review headlines made clear: 'Carnival is Delightful to Look at But *Slushy*' (*Stage*),[7] 'Sweet for kiddies or auntie – but not for me' (*Hendon Times*),[8] 'A Little Too Much Sugar' (*Manchester Saturday Chronicle*),[9] 'Horrible Henry Apart, This Is All Goo' (*Daily Mail*).[10] Herbert Kretzmer's notice was headed 'Yum?

30 As well as being the leading lady of *How to Succeed in Business Without Really Trying*, this publicity shot has Patricia Michael renovating the old Princes Theatre in preparation for its reopening as the Shaftesbury in 1963

It Didn't Ticky, Ticky in *My* Tum', a reference to the puppets' song 'Yum Ticky, Ticky, Tum, Tum'. For Kretzmer, *Carnival* 'must appal all but the most retarded adults. This American musical walks a tightrope like a spangled acrobat, and a dozen times totters off the wire into a candy-floss abyss of squirming whimsy.'[11] It meant nothing that the show had won the New York Critics' Award as best musical of the 1960–61 season: in London it was cast into the critical dustbin.

The best of the warm-hearted songs were sung by Logan: 'A Very Nice Man', 'Mira' (also known as 'Can You Imagine That?'), 'Yes My Heart' (in which she was joined by the male roustabouts), the show's romantic theme 'Love Makes the

World Go Round', and the rousing 'Beautiful Candy'. Perhaps if Tennent had played safer and induced Miss Alberghetti to make the journey (the *Daily Mail* reported that she was available and indignant not to have been asked),[12] perhaps if they had put Mr Champion up at the Savoy for a couple of weeks to ensure the original magic he had worked on the Broadway show was in place, *Carnival* might have fared better. As it was, Champion's work was replicated by his assistant Lucia Victor, unsuspecting British theatregoers were probably unaware that the show was based on a famous film, and there were no star names to bring audiences in. When the show closed, Logan went back to live with her parents in Glasgow, and subsequently established a popular singing duo act with her husband. Neither Logan, Maurel, Sands or Harris were ever again to star in a West End musical, but there was something touching in Champion beginning the show with a bare stage on which the carnival folk struck up their tent and paraphernalia, and having them remove everything before the orchestra struck up the final chords of 'Love Makes the World Go Round'. In just such a way did the British *Carnival* depart, as if it had barely existed.

If *Carnival* dripped with charm, the next entry threw it overboard. New York had kept Frank Loesser's bucolic idyll *Greenwillow* (1960) to itself – it was the only one of his Broadway musicals not to reach Britain – but there was the warmest of welcomes for his last, the already award-burdened ***How to Succeed in Business Without Really Trying*** (Shaftesbury Theatre,[13] 28 March 1963; 520), thoroughly deserving of its Pulitzer Prize, New York Drama Critics Circle and seven Tonys. An American *ironic* musical play, which took nothing seriously and never descended into the genuinely romantic or sentimental, was a rarity, although some of the way had been paved by *Bye Bye Birdie*, even if that show hadn't eschewed sentiment or romance. *How to* had not only the air, but the airs, of satire, of irreligiousness. Abe Burrows, Jack Weinstock and Willie Gilbert adapted Shepherd Mead's handbook of how to climb the greasy pole of business achievement, taking a swipe at absurdities that would have found a response anywhere in the capitalist world. Loesser's untiringly resourceful score displayed the clarity of his ideas, his identification of targets, all of them achieved with a bullseye, whether it was the institution of the 'Coffee Break' (here taking on a life-or-death importance in the daily round) or the professional etiquette around clerical staff, 'A Secretary is Not a Toy'. There was nothing unkind in *How to*'s relentless cynicism, and the characters, although at a remove from reality, were more than cardboard. How could one not be concerned at the fate of J. Pierpont Finch, a window-cleaner gazing in through the glass at World Wide Wickets, a mop in one hand and a copy of Mead's helpful guide to self-progress in the other.

American actors, though hardly known to the British public, were drafted in as leading men: Warren Berlinger as Finch, and Billy De Wolfe as J. B. Biggley, the President of WWW. Berlinger's only Broadway musical credit had been as the Little Boy in the 1946 *Annie Get Your Gun*, but he had recently made a Broadway success as the young hero of the comedy *Come Blow Your Horn*. Producer Cy Feuer's choice of Berlinger had to be sanctioned by Loesser. Meeting Berlinger, Loesser said, 'I want you to scream at the top of your voice, *Somebody is stabbing me in the balcony.*' The baffled Berlinger screamed as he had never screamed before, and was thus catapulted into musical theatre stardom, although his only subsequent Broadway musical was appropriately titled *A Broadway Musical*, a one-night 1978 fiasco. Meanwhile, Berlinger protested that he was 'dead scared about the music [...] I'm not really a singer at all and never wanted to be in the show anyway'.[14] The sedate De Wolfe had a more substantial pedigree, having played *John Murray Anderson's Almanac* in 1953 with Hermione Gingold, and *Ziegfeld Follies (of 1957)* with Beatrice Lillie. Joining the men was a small army of British actresses perfectly cast, not least Patricia Michael as Rosemary, incisively affirming her selfless support for the upwardly mobile husband she would one day marry in 'Happy to Keep His Dinner Warm'.

> At the audition, after I sang 'Everything's Coming Up Roses', it seemed that everyone suddenly surged up on stage with tremendous enthusiasm. Abe Burrows put his arm around me and yelled 'She *feels* like a Rosemary!' Then, since I was a blonde and they needed a brunette, I was hustled into a cab off to Wig Creations to be fitted with a brunette wig. Back onstage with my dark hair there was more bonhomie and laughter. 'Hey, she looks so different, maybe we should get her to sing again!'[15]

As the dumbest of secretaries Hedy La Rue, Eileen Gourlay had an outstanding moment with her aria 'Love from a Heart of Gold', and there was a sterling contribution from the granite-voice Josephine Blake. That *habitué* of so many British productions of American musicals of the period, Bernard Spear, played Mr Twimble in a company that included many names familiar to the genre. For once, the British players seemed able to bring a sharpness to the material that would not have disgraced New York.

Despite being directed by its Broadway director Abe Burrows, part author of its book, and retaining the choreography of Bob Fosse, an element of British amateurism had not been eradicated by the second night. *Theatre World* reported that 'Such a fast-paced show needs expert stage management, and the second-night performance was marred by several misjudgements of timing and lighting, throwing grit into the wheels of an otherwise smoothly running machine-precision musical'.[16] Beyond the theatre, two numbers achieved a measure of popularity. One was the evangelist eleven o'clock hymn 'Brotherhood of Man'. The other was 'I Believe in You', which Finch sang to his reflection in the male executive washroom mirror, and which the male chorus – washing its hands and gazing at itself in the same mirror – endorsed. There was a further irony in that the song, freed from its context, served as a romantic ballad. Britain's fine cast recording was supplemented by a cover studio edition involving Maggie Fitzgibbon as Rosemary, and Mary Preston as Hedy.

CARNIVAL

ORIGINAL LONDON CAST

mono

HIS MASTER'S VOICE

H. M. TENNENT LTD.
present DAVID MERRICK'S production

Carnival

SALLY LOGAN · SHIRLEY SANDS
MICHAEL MAUREL · BOB HARRIS
FRANCIS de WOLFF
and
JAMES MITCHELL
Music and Lyrics by BOB MERRILL
Book by MICHAEL STEWART
Based on Material by HELEN DEUTSCH
Musical Adviser CYRIL ORNADEL

Original New York Production Created
and Choreographed by
GOWER CHAMPION
Staged by LUCIA VICTOR

31 A substantial hit in New York, but the British casting of *Carnival* proved
disastrous, despite the importation of its Broadway second male lead,
and Sally Logan's only London musical appearance as Lili

On the Town (Prince of Wales Theatre, 30 May 1963; 53) had been a long time
coming. The show had opened on Broadway in 1944, turning into a movie five
years later, and an off-Broadway revival in 1959, but by 1963 musicals had moved
on, and the cracks in the show's structure appeared more obvious. Inspired by
Leonard Bernstein's ballet *Fancy Free*, conceived with Jerome Robbins, *On the
Town* fused substantial dance sequences with conventional musical comedy
elements. It had been the composer's Broadway debut, but its delayed arrival
in London meant that British audiences had already been offered *Wonderful
Town* (1955) and *Candide* (1959) and – the only Bernstein to achieve West End
success – *West Side Story* (1958). It was Comden and Green's book and lyrics
that turned Robbins' original into an all-singing, all-dancing Big Apple fairytale,
a genre that found no better practitioners than Comden and Green, who had
also played in the Broadway *On the Town*. The show was the first of the Comden
and Green canon to mythologise American culture and, specifically, New York,
as later they did with *Wonderful Town* and *Bells Are Ringing*. Within the space
of a single day, the play followed the adventures of three young American sailors,
Gabey, Chip and Ozzie, freed on shore leave in New York. The British sailors,
according to the *Daily Telegraph*, were 'long, lean and galvanically fit'.[17] Before
going back on board they have fallen in love with the ballet dancer Ivy (the
Miss Turnstiles of the moment), anthropologist Claire deLoon and taxi-driver
Hildegarde Esterhazy.

H. M. Tennent's production seemed solid. Joe Layton, who had directed the
off-Broadway revival, was brought over as director and choreographer, and
the settings, as in 1944, were by Oliver Smith. The original orchestrations by
Bernstein, Hershy Kay, Don Walker, Elliot Jacoby and Ted Royal were essential
to the authenticity, and in London the orchestra was recruited from some of
the finest players around. The casting was near perfection. Tennent hired
three American actors for the leads: as Ozzie, Elliott Gould, fresh from the
New York *I Can Get It for You Wholesale* which had closed December 1962; as
Gabey, Don McKay, the original Tony for the London *West Side Story*, and, as
Chip Offenbloch, Franklin Kiser who the following year would have a lead in
the Broadway *Ben Franklin in Paris*. Gillian Lewis, whose only other West End
musical had been Julian Slade's *Free as Air* in 1957, was unexpectedly ideal as
the getting-carried-away Claire. She would have been an asset to many other
musicals, but was never used. As Hildy, the Martha-Raye-like big-voiced Carol
Arthur excelled, although her subsequent Broadway career in musicals was
muted, consisting of supporting roles in *High Spirits* (1964) and the 1980 revival
of *The Music Man*. The American Andrea Jaffe's Ivy was much praised, as was
Elspeth March's comic turn as the singing-teacher Madame Dilly. This was an
impressive collection of talent, and there was critical praise, especially for Lewis,
Arthur and Jaffe, but no producers seemed interested in helping them build
musical theatre careers.[18]

So far as the British critics were concerned, the show was dead on arrival.

'In two words: too late' explained the *Daily Mail*.[19] The production exposed the elements, dance, drama and song, and a lack of fusion was noted. Now, 'somehow the Cinderella motif of the twenty four hours slipping away fails to register until the very last parting; somehow the energy expended is out of all proportion to the effect achieved; somehow the sound of the pieces clicking together effortlessly together is missing'.[20] For the *Guardian*, there was 'no disturbing fury'.[21] 'The score is pleasant,' wrote J. C. Trewin, 'but through most of the night I had an uncomfortable feeling that the ball was over, the garlands dead. Even the ballets are tame.'[22] The *Daily Telegraph* predicted a long run, but it was Milton Shulman's prophesy that proved correct: '*On the Town* suffers from the fact that we have already seen musicals like *Pal Joey*, *Guys and Dolls* and *West Side Story* that leave it light years behind. I cannot see why anyone should want to catch up with it in 1963.'[23]

The London cast got to make a recording before early time was called; the result is the most convincing souvenir of *On the Town*. McKay's 'I'm So Lucky to Be Me' has a true theatrical fire to it, as does his chorus. There are definitive versions of 'I Can Cook Too' (done to a turn and at the appropriate tempo, unlike Tyne Daly's garbled rendering on a later studio recording, and with exemplary attack from Arthur) and, sans sentimentality, the 'parting' song 'Some Other Time'. A feeble revival by English National Opera in 2004 had an unimpressive cast, ramshackle sets and everything about it dull, brightened only by Sylvia Syms' non-singing turn as Madame Dilly. There was little evidence that anyone involved understood the first thing about Broadway musicals. Greeted by many as manna from Heaven, the cheapskate production emphasised the play's disparate parts, none of them well delivered, and cobbled together in Jude Kelly's ungainly direction. Time, anyway, had dimmed the appeal of *On the Town*, once distinguished by the daring medley of its elements, but now showing the joins. Compared to the ENO's revival, the Prince of Wales' production was a miracle of taste and casting.

It was four months later when the next Broadway entry opened in London. Less a musical than a comedy with songs, it was as its opening number declared a 'Comedy Tonight', ***A Funny Thing Happened on the Way to the Forum*** (Strand Theatre, 3 October 1963; 762). One of Britain's best-loved comedians, Frankie Howerd, must be held principally responsible for its West End success; good as was his supporting cast of subsidiary comics, it was Howerd who gave it potency. On the evidence of his performance in the 1966 film, Broadway's Zero Mostel would possibly have appealed less to the British, who had a special relationship with Howerd. Howerd specialised in a sort of constant vulgar affront that the domestic audience relished, as the slave Pseudolus escorted his spectators through an ancient Rome made obscene by innuendo. By now British audiences (the few that had sat through it) had forgotten Howerd's only other appearance in a musical, the disastrous 1958 *Mister Venus*. Now a battalion of experienced comics supported Howerd in a show that was comedy over musical: Kenneth

Connor, sustained in the British memory by a string of roles in *Carry On* films, 'Monsewer' Eddie Gray from the Crazy Gang, Jon Pertwee and the veteran comedy actor Robertson Hare, whose career reached back to the Aldwych Theatre farces. In such company the rest of the 'straight' cast seemed incidental, but the supporting comics were themselves of minor importance beside the star. This, indeed, was one occasion in which the casting of a British player in an American musical ensured its success. For Milton Shulman, Howerd was 'deliciously funny [...] Whether he is playing noughts and crosses on the midriff of a statuesque brunette or announcing his powers as a soothsayer ("Silence! I am about to say the sooth"), there is a mad anarchy about his activities which are never less than hilarious.'[24] Transatlantic understanding had been enhanced by Howerd flying out to New York to watch Mostel in the Broadway production, and by the show's writers landing in Coventry and manfully sitting through Howerd in *Puss in Boots*.

The production, directed as it had been in New York by George Abbott, brought with it the accoutrements that had helped it to Broadway success, including settings and costumes by Tony Walton, and orchestration by Irwin Kostal and Sid Ramin. The book by Burt Shevelove and Larry Gelbart was extraordinarily loosely based on the plays of Plautus, over twenty of whose plays had survived into our own age. The theatre programme explained that 'In fact the traditional situations in them formed the basis for almost all subsequent stage humour.' Stephen Sondheim provided his first full score (lyrics and music), from which two of the numbers, 'Comedy Tonight' and 'Everybody Ought to Have a Maid', remain the most popular. The show set Howerd up for one of the greatest television successes of his career, playing Lurcio (in effect, the same character he had played in *A Funny Thing*) in *Up Pompeii!* When Howerd left the cast in May 1965, he handed over to a lesser British comic, Dave King, whose star was already deep in the descendant; by now King had all but retired from show-business and taken up dog-breeding. This was perilous recasting by Tennent, almost as if the management had a death wish. After a handful of performances King became ill, and for the last week of the run his understudy took over, but, as Howerd might have said, 'The end is nigh.' As a goodwill gesture Howerd returned to play the final night.

Twenty-three years after its initial success, the same production's sets and costumes were dusted off for a season at Chichester Festival Theatre and brought back to London with an older and not so agile Howerd. The Piccadilly Theatre revival offered a new troupe of supporting clowns, less felicitous than that of the original production. Howerd sat out some of the concerted numbers and would wander off stage during the finale. The notices varied from adulatory to putrid, and the production was turned out of the Piccadilly Theatre after only forty-nine performances. According to *Time Out* it was limp, tacky and dated. Nevertheless, people turning up to see the ageing comedian had probably made the effort to see him, not the show. It might almost have been

'An Evening with Frankie Howerd', at which audiences relished those moments when Howerd came out of context and took them into his confidence, as he did in his curtain speech at the end of the play: 'In the words of Cleopatra to Mark Antony – if you've enjoyed it, tell your friends'. Desmond Barrit was a much-praised Pseudolus in a National Theatre revival in July 2004, playing in repertory.

 On the Town had taken almost twenty years to get to London, a hold-up *en route* that had cost it dear. Also delayed on voyage was ***The Boys from Syracuse*** (Theatre Royal, Drury Lane, 7 November 1963; 100), a disastrous exercise made the more obvious because it followed on the heels of the Lane's *My Fair Lady* which had closed in October after 2,281 performances. New York had seen Rodgers and Hart's Shakespearean musical in 1938, but the London production had to wait on the off-Broadway revival that had opened in April 1963, directed by Christopher Hewett. One of the mistakes was to select the Lane for the London restaging; of all the West End theatres this was probably the least suitable for what was essentially a modest affair. Even those off-Broadway shows that sensibly put themselves into small London houses, *The Fantasticks* at the Apollo, *Little Mary Sunshine* at the Comedy and *All in Love* at the May Fair, signally failed, and *The Boys from Syracuse* showed once again how much London could have done with a fringe theatre of its own. Shakespeare *per se* was not something to put audiences off: neither *Kiss Me, Kate* or *West Side Story* or, later, *Two Gentleman of Verona*, found him a disadvantage, and even off-shoots like *Your Own Thing* had a following, and there seemed no reason why *The Comedy of Errors* should not be a sound basis for another successful musical.[25] Only two lines of the play were retained in George Abbott's adaptation – 'The venom clamours of a jealous woman / Poisons more deadly than a mad dog's tooth' – but the British critics were left unimpressed by the script with its antique quips. The *Tatler* noted 'the abysmal level of the humour'.[26] When the curtain fell on the opening night, there was tepid applause, and the review headlines left no doubt: 'The moral is plain – never revive a musical' (*Daily Mail*), 'U.S. musical that drags drearily' (*Daily Telegraph*), 'One-Laugh Evening' (*Tatler*). For Bernard Levin it was 'the loudest, crudest, hammiest parade of mugging, grimacing, camping, nudging, yelling and falling down [...] that has been seen at Drury Lane since Sweet Nell was an orange seller'.[27]

 Rodgers, who was in London attending rehearsals, was asked if he was contemplating a collaboration with Lionel Bart. He replied 'My next partner must bring ideas and high ability with him, not just friendship.'[28] Two days later, after the critical drubbing his *The Boys from Syracuse* had received, the *Daily Mail* reported 'Music man Rodgers is angry with British theatre critics.' Rodgers was unaffected.

> I don't give a damn any more. I have never had a good notice in London since *Oklahoma!* – and I've never had a failure here. *Carousel* got a bad

press. They almost seemed to be trying to take back the good notices they gave *Oklahoma!* I would like to emphasise it's not the people who are anti-American. It's the Press.[29]

The Boys from Syracuse came from an earlier age, but more sympathetic handling of the London production may have had a happier result. For the comedian Bob Monkhouse it was his first musical (if you didn't count his 1959 *Aladdin*), playing Antipholus of Syracuse (his twin was played by the more musically experienced Denis Quilley), but the experiment was unrepeated. *The Times* thought 'he plays with a bloodless charm which fits the pantomime-like character of the show, but fails to raise him into a star position'.[30] Most pleasure was found watching its leading ladies, including Paula Hendrix as Luciana, and a sassy Courtesan in the American Pat Turner with her 'Oh Diogenes!'. Maggie Fitzgibbon, in Martha Raye mode, had the funniest numbers in 'What Can You Do with a Man?' and 'He and She' (both duets); not without reason did B. A. Young remember Fitzgibbon's 'brassy lungs',[31] and Levin wished she would quieten down by about 80%. The other female star was Lynn Kennington, who had been discovered by Jerome Whyte and put into a small role in *The Sound of Music. The Boys from Syracuse* didn't promote anyone to greatness, although it did provide an interesting cast recording, where, divorced from the stage proceedings, everything seems satisfactory, and the glories of the score reveal themselves. Perhaps the supposedly sophisticated atmosphere of Lerner and Loewe's *Pygmalion* musical had so permeated the Lane that the Syracuse boys had no place there in 1963. The score can hardly be blamed: its brilliant love songs (Kennington singing 'Falling in Love with Love' in a style at once meaty and swooping; Quilley in the disarmingly despondent 'The Shortest Day of the Year'; 'This Can't Be Love' and Monkhouse and Hendrix duetting in the lamenting romance of 'You Have Cast Your Shadow On the Sea') set among strongly characterful point numbers, topped by Hugh Martin's arrangement of 'Sing For Your Supper', trioed by Kennington, Hendrix and Fitzgibbon. Ultimately, the 1963 critics were out of sympathy with Rodgers when aligned with Hart, and the long residency of the sedate Lerner and Loewe at the Lane made the successor appear a vulgar intruder.

The American Indian Pocahontas arrived in London in 1616, when she was treated as a superstar because she had saved the life of the English Captain John Smith, who had been sent to North America to establish the British colony of Virginia. Subsequently, Pocahontas became a Christian, marrying the puritanical John Rolfe. In 1617, the year of her death, she was received at court. 350 years later, her name was once more heard in London. An American musical that chose not to brave Broadway, **Pocahontas** (Lyric Theatre, 14 November 1963; 12) was Kurt Goell's only musical, all book, music and lyrics of it. The *Stage* was unimpressed with all three. The book 'trundles along with all the sogginess of an uninspired pantomime libretto. The lyrics match the book more or less perfectly, and when the music is not vaguely reminiscent of something else it is largely forgettable.'[32] One of the love songs proclaimed 'I love you so, need you so, I'll cherish you and heed you so.'

At least Goell knew his subject, having written a book about it, along with a mildly successful pop song 'Near You'. Producer Stephen Mitchell took up Goell's property and lined up a strong production team: Carl Toms as designer, lighting by Michael Northen, orchestration by Peter Knight and Ken Thorne, the experienced West End musical director Philip Martell and director Michael Manuel. The ace in Mitchell's pack was his American star, Anita Gillette, already seen on Broadway in *Carnival*, *All American* and *Mr President*. Terence Cooper, whose West End leads were mostly in American musicals (*Where's Charley?*, *The Fantasticks*, *Little Mary Sunshine*), was cast as Smith, and Franklin Fox as Rolfe. The show opened as *The Princess Pocahontas* at Glasgow in October to an insipid reception. By the time the show reached London, Fox had gone, and Cooper had taken on the extra role of Rolfe. Toms' name as designer was sidelined to the minor credits in the London programme, where he was held to be responsible only for the Virginia settings. This may explain why more perceptive members of the audience noted that the shaky backcloths showed London buildings that had not existed in the mid-seventeenth century. W. A. Darlington detected 'a complete lack of sophistication',[33] while Bernard Levin thought 'no show more preposterously unsuited for a professional stage has been seen on one for years [...] it has the feeblest words, the emptiest music and the shoddiest scenery that can ever have come together in a ghastly congruence'.[34] Nevertheless, the *Guardian* considered the story had 'the making of a good musical. This Mr. Goell has not written.'[35] As the hapless princess, Gillette was absolved of blame – *The Times* thought her 'fizzingly impetuous'[36] – but it was her only West End endeavour, and the folly of *Pocahontas* was set aside.

Richard Rodgers was back, unencumbered by a lyricist, for **No Strings** (Her Majesty's Theatre, 30 December 1963; 151), his first effort without Hammerstein, for which he wrote both the music and words of the score. This was little more than conventional and highly competent Rodgers, but the musical itself was probably the first of the 1960s imports to strike out in new directions. The title had resonances. The orchestra had no strings (although the recording borrows a harp), the scenery was moved about by the cast (no 'strings' pulling it into place), and the story itself was about a 'no strings' love affair. Now, Rodgers was free of the strings tying him to Hammerstein and Hart, although the lyrics of *No Strings* tend to the Hammerstein school. The title suggested the show's form and reason for being, from the first beguiling number, 'The Sweetest Sounds', but the sweetness had its bitters, with no happy ending. Here is the collision of two definitive cultures – white (the novelist David Jordan) and black (the model Barbara Woodruff) – told through a chamber work, a handful of characters, no singing chorus, only dancers. The show's musicians provided other on-stage characters, with the leading lady's opening solo backed by wind players strolling behind her. The score has more than its fair share of duets for its two lovers, all except one of them reflective: 'The Sweetest Sounds', 'Nobody Told Me', 'Look No Further' and 'No Strings'; the exception, in lighter mood, is 'Maine'. Left to his own devices, Rodgers equips the show with some of the quietest of his music, in a score that deserves to be better known. For some the mechanics of the 'no strings' concept got into the weave of the piece in the wrong way. To W. A. Darlington it seemed a restless occasion, the effect of which 'is to dehumanise the people of the story and make puppets of flesh',[37] but others noticed a freshness of style and treatment.

Richard Kiley and Diahann Carroll had won plaudits in Joe Layton's Broadway production, reproduced and choreographed for the West End by Wakefield Poole, and 'supervised' by Jerome Whyte. In London, theatregoers got Art Lund, who had established a West End presence in *The Most Happy Fella*, and Beverly Todd, who for a time had played Barbara on Broadway. Lund yielded nothing in masculinity to Kiley, and if you preferred your men of the world (on this unlikely occasion, it seemed, a Pulitzer Prize winning writer) weather-beaten and sounding as if they would be good on a horse, then Lund excelled. Where Kiley had a metallic quality, Lund offered tough tenderness, a kisser with stubble, but *The Times* thought him 'a somewhat blockish lover',[38] described on stage by another of the characters as a 'Eurobum', and J. W. Lambert thought him a 'marzipan Hemingway'.[39] Much attention had been focused on Carroll, for whom Rodgers had written the show, but although Todd attracted some good notices ('the most bewitching of wide-mouthed, bright-eyed self-possessed waifs'[40] according to J. W. Lambert, but *The Times* considered 'her appearance more remarkable than her performance',[41] contradicted by Bernard Levin who found her 'beautiful and vigorous')[42] she failed to break into the public consciousness, and London would never see her again. For *Theatre World*

> Of the cast, the ladies come off best. Beverly Todd, though not a powerful singer, gives a remarkably poignant acting performance, cleverly suggesting the mental upheaval which must follow when a girl from an underprivileged background suddenly finds herself the toast of Paris. Marti Stevens also makes a good impression as the strident young millionairess surrounded by a bevy of fortune-hunting males. And Hy Hazell, in what is for her a typical role, and Erica Rogers take their chances.[43]

Interesting and melodic and inventive as *No Strings* was, it wasn't taken up, and has been little heard of since. If Hammerstein had lived to make this his final collaboration with Rodgers, would British audiences have flocked? New writing partnerships would introduce their works to London through the rest of the 1960s, but none established themselves with anything like the household quality of Rodgers and Hammerstein.

The British musical had two successes, **Half a Sixpence** adapted from H. G. Wells' novel *Kipps* as a vehicle for Tommy Steele, and **Pickwick**, taken from

Dickens' *Pickwick Papers* and fronted by Harry Secombe as the egg-shaped hero. Both would go on to Broadway. *Half a Sixpence* lingered; *Pickwick* was sent home. Managements and writers began to think that adapting well-known books and plays might yet be the salvation of the British musical. ***Virtue in Danger*** was a Restoration romp by James Bernard and Paul Dehn, superior to the Mermaid Theatre's previous musical *Lock Up Your Daughters*, of which it was a worthier cousin. Peter Greenwell and Peter Wildeblood's successor to *The Crooked Mile*, ***House of Cards***, was hustled quickly into the West End and speedily ejected. Sneaking into the frame was ***The Man in the Moon***, mounted at the Palladium as a 'space-age musical' in place of the usual Christmas pantomime. In ***Enrico***, revue writers Peter Myers and Ronald Cass turned out an English version of an Italian musical for no discernable reason.

1963 Broadway Exports

She Loves Me (301) and ***110 in the Shade*** (330).

1963 Broadway Only

Sophie (8) had the feisty Libi Staiger's red-hot momma version of Sophie Tucker, but was otherwise reckoned inferior. There was a major disappointment in Judy Holliday's new vehicle, ***Hot Spot*** (43), with music by Mary Rodgers, and even Mary Martin could not save from a speedy death ***Jennie*** (82), with its songs by Arthur Schwartz and Howard Dietz. ***Here's Love*** (338), Meredith Willson at his most whimsical, proved a success despite its obvious deficiencies, while Vivien Leigh made it to Broadway with her only musical ***Tovarich*** (264). Noel Coward's operetta ***The Girl Who Came to Supper*** (112) marked the end of his career in musicals. It found little favour and was never returned to Britain where it properly belonged. There was a failed attempt by Rick Besoyan, author of the long-running *Little Mary Sunshine*, at another pastiche, ***The Student Gypsy*** (16).

32 A gentle chamber work, *She Loves Me* never really established itself as a West End success despite two attractive productions

1964

All In Love
She Loves Me
Camelot
High Spirits
Little Me

B Y THE MID-1960S the British musical was in a parlous state, with Lionel Bart's career fizzling out, as had the reputation of most of the British composers and writers who had come up through the 1950s. American musicals still comprised an industry, and new names were establishing reputations through their transfers to London: Jerry Bock and Sheldon Harnick, Charles Strouse and Lee Adams, Cy Coleman, Jerry Herman, Tom Jones and Harvey Schmidt, at a time when the West End had almost nobody of note coming through the ranks. Older hands such as Jule Styne still provided first-rate work. Not surprisingly, the old-established might come up with essentially old-fashioned shows, of which *Funny Girl* was an example, a sturdy no-nonsense star vehicle, and Lerner and Loewe may have receded further into operetta with *Camelot*, but the spirit of the American product was not diminished but in one of its last fine floods.

Of the five New York offerings of 1964, only **All in Love** (May Fair Theatre, 16 March 1964; 22) came from off-Broadway. The British cast must have wondered what it had done to deserve the May Fair Theatre, in the bowels of a smart London hotel. The adaptation of Richard Brinsley Sheridan's *The Rivals* had a sprightly but unremarkable score, occasionally inventive (as in the chorally diverting 'Why Wives?'), but Sheridan's comedy was not improved by the interruption of songs accompanied by harp, clavichord and vibraphone. Some capable British actors were engaged: Peter Gilmore, Ronnie Barker (yet to be a major star), James Fox (ditto), and ex-D'Oyly Carte comedian Peter Pratt as the leading men, with the magnificently grumpy Gwen Nelson as Mrs Malaprop, jazz singer Annie Ross as Lucy, and Mary Millar as Lydia Languish. Some fluidity was ensured by the choreographer Douglas Squires doubling as director, but the show made no impact, and served as a warning about transferring such a peripheral work, which sounded as much like a so-so British musical as a so-so American musical. Adaptations of classical works were at this time proving popular with producers of British musicals, if not audiences. The early 1960s offered many home-grown shows worked up from plays and novels: Shakespeare (*The Three Caskets*), Fielding (*Lock Up Your Daughters*), Thackeray (*Vanity Fair*), Wells (*Half a Sixpence*), Ostrovsky (*House of Cards*), Dickens (*Oliver!* and *Pickwick*), Vanbrugh (*Virtue in Danger*) and Barrie (*Our Man Crichton*) among them. Only a few were conspicuously successful, but *All in Love* was not of their number. Bernard Levin agreed that 'It's unrivalled! It's dreadful, lumpish, dull, flat [...] and most of the cast would not make buskers.'[1] Philip Hope-Wallace reported 'pitiable goings-on [...] impeded by alleged songs and lyrics of such extreme poverty of invention and wit',[2] while Eric Shorter witnessed a 'mediocre travesty'.[3] For the *Stage* R. B. Marriott thought it 'brash, blustering and thoroughly inept, and kills the glorious comedy of the play. Surprise, the effect of situation and a comic sense of character relationship and idiosyncrasy are all badly managed.'[4]

Refinement, intelligence and craftsmanship arrived with **She Loves Me** (Lyric Theatre, 29 April 1964; 189) in its original Broadway package with director Harold Prince and choreographer Carol Haney, newly invigorated by an all-British cast. Sheldon Harnick and Jerry Bock had been unlucky with their first British transfer *Fiorello!* and their *Tenderloin* had stayed at home. Joe Masteroff's book was based on the Hungarian Miklos Laszlo's 1937 play *Parfumerie*, which Hollywood had already plundered for two movies, the Ernst Lubitsch *The Shop Around the Corner* and the Judy Garland feature *In the Good Old Summertime*. In one way and another, by 1964 the piece had been around for a long time. A moderate success in New York, the musical presented as neither fish nor fowl, with a sort of innate modesty about it. There was no chorus to speak of, the non-parted ensemble having only one musical number, no set-pieces, no spectacle, and in London (despite what the cast may have thought) no stars. Here was a work that stayed close to its characters, exploring each of them sympathetically, with most of the songs working as characterful vignettes.

At its heart is Maraczek's Parfumerie in Budapest 1934, where two of the assistants, Georg Nowack (Gary Raymond) and Amalia Balash (Anne Rogers), do not care for one another. Each has a penpal. The penpals arrange to meet. Georg cannot wait to at last see his beloved correspondent at the Café Imperial ('Tonight at Eight'), while Amalia is beside herself with anxiety as to whether her unknown admirer will be disappointed in her ('Will He Like Me?'). When Georg arrives at the Imperial he recognises Amalia waiting for him at her table but departs without revealing himself, leaving Amalia believing her 'Dear Friend' has stood her up. The realisation that Georg has all along been her 'Dear Friend' is stored for the very final moments before curtain-fall. In a subsidiary plot, Ilona Ritter (Rita Moreno), plaything of the lecherous shop employee Steven Kodaly (Gary Miller), discovers a better life and a new man after 'A Trip to the Library'.

The story is a simplicity, and sweetness and light might have overcome it without Bock and Harnick's expert handling. They showed interest even in the minor characters, as when the fledgling errand-boy Arpad Laszlo begs Mr Maraczek to 'Try Me' as a shop assistant. Without straining, there was an air of goulash about it, and here and there spasms of czardas, notably in Amalia's Act Two aria 'Vanilla Ice Cream' when, visited on her sick bed by the detested Georg, she begins to awaken to his charms. Above all, the show stayed true to its sense of proportion, never misleading the audience into thinking these were remarkable or particularly interesting people. An almost silent ensemble broke into song only once in 'Twelve Days to Christmas', in which increasingly frenetic shoppers invaded the store for seasonal gifts. Literate and resourceful as it was, *She Loves Me* stayed at the Lyric for only six months. Anne Rogers was a good choice for Amalia, but she would find it difficult to capitalise on her reputation as Julie Andrews' successor in *My Fair Lady*, despite a career that now and again returned to America. Nyree Dawn Porter, signed up as Ilona, had to withdraw through illness before the opening, and was replaced by the lesser known Moreno, who would be followed by Amanda Barrie. There was also the advantage of an appealing Georg in Gary Raymond. A 1994 London revival was given an extra frisson by casting Ruthie Henshall and John Gordon-Sinclair as the two lovers, but the smallness of the piece was probably even more of a handicap to its popularity than it had been thirty years before. Neatly done as it was, Gordon-Sinclair seemed overparted, and Henshall had a coolness that made one care little about Amalia's fate.

The inherent difficulties of the piece had been noted by the British critics in 1964. Levin thought it 'better than some but worse than most. Though not often actively bad, it fails for its lack of any real distinction.' Further, 'Without the music to bolster up the lack of distinction elsewhere, and with the sugar-content dangerously high, there is little to make an evening. Which is a pity, because the intentions are good.'[5] Eric Shorter was no more impressed, noting that it 'harks back to the thirties with all the insipid authenticity of a revival [...] the general effect, though gay and pleasantly innocuous, remains vapid and distinctly patchy.'[6] Most of this was in stark contrast to Broadway's welcoming reviews. Public dissatisfaction was voiced in a letter to the *Stage*: 'The West End has no need of these current third-rate shows. Broadway writers have sunk to what must be an all-time low in the quality of their musicals. There has not been an American musical with a decent score in London since Rodgers and Hammerstein's *The Sound of Music*.'[7]

In the summer, Lerner and Loewe returned to London with their resplendently attired **Camelot** (Theatre Royal, Drury Lane, 19 August 1964; 518). Following the Broadway production a company headed by British actor Paul Daneman had embarked on a long-running Australian edition, but only after three and a half years did Jack Hylton's new production premiere in London. Critical reaction in New York had been lukewarm, with considerable praise for the songs, especially two ballads which would achieve popularity in Britain, 'How to Handle a Woman' and 'If Ever I Would Leave You', but there were reservations about Lerner's libretto, adapted from the T. H. White novel *The Once and Future King*. The king being Britain's own legendary Arthur, *Camelot* seemed by rights to belong to the British rather than the Americans. Here, Lerner had to concoct dialogue, whereas for *My Fair Lady* he had enjoyed the luxury of lifting much of it from Shaw's unimprovable original. Broadway had earlier visited the King Arthur story in Rodgers and Hart's *A Connecticut Yankee*

(1927), revised and restaged in 1943, redolent of Hart's irreligious wit. Nothing so scurrilous would contaminate *Camelot*, in effect the most refined operetta, lacking the zest of some of the team's earlier works. Lush and mightily romantic in tone, there was none of the bite that had punctuated *My Fair Lady*. By the time the show manifested in London, it had assumed some sort of mythological status in America through the assassination of President Kennedy in November 1963, although how much this resonated with potential patrons of the British production is unclear.

R. B. Marriott found it 'very much better than one had learned to expect, worse than one would have thought' and noted 'a lack of music, or at any rate of music that has a striking effect; the book is often stiff and dull; there is some dreadful dialogue. Yet in a curious and surprising way the whole thing works.'[8] The review headlines were not encouraging: 'Camelot is gorgeous but uncertain' (*Daily Telegraph*);[9] 'Arthurian Pomp and Little Else' (*The Times*);[10] 'Catastrophe! Wrong Show in the Wrong Place at the Wrong Time' (*Daily Mail*).[11] To Levin the play was 'a broken-backed mess' which should have been offered as a Christmas show at the Palladium; it was, in fact 'a rather inferior Robert Nesbitt pantomime'.[12] *The Times* acknowledged that it outdid in opulence anything that had been seen in London for years, but 'the rest of the production is an almost total blank'. For the length of its three and a quarter hours it was 'best understood as a product of America's taste for British pageantry. And if that is the case, there seems little enough point in showing it over here.'[13]

In fact, British critical opinion was married to the American reviews. Producer Jack Hylton dismissed the critics, insisting that 'This is a good entertainment show, and a grand night out for the public. It's not the Old Vic. What do critics expect?'[14] As he decamped to his French home Loewe was equally unimpressed, telling the *Daily Mail* that he thought the London production better than the original, and that he found the London papers' verdict 'ununderstandable'.[15] The day after the first night its leading man Laurence Harvey bought himself a £11,000 Rolls Royce, telling the press that *Camelot* was 'just a lovely fantasy [...] We all know there aren't any virgins left.'[16] It appears that Harvey, Hylton and Loewe were not too concerned about the musical as an art form.

Hylton's casting was odd but very Hylton. As Arthur, Harvey came with a whiff of hell-raising hedonism, not much theatrical clout and no reputation in musicals. The film critic David Shipman remarked that 'Laurence Harvey's career should be an inspiration to all budding actors: he has demonstrated conclusively that it is possible to succeed without managing to evoke the least audience interest or sympathy – and to go on succeeding despite unanimous critical antipathy and overwhelming public apathy.'[17] Harvey had been born in Lithuania as Zvi Mosheh (Hirsh) Skikne, although he claimed to be Larushka Mischa Skikne. His only previous brush with musicals had been in the resolutely *non*-musical film of *Expresso Bongo*, in which he cluelessly played the role created on stage by Paul Scofield. His leading lady for *Camelot* was the Jack

Hylton discovery and favourite Elizabeth Larner. Bernard Levin wrote that she 'raises insipidity to the status of a new art form'.[18] Hylton probably never considered casting the British Patricia Bredin who had taken over from Julie Andrews in the Broadway production two years earlier. Harvey and Larner were substitutes for Broadway's stellar pairing of Richard Burton and Julie Andrews. Where was the allure or stature of the original New York stars? Nevertheless, in *Theatre World* Mawby Green was impressed: 'Laurence Harvey and Elizabeth Larner transform stock sentiments into something personal and momentarily believable. In Vancouver, the [different] leads behaved like two ex-movie stars, not on speaking terms, but forced to make a personal appearance on the same bill.'[19]

Surprisingly, Harold Hobson declared Harvey's performance one of the greatest he had witnessed. How deceptive theatre can be! The London cast recording reveals Harvey's laboured attempt to sound like Burton, and Harvey's placing of the lyrics is unatural. The almost unknown Barry Kent was hired as Lancelot. The role had propelled a *Broadway* unknown, Robert Goulet, to stardom, but Kent subsequently headed for oblivion via a leading but small role in *Mame*. Elsewhere the casting was more interesting: moon-faced Miles Malleson as Merlin, the revue artiste and dancer Moyra Fraser as Morgan LeFay and minor British comic Cardew Robinson as a chinless King Pellinore, given some excruciating 'modern' gags. Interpolating such material into an Arthurian setting recalled a much earlier age of musical comedy, and seemed unworthy of the creators of *My Fair Lady*, but Lerner's lyrics happily verged away from any period authenticity. (Would Arthur have understood the feeling of being 'blue'?) Could it be that Lerner struggled with majesty? He means to make Arthur sound stately and possessing something above human mettle, but, certainly in Harvey's hands, the effect is forced, and when Arthur intones 'How to Handle a Woman' he is diminished by the trite lyric. Stripped of its technical glamour, *Camelot* seems inferior to *Paint Your Wagon*, *Brigadoon* and *My Fair Lady*, despite recalling moments of all three.

The West End version was not a reproduction of the Broadway original. During the New York run Lerner was reported as having made considerable revisions to the much criticised script, and it was reported that more alterations were made for London, but much of the piece remained heavy-going, as if dragged down by the heavily brocaded costumes. At the Lane there was a predictably balletic quality to the direction and choreography of Robert Helpmann, and sumptuous new costumes and sets by John Truscott who had decorated the Australian production. *Camelot* took the Lane back to its reputation for unbridled operetta spectacle. Audiences attended its glamorous presence until November 1965, a creditable run although nothing like the two-year stay claimed by Lerner and Loewe's biographer.[20] When Harvey left the production at the end of his six-month contract, Paul Daneman took over, remaining until the close of the show, eventually playing the role for three months longer than Harvey. In 1982 there was a revival with Richard Harris and Fiona Fullerton, but the lasting memory of *Camelot* is of an over-iced cake.

Although Noel Coward's name was spread all over **High Spirits** (Savoy Theatre, 3 November 1964; 94), adapted from his comedy *Blithe Spirit*, he had no hand in its transformation into a musical; nevertheless the legend 'The production supervised by Noel Coward' hung over it. The idea of musicalising the play seemed promising, and the sunny songs by Hugh Martin and Timothy Gray were friendly but uninspiring. In America, the central role of Madame Arcati had been taken and overtaken by the irrepressible Beatrice Lillie. Eric Johns wrote

> She, rather than the show, had been the success, so by the time it reached London Cicely Courtneidge was presented with a part which had been turned into a vehicle for Beatrice Lillie [or, perhaps more correctly, which Lillie had turned into a vehicle for herself] which did not happen to work for anyone else. Cis was devastated at rehearsal, but it was too late to turn back. She had expected a part not unlike Margaret Rutherford's creation,[21] but who could be further from Dame Margaret than Bea Lillie?[22]

The role had been cranked up for Lillie: now, far off beam from the original play, Arcati was the proprietress of a modern coffee club peopled by all manner of young people eager to benefit from her spiritual gifts. A séance was never far away. Courtneidge's performance delighted some and appalled others. The *Illustrated London News* insisted that she was

> the most professional of comediennes [...] In any song or dance she still comes tirelessly to the attack. Now whatever one may think of the material, or of Miss Courtneidge's special sense of comedy, one has to record that in such a libretto [...] her authors must be deeply grateful for her. This loyalty and attack are needed; the high spirits of the night are hers.[23]

Coward did not share this kindly appreciation of his elderly star's contribution. W. A. Darlington, usually a mild critic, wrote that 'the plot has been retained as a lumbering and creaking machine where before it was a beautiful vehicle with a load of laughter',[24] and that Courtneidge was 'admirable, but Mme. Arcati's character had been lengthened without being strengthened, and could not really bear the actress's weight'. Lillie's presence might have radically improved the show's chances in London. Swimming against the tide, Michael Thornton lambasted the critics for their demolition of the show, citing Courtneidge's as 'the most vigorously funny performance seen on the London stage for years and years'.[25] But Courtneidge had always been a matter of taste, and her style of comedy was becoming unfashionable by the mid-1960s.

The Condomines were played by the excellent Denis Quilley and Jan Waters, 'Coppernob' to Coward, who wrote in praise of her in his diaries, and who regularly called in at her dressing-room, collapsing on her *chaise-longue* and declaring on each occasion 'Give me a glass of *acqua minerale*, and keep the marauding hordes from the door!' Quilley and Waters had the best sentimental song of the night in 'If I Gave You'. Fenella Fielding had been cast as the ghostly Elvira, but didn't get on with Coward. 'Fenella was absolutely perfect for the part,' Waters recalls. 'They didn't realise that if you cast Fenella Fielding you get Fenella Fielding.' At the flying rehearsal, the technical team mistimed Fielding's landing, causing her to smack into one of the stage towers. This seems to have been used as the excuse to replace her. She explained to the press that there was nothing seriously wrong with her except a general malaise (a bad cold, according to Waters) and a pulled muscle caused by the on-stage flying. The following morning the principals were informed that her role was being taken over by the American Marti Stevens. Miss Stevens arrived suspiciously word perfect at rehearsals.

Although the British *High Spirits* coincided with a restirring of interest in Coward's work, it collided with a well received revival of his play *Hay Fever* at the National Theatre, beside which the musical appeared small fry. Matters were not helped by having Coward's partner Graham Payn share the directing with Gray under the eagle Coward eye. It was an occasion riven by internal politics. The production was redressed for London by Hutchinson Scott, whose innovations included a hat for Courtneidge that resembled a demented waste-paper basket. Despite desperate efforts to liven things up with gyrating chorines and hysterically energetic chorus boys, notably in Arcati's entrance number 'The Bicycle Song', the first act closer 'Faster Than Sound' (flying by Kirby), and 'Something is Coming to Tea' with the chorus transformed into beatniks, *High Spirits* was quickly deflated. When the curtain fell on 23 January 1965 it left the production in the red, and marked the end of Courtneidge's long career in musicals, begun in her father's 1909 production of *The Arcadians*. Perhaps the verdict of the *Sunday Times* echoed in her mind: her last show had been 'grotesquely unfunny, acted with sledge-hammer clumsiness, and, with its immemorable music, it is an appalling bore'.[26] For Coward, there was a castigation of his original enthusiastic approval for the adaptation from Bernard Levin, for 'although I have not, in fact, liked any of Mr. Coward's post-war musicals very much, the worst of them was a thousand times better than this dreary waste, as pallid and nugatory as the ghostly make-up affected by the returning Elvira'.[27]

Waters' memory is of Courtneidge seeming 'very old. She'd be there in the wings at rehearsal dressed in a suit and hat. And lots of tears. I think one of the main problems was that she couldn't remember the lines.' In one scene Waters sat at a table, at which Courtneidge had to join her. On arrival, Courtneidge would move her chair to upstage Waters. ('I knew what she was up to. It didn't bother me. She was such a wonderful artist.') One night Courtneidge's chair leg got caught in the table-legs and she couldn't move it as she always did. 'It completely threw her. It had become so much of her routine, and she

33 One of the funniest American musicals to play London: *Little Me*

couldn't remember a word of the scene.' Courtneidge left the stage door after each performance dressed as if *en route* to a sophisticated cocktail party. She informed Waters that all respect for actors had been lost 'when Albert Finney walked out a stage door wearing a cloth cap'. Waters sent Coward a first night telegram: 'Hello West End, here we come'. Coward replied: 'Goodbye West End, there we went'.[28]

Little Me (Cambridge Theatre, 18 November 1964; 334) was the final funniest American musical of the 1960s. Its closest relative of the decade was *How to Succeed in Business Without Really Trying*, with which it shared irreverence, a sense of irony and refusal to take the human condition seriously. Such qualities were plain to see in Patrick Dennis' spoof 1961 autobiography of the self-obsessed Hollywood star Belle Poitrine. Neil Simon's adaptation of Dennis' book was skilful, and the score by Cy Coleman and Carolyn Leigh resourceful and amusing. Britain had not seen Coleman and Leigh's first collaboration, *Wildcat* (1960), a troubled vehicle for Lucille Ball; *Little Me* was altogether happier. At the Cambridge Theatre the New York direction by Cy Feuer and Bob Fosse (who doubled as choreographer) was reproduced by Merritt Thompson, ensuring that the Fosse style remained a critical component of the show.

The musical retained Dennis' original female star, now played by two actresses, the 'young' and the 'older'. Simon cleverly shifted the focus to her boy-friends and husbands and male associates, all played by one actor. On Broadway Sid Caesar headlined; in London, the popular comedian Bruce Forsyth was signed. Forsyth's only book musical brought him a personal success in a show that was critically welcomed, and it was his drawing power that helped the production to 334 performances, a run which, according to its producers, was only ended by a general West End slump. Philip Hope-Wallace detected that 'His touch is sure; there is a suggestion of Max Adrian about him, a memory of Ralph Lynn, too, and I felt that the mantle of Cyril Ritchard might at any moment fall upon his shoulders.'[29] A displeased voice among the generally rave notices was Michael Thornton, who thought it 'puerile American rubbish [...] unimaginably vulgar, boring, and banal burlesque', and that Forsyth had been forced into 'some sort of extension of Beat the Clock on *Sunday Night at the London Palladium*. Unhappily it is not. It is a three-hour travesty of brash schoolboy humour and instantly forgettable music'.[30] *The Times* disagreed: 'After a dismal series of musicals [presumably British as well as American] we have seen recently, it comes as a delightful shock to encounter one that is as logically built as a play and in which all the separate production elements support one another.'[31]

The producers bolstered their star with sound support, not least Eileen Gourlay as the younger Belle. Gourlay had been one of the joys of the previous year's *How to Succeed in Business Without Really Trying* as Hildy, a role created in New York by Virginia Martin, who had also been the Broadway Belle. Gourlay was excellent, whether wonderingly lost in innocence as she contemplated the impossibility of upward social mobility in 'At the Very Top of the Hill' (also

known as 'On the Other Side of the Tracks') or going emotionally over the top
in her Act Two aria 'Poor Little Hollywood Star'. It was a particular sadness that
after *Little Me* her talent was more or less ignored, and London saw no more
of her. As the older Belle, Avril Angers had a rare role in an American musical,
and at curtain fall had the only 'reality' song of the night, 'Here's to Us'. Swen
Swenson, who had won a Theatre World Award on Broadway for his featured
performance (notably in 'I've Got Your Number') was shipped to Britain and
given better billing than in New York. The critics picked up on this highlight,
'like early Astaire'.[32] The useful Bernard Spear, who seems never to have been
far from an American musical throughout the 1960s, turned up in a variety of
disguises.

In telling Belle's ridiculous story, *Little Me* took its audience on a madcap
journey from Belle's humble beginnings at the bottom of Highgate Hill to her
butlered existence at the very top, taking in France, the North Atlantic, Monte
Carlo and a Mitteleuropean principality via Belle's beloved, although not always
loving, Hollywood. Forsyth was brilliantly cast in the many roles that provided
a showcase for his singing, dancing and comedic skills, but the show was always
more than a vehicular device, with its absurdly heightened numbers, routines
and ideas. Listening to the American cast recording, one suspects that the
British would not have taken to Mr Caesar, who sounds flat-footed and less able.
A London revival in 1984 was built around the comedian Russ Abbot and ran
for the same number of performances as the Forsyth version. Both had out-run
Broadway's 257.

It was August by the time the first British musical, ***Instant Marriage***, opened.
A mongrel cross between a Brian Rix farce and a *Carry On* film (one of the
Carry On regulars, Joan Sims, was its leading lady); the level of achievement
was not high. Things improved with ***Maggie May***, the legendary Liverpool lady
of pleasure canonised in Lionel Bart's last successful musical. Rachel Roberts
was its husky star, succeeded by Georgia Brown (for whom the part had been
written) and Judith Bruce. Everything about ***Robert and Elizabeth*** seemed to
belong to an earlier age, as did its story of the love between Robert Browning
and Elizabeth Moulton-Barrett. Sandy Wilson's ***Divorce Me, Darling!***, successor
to *The Boy Friend*, brought the original show's characters back ten years on for a
pastiche of the 1930s. It must have seemed a good idea to make a musical of J. M.
Barrie's *The Admirable Crichton*, but ***Our Man Crichton*** laboured under several
difficulties. A Moral Re-Armament musical, ***Give a Dog a Bone***, came and went
for many a Christmas season.

1964 Broadway Exports

Hello, Dolly! (2,844), *Funny Girl* (1,348), *High Spirits* (375), *Fiddler on the Roof* (3,242) and *Golden Boy* (569).

1964 Broadway Only

Of the four major flops of the year three are long forgotten – *Café Crown* (3), *Something More!* or less (15), and the Italian *Rugantino* (28) by Giovannini and Garinei, three of whose musicals reached London – but one, *Anyone Can Whistle* (9) has passed into legend. The first score by Stephen Sondheim, it starred Angela Lansbury and Lee Remick. Most of the rest of the year's stay at homes were undistinguished: Bert Lahr in *Foxy* (72), an adaptation of Ben Jonson's *Volpone*, Carol Burnett in a lesser Comden-Green-Styne piece *Fade Out – Fade In* (271), the lively but vacuous *Bajour* (232) and the Buddy Hackett vehicle *I Had a Ball* (199). Robert Preston was the titular hero of *Ben Franklin in Paris* (215), but the score was ordinary. The stay-at-home with the longest run was *What Makes Sammy Run?* (540), a 'serious' musical about the Hollywood jungle headlined by the nightclub singer Steve Lawrence. It might have run longer had he not earned the reputation of regularly not bothering to turn up for the show.

1965

The Wayward Way
Hello, Dolly!

RATHER THAN ARRIVING in the West End early in the year, *The Wayward Way* (Vaudeville Theatre, 27 January 1965; 36) would have done better to utilise whatever festive spirit had been around two months earlier. Broadway had never seen it, but Los Angeles had seen rather a lot of it. The history of *The Wayward Way* is long, going back to the temperance melodrama that proliferated in Victorian England, offering such enticements as *The Fruit of the Cup*, *The Drunkard's Doom* and *Aunt Dinah's Pledge* in which the audience was urged to repudiate not only alcohol but tobacco. The degradation that would inevitably follow on unstopping a bottle pervaded Douglas Jerrold's *Fifteen Years of a Drunkard's Life* in which the hopelessly inebriated hero inadvertently kills his wife. In T. P. Taylor's 1828 play *The Bottle* a hapless working man loses his home, appears insensible by the side of his young child's coffin, in a drunken frenzy despatches his wife, and ends his life in an asylum. These would doubtless have been too strong meat for those creating an entertaining temperance musical, but *The Drunkard*, written by W. H. Smith and 'A Gentleman' and first seen in London and Boston in 1844, proved eminently suitable.[1] Almost a century after its premiere *The Drunkard* was presented at the Los Angeles Theater Mart in 1933, where it stayed for twenty years. In 1953 it was succeeded by its musical adaptation, *The Wayward Way*, the creation of Dan Eckley (then director of the St. Louis Municipal Opera), with music by Lorne Huycke and lyrics by Bill Howe. This played Los Angeles before shutting up in 1959, and six years later opened at the Lyric Theatre, Hammersmith in mid-November 1964 before transferring to the West End.

In the twentieth century Britain's acquaintance with melodrama had been at its height with the actor-manager Tod Slaughter, he of the evil giggle, overworked eyebrows, lecherous leer and corseted midriff. Slaughter was magnificently equipped for melodrama, although it has never been established whether he was acting badly or brilliantly. His barnstorming journeying around the lesser theatres of Britain was greeted with boos and hisses, while the pathetic heroines and heroes that had the misfortune to encounter him had more encouraging welcomes. Slaughter would have relished the role of the black-hearted Squire Cribbs in *The Wayward Way*, whose audiences were invited to make vocal contributions throughout the show. Eckley insisted that, 'The musical is played seriously, like the play was, and no matter how much the audience may join in, there is no ad-libbing on the stage. The production is firmly controlled, part of the impact being that it is *not* altered in any respect by the reactions of the audience.'

The 'serious'-ness was different to that with which Vida Hope had imbued

Sandy Wilson's 1920s pastiche *The Boy Friend*. Theatrical legend has it that Hope
and her cast never guyed the material (oh no?), but *The Wayward Way* selected
to send up the style of playing at every turn. W. A. Darlington complained that
'Instead of allowing the play's temperance message to come across, the actors
were making mock of it.' He also saw that the audience overplayed its part,
'was too quick on its cues and too noisy'.[2] *The Wayward Way* never hammered
on the door of musical immortality, but its songs were welcome stopping-off
points, and there was mild pleasure to be had from Cheryl Kennedy playing
the mad, Ophelia-like Agnes singing 'Why do they call me dotty when Agnes is
my name?', and Roberta D'Esti as the heroine in her New York garret emoting
the title song. John Gower offered a fruitier but less entertaining Cribbs than
Slaughter would have delivered, David Holliday was the burly hero Edward
Middleton, and Jim Dale made his London debut as the sparky William Dowton.
After the play was done Dale introduced the 'turns' performed by the company
in the 'Olio'.[3] It was all good fun, but audiences (all that booing and hissing and
cheering) probably had to work as hard as the cast, and when attendance quickly
fell away there seemed little reason for the cast to perform to silence. D'Esti
complained that Winston Churchill's death had undermined the show. Her
suggestion that the company should work on without payment was vetoed by
Equity.[4]

Jerry Herman was probably the only American composer between the
closing down of Rodgers and Hammerstein and the arrival of Stephen Sondheim
to write with such individualism that audiences recognised his work, even
if that recognition was largely subliminal. Rodgers and Hammerstein had
pursued a theme of cultural clash, but Herman's manifesto was to write musicals
dominated by their leading lady, and to compose take-away songs. Remove the
feminine core of *Hello, Dolly!* or *Mame* or *Dear World* and too much of the fabric
of Herman's work is removed. There was nothing new in this; Herman's shows,
up to a point, are girlie shows, but these girlies are well advanced in years, and
not a dumb one among them. Maturity and feminine wile rather than feminine
sexuality are at the core. The leading ladies of the three aforementioned musicals
are much too intelligent, too full of knowing, to reduce their success to sex. This
is only one reason why Herman's musicals, Herman's *ideas* for musicals, are
more sophisticated than they appear. Before **Hello, Dolly!** (Theatre Royal, Drury
Lane, 2 December 1965; 794) Gerald Herman had written four scores for shows
that had stayed in New York, beginning with *I Feel Wonderful*, a revue staged
in 1954 off-Broadway in Greenwich Village. *Parade*, another revue for which
Herman wrote book music and lyrics, originally played in a nightclub milieu
as *Nightcap*, and had an off-Broadway run of ninety-four performances in 1960.
Milk and Honey, his highly successful 1961 Broadway debut, was set in Israel
and involved – rather in the style of Rodgers and Hammerstein – the cultural
difficulties encountered by its middle-aged lovers. There had also been the
short-lived off-Broadway *Madame Aphrodite*.

The New York success of *Hello, Dolly!* in 1964 was repeated around the world, not least in London, in effect a stopping-off date for the company that had been on the road (America, South Vietnam, Korea, Tokyo and Okinawa) for eight months. If the players were exhausted by their travels, they didn't betray it. Mary Martin had not played Dolly on Broadway, but joined the show for the touring edition, as had many of the all-American cast. Any of the leading ladies who had played the show in New York would have been more than welcome in London (Carol Channing, Ginger Rogers, Martha Raye, Betty Grable, Bibi Osterwald, Pearl Bailey, Phyllis Diller and Ethel Merman) but there was something appropriate about Martin, who fourteen years earlier had been the toast of the West End in *South Pacific*. When she made her entrance for *Hello, Dolly!*'s title number, when those waiters welcomed her back to where she belonged, there was another whole something else going on at the Lane – much of the audience brought its own nostalgia with it. *The Times* declared that the show was 'single-mindedly bent on mobilising public enthusiasm for Mary Martin'.[5]

A sense of going back was anyway built into *Hello, Dolly!* – what else was its title song about? – and Martin was the perfect choice for the specific London nostalgia. Its book-writer, Michael Stewart, could not be applauded for the in-depth characterisation. Such stuff would have held up the proceedings, when all that anyone who goes to see *Hello, Dolly!* cares about is meeting the woman herself. Thornton Wilder's play *The Matchmaker* had been around for ever, itself squeezed out of various other plays, including one of his own, *The Merchant of Yonkers*, and a British one-act farce of 1835 by John Oxenford called *A Day Well Spent*. The story of *Hello, Dolly!* goes back 130 years, at least one justification for the old-fashioned air of the musical. This music had nothing of the modernity of most of the American musicals that were now finding their way to Britain. This is music one can imagine being churned out of the pianola. Perhaps we should not be surprised that the American impresario David Merrick screamed at Herman during the show's rehearsals, 'I am ashamed of these songs.'[6] In a way, Merrick's outburst is understandable, but hopefully there is a subtext; perhaps what he meant to say was that he could swear he had heard many of these tunes before, in some primeval state, that there was something about their insistent rhythms ('Put On Your Sunday Clothes' and 'Elegance', and the never-ending thump of 'Before the Parade Passes By', and that title song) that invaded the consciousness and wouldn't depart. Stephen Citron subtitles his monograph on Herman 'Poet of the Showtune', dignifying Herman as, indeed, a 'poet' but also as a tunesmith rather than a composer. Such a description does not detract from what is a natural brilliance, an affinity with theatricality that puts Herman in the front rank of Broadway composers.

That very theatricality, that tunesmith-ship, his fondness for the cakewalking title songs, has left Herman with a reputation as a composer-lyricist unable to advance into 'serious' musical theatre, but this is the man who will fashion musicals from the tragedy of the persecuted Jew in *The Grand Tour*, homosexual love in *La Cage aux Folles*, and the hinterlands of sanity in *Dear World*. But how to get to the heart of *Hello, Dolly!*? I think there is a sort of alchemy here, something inspired, natural and organic. Hugh Leonard's review for *Plays and Players* takes us a little further.

> Until the second half, *Hello, Dolly!* is never dull, but never remarkable; and one wonders what Mary Martin is doing in it. Then comes a wonderful number called 'Elegance', and a few minutes later we begin to see what all the fuss was about. After a beautifully choreographed piece of tomfoolery by the aforementioned waiters, Miss Martin appears, dressed to kill, at the top of a stairway, and proceeds to sing the title song. By the time the scene is over, the audience is limp with emotion, caught up in the schmaltz of it all, wracked by nostalgia, and bleary-eyed from sheer delight. It is the show-stopper of all time; and Miss Martin – whose business it is to be irresistible – has cemented her own legend for ever.[7]

Puccini had done it all before. Minnie, the heroine of *La Fanciulla del West* has to wait for twenty minutes before making her Act One entrance into her Polka Saloon. Minnie, Puccini's *Annie Get Your Gun*, deserves no less than an extraordinary ovation. The brawl that has just broken out among the gold-digging miners of her bar-room is interrupted by her sudden appearance, at which moment the hard-drinking men turn into soft-hearted, adoring angels, throwing their hats in the air and shouting 'Hello, Minnie', 'Hello, Minnie', 'Hello, Minnie'. It is a heart-stopping occasion of theatrical brilliance, the piercing subtlety of which shows up Herman's effort as existing on an altogether lower plane. Herman hangs about for five minutes, having his dancing waiters helloing Dolly all the time, but having given Minnie that extraordinary tribute from her unwashed and untutored customers, Puccini goes on to build a character (no matter how implausible), with emotions and values that Miss Levi could never aspire to. The moment when Dolly arrives at the top of the staircase at the Harmonia Gardens Restaurant is preserved on the British cast recording, vivid, almost life-like, in its immediacy. Here is a historical document of American (and British) musical theatre that delivers something very much like the experience playgoers experienced in the theatre.

Hello, Dolly! was also notable for bringing a gay sensibility to the American musical, and thus to Britain. This had been obviously lacking in Rodgers and Hammerstein, for whom even the thought of any gay referencing would have been anathema: what would they have thought of gay audiences looking forward to the sailor sequences of *South Pacific*? Nothing would have been further from the writers' minds! There is no gayness in the work of Lerner and Loewe or Frank Loesser or many other Broadway composers. Harold Rome's *Fanny* might have held its male audience in thrall at the appearance of the seafaring, bare-chested Marius, but the authors' intention is clearly heterosexual. Musical theatre enthusiasts of the 1960s might detect the gay element in the handsome stewards that surrounded Elaine Stritch in *Sail Away*, but it was essentially true of the waiters who welcomed back Dolly Levi to the Harmonia Gardens restaurant. Overexcited about the return of Dolly as they might be, we have the feeling that they were probably much more interested in one another. It is obvious that Herman's dealings with theatrical gayness reach their apogee in *La Cage aux Folles*, but it is already in evidence in *Hello, Dolly!* Of course other composers had made females the centre of their musicals – *Funny Girl*, *Gypsy*, *Bells Are Ringing* (the list is almost endless) just as Puccini would have been lost without his Minnie or Mimi – but Herman's take on his central female is from the gay sidelines. It imbues some of his best works, at least in those that revolved about an eccentric, formidable and domineering woman (Dolly Levi, Mame Dennis Burnside, and Countess Aurelia, the Madwoman of Chaillot). As Citron has pointed out, probably the least successful of Herman's musicals, the Broadway-only *The Grand Tour*, is hampered by *not* having an eccentric, formidable and domineering woman as its focus.

And the alchemy of *Hello, Dolly?* Here, I think Herman ranks as a near genius (a lesser one than Puccini). Look at the sequence of its songs. The opening brief chorale bringing Dolly on for Act One is little more than a musical gesture, before our star explains the credo of her existence in 'I Put My Hand In'. Horace Vandergelder (in Britain, Loring Smith) gives his views on the usefulness of the female in 'It Takes a Woman', before Dolly and the company jolly things up with the chugging 'Put on Your Sunday Clothes', a number dazzling in its persistent brightness, and a fair example of Herman's pianola style. The secondary leading lady Irene Molloy (in Britain Marilynn Lovell) has the outstanding rhapsody of the night, 'Ribbons Down My Back'. This is magical enough, an attempt to recapture the feeling of young love, but from this point on the score gathers momentum. The happy numbers pour out: 'Motherhood', 'Dancing' and another ecstatic claim to immortality from Dolly as she demands to extract everything from life 'Before the Parade Passes By'. At this point we might expect the emotional roof to have been reached, but Herman has more, two brilliant tricks more: 'Elegance', a cake-walking, snorting show-stopper, followed by the title song, which, in its way, has never been bettered. After this the score settles, calms down, but the job has been done. Somehow Herman has married the show-business dazzle to the human interest. Why should we be in the least interested to know how Dolly feels about stepping foot in some overpriced restaurant? By the end of it, or even by the middle of it, we know why – because the song, the moment, strikes a chord about belonging, returning, going back to what was known and loved. Like *Mame* and *Dear World* and *La Cage aux Folles*, *Hello, Dolly!* also stands at the door of old age, its main characters with most of their lives behind them.

Despite rumours that Carol Channing or Ginger Rogers would follow Martin into the Lane, in May 1966 she was replaced by Dora Bryan, who in Britain had played another role created by Channing on Broadway, Lorelei Lee in *Gentlemen Prefer Blondes*. For all this, Bryan was essentially a *revue*, not a *musical* actress, and the contrast with Martin was pronounced. Martin's allure had no dependence on quirkiness or outrageous comedy techniques, but Bryan's arrival marked a happy development in the history of the British production. Simultaneously, the ever-ready Bernard Spear took over as Vandergelder. In 1979 Channing made it to London for a revival at the Lane which went on to the Shaftesbury Theatre, and five years later the female impersonator Danny La Rue was the Dolly for a production at the Prince of Wales Theatre. The most recent revival at the Regent's Park Open Air Theatre had Samantha Spiro as its Dolly, suggesting (but not necessarily proving) that star names are not necessary to its success.

Friendly to its core, this show has always welcomed newcomers to its ranks, but in London, on its first showing, it proved less than universally popular with the critics. David Merrick's New York production had been rapturously received, but any London critic considered 'serious' was not throwing his hat in the air. Merrick complained that 'We had to come to London to get our first adverse criticism.' Merrick was defiant, even after he was in trouble for placing a television advertisement on Rediffusion in which he used reviews from the American production as if they were London reviews. The *Daily Telegraph* reporter enquired if Merrick approved of the use of the word 'rave' in this advertisement. 'Rave is a word I always use as applied to lunatics,' replied Merrick. 'From my own private opinion poll there is a monumental contempt for the London critics who have sent the public to some pretty tawdry shows.'[8] Always happy to accept and promote the critics' comments when they were pleasing, Merrick did not choose to accept them when they were not. Peter Lewis decided that 'By our current dud standards, Dolly is the best musical of a bad year; but by the standards of *South Pacific*, *Kiss Me, Kate*, or *My Fair Lady*, it is sadly non-vintage, indeed mediocre stuff'.[9] Milton Shulman was unimpressed: 'The arch squirming, the naïve slapstick, the gauche lines that are proffered as comedy in this situation makes our weariest Whitehall farce a masterpiece of intellectual wit by comparison.'[10] Hobson's *Sunday Times* review noted the 'trivial story, its laborious jokes' and the fact that the disparate elements of story, music and dance had seemed to fall apart.[11]

With only one major American musical, the year gave way to the British, but the only commercial success, **Charlie Girl**, endured terrible reviews. The teaming of Anna Neagle with pop-singer Joe Brown and comic Derek Nimmo, tied into a Cinderella-story, pulled in the crowds. Reviews were just as appalling for Lionel Bart's treatment of the Robin Hood story, dragged into the West End after endless problems during rehearsal and its Manchester try-out. **Twang!** sadly confirmed that Bart had not only peaked but gone over the hill. The British musical's contribution to the permissive society was **Passion Flower Hotel**, enlivened by its youthful cast and John Barry's neon-bright music. Bernard Miles adapted John Dryden's *Amphitryon* for the Mermaid Theatre's **Four Thousand**

Brass Halfpennies, and there was an attempt at musicalising Stella Gibbons's novel *Cold Comfort Farm* in **Something Nasty in the Woodshed**.

1965 Broadway Exports

Do I Hear a Waltz? (220), **On a Clear Day You Can See Forever** (280) and *Man of La Mancha* (2,328).

1965 Broadway Only

The year was pockmarked by several failures including **Drat the Cat!** (8) with Elliot Gould and Lesley Ann Warren, and **La Grosse Valise** (7), supposedly based on a French revue by the creator of an earlier Parisian revue *La Plume de ma Tante*, but despite its insistence that it was now a musical *La Grosse Valise* was still a revue. A Wright-Forrest musical adaptation from the works of Rachmaninoff, **Anya** (16) was a quick casualty, taking with it a cast that included Irra Petina, Constance Towers and Lillian Gish. **Flora, the Red Menace** (87) was a moderate success for Liza Minnelli, singing the songs of Kander and Ebb. More successful but less happy backstage (its lyricist Sammy Cahn found it 'a devastating experience') was **Skyscraper** (248). A Sherlock Holmes musical, **Baker Street** (313), sounded promising but though Peter Sallis and Teddy Green were sensibly imported to add some authenticity to the London setting, the songs were plain. **The Yearling** (3), an evening of death and gloom, found no favour, but was a long runner compared to *Kelly* (1). *Kelly* had the finest of attention, including direction and choreography by Herbert Ross, costumes by Freddy Wittop, sets by Oliver Smith and orchestrations by Hershy Kay, and a plot about a man who jumped off Brooklyn Bridge. Among its players were Anita Gillette and Wilfrid Brambell, on holiday from the British TV comedy series *Steptoe and Son*.

1966

Funny Girl

AMERICA SANCTIONED LONDON as 'swinging' in the *Time* issue of 15 April 1966, two days after one of its youngest and biggest Broadway stars had stepped out for ***Funny Girl*** (Prince of Wales Theatre, 13 April 1966; 112). The city had probably been swinging at least a year earlier, when *Hello, Dolly!* had been Broadway's only contribution. The only thing that swung in that show had been the hips of the Harmonia's waiters; the only thing to swing in *Funny Girl* would be an understudy. *Funny Girl*, music by Jule Styne, lyrics by Bob Merrill, book by Isobel Lennart, won much acclaim at the time, but now sounds like an old-fashioned Broadway musical, some of its score veering to the ho-hum. As it happened, the British musical itself didn't take much notice of the 'swinging' reputation of London: in a sense those feelings of sexual emancipation, of social shifts, had to wait for the advent of the American *Hair*. Neither had the British made much effort to present bio-musicals, and those that were attempted – among them *And So to Bed* (Pepys), *Joey Joey* (Joseph Grimaldi), *Man of Magic* (Houdini), *The Stiffkey Scandals of 1932* (the Revd Harold Davidson), *Sing a Rude Song* (Marie Lloyd) – were not very successful. America made rather more of the bio-musical with such works as Styne's *Gypsy* (Gypsy Rose Lee), *Annie Get Your Gun* (Annie Oakley), and *Mack and Mabel*, all of which travelled to Britain. Others, less well received in New York, didn't make the journey, among them Anthony Newley as Charlie in *Chaplin*, which closed on the way to Broadway in 1983, Libi Staiger as Sophie Tucker in *Sophie* (1963), Alfred Drake as *Kean*, with its original score from Robert Wright and George Forrest in 1961, the 1968 *George M!* about George M. Cohan and the 1970 *Minnie's Boys* about the Marx Brothers.

Lennart's biographical *Funny Girl* was based on incidents in the life of Fanny Brice shortly before and after World War I. It was originally intended for Anne Bancroft, but, as Styne wrote, after hearing the music Bancroft 'knew immediately that she was not capable of singing the score and withdrew. I had written for a big voice, and now the search began for that voice.'[1] Styne suggested Barbra Streisand, who had recently made an impact on Broadway in the small role of Miss Marmelstein in *I Can Get It for You Wholesale*, a show with Harold Rome songs set in the New York garment district. By the time *Funny Girl* opened in London, Streisand had achieved star status, making this one of the most looked-for occasions. Along with Streisand came London director Lawrence Kasha, who had been associate director for the Broadway version, and Kay Medford repeating her role as Brice's mother. It was reported that Streisand asked for Michael Craig, best known as a film actor, to play opposite her as Nick Arnstein. On Broadway Sydney Chaplin had shared billing with Streisand above the title, but in London Streisand remained above and Craig was sent below.

There was some justice in this, as Streisand was involved in twelve of the sixteen numbers, including several solos, while Craig only got to share two duets with her, one of which, 'You Are Woman', had originally been intended for Broadway as a solo for his character of Nick Arnstein before being altered to accommodate Streisand.

There was little doubt that Streisand *was* Funny Girl, despite whatever efforts the rest of the cast put in, and this proved the kernel of the London production's difficulties. Rumours soon circulated about Streisand's relations with the rest of the cast, although one of its producers, Richard Mills, has denied them, saying that Streisand behaved impeccably throughout. The engagement was for three months only, with the star paid the then considerable fee of £1,000 a week, but early in the run Streisand became unwell with intestinal influenza, and then became pregnant and unable to play all seven shows a week. Her understudy, a Dublin girl called Lisa Shane (real name Hazel Yeomans), was sent on. When Craig manfully stepped out before the curtain to make the announcement that Streisand would not be appearing, 400 of the audience stampeded into the theatre vestibule baying for reimbursement. Shane had been in her dressing-room studying shorthand when she was told she was on. She thought the audience sounded like a lynch mob, although Streisand had considerately sent her a message of encouragement and a bouquet. The audience booed Shane's entrance. At the close, she was given a five-minute standing ovation and six curtain calls of her own. By the end of April, impresario Arthur Lewis announced that he and Bernard Delfont were considering giving Shane the role when Streisand's contract expired.

Unlike Broadway understudy Lainie Kazan, who was acclaimed for the only performance at which she took over from Streisand ('after which,' according to Kazan, 'she never got sick again'),[2] Shane regularly played for Streisand. She did this so impressively that, four weeks after opening, the *Daily Telegraph* reported that she would indeed be replacing Streisand when the star returned to America in mid-July. Shane was undeterred by the fact that she was to get £100 a week, a tenth of what Streisand had received. Her ecstasy was shattered three weeks later when the management announced that the show would close when Streisand left. This may have been affected by the fact that Craig, Medford and the American Lee Allen, cast as Eddie Ryan, announced they too would be leaving the production at that point. There were rumours that Shane would be sent out on tour, but this didn't materialise either. The show's musical director Marcus Dods accompanied her into the Pye recording studios to record four of the show's numbers. If they give any idea of what Shane was like on stage, she must have been worth seeing. The same year she made a single for Pye, Burt Bacharach's 'Come and Get Me'. The rest seems to have been silence. Shane's talent had fallen victim to a system that didn't give a damn. Hopefully, her shorthand came in handy.

NOTICE
—
Owing to the indisposition of
BARBRA STREISAND
the part of Fanny Brice at this performance
will be played by
LISA SHANE

The Prince of Wales
Theatre

Playbill

34 An apology for not being able to see Barbra Streisand in the West End's
Funny Girl: an insert that frequently slipped out of the theatre programme
at the Prince of Wales Theatre in 1966

Total gross receipts for the three-month run were put at £225,000, with a full house and maximum standing capacity for every performance Streisand played. However, although they had already been printed, the box office had been unable to sell a single ticket for performances after Streisand left. It gave an ironic slant to Styne's programme note that '*Funny Girl* will be played by many ladies in the future as the years roll by, and I hope they will all feel we did right by Fanny Brice.'[3] In fact, the show has had little afterlife beyond the film version. It may be that it is too tied in to its association with the original star; compare something like *Hello, Dolly!* which welcomed a queue of leading ladies, continually freeing itself from being locked in to Carol Channing. Away from Streisand, though, is the show unusually good? Styne and Merrill's ballads are undoubtedly the best things in it: 'People', the first act closer 'Don't Rain on My Parade' and, possibly finest of all, 'The Music That Makes Me Dance'. Aside from these, the score is no better than many Broadway shows of the period, and many of the numbers seem weak out of (and sometimes even in) context. Perhaps advancing without Streisand would have been a dangerous adventure. For Hugh Leonard the show 'reached a high level of adequacy, but lacked an over-riding sense of style and taste. Compared with, say, *Hello, Dolly!*, it comes in a rather shambling second-best.' And

> One could also take issue with the basic premise of the show: that its leading character was as funny off-stage as on (I don't want to seem prejudiced towards the acting profession, but almost every comedian I have met has turned out to be a regular bastard in private life); but the thought of a doleful Barbra Streisand makes me drop that objection in a hurry.[4]

Styne and Merrill subsequently worked together for the 1971 *Prettybelle*, a work that dealt with prostitution, nymphomania, alcoholism, racial murder and schizophrenia, and the 1972 Broadway *Sugar*, seen in London as *Some Like It Hot*.

As the Broadway incursion into Britain diminished, the British musical went for quantity above quality. **The Matchgirls** was an attempt to do something new: a British show that played out in near darkness with a jazz-based score, directed with choreographic intensity by Gillian Lynne. The Victorian story of the Bryant & May factory strike was not told with sufficient skill, but the try was laudable. Another musical on the same theme, **Strike a Light!**, followed swiftly on *The Matchgirls*' heels, with bigger names over the marquee: Evelyn Laye, Jean Carson and John Fraser. Parts of **On the Level** by Ron Grainer and Ronald Millar seemed aware of modern Britain, but the public stayed home. The female impersonator Danny La Rue starred in **Come Spy with Me**, which, despite making no pretence to be a major musical, achieved a long run. **Jorrocks** had Joss Ackland as R. S. Surtees' bluff fox-hunting hero and songs by David Heneker. Ron Moody's bio-musical of the Regency clown Joseph Grimaldi, **Joey Joey**, crept quietly in and out of the West End. There was compensation in the spectacle of some scary stage trickery in a bio-musical about Harry Houdini, *Man of Magic*, but an ineffective book and second-grade score could not prolong its stay.

1966 Broadway Exports

Sweet Charity (608), *Mame* (1,508), *Cabaret* (1,166) and *I Do! I Do!* (561).

1966 Broadway Only

The successes were substantial, and the failures interesting. The longest runner was made up of three one-acters: *The Apple Tree* (463), with a Jerry Bock–Sheldon Harnick score. The outright flops were *Pousse-Café* (3) with music by Duke Ellington, and *A Joyful Noise* (12) which audiences didn't endure. *It's a Bird ... It's a Plane ... It's Superman* (129) was a bright adaptation from the famous American comic strip with an excellent score by Charles Strouse and Lee Adams. *A Time for Singing* (41) was based on Richard Llewellyn's novel *How Green Was My Valley* – very Welsh. The music by John Morris was at once apposite, immature and stirring, with intermittent flashes of ingenuity; at times it seemed to point a way forward. The cast was headed by British stalwarts Tessie O'Shea, Laurence Naismith, Ivor Emmanuel and Shani Wallis. Harold Brighouse's play *Hobson's Choice* became *Walking Happy* (161) with songs by James Van Heusen and Sammy Cahn. Norman Wisdom excelled as the timid cobbler Will Mossop.

35 Despite the presence of its much appreciated Broadway leading lady, *110 in the Shade* failed to excite critics or theatregoers at the Palace Theatre in 1967

1967

110 in the Shade
Fiddler on the Roof
The Desert Song
Sweet Charity

TOM JONES and Harvey Schmidt's phenomenally successful *The Fantasticks* had failed to make any impression on London in 1961, but the team reintroduced themselves with the more substantial *110 in the Shade* (Palace Theatre, 8 February 1967; 101), an adaptation by N. Richard Nash of his 1954 play *The Rainmaker* about Starbuck, a charlatan miracle-worker passing through a one-horse hick settlement in the American West during a drought, along the way helping a plain Jane of a spinster, Lizzie Curry, to realise she is beautiful and that the town's sheriff File is in love with her. The headlines following its opening night in London were not encouraging: 'A shadowy musical' (*Illustrated London News*), 'A Wash-Out Waiting for the Rain' (*Daily Mail*), 'At Least the Rain Water Was Real' (*The Times*). Alan Brien wrote that 'By the end of the evening, the dry-throated inhabitants of the drought-stricken town looked less in need of a drink than the audience.' Furthermore, the book 'does little to make an audience care about the people in its small-town world. Their names are more individualised than they are and I defy anyone to describe who are Geshy Toops, Bo Dollivon, Wally Skacks III or Tom Kitch. Music, song and dance are thin on the ground.'[1]

To some *110 in the Shade* was second cousin much removed to *Oklahoma!*, although there was a genuine welcome for its Broadway star Inga Swenson as Lizzie, her bunned hair ready to stream down her back when she is emotionally freed by the bewitching Starbuck, who promises to bring rain to the sun-drenched earth. Starbuck was played by American Stephen Douglass, remembered for his Billy Bigelow in the British *Carousel*. The Palace programme explained that he had already 'starred in the Broadway production of *110 in the Shade*', but neglected to mention that in America he had played File, not Starbuck; a rare example of a leading man switching roles between New York and London. File, the sheriff mourning the death of his wife and unable to express his feelings for 'old maid' Lizzie, was now played by the Welsh singer Ivor Emmanuel. After unsuccessfully auditioning for the D'Oyly Carte Opera Company, Emmanuel had, through the influence of his Welsh compatriot Richard Burton, got into the chorus of the British *Oklahoma!*, after which D'Oyly Carte took him on for eighteen months. This was followed by small parts in *South Pacific*, *The King and I* and *Plain and Fancy*, after which he played Joe Hardy in *Damn Yankees*. A year before *110 in the Shade* he had played the lead in the Broadway *A Time for Singing*. Back in London, *110 in the Shade* was the full stop to Emmanuel's career in musicals. Swenson's performance was praised, but the score raised none of the enthusiasm it had created on Broadway. When by curtain-fall Starbuck's promise apparently (and as much to his surprise as anyone else's) came true, the skies opened and a torrent of water deluged the Palace stage. But the whole affair had already been drowned by the critics, among them John Russell Taylor, for whom 'The energy here is all faked-up, and the tunes are terribly wishy-washy affairs which hardly stay with one as far as the foyer'.[2] Why, he asked, hadn't the management opted for the Richard Rodgers and Stephen Sondheim *Do I Hear a Waltz*? But no British management was prepared to take a risk on the Rodgers–Sondheim show, and meanwhile audiences were not drawn to *110 in the Shade*, of which they had never been much aware.

A very different beast opened a week later. ***Fiddler on the Roof*** (Her Majesty's Theatre, 16 February 1967; 2,030) would live on into old age. At the time of the London opening the New York production was already into its third year, had opened in Helsinki and Amsterdam, and was about to play Paris. Its appeal was universal, and of how many other musicals of its time may this be said? Taken from some stories by Sholom Aleichem that included 'Tevye's Daughters', the play was set in Tsarist Russia in 1905. In an isolated village the poor dairyman Tevye struggles to keep his wife and five daughters. An exemplar of the good, honest Jewish father, Tevye can only dream of becoming a rich man as his Jewish settlement is threatened by far-off stirrings of revolution. His need is to marry off his daughters, but even in this he has to face changing attitudes. At last, the threatened pogrom begins and the village is razed. Tevye and his family pack their paltry belongings and make their escape in search of a new beginning. Although focused on the ordinary lives of one seemingly unimportant family, the piece resounded with a humanity that knew few barriers. Some remembered that its songwriters had written the score for two other musicals that had reached London, the disastrous *Fiorello!* and the commercially disappointing *She Loves Me*, neither of which had equalled their Broadway success. *Fiddler on the Roof* was to eclipse all expectation.

In the *Stage* R. B. Marriott declared it the best American musical to reach London since *My Fair Lady* and *West Side Story* a decade earlier: 'There is sentiment in plenty, but of a kind that gives expression to genuine feelings, and is an indication of personal, racial, and religious motivation [...] The story is told with delicacy and intelligence; it has power and wit and simple but true emotion.'[3] The work made a London star of the Israeli actor Topol, whose interpretation proved as memorable as that of Broadway's Zero Mostel. Topol brought a peculiar intensity to the part, and an easy appreciation of what it was about.

> *Fiddler on the Roof* is a play – with music – a theatrical production. But it is not meant to be heavy. It brings some understanding between people. It makes what Aristotle says you feel clean after. Catharsis. I would like

theatre to be much more happy, as Joan Littlewood makes it. I think the audience deserves [...] you see, if the audience comes to the theatre after a day's work, they have enough troubles in their life. I would like them to enjoy themselves. Otherwise, you are stealing their money.

As for the Jewishness of the piece, Topol considered

It is part of the human condition to suffer, but the Jews thank God for suffering as for everything else. They believe the Messiah is still to come and that they must suffer until this golden day: but they make happiness in the middle of their suffering. A human being must be happy even then. The Jews in Russia always agreed to accept, to submit, to live in ghettos. But to live.[4]

Frank Marcus' perceptive review in *Plays and Players* extolled the 'miracle' that director Jerome Robbins had wrought on the piece, seeing that 'His gift is for lyricism and his medium is movement [...] He has the knack of getting to the core, to the poetry, of his subject', just as he had in *On the Town* and *West Side Story*, and in *Fiddler on the Roof* 'he spreads his genius evenly over the whole work, the good parts as well as the bad'. After praising Aronson's décor and Richard Pilbrow's lighting, the dancing (almost as good as in New York) and the acting (better), Marcus' doubts were about the work itself. Jerry Bock's music

has no surprises: it is predictably derivative from traditional sources. There are only two or three tuneful numbers, of which 'If I Were a Rich Man' is the best. The lyrics (Sheldon Harnick) are clever in the accepted Broadway idiom. The book, by Joseph Stein, is workmanlike rather than inspired. The episodes are shrewdly selected, but the dialogue – except for a generous sprinkling of Jewish jokes – is often woefully prosaic and unsubtle.[5]

Topol stayed with the London production for a year, but thereafter probably remained more associated with his role than any other actor in musicals; the male equivalent of Carol Channing in *Hello, Dolly!* When in June he returned to Israel for a few days because of the conflict raging there, the role was temporarily taken over by his standby George Little; Topol explained to the audience in a programme note that 'It's a great show – whether I am in it or not [...] the kind of plea for understanding which would make war like this impossible.' He was succeeded by Alfie Bass, and Bass was replaced in August 1969 by the Dutch actor Lex Goudsmit, who had played the role in Holland. Bass returned when Goudsmit left to lead the British tour, but when Bass left again in 1971 Goudsmit came back, to be followed by Barry Martin. As Golde, Miriam Karlin was succeeded by Avis Bunnage, who after eighteen months gave way to Hy Hazell. When Hazell died during her tenure, Bunnage returned to the role, to be followed by Stella Moray, whose singing voice was used to dub Norma

Crane's songs in the 1971 film. In 1983 Topol was back for a season at the Apollo Victoria Theatre with Thelma Ruby at his side, then played the show for the first time on Broadway for a 1990 seven-month revival, and twenty-seven years after first playing Tevye went to the London Palladium for a two-month engagement in 1994. In 2006 he was still playing the role, now in New Zealand. The British tour went out in 1970 with Vivienne Martin, another ideal for Golde, playing opposite Goudsmit.

A provincial British production directed by Lindsay Posner for Sheffield's Crucible Theatre with Henry Goodman as Tevye transferred to the Savoy Theatre in May 2007, receiving some good reviews. The *Guardian*'s critic thought it 'a show that had been mothballed in the kitsch and picaresque', and that Posner had offered no more than 'a big, jolly night out'. It seemed that for some *Fiddler on the Roof* was in danger of suffering from the sort of treatment meted out to the British *Oliver!* – production after production moving further away from the original.

The day of Sigmund Romberg operettas had surely passed by the time London was offered **The Desert Song** (Palace Theatre, 13 May 1967; 433) in what was effectively a fortieth anniversary production, the original having been seen at Drury Lane with Edith Day and Harry Welchman in 1927. Now, the Red Shadow, alias Pierre Birabeau (or vice versa), was the much-travelled tenor John Hanson, and his Margot, Patricia Michael. Their undersized and under-cast road tour of this romance of the sands was unexpectedly pushed into the Palace following the collapse of the poorly attended *110 in the Shade*. No one involved can seriously have considered that Romberg's museum piece would take hold, but it ran and ran. The first-night audience was reported to be in a paroxysm of delight. As Hanson stepped forward to make a speech to a wildly enthusiastic house (in which sat London's original Margot, Edith Day), a voice from the audience called out 'This is what we want.' A Miss Maud Abrahams, seventy-two, from Bethnal Green, had seen Harry Welchman play the Red Shadow in 1927, 'but I think John Hanson is wonderful'.[6] Michael Billington observed that 'There is a large, undemanding audience for the third-rate. And here, by George, they have it.'[7] For the supporting players it was a rare chance to be in the spotlight, which revealed to Billington a company with

> rather a long tail. As the hero's father, Martin Carroll bears an uncanny resemblance to Sir Tyrone Guthrie, which is about all the praise I can give him. Lita Scott, playing a treacherous slave-girl, displays a sumptuous figure with justifiable pride but delivers her lines rather as if she were acting to an audience of backward foreigners. In the chorus, there are some very stiff Riffs indeed who, lustily though they sing, appear to know only two acting positions – arms resolutely folded and hands placed saucily on hips. As I watched them, at one point, queuing up to get off, I began to wonder if I was really and truly in a West End theatre.[8]

Felix Barker noted 'a heady mixture of stirring songs and sublimely silly plot',[9] while *Punch*'s Jeremy Kingston decided that 'people in those days must have been fitted with hearts of marshmallow and minds of fudge to [...] not shriek with hysterical laughter at such pasteboard heroes, such stupid plots and dialogue that never was heard outside Ruritania and the Garden of Allah'.[10] At one performance as an elderly lady was taken to her seat she said to the usherette 'I'm so looking forward to seeing the show – is it the original cast?'[11] After years of travelling up and down the country, this was Hanson's first West End adventure, in which he invested his own money. There is no denying the scale of its success; Hanson was still going up and down England with it years later (by 1979 his Margot was the ex-D'Oyly Carte soprano Pamela Field), and still having difficulty in arriving on stage with his Red Shadow mask in position. He would return to London with two more shows, a revival of *The Student Prince* and a concoction of his own, *When You're Young*.

The arrival of **Sweet Charity** (Prince of Wales Theatre, 11 October 1967; 476) marked a distinct change of tone for the West End Broadway musical, uniting the music of Cy Coleman with the lyrics of Broadway veteran Dorothy Fields in the score of a work written as a vehicle for Bob Fosse's wife Gwen Verdon. Based on Federico Fellini's film *Nights of Cabiria*, Neil Simon's book rolled out the story of Charity Hope Valentine, dance-hall hostess at the low-life Fan-Dango Ballroom; the saga of a 'Girl Who Wanted to Be Loved'. The bitter-sweetness was skilfully achieved in a zippy score that achieved great popular success, its numbers including 'Big Spender', 'If My Friends Could See Me Now', 'Rhythm of Life' and 'I'm a Brass Band'.

For Bernard Delfont and Harold Fielding's West End edition, Fosse's original direction was reproduced by Lawrence Carr and Robert Linden, and Fosse's choreography by Ed Gasper, set among Robert Randolph's Broadway décor and the costumes of Irene Sharaff. Verdon never transferred any of her Broadway roles to London: instead, Charity was Juliet Prowse, who had made her West End debut as a princess in *Kismet* twelve years earlier. She took the notices in *Sweet Charity*, and would return to London as a holiday replacement for Ginger Rogers in *Mame* in 1969, and in 1976 opposite Rock Hudson in a brief revival of *I Do! I Do!* When her *Sweet Charity* work permit expired she was replaced by Gretchen Wyler in her London debut. Wyler, who had made an early impression on Broadway in *Silk Stockings*, subsequently took over from Verdon in *Damn Yankees* and Chita Rivera in *Bye Bye Birdie*. Sheila O'Neill took over from Wyler in May 1968.

There was nothing revolutionary about *Sweet Charity*: the work went through most of the well-rehearsed hoops that had forever been known to American musical theatre. It was not that this was a 'serious' musical in the manner of the forthcoming *Cabaret*; rather, it had an undertow of profundity that you might search for in vain within a Lerner or Loewe, or a Jerry Herman, or a Rodgers and Hammerstein (for whom the premise of *Sweet Charity* would have been unthinkable). *Sweet Charity* has no pretensions, but it has meaning, and isn't global in the more portentous manner of *Fiddler on the Roof*. Despite its low-life showbiz milieu, it avoids the obvious artificiality of the 'shows within a show' hidden in so many earlier pieces. After the canonization of such characters as Eliza Doolittle, Dolly Levi and Fanny Brice, in its way it is an example of democratization in the American musical. The whole of *Sweet Charity* takes us back to parts of Rodgers and Hammerstein's *Pipe Dream*: low-life dressed up with songs, for Charity's story is set in shade, her life lived out in the underbelly of society.

So far as London was concerned in 1967, *Sweet Charity* was an adventure in subculture that happened to coincide with a time when British society was undergoing radical shifts in sexual and social values. It happened to reach London when that city was said to be swinging, and showed that swinging did not always lead to happiness. It's the common-man musical, with none of the pretty accoutrements that come with Wilder's matchmaker in *Hello, Dolly!*, Fanny Brice in *Funny Girl*, or Guenevere in *Camelot*. There is little artificiality about Lizzie in *110 in the Shade*, but her story is one of purity transformed into joy; Charity's story doesn't have the same starting-point. Perhaps this was the first London Broadway arrival to strike a note of social verity since the interesting effort of *No Strings* four years earlier. It was *Sweet Charity* that cleared a path for such of its cousins as *Golden Boy* and the even more closely related *Promises, Promises*. In fact, the British musical had done much more work on the darker side of society with its clutch of 'kitchen sink' musicals in the late 1950s, but by 1967 these had long gone into the mist.

The music of *Sweet Charity* struck *The Times* as 'more verve than tune', but Simon's dialogue was 'full of oblique humour and bursting with good-natured energy'.[12] The *Daily Mail* thought it 'a not very original throwback to the traditional post-war Broadway musical – but what's wrong with that tradition? [...] the reliable old mixture of vinegar and schmaltz'.[13] For the *Guardian* Philip Hope-Wallace was not keen on the show's sentimentality, but praised Prowse, Paula Kelly and Josephine Blake in 'There's Gotta Be Something Better Than This', and found Coleman's music at its best when 'racy and gay'.[14] R. B. Marriott thought that Prowse 'puts over her songs with energy and concentrated effort but her voice seems small in range and power, with the result that some of the numbers are by no means as rousing as they ought to be'.[15] *Sweet Charity* has twice been revived in London, in 1998 with Bonnie Langford and in 2009 with Tamzin Outhwaite. Fosse directed the 1969 film version starring Shirley MacLaine.

The British musical was not at its best. **Queenie**, a curiosity about a widow (Vivienne Martin) who runs a London pub and is courted by various suitors, had dialogue written in rhyming couplets. Despite Martin being referred to by one critic as a budgerigar, it was a quick flop. A Moral Re-Armament musical, **Annie**, had the most modest book, music and lyrics. A dismal adaptation from Dumas,

The Four Musketeers, opened at Drury Lane, reaching a low-point in the genre. Of marginal interest were a political lampoon with songs *Mrs Wilson's Diary*, and the bio-musical *The Marie Lloyd Story*.

1967 Broadway Exports

None.

1967 Broadway Only

It was not a vintage year. *Sherry!* (72) was a mistaken attempt at adapting George S. Kaufman and Moss Hart's play *The Man Who Came To Dinner*, but the tightness of the source material was weakened. *Ilya, Darling* (320) was memorable for featuring Melina Mercouri and the song 'Never On Sunday'. The new Styne–Comden–Green *Hallelujah, Baby!* (293) had Leslie Uggams as its star but was second division, as was *How Now, Dow Jones* (220), the very title of which consigned it to the Broadway-only category. *Henry, Sweet Henry* (80), based on Nora Johnson's novel *The World of Henry Orient* had one of Bob Merrill's less remembered scores.

may 1968   incorporating theatre world & encore   4s 6d

plays
and players

Full text of
Peter
Luke's
HADRIAN
THE
SEVENTH

36 'Seriousness' in the Broadway musical in London, with Judi Dench as Sally Bowles in *Cabaret* at the Palace Theatre in 1968, but the public resisted its call

1968

You're a Good Man, Charlie Brown
Cabaret
Man of La Mancha
I Do! I Do!
Cindy
Golden Boy
The Student Prince
Lady, Be Good!
Hair
Man with a Load of Mischief

You're a Good Man, Charlie Brown (Fortune Theatre, 1 February 1968; 116) was the first of the year's off-Broadway imports. A chamber work for six players, this was 'a musical entertainment' (after opening night the programme description was changed to 'An Intimate Review [*sic*]') based on Charles M. Schulz's comic cartoon strip *Peanuts*. It was greeted with mild enthusiasm. The *Tatler* announced 'Gesner's music and lyrics tend to be of the Julian Slade variety',[1] and Peter Lewis in the *Daily Mail* found 'the music tinkly and the entertainment very mild indeed'.[2] The music and lyrics of Clark Gesner, who also wrote the book under the pseudonym John Gordon, locked in to the cartoon's feyness, exemplified in the final number 'Happiness'. Warm-hearted and inoffensive as it was, it failed to ignite much interest. Gesner would go on to write songs for the 1979 Broadway musical *The Utter Glory of Morrissey Hall*, an odd score that repays attention, although it closed on its first night. Another *Peanuts* musical, *Snoopy*, by other hands, played London in 1983 with more success.

Cabaret (Palace Theatre, 28 February 1968; 336) was the first of two 'serious' Broadway musicals of the year. Britain's Sandy Wilson had already adapted Christopher Isherwood's tale of Sally Bowles for his musical *Goodbye to Berlin* (at one stage no less than Julie Andrews had considered playing it), but the project foundered. Wilson's timidity was overcome in the songs by John Kander and Fred Ebb for *Cabaret*, the American adaptation by Joe Masteroff which played New York from November 1966, and was still playing when the West End production premiered. All seemed to be as on Broadway, with the major production personnel intact: director Harold Prince, choreographer Ron Field, costumes Patricia Zipprodt, lighting Jean Rosenthal, and the orchestrations of Don Walker perhaps (as too often) watered down for London. Difference was focused on the casting, with the 'straight' actress Judi Dench cast as Sally, Barry Dennen as the menacing MC of the Kit Kat Klub, and Lila Kedrova as Fräulein

Schneider, originally played in America by Lotte Lenya. Dench would go on to be almost the only exceptional thing about another 'American' musical seen only in London, *The Good Companions*, in 1974, and a fine Desiree Armfeldt in the Royal National Theatre production of *A Little Night Music* in 1995. All three musicals made use of Dench's ability to plumb depths of the soul.

There was much soul-searching about *Cabaret*; and a sense of bravery attached to this serious musical, without the portentous overlay of *Man of La Mancha*. Central to the piece were the numbers set in the context of the Kit Kat Club, raising pastiche 'to the level of art' according to Frank Marcus, utilising these scenes to darken the Nazi cloud that hung over all, although Marcus had reservations about the piece as a whole. He thought it 'almost beyond belief' that Bowles and Isherwood's relationship in Isherwood's original should have been reduced to 'a boring and commonplace *affaire*', not helped by Dench's abundance of 'warmth and intelligence'. For Marcus, the introduction into the proceedings of the character of Herr Schultz (Peter Sallis) was no more than 'a sop to the vast Jewish audience of Broadway'; Marcus could recall no Jewish greengrocers residing in Berlin. He thought the romantic scenes between Schultz and Fräulein Schneider 'including a very silly song about a pineapple' recalled the romance between Canon Chasuble and Miss Prism in *The Importance of Being Earnest*, and 'they are not evocative of Berlin'.[3]

It was a characteristic of *Cabaret* that, while it seemingly broke barriers, breathing of the Holocaust, it mostly stayed close to conventions of the musical play. There was, after all, nothing fresh about the device of having 'show within the show' numbers regularly peppering the evening: just as had happened in Noel Coward's *Ace of Clubs* or Rodgers and Hart's *Pal Joey*. The difference now was that these 'in-house' numbers *meant* something beyond another ensemble number for the girls and for the eleven o'clock number Sally stretched the convention by singing 'Cabaret', a song that came with two flavours, sweet and bitter. The seriousness of *Cabaret* inhabited the Kit Kat's repertoire as much as the rest of the score.

The London notices were mixed. 'Certainly the best numbers we have heard since *Fiddler on the Roof* said *The Times*, with the *Financial Times* announcing '*Cabaret* is a work of art'. In the *Daily Mail* under the headline 'Sentiment and the Nazis just don't mix' the show was declared 'a disappointment [...] One of the troubles here is the music, which entirely fails to get the injured howl into it that Kurt Weill did in, for instance, *Mac the Knife*'.[4] Eric Shorter suggested 'the central flaw [...] It boldly tries to mix the tawdry glitter and vulgarity of 1930s Berlin night-life with the creeping shadow of Nazism. The music, by John Kander, is insufficiently astringent to bridge the contrasting moods. The result, despite the strength and diversity of the acting, is a feeling of sentimentality'.[5] Elizabeth Seal had been announced as taking over when Dench's contract expired, but declining audiences forced the show's closure with Dench still in place on 30 November 1968.

Gillian Lynne directed a revival that originated at Hanley and moved to the Strand Theatre in July 1986, with Lynne and musical director Ray Cook 'extending' the songs. Lynne noted that Cook 'wrote wonderful links, based on the original Kander and Ebb stuff, but tailored very specifically to what I wanted'.[6] The songs for Sally Bowles were bolstered by introducing 'Maybe This Time' from the 1972 film. Kelly Hunter had played the title role in the disastrous *Jean Seberg* (songs by lyricist Christopher Adler, music Marvin Hamlisch) at the National Theatre in 1983, but casting her as Isherwood's flawed heroine proved a mistake. Charles Spencer thought her 'lucky to get another major starring role' in what was 'another let down [...] entirely sexless [...] her movement is awkward and she entirely misses the character's appealing vulnerability'. Wayne Sleep – 'an unhappy bystander on the sidelines' – failed to impress as Master of Ceremonies in a production that was 'a bitter disappointment' with its choreography 'depressingly wan'.[7] Toyah Willcox's takeover of Sally improved matters, but Sleep remained with the show until it closed in disarray. Subsequent British productions have worked at different levels, often benefiting from imaginative and occasionally more starkly horrific touches, but few have overcome the lack of a Miss Dench.

And then, the show with an impossible, possibly *the* impossible song of 1960s' musicals, a melody and lyric that transmuted into 'The Impossible Dream'. In fact, there are several apparent impossibilities about **Man of La Mancha** (Piccadilly Theatre, 24 April 1968; 253), an unlikely musical from an unlikely source, Cervantes' *Don Quixote*, that became an unlikely world-wide success, although in London the success was less obvious. To begin, no less than W. H. Auden and Chester Kallman were to write the book for the show's originator and director Albert Marre, but the book was eventually worked up by Dale Wasserman from his television play *I, Don Quixote*. The *Man of La Mancha*'s lyricist was Joe Darion, who had previously written the lyrics for Broadway's *Shinbone Alley*, and the composer Mitch Leigh, who had made a career of writing jingle music for commercials.

The pairing of Leigh and Darion didn't sound promising, but the work they came up with has a dignity, a sense of gravitas, a *seriousness* that commands attention. The affectation of classical endorsement has always been a vital component of *Man of La Mancha*'s potency. This isn't George Bernard Shaw or Damon Runyon or Thornton Wilder or Christopher Isherwood: this is Cervantes. As such, we are expected to listen out for its nuances in a quite different way to the way we listen to *My Fair Lady*, *Guys and Dolls*, *Hello, Dolly!* and *Cabaret*.

What no one was allowed to forget was that the American musical was now *seriously* serious. Leigh explained that 'I see *Man of La Mancha* as a plea for idealism [...] The only things I reject are pomposity, the "grand compositeur" outlook, which just makes you self-indulgent and narrow, and subservience. Subservience is a pain in the ass.' In the London production's souvenir brochure Brooks Atkinson informed theatregoers that '*Man of La Mancha* is stage literature.' Difficult as it may be to swallow, Arthur Rubinstein, the 'venerable musical figure and lifelong fan of Cervantes' claimed 'That score is the finest work by any composer who ever wrote for the American musical theatre.'[8] At this point we have to pull ourselves up sharply: can these serious comments about this oh-so-serious musical be taken *seriously*? Much as we might want to pin Mr Rubinstein down and get him to expand his argument, we must sigh and pass on.

Having studied the music of the time of Cervantes, Leigh considered it uninteresting and a poor imitation of other European music of the period. He turned to Spanish gypsy flamenco music and decided at the risk of anachronism (perish the thought: anachronism in a musical theatre score!) to exploit flamenco as the core of his score. 'Strings are too slick and smooth for the style I wanted,' he wrote, 'woodwinds, brass and percussion are more caustic and commanding.'[9] There were other tricks up this score's sleeve. The orchestra would be split on two sides of the stage, creating an effect (it was hoped) of church music. Darion's belief was that 'We [the authors] never took the easy road or tried for a cheap effect.'[10] There is no reason to doubt it, for *Man of La Mancha* always wanted to be more than mere musical.

The stage and orchestra pit at the Piccadilly were taken out and replaced by designer Howard Bay's 25-feet-deep platform, with a 35-foot-high staircase rising from it. Keith Michell, whose previous musicals had all been British (*And So to Bed*, *Irma la Douce* and *Robert and Elizabeth*) was a sound choice of leading man (subbed by Emile Belcourt) playing opposite Joan Diener, Broadway's original Aldonza, with an all-British cast in support, among them Ivor Novello's contralto Olive Gilbert, Bernard Spear whose Pancho according to Milton Shulman 'was called upon to do little more than look as doleful as a delicatessen owner on a bad Saturday night',[11] and Patricia Bredin.

The critics were mixed in their reactions, although it was obvious that Michell was worthy of the responsibility. Dale Wasserman in *The Times* considered the show 'a heady theatrical tonic. It proves that a simple dramatic idea and some excellent tunes are worth any number of spectacular set pieces and coatings of irrelevant sentimentality'. Furthermore, Diener was 'a sight for the sorest of eyes. Radiating sexual ferocity and singing like an angel, she gives the best female performance in a musical since [Chita] Rivera in *West Side Story*.'[12] Sheridan Morley was less sure of 'a curiously old-fashioned entertainment' but the songs were 'superlative; where in *Cabaret* or *Sweet Charity* they are often incidental to the plot, here they seem to be the very reason for its existence as a musical, and the overall effect is operatic rather than dramatic.' What was more, Michell 'invests the whole thing with a classical almost Shakespearean grandeur which would otherwise be lacking'.[13] Eric Shorter for the *Daily Mail* decided 'It should give a lot of easy pleasure, but it hardly gave me as much as I had wished.'[14] 'I do wonder a little,' wrote J. C. Trewin, 'whether, like other publicized Broadway musicals, *Man of La Mancha* may not suffer from an illusion of greatness.

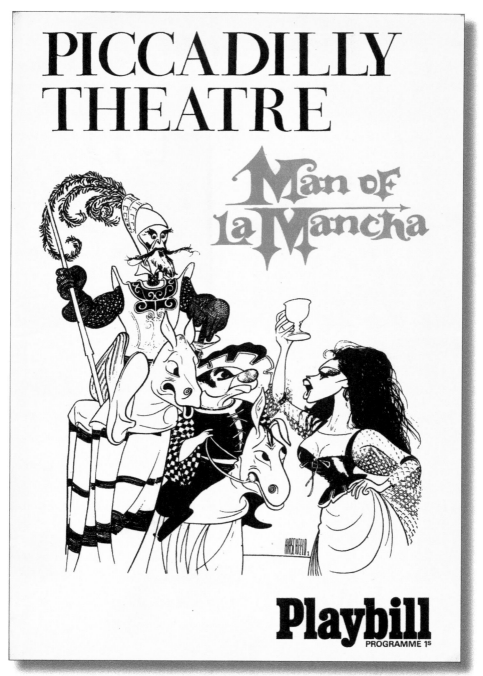

37 Did seriousness get more serious than in the impossibility of Don Quixote's musical dream? Keith Michell, Bernard Spear and Joan Diener caricatured on the *Playbill* theatre programme of *Man of La Mancha* in 1968

That is not the word. It is just a very good musical, more imaginative and unexpected than most.' It didn't help that, thinking about it afterwards, Trewin found Diener 'slightly comic'.[15]

Perhaps the producers' coup was to bring the show's original leading lady to play opposite Michell. In New York she had broken two ribs and suffered innumerable bruises during the play's rape scene, and by the time she met Michell and Spear at the Piccadilly she had already played opposite eight Don Quixotes and six Panchos. If not a wonder of the world she was once again, as she had been for a time in the British *Kismet*, a physical wonder of London's theatreland. London had seldom seen a musical actress whose physical construction was as startling as her voice and manner, and in *Man of La Mancha* she attacked her role with vigour and a style that none might wish to imitate. As had happened in *Kismet*, Diener did not wait for the show's old age but was replaced by Ruth Silvestre, who had followed her into the show in New York.

It was left to Harold Hobson to put *Man of La Mancha* in its place. He hated it. He reminded his readers that he had loved the previous year's revival of *The Desert Song* although he had missed its first night at the Palace Theatre because he was watching a performance of *The Desert Song* by the Bognor Amateur Operatic and Dramatic Society. As for 'the man at the Piccadilly [he] is not a Fool of God, he is just a fool.'[16] But when the production closed after 253 performances and a loss of £40,000, *Man of La Mancha* was not done with. The following year it was back at the Piccadilly with its original Broadway star, Richard Kiley, as Quixote, enjoying what R. B. Marriott called 'an artistic triumph'. Because Diener was now back playing the role on Broadway opposite Jacques Brel, Silvestre, 'an English actress known in cabaret but new to the stage', reappeared as Aldonza, enjoying 'a triumph only lesser than the memorable one of Mr. Kiley'. Once again Marriott noted how in the production 'the drama, the passion and sentiment of it all, even something of the metaphysical import, are treated with intelligence, sensitivity and dramatic power'.[17] The *Illustrated London News* thought it 'an even better performance than the first' and in Kiley the critic found himself 'responding also to an actor uncommonly moving and dignified; often he reminded me of the late Baliol Holloway at his prime'.[18] The production would have run longer than its 118 performances if Kiley had not had Broadway commitments. Despite the world-wide celebrity of *Man of La Mancha* Leigh's subsequent scores written with other collaborators – *Cry for Us All* (another decidedly 'serious' work) and *Home Sweet Homer* stayed but briefly in New York.

The team of Tom Jones and Harvey Schmidt are as good an example as any of the American writing partnerships who were notably more successful at home than in Britain. *The Fantasticks* went into American theatrical history, but in Britain sank (twice) without trace. Their much more ambitious *110 in the Shade* had not disgraced itself on Broadway, where it had decent reviews; Britain had rejected it, critically and commercially. Their latest work, *I Do! I Do!*

(Lyric Theatre, 16 May 1968; 116) was what it suggested: the celebration and acting out of a very long and unspectacular marriage. The American musical could hardly, in the mid-1960s, have been more heterosexual, although this was heterosexuality without the sex. Helen Dawson in *Plays and Players* was not impressed.

> I think that one would have to be going through a fairly bleak patch of married life to get much pleasure from the new American musical, *I Do! I Do!*, at the Lyric. Presumably there must be enough people thus afflicted for the backers to feel reasonably confident. But this musical version of Jan de Hartog's unmemorable play, *The Fourposter*, struck me as being one of the most unctuous New York offerings for some time. Hard-pedalling on the whimsical-marital button, one can understand why it's had such a run on Broadway: nothing could fit more neatly into the expense account or anniversary jelly mould.[19]

In Britain, then, one for the tired business man; indeed, here was a show that probably explained why the business man *was* tired, although the message of the show, underlined in one of its final lyrics, left no doubt: 'Marriage is a very good thing' it ran, 'though it's far from easy.' The message could not have been more obviously delivered: the curtain went up on He and She, waiting to be wed, ready to repeat the eternal cry of 'I Do!'. The time was the turn of the century, through which the newly-weds passed with a number always on hand to illustrate the moment; the wedding night ('Goodnight'), She's pregnancy ('Something Has Happened'), marital contentment ('My Cup Runneth Over'), financial stress ('Love Isn't Everything'), argument, disillusion between He and She and the prospect of divorce ('Nobody's Perfect'), She letting her hair down and breaking the bounds ('Flaming Agnes'), the less demanding contentment that comes with age ('Where Are the Snows?'), the realisation that both He and She can now do whatever they wish ('When the Kids Get Married'), He's emotional tussle with the fact that He's daughter is getting married ('The Father of the Bride'), She adopting a more mature attitude to femininity ('What Is a Woman?'), packing away the past ('Roll Up the Ribbons') and ultimately the move to a smaller home, and different bed ('This House'). That bed was the third character of Hartog's play and Jones's libretto, gliding into position centre stage after the show's opening number and remaining there all night, a symbol of the ties made by He (in London's case Ian Carmichael) and She (Anne Rogers) at the altar.

Broadway's Robert Preston and Mary Martin, bigger names than London's pairing, had probably been the best thing going for *I Do! I Do!*, helping it to a long stay. In Britain, although the performances seem to have been exemplary, Carmichael was a star associated with light comedy and revue, not musicals, and Anne Rogers was several years on from her success in *My Fair Lady*. Her reputation for taking-over was unhelpful; after *My Fair Lady* she had been replacement in New York in *Half a Sixpence* and *Walking Happy*. There had been little success, either, with London's *She Loves Me* and Broadway's *Zenda*. Nevertheless, as the London recording attests, she and Carmichael were as good as London was able to provide. Faced with a two-hander, the audience had no choice but to accept the situation: if it didn't like these two characters, or the performances, there was nowhere else to go. Carmichael was confident that the show would be a huge success. Gower Champion came to supervise rehearsals, although a restaging is credited to his assistant Lucia Victor. A sixteen-piece orchestra was placed behind a gauze at the back of the set, and standbys Ian Burford and Maureen Hartley looked on from the wings.

There were various problems with the premise of *I Do! I Do!*, quite apart from its dangerously high sugar content. The score was serviceable but unexciting, and unmemorable except for 'My Cup Runneth Over'. There was no escaping the difficulties of having two people on stage all evening. The marriage they depicted didn't seem particularly relevant to Britain. The *Tatler*'s critic likened the show's book to a pamphlet, informing his readers that here was 'a coy, cloying, soggy and deeply unreassuring microcosm of married life in which two characters sing and dance their way through fifty years of sickly connubial bliss',[20] while Philip Hope-Wallace teetered 'on the precipice of boredom'.[21] People looking to the review headlines cannot have been encouraged to hasten to the Lyric: 'Fifty Years and it does seem a bit too much' (The *Evening Standard*); 'It's just a rotten cliché for two' (*Daily Mail*); 'Marriage without conflict' (*The Times*). The production had been rapturously received on its long pre-West End tour. The show was subsequently revived for a season at the Piccadilly Theatre with Rock Hudson and Juliet Prowse, but the critics remained unimpressed.

The second off-Broadway casualty of the year, **Cindy** (Fortune Theatre, 29 May 1968; 29) had an unpropitious start in Britain with two weeks at the Palace Theatre, Westcliff, on which occasion the comedienne Avril Angers was announced as heading the cast alongside Hy Hazell. By the time *Cindy* washed up in the West End, Angers had gone, replaced by Rose Hill. An updating of the Cinderella story with Geraldene Morrow as Cindy Kreller, now happening in a modern New York delicatessen, the songs were by Johnny Brandon, who had been a featured player in *Love from Judy*. All the old pantomime favourites were in place, but transformed: Buttons became Lucky, Prince Charming became Chuck Rosenfeld and there were two female ugly sisters. Off-Broadway had succumbed to its charms, but not R. B. Marriott, who thought that 'A good deal of *Cindy* is merely shoddily vulgar and brashly sick. The comedy, such as it is, belongs to a familiar, corny line of Yiddish humour', although he conceded that Hazell 'puts over her numbers brilliantly'.[22] There were few patrons and the closing notice must have been a relief to all.

Golden Boy (London Palladium, 4 June 1968; 118) pronounced itself a star vehicle by the very theatre it played; this was the first book musical ever to play London's most famous variety theatre, and without doubt more 'serious' than any of the others that followed there. The star was Sammy Davis, who had opened the show in New York four years earlier, taking it to 569 performances; for London a three-month season was announced. The cast came from America, with Gloria DeHaven as Lorna (it had been Paula Wayne on Broadway), and Lon Satton (Davis' understudy) as Eddie Satin, the role originally played by Billy Daniels. Arthur Penn had directed the Broadway production, replaced now by Michael Toma, and Donald McKayle's original choreography was warmed through by Jaime Rogers and Lester Wilson. Based on Clifford Odets' play by the author and William Gibson, who was brought in when Odets died, the songs were by Charles Strouse and Lee Adams whose *Bye Bye Birdie* had brightened the London scene in 1960. (The 1962 *All American* did what its title said and stayed home, as did the work that followed it – *It's a Bird, It's a Plane, It's Superman.*) And although *Golden Boy* was in no way brilliant, and its score unmemorable, it remains one of the most significant Broadway shows of the 1960s to reach London. It may have been dwarfed by *The Sound of Music, Camelot, Hello, Dolly!* and *Fiddler on the Roof*, and blockbuster it was not, but Odets had provided the basis for a musical that was more important. In some way, *Golden Boy* has slipped from the collective British memory, and doesn't deserve its fate.

People who hastened to the Palladium expecting Strouse and Adams to have written a snappy score like that of *Bye Bye Birdie* were in for (a) disappointment or (b) revelation, for at the heart of *Golden Boy* were much duller colours, and the darkest of them all: black. The original play reached London in 1938, and the following year Hollywood cast William Holden as the boxer who thinks he would rather be a violinist, Joe Bonaparte, who falls for Lorna Moon (Barbara Stanwyck). At this time Harold Clurman wrote of the play:

> *Golden Boy* has already been praised as a good show, common-sense entertainment, and effective melodrama. It has also been blamed for betraying Hollywood influence in its use of terse, typical situations, story motifs which resemble that of either popular fiction or movies, and possibly too in its use of an environment (the prize-fight world) that somehow seems unworthy of the serious purpose professed by its author. There has been, in addition, almost universal admiration for many separate scenes and long passages of brilliant dialogue.[23]

The most blatant alteration from play to musical is of its hero, Joe Bonaparte, who becomes Joe Wellington, and in the process turns from white to black. This is the essence of *Golden Boy's* musical, and the reason why Davis, politically committed to black issues, was central to it. To have cast a black singer-actor who had never given a suggestion that he might be an activist would have taken the wind out of the show's breath before it left the starting-post. By the time play became musical, black is at the back of most of its songs; the shift from straight play through to musical play is extraordinary. Strouse has detailed some of the transformations that Joe underwent during the development of the musical: *en route* to Broadway for four months, Joe had at and on various stages been a violinist, a pianist, and by the time the show reached Detroit, a medical student. There were those who thought the Detroit show preferable to the version that wound up in New York: keep the stethoscope closer than the boxing glove.

Perhaps Odets' original plot would not have undergone such emasculation had he not died before the Broadway opening, by which time Joe Wellington was no longer a medico but a relentlessly ambitious black (and wanting to be golden) boy who sees a way to get out of the Harlem ghetto via boxing, the no-hope boy's escape route to fame and riches. His white manager Tom's girl friend, Lorna Moon (also white, as her lunar name suggests), is sent to Joe to urge him to fight harder. The black boxing promoter Eddie Satin sees Joe's potential and stages a major New York fight. Before the match Joe's father tries to persuade Joe to give up the ring, but Joe is driven on by his love for Lorna. Tom and Lorna's relationship is crumbling, as is Tom's hold over Joe's career. Joe and Lorna's love becomes physical, and Tom threatens to kill himself if she leaves him for Joe. Knowing this to be true, Lorna breaks off with Joe, who now has to face a big title fight against Lopez. His father, thinking Joe will surely lose against Lopez, at last gives his consent to the path Joe has taken. Lopez beats Joe to the ground, but Joe gets back up and floors Lopez. Later, in his dressing-room, Joe learns that Lopez has died. This is not what Joe wanted, and driving from the scene in his Ferrari, Joe is killed.

Racial prejudice against blacks and the difficulties they encountered is always present in *Golden Boy*: look at the songs. Davis' entrance number, the urban lament 'Night Song', has an Edward Hopper desolation about it, an expression of isolation that of course was not a new device for a hero's song in American shows. (How about 'A New Town is a Blue Town' in *The Pajama Game* or, rather more operatically, 'Lonely Town' in *On the Town*?) But this is Davis singing it, set in the middle of Harlem, where the rats are as big as Lassie and poverty reigns: the very blackness of the hero underlines the unfriendliness of the landscape. Then there is 'Colourful' with every hue in the rainbow brought up merely as a stepping-stone to Joe's insistence that 'black is chic, it goes with everything and doesn't try too hard'; ultimately, as Joe sings, 'Black suits me best'. This, no matter what else was to come later in the show, flung the show's philosophy in the face of the audience. There is blackness, too, in the songs for the villain of the piece, Eddie Satin, the promoter who wants to exploit Joe for everything he's worth. Then, there is *Golden Boy*'s travelogue for Harlem, 'Don't Forget 127th Street', once described by Strouse as 'patently vulgar music with no compositional subtleties'.[24] Perhaps, but Davis knew he wanted a song-and-dance and comedy number with the company and this was it, the full Davis package in one song, which regularly stopped the show. The number was black, with its uncomfortable message to white audiences that Harlem was 'the place that white folks think we love'.

The emotional highlights of the score came in Act Two, the first when Joe and Lorna – black boy and white girl – finally realise their lives are forever linked, cling to one another and begin to make love, in 'I Want to Be with You', a number that took Strouse and Adams beyond anything that most of the other much more successful musicals of the period were attempting. Again, black (and white) skin (and now, on stage, skin touching) was at the core of the song. Finally came *Golden Boy*'s spiritual 'No More', with Davis and the company forcefully informing the audience (and in Britain it must have been predominantly a white one) that blacks were no longer prepared to bow down. According to Davis, 'No More' turned into Martin Luther King Jnr's favourite song.

Golden Boy's London season was not without incident. As in America, Davis (and perhaps others in the production) was sent hate mail; Davis himself received death threats, and was given police protection. He was unable to play some of the first performances because of throat problems, on which occasions Satton took over. On 6 June, two days after opening, the curtain rose at 7.50 p.m., twenty minutes late. According to Hugh Leonard

> it was quickly apparent that something was wrong. The pace was leaden, the dialogue thrown away; the star [...] walked through his role; while of Mr. Davis' co-star Gloria DeHaven, there was no sign – the part being taken by her understudy [Marilyne Mason] and without any announcement or explanation to the audience. Then, at the beginning of the second act, Mr. Davis came forward, and, to use a metaphor straight out of *Golden Boy*, threw in the towel. In a lengthy speech he explained that because of the shooting of Robert Kennedy [the previous day] he would not continue with the performance; an understudy would take his place. The show would go on, but not, apparently, its stars.[25]

As Leonard pointed out, Davis' sentiments could not be questioned, although he had abandoned the rest of the cast to get through the night as best they could. Ultimately, there was no denying Davis' stardom, but the box-office was not overrun in the way that the management had expected. Best known for his variety and cabaret and one-man shows, perhaps audiences couldn't be bothered with Davis working his way through a book musical that went for tragedy above song and laughter, and a show that nobody knew a song from (so different from Rodgers and Hammerstein).

Even so, the run was extended to 14 September, leaving a leading lady vacancy when Gloria DeHaven left at the end of her three-month contract. As take-over, producer Richard Mills suggested one of his clients, Vivienne Martin, already a veteran of British musicals,[26] and an audition was arranged at the Palladium. Davis and the producers were in the auditorium when Martin walked on stage and did her stuff. They were impressed, and Davis agreed that she would be suitable. He did not, however, speak to her. Martin rehearsed with Davis's understudy and then moved into the leading lady's dressing-room. On her first night, as she was making-up, the company manager knocked on her door and suggested that it might be a good idea if she went along to Mr Davis's room to introduce herself. Martin replied that if Mr Davis wished to introduce himself he knew where she was. She met her co-star for the first time when she walked on stage that night. Such was the care taken for audiences with the British *Golden Boy*.

One wonders if Davis or anyone else in the cast appreciated Martin, for whom this was a rare American musical. Although Strouse and Adams' songs for Lorna ('Lorna's Here' and 'Golden Boy') are not the strongest, Martin gave them an intensity and strength that was deserving of something better, but almost everything she did in her long career was deserving of something better. After a handful of performances, her involvement with *Golden Boy* was done, and the show's reputation slipped away. Rather in the manner of Streisand and *Funny Girl*, Davis' flirtation with London's *Golden Boy* was brief. His popularity was fêted on British television, and theatregoers rightly had high expectations of him in a dramatic book musical. In London he had better notices than the show. Milton Shulman reported 'The music [...] is lively without being particularly memorable. The lyrics [...] are clever but spoiled by linguistic over-heating.'[27] For J. C. Trewin it was 'a long and vigorous night',[28] for Peter Lewis in the *Daily Mail* 'turgid stuff'.[29] The apple-pie sweetness of Strouse and Adams' orphaned *Annie* musical would prove much more to the British public's liking, as did pop singer Cliff Richard, who was moved into the Palladium the week following *Golden Boy*'s closure, and stayed for eleven weeks, almost as long as *Golden Boy* had been able to chalk up.

Following his unexpected West End success with *The Desert Song* John Hanson returned to London in a revival of **The Student Prince** (Cambridge Theatre, 8 June 1968; 282). 'It's escapism not realism they want,' said Hanson, 'away from the kitchen sink and all that – romance, melody, colour, the sweeter side of life.' Of the young, Hanson said that 'they come to laugh but stay to cheer'.[30] Indeed, in ten years of touring the provinces Hanson had taken over £1.5 million, and *The Desert Song* had made West End managers sit up to the possibility that there was still an audience for such stuff, much of it willing to be bussed in from outside London. Across the road at the Saville Theatre, a revival of Ivor Novello's *The Dancing Years* with soprano June Bronhill suggested a sudden thirst for the entertainments of yesteryear, although the Novello got far worse notices than the Romberg.

At least two patrons eagerly looked forward to the return of Mr Hanson. Sixty-five-year-old twins Violet and Gladys Bennett travelled from Whitechapel each weekend to sit through every Saturday matinee and evening performance of *The Desert Song*, an escapade on which they estimated they had spent over £350. The ladies worked for a theatrical costumier, and dressed in grand style for their outings up West. Hanson (possibly sensing some press coverage) asked Violet, who had lately taken up making georgette roses, to create one for him

to use during this revamped *Student Prince*, in which Barbara Strathdee made
her first West End appearance as Kathie. The critics were tactful, the *Daily
Telegraph* suggesting 'it's all very jolly indeed until the music stops and the
stilted acting begins',[31] and the *Illustrated London News* confirmed 'everything
going, according to mechanical plan, among sundry pasteboard grandeurs'.[32]
Hopefully the result pleased the Bennetts, who had by now perhaps shaken off
the opposition of a glamorous Swedish widow who always sat at the end of their
row throughout their long hours at *The Desert Song*.

A revival of **Lady, Be Good!** (Saville Theatre, 25 July 1968; 155) was Revival
of the Year because it was the only one. First staged at the Forum, Billingham,
Hugh Goldie's production starred a patented dumb blonde of the 1960s, Aimi
Macdonald, in the Adele Astaire role of Susie Trevor, with Lionel Blair in Fred's
old role of Dick Trevor. Better cast than the following year's revival of *Anything
Goes*, the new *Lady, Be Good!* had reasonable reviews and a fair run at the Saville,
whose previous installation, Ivor Novello's *The Dancing Years*, had been savaged
by critics and died after a few weeks. Milton Shulman considered it 'Very
uncertain as to whether they are sending up the original or trying to catch its
early quality, this production is neither sharp enough for chuckles nor serious
enough for any involvement in anything transforming on the stage.'[33] It seemed
to be a question of style. Irving Wardle agreed that 'By hedging its bet, the show
loses any claim it might have to style, either the satiric consistency of *The Boy
Friend* or the homespun integrity of John Hanson's revivals.'[34] For the *Daily
Mail* Peter Lewis praised the well-trained chorus (one of the best for years, he
said) and the comic Joe Baker who stole the show as Watty Watkins. The likeable
Baker had been wasted in a British musical, *Joey Joey*, in 1966.

And then, for one brief shining moment, not a Camelot, but surely the most
noteworthy musical of the 1960s so far as the West End was concerned. The
title was unpromising. How was a British public at least sometimes attuned
to the likes of all those shows that had wafted across the Atlantic to respond
to its title? A musical about the stuff that never ceases to grow on the human
body? With *Cindy* you knew where you were, *Cabaret* seemed self-explanatory
until you had sat through it, *Oklahoma!* told you everything you needed
to know. But **Hair** (Shaftesbury Theatre, 27 September 1968; 1,998)? How
was this to attract audiences who every now and again roused themselves to
Rodgers and Hammerstein? How could the West End cope with a musical that,
above all others that followed in its shadow, including one or two in which
Jesus made a guest appearance, seemed to change the face of the American
musical in London? To some it was as if the very genre had been indecently
assaulted. On that September night, Britain welcomed the arrival of a musical
of almost biblical importance, a work that was to have far more significance
in musical theatre than those of the past remembered as world-changers,
except that it changed very little about American musicals or their London
doppelgängers.

It had been supposed by many that the Lord Chamberlain would refuse to license a British production, but by the time the script was submitted for consideration the end of theatre censorship in Britain was inevitable. The Lord Chamberlain had recommended that the show should be licensed providing that cuts were made; effectively, *Hair* could go on but would be neutered. When a second script was submitted, a reader to the Lord Chamberlain, Charles Heriot, described 'a totally reprehensible affair. Satire is one thing, but the "knocking" at every convention and the tacit glorification of drugs and general intransigence inclines me to agree [...] that, in effect, this piece is dangerously permissive.'[35] A month later the Lord Chamberlain was still displeased, Heriot complaining that the resubmitted text was 'a curiously half-hearted attempt to vet the script. All the drug references seem to be removed and all the f...s but there are still a lot of cuts to be made.'[36] Even so, the production was licensed, but the passing of the Theatres Act 1968 stipulated that after 25 September new plays no longer had to apply for licensing from the Lord Chamberlain. By announcing an opening date of 27 September *Hair* had freed itself of that official's strictures.

The Times review by Irving Wardle was headlined 'Plenty to alarm unwary in hymn to freedom'. Noting that much of the plot seemed to have been lost on the way from New York, Wardle thought 'the unmistakable purpose of the show – behind its strobe light massacre and transvestite parades of Western heroes – is to send up a great hymn of freedom and love, and for once the message really comes across'.[37] The show represented the final bow for the elderly critic of the *Daily Telegraph*, W. A. Darlington, who had sat through 'a complete bore – noisy, ugly and quite desperately unfunny',[38] while Herbert Kretzmer in the *Daily Express* considered the nude scene 'totally innocent' but warned those hoping for 'craftsmanship, professional performance and coherence' that they were in for 'a crushing, shambling disappointment'.[39] The performance was interrupted by booing, but even B. A. Young in the *Financial Times* reported 'not only a wildly enjoyable evening, but a thoroughly moral one'. Harold Hobson was so overcome by 'this conquering charm'[40] that he admitted he had almost ended up on stage when the audience were invited to join the cast in celebration, a fifteen-minute event that J. C. Trewin claimed was 'quite the happiest thing of the night'. As for the piece itself, 'If only there had been a reasonable book, and the production had arrived before the Lord Chamberlain's official death, we might well have applauded some of *Hair* as an exhilarating youthful outburst.'[41]

In Britain *Hair* proved to be more than a five-minute wonder, its long run stalked by incident. The producers of ITV's *Eamonn Andrews Show* planned to show a live performance of the nude scene (strangely, as Andrews was of notably prim character). His blushes were saved when the cast refused to appear. In 1969 forty of the cast demanded to be auditioned for *The Black and White Minstrel Show* which was due to return to the Victoria Palace. They considered white performers blacking up and dressing in 'coon' costumes an insult to black people, as well as cheating black actors out of jobs. News that a service of thanksgiving for the third anniversary of the show's London production was to take place at St Paul's Cathedral renewed some of the outrage that had been around since 1968. Peter Dawson complained to the *Daily Telegraph* from Morden Rectory that 'the celebration of three years portrayal of filth and perversion is totally at variance with that faith and life which the Cathedral exists to proclaim'.[42] Eighty-seven members of the London Diocesan Synod signed a petition of no confidence in the Dean and Chapter, and the Prebendary of St Paul's threatened to resign. The eighteen-year-old Princess Anne saw the show, as did (twice) the Reverend Michael Botting, Rural Dean of Hammersmith, who helped organise the petition, finding the piece 'pornographic and blasphemous [...] I would never encourage masturbation'. As for the simulated acts of homosexuality, 'I believe it's wrong in the same way as adultery.'[43] The playwright William Douglas-Home suggested to *The Times* that his local vicar might put on a service to celebrate the fourth anniversary of Douglas-Home's comedy *The Secretary Bird*, as well as a memorial service for his recent flop *The Douglas Cause*.

Throughout its West End tenure, the show provided an easy focus for such as the Festival of Light, an organisation of conservative Christians associated in the public consciousness with Mary Whitehouse, Malcolm Muggeridge, Cliff Richard and Lord Longford. Having his photograph taken in front of a poster for the stage comedy *No Sex Please, We're British* was a trifling example of his lordship's antics, that play being one to which most maiden aunts would have taken little exception.

Despite its well-established reputation, *Hair* never ceased to shock. As late as 1973 a school party of eleven-year-old children from a Brixton comprehensive attended a performance. An organisation called the Society for Individual Freedom pointed out that 'A carefree attitude to drugs, the idea of easy sex, an irresponsible attitude to life, blasphemy and obscenity are all present in *Hair* and they are not the sort of things that eleven year olds should be taken to see.' The school announced that 'The housemaster was quite horrified by what he saw and heard at the theatre.'[44]

On the eve of its 1,999th performance at the Shaftesbury, the night watchman was alerted by crashing sounds in the thankfully vacated auditorium. Part of the ceiling had collapsed onto the stage and stalls. The theatre was closed and the production halted. For some this seemed an act of God. In October 1973 members of the company gathered outside the theatre (now threatened with demolition) to give a farewell *al fresco* performance. At its beginnings Jeremy Kingston in *Punch* had discovered in the nude scene and the final lines of 'Where Do I Go?' scenes 'intended neither to affront nor to turn us one and all into sex maniacs but expressing the gentle, earnest, pathetic attempt to recapture primal innocence. It is the desire to start the world again.' Of how many American musicals could as much be said? *Hair* nailed colours to the mast that would not be raised by others. Its contribution to radical alterations in British society was so considerable that it seems incredible that the genre that offered it birth turned its face away from its innovation.

A Broadway production was imported into London in 2010, giving ageing hippies and newcomers the chance to rediscover its potency, but despite excellent notices the moment had passed. Two years after the London opening of *Hair*, Galt MacDermot's music was heard in the London-only *Isabel's a Jezebel*, and subsequently in the Broadway import *Two Gentlemen of Verona*, but neither had the shock or freshness of *Hair*. No other musical had so alarmed British conservative reactionaries, but by the end of its run the British had begun their worship of the pop-opera religioso confections of Andrew Lloyd Webber: *Jesus Christ Superstar* and *Joseph and the Amazing Technicolor Dreamcoat*. Webber's work took the public in the opposite direction from *Hair*, establishing the godly musical imbued with all the fervour of a novel by Marie Corelli, with no impropriety of any kind. Eleven-year-old boys, subscribers to the Festival of Light, and millions who had never before darkened the door of any musical, had been shown the way.

The Broadway musical took little note of the changes *Hair* had introduced, but the springing up of the 'alternative' off-Broadway musical claimed *Hair* as antecedent. *Hair* had to be content with opening the door to such unexpurgated works as the off-Broadway *Oh! Calcutta!* which began its phenomenally long London run at the Roundhouse in 1970, off-Broadway's *The Dirtiest Show in Town* at the Duchess Theatre for two years from May 1971, and in 1974 *The City*, a 'motorcycle' musical with the Tokyo Kid Brothers. The 'sexual musical' *Let My People Come* at the Regent Theatre in 1974 was a sure love-child of *Hair*, with songs called 'Come In My Mouth', 'I'm Gay' and 'Whatever Turns You On', but *Plays and Players* reported that 'our theatre has seen scores of much inferior entertainments by casts who keep at least half-clothed'.[45] Its director Phil Oesterman considered that '*Hair* was a mile-stone, but [*The Dirtiest Show in Town*] is just a fun, entertaining evening. What I can no longer produce, or feel very involved about, is a show that I think is not communicating any ideas. I could never do *Irene* or *No, No, Nanette*.'[46]

The least-remembered import of the year was **Man with a Load of Mischief** (Comedy Theatre, 9 December 1968: 26), based on the 1924 romantic comedy by Ashley Dukes, a prolific British playwright (in *Who's Who in the Theatre* he names 'Sleep' as his recreation) almost forgotten today. His works, many of them taken from the French, included *The Comedy of a Man Who Married a Dumb Wife* and *The Dumb Wife of Cheapside*; what was it about Dukes and dumb women? He created London's Mercury Theatre, wrote theatrical criticism and books on the drama. With so strong a British pedigree, it seemed a bit rich that in musical theatre the only work to bear his name had originated in New York.

The musical version of *The Man with a Load of Mischief* had already made its debut in London at the modest Intimate Theatre, Palmers Green, where it sported a surprisingly good cast. The only cast member (of five) to survive the transition to the West End was Roberta D'Esti in the role of Lady. The choice of venue accentuated how difficult it was for an intimate off-Broadway production to find a suitable resting place in Britain. The notices for the Comedy Theatre production directed by Tad Danielewski had muted headlines: 'Mild Diversion for the Unsophisticated' (*Daily Telegraph*), 'Baffling Load of Olde English Moody' (*Daily Mail*), 'Charming but a Bit Fragile for the West End' (*Evening Standard*) and 'Comedy Just for Fun' (*The Times*) unlikely to start a rush for tickets. The adventure of a Regency actress on the run from a royal lover, her servant and a comical nobleman and an innkeeper's wife, seemed little enhanced by the words and music of Ben Tarver and John Clifton, although the work has several times been revived in New York.

The cast was not blamed. Philip Hope-Wallace considered it 'daintily done [...] with rather charming performances from Roberta D'Esti, Valentine Palmer and Julia McKenzie, and I could imagine the *Salad Days* public feeling reasonably at home with it'.[47] For Milton Shulman, 'Its most positive ingredient is charm and this is slapped on so thick that one does not so much experience it as wade through it.'[48] The critic of the *Lady* reminded readers that 'the original play depended upon its style and verbal rhythms to which the present business [...] is quite insensitive',[49] but by the time this review appeared the company had dispersed. Not a shred of its music permeated the British consciousness, with tunes 'particularly those treated to a reprise, [which] are all extremely conventional'.[50]

The Dancing Years brought back Ivor Novello's old British hit with June Bronhill, with little return. **Canterbury Tales**, the only musical ever likely to be made from Chaucer, was a hybrid: part pop, part swinging London, part music-hall, part medieval (or modern) smut. It established itself for a hugely successful run, despite having no songs of note. Two of the more interesting productions of the year arrived in December, but neither found favour. **Mr and Mrs** was an extraordinarily loud and vulgar version of two Noel Coward plays, while **The Young Visiters** turned Daisy Ashford's childhood novel into an evening of considerable delight.

1968 Broadway Exports

Hair (1,750), *Zorba* (305) and *Promises, Promises* (1,281).

1968 Broadway Only

The most ill-chosen title of the year was **Here's Where I Belong** (1). Lumbered with another impossible title, **The Education of H*Y*M*A*N K*A*P*L*A*N**

(28) sparked little interest, as did *Maggie Flynn* (82) and a 'musical fable' *I'm Solomon* (7). *Golden Rainbow* (385) lasted for a year without leaving an aftertaste, and the folly *Her First Roman* (17), about Caesar and Cleopatra, was the sole work of Ervin Drake. John Kander and Fred Ebb wrote the score for *The Happy Time* (286), a delicate piece that deserved a London outing. Potentially of more interest to the British was *Darling of the Day* (33), a much troubled adaptation of Arnold Bennett's novel *Buried Alive*, from which Hollywood had already fashioned the 1943 film *Holy Matrimony* with Monty Woolley and Gracie Fields. Jule Styne wrote the music to Yip Harburg's lyrics, but book and production problems seem to have scuppered the enterprise, most notable because Patricia Routledge won critical acclaim in the leading role opposite Vincent Price.

1969

Your Own Thing
Mame
Belle Starr
Dames at Sea
Promises, Promises
Anything Goes

Y*our Own Thing* (Comedy Theatre, 6 February 1969; 42) was a little musical being very modern, and clever in being suggested by Shakespeare's *Twelfth Night* and turned into the book by Donald Driver (who also directed) and music and lyrics of Hal Hester and Danny Apolinar. Producers Oscar Lewenstein and Binkie Beaumont of H. M. Tennent brought over the American company, but the Comedy, one of London's smallest theatres, was still too big for the piece. Which theatre would have been right for doing *Your Own Thing*, a little outpost of the hippie revolution? There was nothing suitable in the West End. With its complex sound system and fourteen projectors, the mixed-media production was a technological challenge. Driver told *The Times* he had written a piece that was as much message as musical, which for him centred on

> the asexuality of the twins. [...] *Twelfth Night* bores me. What I'm saying is that one should be exactly what one is. Do your own thing. I'm tired of the uptight world which is against change in hair styles, dress, philosophy, politics, when what we so obviously need is change – including man's dress which is dull, dull, dull.[1]

Your Own Thing came from off-Broadway, riding the wash from the Atlantic crossing of *Hair* and trailing awards, and went on to win not inconsiderable plaudits from the British critics. Peter Lewis in the *Daily Mail* found 'a lot of youthful fizz [...] it is quite a pretty bauble. I wish the music had been better.'[2] 'Brash but beguiling' was the verdict of the *Daily Telegraph*, for whom 'Gaily it exalts what is natural over what is legal. All in all, a light, slight frolic of unassailable charm.'[3] In the *Financial Times* B. A. Young applauded the idea but 'the script is neither deep enough nor witty enough',[4] while David Nathan in the *Sun* declared it 'basically televisual, a mixture of the *Laugh In* and the Monkees'.[5]

The hullabaloo surrounding London's **Mame** (Theatre Royal, Drury Lane, 20 February 1969; 443) had all the fingerprints of impresario Harold Fielding. Everything about the British production of Jerry Herman's latest work was ostentatious and classically camp. The tone was set before the first rehearsal. Its star, Ginger Rogers, making her British debut and earning £5,000 a week for the engagement, was not to be allowed to slink quietly into the country. Her arrival at Southampton on 20 December 1968 was greeted by a fifty-two-piece band from the 1st Battalion Worcestershire Regiment, as dockers in gumboots danced in celebration. She was whisked to Waterloo in a train which was emblazoned 'Ginger Rogers Mame Express'. The journey was whiled away with a showing of the Astaire–Rogers movie *Top Hat*, as her coterie dined on stuffed turkey (very *Mame*) and Miss Rogers' favourite ice-cream, chocolate chip, renamed for the occasion 'Ginger Rogers' Delight'. At Waterloo there was a trumpet fanfare provided by musicians from the Royal Military School of Music, Kneller Hall, after which the theatrical immigrant rode off in an open horse-drawn carriage. £2,000 had been spent on decorating her dressing-room at Drury Lane, its walls and ceiling lined with 194 yards of dyed raw silk in a pale pink design by the fashionably in demand Adam Pollock, who subsequently spent much time running around London in pursuit of exotic ice-creams for the star. Other of the dressing room's features were a canopied couch and mirrored pillars that supported an overhanging canopy. All that was possible was done to eliminate any memory of the previous occupant of the Lane, the British musical *The Four Musketeers*, so tasteless that it remains a prime example of how low British musicals had sunk by the end of the 1960s. Its star, the comedian and singer Harry Secombe, was so essential to the piece that on those nights when he was too ill to sing he remained on stage and mimed to a recording. *The Four Musketeers* might just have redeemed itself by being as camp as *Mame* meant to be, but decided to make do with being unspeakably bad. In doing so, it endeared itself greatly to the British public, who made sure it had a good run.

In truth, Rogers was just as important to *Mame* as Secombe had been to that Dumas disaster, and had once been considered for the Broadway opening, which eventually went to Angela Lansbury. The confidence attached to *Mame*'s arrival was palpable, and not without reason. Patrick Dennis's popular novel about an eccentric, larger-than-life socialite and her bohemian relationship with her nephew had already enjoyed a second life as a successful play on Broadway with Rosalind Russell and in London with Beatrice Lillie. Hollywood gave it new life, once again with Russell, in the 1958 film. It seemed that the public thirsted for *Mame*'s credo that 'Life is a banquet and most poor sons of bitches are starving to death.' Hardly the sort of statement one of Rodgers or Hammerstein's females would have made (imagine Nellie Forbush or Anna Leonowens or Julie Jordan coming out with such things), but Mame, from her birthplace of Dennis' novel, had always been a product of a gay sensibility. Neither Rodgers nor Hammerstein would have tolerated Dolly Levi or Mame Dennis as either the subject of a musical or as consort of one of their leading males; imagine Dolly or Mame reduced to consorts! Indeed, Rodgers and Hammerstein's works are the antithesis of Herman's œuvre. In their way, Herman's musicals repudiate the heterosexual, male-dominated, middle-class 'niceness' of Rodgers and Hammerstein; their subjects were chosen because Herman could respond so personally and effectively to them, welcoming the formidable women into the spotlight, whereas Rodgers and Hammerstein, confronted by such a strong character as the brothel keeper Fauna in *Pipe Dream* reduced her to milk and water. Herman, consciously or unconsciously, or just *naturally*, was making some sort of commitment to sexual politics, as he had throughout his career. That commitment would emerge fully from the closet in *La Cage aux Folles*. Meanwhile, he understandably let out a whoop of delight when asked to be the composer-lyricist of Dennis' work. Just as Carolyn Leigh and Cy Coleman had been the ideal collaborators for the musicalisation of Dennis' *Little Me*, Herman was right for *Auntie Mame*.

Herman's women are unusual in that they do not pin hearts on their sleeves in the anticipated heroine fashion. Neither Dolly nor Mame wastes time on romance, seemingly much more content to be surrounded by a male chorus and meddling in other people's affairs – Dolly by 'putting my hand in there', and Mame by suggesting that people open windows – than in searching for Mr Right. Mame's love, Beauregard Burnside, is a husband who dies long before curtain call, and one instinctively knows that Mame will not be trying it again. The positivity of *Hello, Dolly!* and *Mame*'s feminism is essentially progressive, even modern, a proof of Herman's signature. The assertive woman is never far from the centre of most of the output. After *Mame* she is there again at the centre of *Dear World* and *The Grand Tour* (both unseen in Britain) and, like her predecessors, the heroine of *Dear World*, the Madwoman of Chaillot, has little time for love, reserving most of her passion for man's mistreatment of the universe.

Although audiences were well used to the story of Mame, Herman's songs added a new dimension, almost bludgeoning them into submission with Mame's Sergeant Major manner, instructing the disillusioned to keep on opening those windows and forging ahead through life with 'It's Today', fiercely encouraging festiveness in 'We Need a Little Christmas'. The martial tone is often to the fore in *Mame*, even in the regimental rhythm of its cake-walk title song, one of those numbers that depends on seemingly endless repetition of the show's name; *twenty two* mentions, and *five* hammered out at the audience just before the curtain falls on Act One. Few can have left the theatre without taking home the name of the show, though there were probably some who remained resistant to the simple declamatory style of Herman's songs. By 1969 *Mame* stood out as a stonkingly old-fashioned Broadway musical. How many realised they were in at something like the death of the old-fashioned Broadway show?

Rogers' performance was mostly appreciated – the *Daily Telegraph* review was headlined 'Miss Rogers stunning in star appeal'- but the overall reaction to the work was general disappointment. 'Just what *would* it be like without Ginger?' asked the *Evening Standard* headline. Milton Shulman went on to review a production that was 'not a musical for anyone really interested in the genre – its development, its advancement or its style'.[6] Peter Lewis in the *Daily Mail* considered that 'The only things to go for are the songs of Jerry Herman – and Miss [Ann] Beach's performance.'[7] The *Lady* found 'the material is indifferent and the evening tepid'.[8] John Barber for the *Daily Telegraph* declared it 'ponderous'.[9] For *The Times* the score was 'pre-Gershwin' in 'an extraordinarily old-fashioned musical'. This is certainly true of the score, marking *Mame* as something quite alien to the London of 1969. Few American musicals of the decade had caught this spirit, or been executed with such bravado, and since *Hello, Dolly!* had opened in December 1965 London had mostly been offered Broadway musicals with a point, or, not quite the same thing, an intended point. There was the intention of added depth to *Funny Girl* (heartbreak of a star), *Fiddler on the Roof* (ethnic persecution), the underbelly of prostitution in *Sweet Charity*, Nazi evil in *Cabaret*, supposedly classic drama in *Man of La Mancha*, the politics of black poverty and inter-racial love in *Golden Boy*, hippie philosophy in *Hair*, love resulting in a suicide attempt in *Promises, Promises*. Dennis' novel eschewed any modern agenda, as did Herman's score, and the focus was on the star. According to *The Times*,

> It is true that in the first act you keep waiting for the show to start, and for Miss Rogers to begin her own night's work; but by half time you are in no doubt that you are in the company of a whale of a star [...] she glows and radiates a blend of sensual magic and athletic pleasure of a kind I have never seen combined in one performer.[10]

It was canny of Fielding to sign Rogers, although it might have been wiser to hire a comedienne; Rogers was not first choice for making audiences laugh. The supporting cast was British. Statuesque Margaret Courtenay played Mame's bosom buddy and embodiment of theatrical camp Vera Charles, and the undervalued Ann Beach was an admirable Agnes Gooch. It hardly signified that Barry Kent returned as leading man to the scene of his former triumph (Lancelot in *Camelot*) when he had next to nothing to do.

Juliet Prowse took over from Rogers for two weeks in September 1969 to allow Rogers a break. Rogers' understudy, India Adams, who had dubbed Joan Crawford's singing voice in Hollywood and was something of a *doppelgänger* for Rogers, stood by for the entire run, but Rogers never missed a performance.[11] Indeed, Adams' only other British appearance seems to have been in the short-lived revue-musical *How Now Brown Cow*. With such a fanfare, it was no surprise that the show made a good start at the box-office, taking £100,000 in its first month, but because production and running costs were high the show proved profit-resistant. When Rogers' contract was drawing to its end Fielding asked her to stay. No attempt was made to replace her when she declined. There was still more to be wrung out of Patrick Dennis's invention. Warner's 1974 Hollywood film of the musical had Lucille Ball, her face bleached out by being strained through too many filters. The movie was given a hard critical ride – the *New Yorker* recommended it as 'So terrible it isn't boring.' The vim seemed to have been surgically removed, and Ball ineffective in a great number of costumes. Her weakness in the part added another layer on to the heap of *Mame's* camp. A 1983 New York revival of *Mame*, again with Lansbury, managed a month's run.

Two months after Rogers had begun *Mame*, another Hollywood star took to the London stage in **Belle Starr** (Palace Theatre, 30 April 1969; 12). While speaking to its director, lyricist and originator Jerry Schafer on the telephone, Betty Grable apparently agreed to star in a London production without ever having set eyes on a script. Originally announced as *The Piecefull Palace* and variously described by its producers as a 'Wild West Musical', 'A Musical Musical' and 'a Wild West Musical Stunt Show', the title was changed to *Belle Starr* by the time it opened at Glasgow. How confusing would it have been to have a show called *The Piecefull Palace* at the Palace, and customers might well complain, if it wasn't for the title's spelling, that the thing was far from peaceful. Its subject was the rootin', shootin' Myra Maybelle Shirley (alias Belle Starr), already portrayed in movies by Jane Russell and Gene Tierney, and her male companions. J. C. Trewin's premonition of disaster for an evening spent at a Wild West brothel in the 1860s proved accurate: 'Tell me that I have an evening before me with Billy the Kid and Jesse James and my blood congeals.'[12] The book, written by Warren Douglas from a short story by Schafer, was joined with lyrics by Douglas, Schafer and the show's composer Steve Allen, whose other main composing credit had been for a 1963 Broadway bio-musical of Sophie Tucker. *Sophie* had starred Libi Staiger (the Cleo of the London *The Most Happy Fella*) and had more or less killed off her career; now, *Belle Starr* was to do the same for Grable.

The £140,000 show had been devised as a 'revolutionary new concept of show business in Las Vegas; the central philosophy is "a violent continuous session of fist fights and gun spins, with breakaway bottles and shattering glass"'.[13] One of the gunfights had thirty-two on-stage shots. Grable had left it late for her West End debut and chosen a dead duck. Though her presence was celebrated by the first-night audience, the critics were unimpressed by the material. Mistakenly thinking itself in *Mame*, the chorus carolled 'Tell me we'll never part, Belle' as Miss Grable's legendary legs descended a staircase. For Irving Wardle in *The Times* 'The music revives memories of the Billy Cotton Bandshow.'[14]

R. B. Marriott found 'the show on the whole is on the tame side', noting Valerie Walsh's Calamity Jane for one of the better songs of the night, 'I'm a Lady', but remarking on one of the most dismal of 1960s scores. As for its star, 'Miss Grable makes some excellent entrances, but her exits are most inconsequential'.[15] In the *Illustrated London News* Trewin wondered at the welcome given its star: 'one asked whether Siddons, Bernhardt, or Duse had ever had so clamorous a reception',[16] but Eric Shorter in the *Daily Telegraph* regretted that

> The centrepiece of comical interest is an imported water closet which flushes at crucial moments. Other jokes concern cowboys in orange combinations affecting sexual exhaustion; a flamboyantly effeminate

baddy; and a man with potently bad breath. The latter is a gag which Feydeau may get away with; but Feydeau did not have a hand.[17]

Barry Norman in the *Daily Mail* pronounced it 'excruciating rubbish [...] comedy of a sort, mostly about body odour and bottoms'.[18] The Palace's owner Emile Littler confirmed, 'You cannot have a lavatory on stage and it flushing three times during a show and get away with it.'[19] Grable ('Some of the things I had to say were absolutely embarrassing. It's a question of taste.') offered to pay for a doctoring writer to be brought in to overhaul the script, but the management refused. *Belle Starr* closed in disarray at the end of its second week. No one blamed Grable, who had not yet been paid. When the final curtain fell, the cast inserted a commemoration in the *Stage*: 'Our Greatest Possible Thanks to Betty Grable for being a lovely lady and a super star from the "Belle Starr" Company. Please Come Back – We Love You.'

The second off-Broadway entry of the year proved yet again that anything originating beyond the Great White Way made the journey to London at its peril. **Dames at Sea** (Duchess Theatre, 27 August 1969; 127) was an amusing pastiche of 1930s American musicals for six actors. Four years earlier, London had rejected Sandy Wilson's pastiche of British musicals of the same period, *Divorce Me, Darling!*, a work requiring much larger forces than the piece written by George Haimsohn and (British) Robin Miller, with music by Jim Wise. The 'Now 1930s Musical' followed the well-worn narrative of the temperamental leading lady who is replaced by a young unknown hopeful, Ruby (read Keeler). Ruby becomes a 'Star Tar' when a new musical is presented aboard ship because the theatre is demolished. Much easy fun was to be had, but the production couldn't turn itself into a success. The troublesome Mona Kent was an opportunity for Joyce Blair, labelled 'superb' by the *Guardian*'s Michael Billington.[20] John Barber confessed that Blair had been his favourite chorus girl in *Guys and Dolls* 'and now suddenly blossomed into a flamboyant, witty, big-voiced personality'.[21] Despite such encouragement, Blair would struggle to establish herself in the public consciousness.

Condemning the piece as 'this unutterably tedious piece of nonsense' Caryl Brahms remembered the dames at sea 'and for my part they can stay there'.[22] The *Tatler* thought the cast 'are for the most part far too inclined to mock what is already a parody, thereby negating the original intention. Say what you like about those early musicals, at least the cast took them seriously.'[23] The bulk of audiences at the Duchess were probably unconcerned about how the company dealt with the pastiche. Should the material be guyed, as in *Little Mary Sunshine*, or played straight, as in the original Vida Hope production of *The Boy Friend*? In truth, the bulk of audiences would not have been able to tell one treatment from the other. Less concerned with such niceties, some critics were happy with the light-heartedness and a score that was consistently inventive: the love song immediately switched on when Ruby meets struggling composer Dick ('It's

You'), the vampy, ageing female star who can sing Dick's big number straight off from memory after a momentary glance at the sheet music ('That Mister Man of Mine'), the comic duet when Mona is reunited with her old flame ('The Beguine'), a natty 'umbrella' number ('It's Raining in My Heart') and the glib final curtain coming together of the three matched couples ('Let's Have a Simple Wedding'). The casting was probably better for a subsequent production by the Cambridge Theatre Company, with Pip Hinton as Mona and Sandra Dickinson as Ruby. A later tour with Josephine Blake as Mona was not so effective. While America continued to mount provincial productions, in Britain *Dames at Sea* has enjoyed less afterlife.

A work that essentially came from outside the mainstream Broadway factory was H. M. Tennent's presentation of **Promises, Promises** (Prince of Wales Theatre, 2 October 1969; 560), but it disappointingly turned out to be the only musical play scored by Burt Bacharach and lyricist Hal David. The promises came in many disguises. Of course there was the promise made to the show's luckless in love hero, Chuck Baxter, one of a mere 31,259 employees at the Consolidated Life Insurance Company, that hiring his flat out to its executives for a quick sexual encounter would get him a foot on the firm's ladder. Then there were the promises of happiness dangled before Chuck, and the promise of a happy relationship with Fran Kubelik, bedded by Chuck's boss J. D. Sheldrake. When Fran, worn out by the inability of life to deliver what she had been promised, tries to end her life, the fulfilment of a promise begins to slide into view for her and Chuck.

Promises, Promises had worked as a movie, *The Apartment*, for Shirley MacLaine and Jack Lemmon, and the musical had the advantage of its screenwriter Neil Simon as book author. In fact Simon claimed that he had changed almost all the dialogue for the musical's much-praised script.

'Energy and Sparkle but formula a bit tired' ran the headline of John Barber's review for the *Daily Telegraph*.[24] Perhaps the formula, the *shape* of things, didn't stray far from standard New York product, but a distinct mood pervaded every moment of the piece. The original Robert Moore direction was re-enacted by Charles Blackwell, with the other New York components in place: choreography by Michael Bennett, sets by Robin Wagner, costumes by Donald Brooks and, crucially, the wholly sympathetic orchestrations of Jonathan Tunick. Here was a case where domestic casting simply would not do. Tennent sensibly compiled an American company headed by Anthony Roberts as Chuck, of whom Harold Hobson wrote, 'The world is a finer as well as a more enjoyable place because of the nature of Mr. Roberts' performance in this rather salacious piece',[25] and Roberts went on to head the US touring production. There was a memorable Fran in twenty-two-year-old Betty Buckley, formerly a Texan journalist and Miss Fort Worth of 1966, who had yet to appear on Broadway.

Of its year, *Promises, Promises* was the only Broadway import that seemed of its time. Whatever the delights of *Mame*, Herman's work clung to a much earlier era; *Mame*'s songs might have inhabited a Hollywood movie of the 1930s. The brief but welcome revival of *Man of La Mancha* should have reminded its patrons that it belonged to no era at all, striving in the impossibility of its dream to create some more meaningful sound-world of its own. In fact, there had been much better and more interesting shows than the Knight of the Woeful Countenance conjured up throughout the end of the sixties. Seriousness had been the backbone of *Fiddler on the Roof, Cabaret, Golden Boy, Hair* and *Sweet Charity*, closest cousin to *Promises, Promises*. Some of these had strong links to 'pop' music, which now and again had even worked itself into British musicals: think *Canterbury Tales* with its indigestible mix of the medieval with sub-Beatles items, the ghastly *Pull Both Ends* (a hopeless charade set in a Christmas cracker factory as an excuse to showcase a TV dance troupe, The Young Generation), and – at the lower end of the market – John Taylor's knockabout score for *Mr and Mrs*. None of these, of course, made a pretence of seriousness, and there was nothing remarkable about 'pop' being used effectively to convey 'issues'. The score of *Promises, Promises* is remarkable because David and Bacharach brought to it a unique sound, mood, energy, experience which they had already established outside the genre.

It may have seemed at the time that *Promises, Promises* was *of* its time, and that time would pale its contemporary effectiveness. But this is a work that will not stay in the shadows. In a 2010 Broadway revival headed by Sean Hayes and Kristin Chenoweth, an attempt to gild the lily by interpolating two David-Bacharach hits, 'I Say a Little Prayer' and 'A House Is Not a Home', did not improve matters. The dollop of sentimentality hidden in the latter didn't sit with the original tone of the work, into which sentimentality doesn't much intrude; it goes beyond the poignancy that makes this score tick. Anyway, this constant drip of numbers with pop rhythms shouldn't work at all, its karaoke overture with its off-stage choral voices threading through the themes (and an old-fashioned overture, too, squeezing in as many of the show's tunes as it can manage), its melodies that seem to exist purely by their beat, but it does work, all of it. Perhaps it's because there is at its root, and essentially in Bacharach's music, a melancholia that pervades even the numbers that are meant to sound happy. When Chuck celebrates the fact that 'She Likes Basketball' he may be all smiles and expectation, but it's the paltry nature of his hope that strikes home. Where is *Promises, Promises* truly happy? It never is, in the same way that another 'pop' score, *The Umbrellas of Cherbourg*, never is, or many of the scores of Andrew Lloyd Webber. It's often more effective to a musical if the undercurrent of sadness turns into a torrent.

So much of *Promises, Promises* is concerned with isolation, the unsatisfactory life. Try 'Half as Big as Life' (Chuck's self-doubt; knowing he's a good guy but ...), 'Upstairs' (Chuck literally as the outsider, killing time in the street while his apartment is being 'used'), 'You'll Think of Someone' (the indaequacy of natural expression), Sheldrake's drug-like addiction to 'Wanting Things'. Most oustandingly, Fran has two of the finest numbers in all of American musicals of the period: a terrible desperation expressed in 'Knowing When To Leave' and 'Whoever You Are, I Love you'. What other songs of this period reach the pitch of 'I'll Never Fall in Love Again'? Far from being modishly parked in the 1960s, *Promises, Promises* may be emotionally immortal.

There was little welcome for a revival of **Anything Goes** (Saville Theatre, 18 November 1969; 15) propped up by a seriously under-cast company and a band of ten musicians. The original score was subjected to interpolations from other Porter works – 'choking the cat with cream' according to Philip Hope-Wallace, who otherwise remained unenthusiastic.[26] The music was newly 'arranged' by Julian Stein, with orchestrations by Alfred Ralston, but asking Marion Montgomery, a subtle jazz singer, to deliver some belting numbers made famous by Ethel Merman did the stuff no justice. The *Illustrated London News* found 'the present version of the book [...] sadly facetious, and the voyage from New York to Southampton appears interminable [...] Porter's songs, the night's justification, are variously treated; we miss the full relish of the lyrics.'[27] The starveling production was quickly gone.

News from the British front was not encouraging. Edward Woodward gallantly took the stage as Sydney Carton in a galumphing adaptation of Dickens' French Revolution novel. **Two Cities** took on the vastness of the Palace Theatre, but the piece was puny. Another adaptation, from H. G. Wells' novel about female emancipation, **Ann Veronica** was an inferior offering from which its leading lady, Dorothy Tutin, fled before the London opening. Nobody much noticed the Moral Re-Armament musical **High Diplomacy**, but it propounded the organisation's beliefs. Fewer patrons attended **The Stiffkey Scandals of 1932**, a 'play with songs' about the decline and fall of the notorious Revd. Harold Davidson. More lavishly staged than any of the above was Harold Fielding's production **Phil the Fluter**, loosely based on the life of the Irish composer Percy French, but the mix of French's compositions and new numbers by David Heneker was unsatisfying, and a starry cast couldn't redeem it.

1969 Broadway Exports

1776 (1,217).

1969 Broadway Only

Success was outweighed by failure. **La Strada** (1), an adaptation of Federico Fellini's movie, had started life as a Lionel Bart musical, but almost his entire score was jettisoned before the New York opening. Equally catastrophic was **Billy** (1). British actor Laurence Naismith played Captain Vere opposite the Billy Budd of Robert Salvio in this musicalisation of Herman Melville's *Billy Budd*, more substantially translated into an opera by Benjamin Britten. Dorothy

Loudon made an impression in *The Fig Leaves Are Falling* (4), with music by Albert Hague, but it failed to reach week two. Other failures were **Buck White** (7) and **Come Summer** (7), Ray Bolger's last Broadway musical, and directed by Agnes de Mille. From the creators of *The Fantasticks*, **Celebration** (110) was much in the same mould. A bio-musical of Jimmy Walker, **Jimmy** (87) failed to take hold, as did **Dear World** (132), adapted from Jean Giraudoux's *The Madwoman of Chaillot*. The Jerry Herman score had some real pearls ('The Tea Party') and an embarrassing title number, plus the advantage of Angela Lansbury. It was an interesting flop, whereas **Coco** (333) was a not particularly interesting success. Its credentials were impressive: libretto by Alan Jay Lerner, music by André Previn, costumes by Cecil Beaton, and star Katharine Hepburn.

1970

1776
The Great Waltz

CONSIDERING ITS SUBJECT, *1776* (New Theatre, 16 June 1970; 168) did well to hold out in the West End for as long as it did; on Broadway it was a three-year winner. On the face of it, there seemed little reason why a British audience would be bothered: its composer-lyricist, and the man who had dreamed the idea, had not been heard of in Britain; its librettist had never written a successful show; there was a lack of extractable songs; the home-grown cast lacked any star name. And then there was the subject: an evening of hot, tetchy men comprising a meeting of the Continental Congress in a sultry Philadelphia room, faced with the decision whether or not to break America's allegiance to Great Britain. Never mind that it ended triumphantly (for America) with the signing of the Declaration of Independence – try explaining this to someone organising a coach party up West for an enjoyable night out. Bringing the piece to London was a bravery in itself, for which the Broadway production personnel was retained: director Peter Hunt, choreographer Onna White, sets and lighting by Jo Mielziner, costumes by Patricia Zipprodt, orchestrations by Eddie Sauter.

Dangerous as it may have seemed for so transatlantic a work, the London edition of *1776* was cast from domestic actors headed by Lewis Fiander as John Adams and Ronald Radd as Benjamin Franklin, with a strong supporting company that included only two females, Vivienne Ross as Adams' wife Abigail, and Cheryl Kennedy as Martha Jefferson. For London, it was decided that this self-confessed 'new musical from the Colonies' would be played without any attempted American accents. What might have been just another impediment for the British audience proved liberating for the production, allowing it to breathe more naturally. Still trying to encourage that coach party to set off for the New, it then had to be explained that the show would be played without an interval (something that audiences in Britain were not attuned to), there were no dancing girls (and no dancing), and at one point the conductor put down his baton for a straight half hour of dialogue. Much safer to book for *The Great Waltz*. And yes, the evening did threaten to be claustrophobic, its action (precious little of it) mainly confined to the debating hall of the second Continental Congress, the passage of days marked only by a calendar at the back of the stage.

In the *Daily Telegraph* John Barber noted 'the superb unarrogant patriotism which is the show's whole message' and that 'its novelty is striking, and it admirably illustrates America's confident use of the musical as a medium capable of expressing, if necessary, serious historical ideas'.[1] *1776* was not only a trailblazer in this regard, but almost a lone voice, although here and there political subjects would be treated with seriousness, even if, as with the Alan Jay Lerner–Leonard Bernstein *1600 Pennsylvania Avenue* of 1976, they were

38 Backstage at the Coliseum: Judith Bruce waiting to go on as Bianca in
the Sadler's Wells Opera revival of *Kiss Me, Kate* in 1970

rejected by critics and audiences alike. There is perhaps more evidence of the musical 'as a medium capable of expressing, if necessary, serious historical ideas' (or at least themes) in British theatre, although even here the manner in which they appeared belonged to the revue format, as in *Oh What a Lovely War* (World War I) and *Hang Down Your Head and Die* (capital punishment). Here, the 'serious ideas' are central to the work, in a way that cannot be said of *Cabaret* (Nazi Germany). Irving Wardle of *The Times* seems to have agreed. 'If the test of a good musical is to extend the territory by absorbing apparently unmusical material, then this treatment of America's secession from Britain ranks as Broadway's more [*sic*] virile contribution to the form since *West Side Story*.'[2]

The fact that *1776* arrived with such a spirit of innovation almost slipped from British interest. On Broadway it pre-dated Stephen Sondheim's *Company*, which arrived in London in 1972, the first of the 'wholly' Sondheim shows to make the journey, and to seem to mark a distinct shift in British perception of what American musical theatre could do. That reputation was not undeserved, but *1776* also deserves credit. From somewhere, composer Sherman Edwards found a distinctive voice, evident as much in the opening 'Piddle, Twiddle and Resolve' as in its moments of high drama, the moving 'Momma, Look Sharp' and 'Is Anybody There?'. *1776* seemed time and again to contradict the profundity of its subject, by the uproarious intervention of 'The Lees of Old Virginia', through the delicious 'He Plays the Violin' and the epistolary duet for Adams and his stay-at-home wife 'Till Then', their gentle argument over his need for saltpetre and her need for pins turning on a sigh into a ravishing love-motif.

Rather in the manner of Ivor Novello's taking over of the Theatre Royal, Drury Lane, in 1935 with his florid operetta *Glamorous Night*, Harold Fielding had sustained tenure of the old playhouse for *Mame* in 1969, and stayed on until *Gone with the Wind* in 1972, an enterprise of which Novello would surely have approved, and one that fully exercised the theatre's machinery. Between these came Fielding's co-production with Bernard Delfont of a Frankenstein of an operetta which had played New York decades before, *The Great Waltz* (Theatre Royal, Drury Lane, 9 July 1970; 605). Before its premiere the historical greats of the house – David Garrick, Richard Brinsley Sheridan and Edmund Kean – had given way to a season of *Carol Channing with Her Ten Stout-Hearted Men*. Now *The Great Waltz* promised a return to a theatrical grandeur, spectacle and opulence. First seen on Broadway in 1934, another version had played Melbourne in 1966, but the magnificence of Wendy Toye's new production, with sets by Oliver Smith and choreography by Edmund Balis, eclipsed the earlier efforts. The lyrics of Robert Wright and George Forrest were supplemented by those of Forman Brown, and the book, some nonsense about the difficulties between Johann Strauss and Johann Strauss Junior in mid-nineteenth century Vienna, had a convoluted authorship in which a dozen writers seem to have played a hand.

The results may be imagined, but audiences turned up for the music and the spectacle. R. B. Marriott reported that 'The corn is thick and rich, high and swaying at Drury Lane. Not, it must be quickly added, corn like the fresh new growth and sturdy power of *Oklahoma!*, but that of another, far away, age.'[3] Fielding had wanted Anneliese Rothenberger to play the leading role of Helene Vernet, but the role went to the Hungarian soprano Sari Barabas, with the American baritone Walter Cassel (succeeded in October 1970 by Inia Te Wiata) as Strauss Senior, British David Watson as Strauss Junior, and Diane Todd as Resi. The enthusiastic public response suggested that audiences were still content with musicals that offered nothing new in the manner of style, imagination or serious intent.

There was little in the British musical to compel public attention. There was worthiness in *'Erb*, a socially aware piece about trade unions written by and starring Trevor Peacock. *Mandrake* was ushered in from the provinces, taken from Machiavelli's *Mandragola*, with music by Anthony Bowles, and was quickly ditched. Efforts to bring the British musical up to the moment were obvious in the short-lived **Lie Down, I Think I Love You**, and Jack Good's rock version of *Othello*, **Catch My Soul**. It was only two years since *Hair*, but Galt MacDermot's music for the 'musical fable' *Isabel's a Jezebel* didn't catch on. The most conventional British entry was a bio-musical of Marie Lloyd. The casting was perfunctory, and the music by Ron Grainer disappointingly wound around the elongated lyrics of Caryl Brahms and Ned Sherrin. The right sort of vulgarity might have helped **Sing a Rude Song**, but even the rudeness was wrong.

1970 Broadway Exports

Applause (898) and *Company* (690).

1970 Broadway Only

Essentially American musical theatre, *The Rothschilds* (505) told its story of overweening ambition, sweetened by a good score from Jerry Bock and Sheldon Harnick, but the show was essentially for the home market. Richard Rodgers scored *Two by Two* (351), a bio-musical with Danny Kaye as a genuinely truculent Noah, but the 'black' satire *Purlie* (689) ran twice as long. The year's flops were potentially more interesting. *Minnie's Boys* (80) told the story of the Marx Brothers and their domineering mother (Shelley Winters) with a personable score from Larry Grossman and Hal Hackady. A quick death awaited *Look to the Lilies* (25), its score by Jule Styne, but there was something unsatisfactory about the casting, with the glorious Shirley Booth as an unlikely Mother Superior. *Cry for Us All* (9) was a descendant of *Man of La Mancha*, but its source – the verse drama *Hogan's Goat* – and its distinguished cast, could not save it. The Yiddish community was served by two off-stream Broadway productions, ***Light, Lively and Yiddish*** (87) and ***The President's Daughter*** (72). In the reject department were ***Lovely Ladies, Kind Gentlemen*** (16) from the successful play *The Teahouse of the August Moon*; ***Park*** (5) in which the audience listened to two couples discussing their predicaments in a public space; ***Georgy*** (4), concocted from Margaret Forster's 'trendy' novel *Georgy Girl*, for which the British actress Dilys Watling was shipped to New York, and the solitary performance of ***Gantry*** (1).

39 *Hair* met the Bible in *Godspell*, a show that suggested the old Broadway musical may have had its day. *Godspell* went on to beget other 'logo' musicals such as *Jesus Christ Superstar*

1971

Show Boat
Ambassador
Godspell

FORTY-THREE YEARS after its London premiere, ***Show Boat*** (Adelphi Theatre, 29 July 1971; 910) reappeared in a lavish production by Harold Fielding, directed by Wendy Toye. Oscar Hammerstein II's original book had the questionable benefit of a 'script editor' in Benny Green, but this did not still John Barber's description in the *Daily Telegraph* of 'a pretty ramshackle old vessel'.[1] Harold Hobson disagreed: 'We are mighty fine fellows nowadays, but we cannot write a musical one-tenth as good as this, so packed with talent, with such sweeping, overwhelming music, so electrical in its dancing [choreography by Toye and Frederic Franklin], with singing so sweet and pure, or with a story that strikes such reverberating chords in the heart.'[2] Caryl Brahms celebrated 'an enchantment of scenes, each set [by Tim Goodchild] as imaginative and well conceived as the last. Lights flicker and rotate in a way that would make Zeffirelli take note. The production is a triumph.'[3] The *Evening Standard* declared Cleo Laine 'the first ethnically correct' performer ever to play the role of Julie.

Following on the closure of *Fiddler on the Roof*, and after a three-week season at Manchester, ***Ambassador*** (Her Majesty's Theatre, 19 October 1971; 86) was substandard fare, notable here because it was a rare example of an American work originating in the West End before chancing Broadway. The adaptation of Henry James' novel *The Ambassadors* was undertaken by a musical theatre novice, Don Ettlinger, who had written for films and television in America. It was also a first for composer Don Gohman, but lyricist Hal Hackady had contributed to Broadway's *Minnie's Boys* and would be lyricist for Broadway's *Goodtime Charley* and *Teddy and Alice*. Many considerable talents had a hand in the production of *Ambassador*: sets and costumes by Peter Rice, orchestration by Philp J. Lang, dance arrangements by Ray Holder, choreography by Gillian Lynne, and direction by Stone Widney who had been assistant to Moss Hart on *My Fair Lady* and *Camelot*.

James' story was of the punctilious, staid Massachusetts lawyer Lambert Strether, who is despatched to Paris to investigate the romantic entanglement of Chadwick Newsome. Once abroad, Strether is thrown off course by his fascination with the glamorous Countess Marie de Vionnet, with whom he falls in love. Not too much to exercise an audience's brain, and a Parisian setting giving opportunities for local colour, and the hiring of two undoubted stars was icing on the cake: Howard Keel and the French film actress Danielle Darrieux, who had played Broadway in the André Previn–Alan Jay Lerner *Coco*. Otherwise, the show offered few possibilities to any of the supporting cast, including

Margaret Courtenay who might as well have stayed at home, a London debut as the Countess' daughter by Isobel Stuart, and the non-singing Ellen Pollock, who had appeared in more George Bernard Shaw plays than any other, as Gloriani.

Gohman and Hackady's numbers included the gruesome comedy items 'What Can You Do with a Nude?' and 'You Can Tell a Lady By Her Hat'; the titles tell you they have nothing to do with the plot. The two stars got the best of the score. Darrieux sparkled her way through her introductory 'Surprise' (there was an old-fashioned 'Parisian' ballet attached to it), and yearned her way through 'Young With Him' (making excuses to Strether about her love affair with toy-boy Newsome) and 'Not Tomorrow'. Keel delivered Strether's impassioned arias with conviction, notably the character's signature number, 'All of My Life'. Lacking in originality as it was, with too much of its score sounding like a bad example of a British musical of the 1960s, there was reason enough in its stars to keep the show alive, but it proved a casualty. The *Stage* had nothing but praise for Darrieux ('She is very welcome on the London stage, and you must certainly go to see her') and Keel: 'between them they 'give the show the brilliance, charm and personality it intrinsically lacks'. R. B. Marriott heard a script heavy with banality ('more often than not reflected on the lyrics') and music that was 'unmemorable if at times tuneful in a reminiscent sort of way'. [4]

A year after the London opening, a revised production opened on Broadway with an American cast headed by the two original London stars, sets and costumes, and London director, but Lynne's name as choreographer was replaced by Joyce Trisler. Now the adaptation was credited to Ettlinger and Anna Marie Barlow, her only Broadway credit. One of the many alterations from London was the excision of the play's opening scenes in Massachusetts, and for some reason the action took place in 1906 rather than in the West End production's 1908. There were many adjustments to the London score. These included two new numbers for Darrieux, 'I Know the Man' and 'She Passed My Way'. 'La Nuit d'Amour' for the prostitutes of Paris was removed. Gloriani became a singing role for Carmen Mathews in 'Why Do Women Have To Call it Love?' Andrea Marcovicci's Jeanne retained the ingenue's two London songs 'Love Finds the Lonely' and 'Mama'. 'What Can You Do with a Nude?' and 'You Can Tell a Lady By Her Hat' were cut. Keel and Darrieux's duet 'That's What I Need Tonight' remained from London, but the just as attractive 'Charming' had gone. Keel had two new songs, 'Something More' and 'Happy Man'; the London 'Am I Wrong?' transmuted into 'Too Much to Forgive'; and his anthem 'All of My Life', sung in London half-way through Act One, was kept back on Broadway until the end of Act Two. Effective as this tinkering may have been, the American *Ambassador* was off after nine performances. It marked the end of Keel's career in book musicals.

The advent of **Godspell** (Roundhouse, 17 November 1971; Wyndham's Theatre, 26 January 1972; 1,128) marked the arrival in London of the biblical musical, a genre that was to radically alter the relationship between Broadway and the West End. The show had survived its off-Broadway beginning of only six months before, eventually blossoming into 2,124 performances. In Britain it seemed an unlikely project for the establishment production company H. M. Tennent, but after a fringe season the musical adaptation of St Matthew's Gospel moved into the West End for its almost three-year run. Presenting as a 'Gospel Rock-Musical' it dealt not in miracles but parables, conceived by John-Michael Tebelak with songs by Stephen Schwartz that seemed to bridge any gap between popular, rock and vaudeville. Its story, unfolded by a group of young people confined in a playground, was of the last days of Christ, with the characters taking on the mantle of Jesus (David Essex) and Judas (Jeremy Irons).

The critics were mixed in their reactions. Jeremy Kingston in *Punch* watched 'a dazzling sequence of performing techniques';[5] Irving Wardle appreciated its reliance on youth and vitality and thought Tebelak had 'most successfully converted his piece into British gesture and speech rhythms' which even included Goons' voices.[6] The *Sunday Times* was enthusiastic: 'magnificent [...] a production full of splendour', noting that although the parables were recited with childish burlesque they possessed a potent vitality that captivated the audience. The *Daily Telegraph* headlined with 'Childlike cavortings of *Godspell*', admitting that the Crucifixion was enacted with total reverence, but that onlookers might be offended by the prevailing 'theatrical puerility'.[7] Complaining that the parables had been dealt a *Sesame Street* treatment, Michael Billington reported that the evening 'turns into an unnerving combination of a Ralph Reader Gang Show, a sterilized version of *Hair* and something a trendy Kingsley Amis vicar might have dreamed up given limitless resources [...] a self-congratulatory uneloquent cartoon-like musical'.[8] Patrons would eventually be lured by posters carrying another press quote: 'You Can Safely Take All The Family'. This was essential to the success of *Godspell*: it offered safe harbour to a morally disturbed Britain at the start of the decade, offering a democritisation, a sanctuary, that was welcoming to all, believers and non-believers. By 1970 attendance at religious services was declining; now, only 1.5 million Britons were regular church-goers.

If you wanted a show about premature ejaculation, the British musical choice of the day was ***Maybe That's Your Problem***; if you wanted a chamber piece that hovered between old-fashioned revue and old-hat musical you made your way (as speedily as possible) to watch the hapless Joyce Blair and Bill Simpson in the short-lived folly ***Romance!***

1971 Broadway Exports

Follies (522), ***70, Girls, 70*** (35), ***Jesus Christ Superstar*** (711), ***You're a Good Man, Charlie Brown*** (1,628), ***Godspell*** (2,124) and ***Two Gentlemen of Verona*** (628).

1971 Broadway Only

The Broadway stay-at-homes were a mixed bag of disappointments. Set in Cyprus in 1947, *Ari* (19) had an unpropitious title and brief existence. The prize turkey was **Frank Merriwell** (1), the adventures of a fictional Yale sporting hero made popular through dime books and comics. **Only Fools Are Sad** (144) was the not altogether encouraging title of a musical performed in English and Hebrew. From Canada came **Anne of Green Gables** (16), an unassuming adaptation of Lucy M. Montgomery's novel; a production had played London two years earlier. A chamber piece based on Truman Capote's novel, **The Grass Harp** (7), had an atmosphere of its own, decorated by Kenward Elmslie and composer Claibe Richardson's score.

1972

Company
Gone with the Wind
I and Albert
Applause

T HE ARRIVAL OF *Company* (Her Majesty's Theatre, 8 January 1972; 344) was well timed. The British musical was at a nadir, with barrel-scrapers such as *Romance!*, a tawdry revival of *The Maid of the Mountains*, shreds of a defunct Lionel Bart in *The Londoners*, yet another rerun of Anthony Newley and Leslie Bricusse's one-idea concept of musicals in *The Good Old Bad Old Days*, and a 'new' operetta composed by and for John Hanson. Against such a background *Company* was bound to stand out, but it also eclipsed its American contemporaries, of which London had been pretty well starved since the 1969 *Promises, Promises*, and three of the few productions in the interim had been revivals: *Anything Goes*, *Kiss Me, Kate* and *Show Boat*.

At any time *Company* would have been an outstanding contribution. There was nothing new about its theme. Love and marriage had been at the heart of musical entertainment since it began. Without infidelities, misunderstandings and emotional chicanery many an old British musical farce would not have got beyond its Overture, and romance had relentlessly stalked the Broadway musical. It was perhaps at the emotional cross-roads that *Company* parted company with almost all that had trodden the, apparently, same path, for *Company* was not in the business of romance. The British musical would have to wait another three years for Monty Norman's *So Who Needs Marriage?*, perhaps the first (and last?) 'serious' home-grown musical to take a Sondheim-like sidelong glance at the marital institution.

London had first welcomed Stephen Sondheim as lyricist to Leonard Bernstein for *West Side Story* in 1958, and then as songwriter for *A Funny Thing Happened on the Way to the Forum*. So far as the West End was concerned Sondheim had scored two hits and three misses: London would have to wait until 1973 to see the 1959 *Gypsy* (Sondheim's lyrics for Jule Styne's music), and had passed on two Broadway flops, the 1964 *Anyone Can Whistle* (music and lyrics) and the 1965 *Do I Hear a Waltz?* (Sondheim's lyrics for Richard Rodgers' music). But it was with *Company* that Sondheim established a completeness of voice.

The production credentials matched those of New York: director Harold Prince, choreographer Michael Bennett, costumes D. D. Ryan, sets by Boris Aronson, and crucially Jonathan Tunick's orchestrations. Authenticity of reproduction was assured by an all-American cast, some of whom had been carried over from the original Broadway edition. As Robert, the unmarried man whose friends are locked into marriages, Larry Kert had been first take-over in New York, and Elaine Stritch, who had established herself as a London name in the 1962 *Sail Away*, repeated the role of Joanne that she had originated in New York. When the original American cast's permits expired in July 1972, Marti Stevens was upgraded from the role of Sarah to Joanne, in a now otherwise all-British recasting headed by the Robert of Eric Flynn.

The Times announced that 'The score is as calculated to please as the book is finely aimed at middle-aged preoccupations, and both are expertly manipulated in the making of a good musical.'[1] For the *Tatler* this was a score that 'sends you out humming the Divorce Act'.[2] The *Daily Telegraph* recognised the work's qualities, for '*Company*, like *West Side Story*, illustrates the American conviction that the musical can say something relevant about modern living, and do it with irresistible gaiety and exuberance.'[3] Michael Billington emphasised the point, finding that 'it divests the musical of its hollowest showbiz trappings and makes contact with common experience'. He wondered if musicals would eventually fade away 'by offering us adaptations of *À la Recherche du Temps Perdu*, the novels of Ivy Compton-Burnett and Kierkegaard's Journals' and hoped that 'songwriters, here and abroad, will now address themselves to the urgent business of writing about today's problems and, like all good dramatists, of telling us how to survive'.[4]

Indeed, not one of the rest of the year's imports could be said to have attempted such a feat: *Gone with the Wind* was an old-fashioned musical melodrama, clinging to the coat-tails of innumerable predecessors; *I and Albert* a costume piece in appearance and sound; *Applause* trailing all the signs of Broadway of an earlier generation, redressed in what its creators imagined to be contemporary style. The late 1960s had seen an influx of 'seriousness' (often mild) into American musicals seen in London, a characteristic much less evident in the preceding years. Earlier musicals might dabble in issues; inter-racial problems in *South Pacific, Flower Drum Song, No Strings, West Side Story*, but there was a harder edge by the time of *Golden Boy* (the physicality of white woman and black man). Few works dealt with anything approaching profundity with marital or sexual matters, although a few (*Pal Joey* at the head of the queue) did so with subtlety. In the mid-sixties the American musical had turned over a stone and glimpsed at what lay beneath, harnessed the underbelly of reality. The works that subscribed to this school did not always shrug off the tried and tested conventions of the musical. What lay beneath *Cabaret*'s stone was the Nazi movement, but the story was told with reliance on the 'show within a show' numbers that had long populated less 'serious' works. *Cabaret* did not always break conventions, but bent them, as did other works of the period such as *Fiddler on the Roof, Sweet Charity* and, ground-breakingly, *Hair*. Perhaps because seriousness can be seriously depressing, after the 1969 *Promises, Promises*, the Broadway musical in London switched away from it. (Or did it? In its way, the 1970 *1776* is a truly serious piece.)

THEATRE ROYAL · DRURY LANE

Chairman: PRINCE LITTLER C.B.E · Manager: GEORGE HOARE · Secretary: S. L. DREW, F.C.I.S

HAROLD FIELDING
presents
JOE LAYTON'S
production of

HARVE PRESNELL   JUNE RITCHIE
PATRICIA MICHAEL   ROBERT SWANN

in

Margaret Mitchell's

Gone with the Wind

with

ISABELLE LUCAS   MARION RAMSEY
BESSIE LOVE   DOREEN HERMITAGE   RONALD ADAM
HARRY GOODIER   IAN HANSON
and BRIAN DAVIES *as Frank Kennedy*

Music & Lyrics · Book
HAROLD ROME   HORTON FOOTE
Scenery Designed by · Costumes Designed by
DAVID HAYS and TIM GOODCHILD   PATTON CAMPBELL
Lighting Designed by · Dance & Choral arrangements by
RICHARD PILBROW   TRUDE RITTMANN
Orchestrations by **KEITH AMOS and MEYER KUPFERMAN**
Personal Assistant to the Director **EVELYN RUSSELL**
Choral Director · Assistant Musical Director · Assistant Choreographer
JOHN McCARTHY   GRANT HOSSACK   HARRY NAUGHTON
Musical Direction by
RAY COOK
Entire Production Directed and Choreographed by
JOE LAYTON
Produced in association with Jove Enterprises Inc.

First Performance at this Theatre Wednesday 3rd May 1972

40 *Gone with the Wind*, the spectacular Harold Rome musical that found a natural resting place in London's Theatre Royal, Drury Lane, with its much praised Scarlett O'Hara.

It was just at this time that seriousness showed it could get no more serious than with utilising an element that had hitherto played very little part in musical theatre: God. Preparing the way of the Lord, *Godspell* represented a new form of musical that would appeal to a vastly greater public audience than even the heady days of Rodgers and Hammerstein had seen. By a judicious mix of simplicity, banality, spectacle, operetta and publicity, the musicals that had gone before would be more or less obliterated by *Jesus Christ Superstar* and *Joseph and the Amazing Technicolor Dreamcoat*. At a time when church attendances in Britain were rapidly declining year on year, the preference for such stuff was to some extent bewildering.

Such works and those 'international' musicals that followed seemed to belong to neither New York or London; at a time when one might have expected the choice and variety of imported musicals to widen and fascinate, the constriction was all too evident, and the one-way traffic that had existed between New York and London was switched. The librettists of the preceding years of the twentieth century would not have recognised most of the characteristics of this new spring of shows; compare the literacy of Lorenz Hart, the cadences of Yip Harburg, the sonorities of Frank Loesser, the liquid poesy of Hammerstein, with what was new. At least in *Company*, the musical started *questioning*. Here was a musical with a message, although what the message was could perhaps not be clearly stated. Essentially, as Robert sings in a final emotional reckoning, is it about the truthfulness of 'Being Alive'?

Gone with the Wind (Theatre Royal, Drury Lane, 3 May 1972; 398) was another quasi-Broadway musical with no Broadway history. Only in 1973 did it set out for New York, but packed up on the road. In London its composer Harold Rome and book writer Horton Foote didn't mean much. *Wish You Were Here* had played the West End in 1953, and in 1956 Rome's *Fanny* had the perhaps undeserved reputation of being a Drury Lane mediocrity. His adaptation of Margaret Mitchell's sprawling Civil War novel was of similar epic proportions, but this time the canvas was even more enormous, and the project impresario-made for Harold Fielding; here was a show that cried out for showmanship. Fielding threw the best at it, bringing Joe Layton from America to direct and choreograph (his name was above the title) and commissioning sets from David Hays and Tim Goodchild, while orchestration was entrusted to the British Keith Amos.

What was being offered was as much an experience as a musical. Nevertheless, there was the suspicion that Rome's score barely excused the making of a musical from material that made such demands. In its adventurous physicality the Lane seemed the ideal place for the show, and the fluidity of Layton's staging was masterful, but the score was lacking in anything memorable or distinguished. There was a 'theme' song, rather in the manner of the title number from *Fanny*, 'Tara', that struck up the Overture and brought the curtain down – a melody with the necessary grandeur, but otherwise the songs seemed to come and go without leaving much behind. This may have been delusion. Milton Shulman considered that 'choreography and music are brilliantly blended in a story-telling exercise that never stops for breath. There are no artificially set numbers to halt the momentum of the tale and every precise dance number propels the action forward.' The American Harve Presnell stepped into Clark Gable's shoes as Rhett Butler, but praise was due to the British Scarlett O'Hara, June Ritchie. The achievement was all the more remarkable because in her only other London musical Ritchie had played a monkey. Another refugee from *His Monkey Wife*,[5] Robert Swann, was the Ashley opposite the Melanie of Patricia Michael, but neither was given much of interest to sing beyond the mild 'We Belong to You'. More crucially, Rome had nothing substantial to offer his Scarlett, a deficiency that Ritchie overcame in a highly skilled performance.

Patricia Michael remembers that

> everyone, including all the men, both straight and gay, was in love with the wonderful Joe Layton. He could pinpoint with deadly accuracy just what was wrong with your performance and then get up and mimic you doing it with hilarious results. His wife, Evie, was a great catalyst to Joe's sometimes caustic remarks. At one rehearsal June Ritchie got in a bit of a state and ended up in tears. 'June, it's too soon to panic,' said Evie. 'We'll tell you when to panic. We'll say: June – panic!'[6]

When the stage pictures of Mitchell's saga had been put away, only dim memory remained. It might have been stirred when a new version of Mitchell's story emerged in London at the New London Theatre in 2008. Once again the score was American, by Margaret Martin. Much was made of the fact that it was directed by Trevor Nunn, who had been associated with some successful London musicals, and was one of the few directors the British had ever heard of. This *Gone with the Wind* (no one involved seemed very aware of Rome's adaptation) was a costly débâcle, with such a dismal score that it was a wonder it had ever been taken up, giving Rome's version the afterglow of a masterwork. It may have been, and it was assuredly in the last of the line for a certain type of musical, where spectacle took precedent over all. Audiences turning up at the Lane wanted to see if the horses would disgrace themselves on stage, and how well Atlanta burned, not how good the score was. Rome's work for *Fanny* had been derided by several British critics, and his work for *Gone with the Wind* has been largely overlooked, but in both he may well have been a master of the epic.

When Joan Buck interviewed Charles Strouse and Lee Adams for *Plays and Players* in 1972, their lives were consumed by preparations for the London debut of *I and Albert* (Piccadilly Theatre, 6 November 1972; 120), announced on its flyers as 'A Royal Family Musical'. The show had been conceived in America, but its producers, who knows how wisely, had decided because of its subject matter – the life of Queen Victoria – that it should premiere in London. John

Schlesinger's production would be one of the most visually impressive of the decade, and there were high hopes of Polly James, assigned to impersonate the monarch from girlhood to exceedingly old age. The British history of musicals about royalty is not a happy one. While films about monarchs have often had box-office success (witness Charles Laughton in *The Private Life of Henry VIII*), musicals on the same subject (Leslie Bricusse's disastrous life of Henry VIII, *Kings and Clowns*; the Edward VIII–Wallis Simpson romance *Always*) have seldom found approval. Schlesinger's production was essentially filmic, but the spread of years from accession to the throne in 1837 to the Golden Jubilee of 1897 was a lot of ground to cover in two and a quarter hours, and Jay Allen's pedantic book could not but seem episodic. The attempt at authenticity and truthfulness was commendable, with Allen acknowledging the usefulness of Elizabeth Longford's biography of Victoria (in his biography Strouse credits Antonia Fraser as the show's consultant), but adherence to events pockmarked the work's progress, when some deeper understanding of Victoria and her consort might have been more interesting.

Ultimately, *I and Albert* was almost as boring as Herbert Wilcox's unimaginative movies about Victoria (the 1937 *Victoria the Great* and the 1938 *Sixty Glorious Years*). Inevitably the show suffered a blow because its leading male character died half-way through the evening, although Allen managed to cling on to him until just after the interval. This left Victoria plunged into widowhood for the rest of the show, with only two mournful musical outbursts ('Draw the Blinds' and 'No One to Call Me Victoria') to her name. There was much concentration on the Queen's Prime Ministers, Melbourne and Disraeli, and the show was obviously in trouble when Disraeli's 'When You Speak With a Lady' (sung by Lewis Fiander as he performed conjuring tricks) sprang out as the most notable moment. But what enchanted recall Strouse enjoys is mystifying when one listens to the cast recording, where the songs refuse to come to life, and even the titles ('Go It, Old Girl!' and 'I've 'Eard the Bloody 'Indoos 'As It Worse') sound like very bad ones from British musicals.

Strouse has offered another reason for *I and Albert*'s failure, citing the fact that the 'openly gay' Schlesinger had a very different attitude to royalty from the writers: 'Thus, from the beginning, there was a stylistic conflict, as Lee, Jay, and I attempted to portray Queen Victoria and Prince Albert with reverence, and the director and *his* queens tried to paint a satirical edge on it all.'[7] It is probably within that *reverence* that the seed for the show's failure lies, but the London production was beset by other problems. On Broadway the Queen might have been played by a star name (Patricia Routledge, after all, played her in the American 1968 *Love Match*), but Polly James, despite delightful bird-like qualities, was not a star. She had already been acclaimed for her title role in the 1969 *Anne of Green Gables*,[8] but the reluctance of British producers to promote British performers as stars seemed to persist with *I and Albert*. The names accompanying her on the Piccadilly marquee were not of the household variety, although the Swedish actor Sven-Bertil Taube made a convincing and attractive Albert. There was no pre-London tryout, and when Taube became ill the opening had to be postponed for five days. Schlesinger was ill-equipped to direct so complicated a musical, in which the 'musical staging' was left to Brian Macdonald, whose experience in musicals was also nil. Alan Barrett's costumes were denounced by some as the ugliest seen on a London chorus in years. Worst of all, despite all the regal nobility enforced by such numbers as 'This Gentle Land', 'This Noble Land' and the (later cut) 'This Dear Paradise', none of the songs asked to be taken home.

The critics were not encouraging. For John Barber it was so much 'trudging through the history of the reign of Queen Victoria' until woken up by Disraeli pulling rabbits out of his hat; 'Nothing has surprised or involved us. It has all been decorous, nicely dressed and soberly factual.'[9] For Michael Billington, Schlesinger's production 'has plenty of movement but no visible destination [...] Admittedly the show has fleeting moments of vitality; but basically I was not amused.'[10] For *The Times* Irving Wardle wrote 'it has action but no plot. Scampering to keep up with the evolving décor, [almost certainly Luciana Arrighi's sets and projections were the most distinctive component of the occasion] it fades in and out with a fluency that has nothing to do with dramatic development'.[11] Summarily, Felix Barker in the *Evening News* wondered why the show needed to be done at all, while Milton Shulman foresaw a precarious post-Christmas future. Alan Brien thoughtfully concluded that

> *I and Albert* (a perversely simple title, hard to say and harder to remember) is stronger on incident than on plot, rich in attitudes but bankrupt of a viewpoint [...] Victoria is too cartoon a creation to epitomise sixty years of British history. Social consciousness flicks on and off, but the people and the soldiers are a long way away on the horizon while the courtiers and the politicians block our sight lines. And even these diminish in theatrical vitality in proportion to their distance from the royal couple. The material is too various and vast to be comprehended by Jay Allen's jackdaw approach – a panorama seen through a periscope, a civilisation reduced to an antique shop.[12]

At the time of *I and Albert* Strouse and Adams had another London opening to look forward to, **Applause** (Her Majesty's Theatre, 16 November 1972; 382). The heroine of that show would have seemed quite foreign, indeed abhorrent, to the old Queen: Margo Channing, a famous, tough weathered and ageing actress whose life and career is threatened by the apparently timid fan Eve Harrington. The piece originated from Mary Orr's story, made into the 1950 Bette Davis movie *All About Eve*. But was it all about Eve? 'It's not so much about an actress as about an ageing woman', Strouse told Buck. Adams agreed: 'We finally saw the universal in it. Every woman is worried about ageing, and a younger woman taking her man away. So that is what it is about.' Strouse added that 'She can only exist in the light, in the light of applause. She cannot have an emotional life unless the hot lights are on her.'[13]

In this case the 'ageing woman' for whom Betty Comden and Adolph Green had fashioned their book was a true Hollywood product, Lauren Bacall, making her London debut following her vivid triumph in the Broadway production. The rarity of having the original New York star make the journey to London was greatly to the show's advantage; indeed, if not Bacall, who? The fact that this was a truly legendary star, the actress so closely associated with the charisma of Humphrey Bogart, elevated Bacall to an icon. Not surprisingly, she would be supported by satellite artists. Her leading man Eric Flynn, one of the most attractive British male leads of his time, had assurance and style, and some experience of Broadway musicals from his take-over lead in the summer of 1972 in the British *Company*. Anne Baxter had memorably played the scheming Eve in the movie, Penny Fuller on Broadway, and now Angela Richards, a distinctive musical actress whose leading roles had included two British works, *On the Level* and *Annie*. One of the brightest dancers in British musicals, Sheila O'Neill, played Sheila.

Critical enthusiasm was mostly confined to the show's leading lady and Sheila O'Neill. Robin Bean in *Plays and Players* considered

> The major mistake [...] was in trying to make a 'now' musical out of [the film]. It just doesn't work [...] Mankiewicz's script was a brilliantly acid put-down of all the grandeur and self-importance of those living idols. Gone is the sardonic wit (gone too is the cynical, urbane critic as played by George Sanders in the movie) and instead we have Betty Comden and Adolph Green's story which suffers from that most deadly of diseases, of trying to be 'trendy'. They may have thought this would have been the great contemporary musical, but somewhere along the line it seems to have ground to a halt in the mid 'sixties (when the 'Swinging' set was the novelty and people still referred to 'pot', as this does). Even worse are such things as everybody toddling off to gay bars.[14]

For Felix Barker 'Few musicals have had less notable numbers', and he thought Bacall the show's only asset: 'she ensures that every word stings'.[15] J. C. Trewin detected 'a special kind of show-business cheering' from the first night audience, and that competent seemed the right word 'for so ably devised a mechanism'.[16] In the *Daily Telegraph* John Barber accorded with several critics in announcing that O'Neill 'scores a triumph'; indeed, O'Neill threatened to steal the show from its American star.

The British musical **Tom Brown's Schooldays** was a not very intelligent stab at bringing jollity to Rugby School in the shadow of Thomas Hughes' novel. There was no welcome for a vacuous piece set in a Christmas cracker factory, **Pull Both Ends**. A Monty Norman-Wolf Mankowitz bio-musical of highwayman Jack Sheppard, **Stand and Deliver**, had no luck. Even more dislocated from the real world was a new operetta part written by John Hanson, who also wrote the songs ('You, Who Have Never Known Love' was a typical title) and starred in *Smilin' Through*, the idea snatched from an old Hollywood movie. *Trelawny*, based on Arthur Wing Pinero's comedy *Trelawny of the Wells*, had a Julian Slade score that seemed effective at the time, but its success was modest. Bridging the gap between opera and musical was *Rock Carmen*. The British musical *Jesus Christ Superstar*, which had opened on Broadway the previous year, marked a clear division from the past, and a new way forward.

1972 Broadway Exports

Sugar (505); subsequently played London as *Some Like it Hot.*

1972 Broadway Only

Broadway product seemed moribund, with a list of quick flops: *Heathen!* (1), *Hurry, Harry* (2), *The Selling of the President* (5), *Hard Job Being God* (7), *Lysistrata* (8), *Dude* (16) and *Different Times* (24); even the titles were dispiriting. Longer lived but now forgotten was *Don't Play Us Cheap* (164), another black mark on the marquee.

Appendix
American Musicals in London, 1939–1972

Key to production details

London: Theatre, date of first performance and number of performances

New York: Theatre, date of first performance and number of performances

Main author credits: Music, lyrics and book, with any details of adaptation of original material

PC: Principal characters, indicated by *Role*: Actor

MN: Musical numbers. This information is taken primarily from the original theatre programmes of each specific production. In revivals, titles of musical numbers may change from the original production. In some cases the spelling and exact titling of musical numbers may be altered; the spelling given here is the one found in the theatre programme for that particular production. Major revivals of works are preceded by information about productions before 1939.

Aladdin

London: Coliseum, 17 December 1959 [145 performances]

Music and lyrics by Cole Porter; book by Peter Coke; additional material by Denis Goodwin

PC: *Aladdin*: Bob Monkhouse; *The Princess*: Doretta Morrow; *Widow Twankey*: Ronald Shiner; *The Emperor*: Ian Wallace; *Abanazar*: Alan Wheatley; *The Diamond Fairy*: Anne Heaton

MN: Aladdin; There Must Be Someone for Me [from *Mexican Hayride*]; No Wonder Taxes Are High; Come to the Supermarket (in Old Peking); Make Way for the Emperor; Opportunity Knocks But Once; Wouldn't It be Fun?; I Adore You; Cherry Pies Ought to Be You [from *Out of This World*]; I Am Loved [from *Out of This World*]; Ridin' High [from *Red, Hot and Blue*]; Trust Your Destiny to a Star

All in Love

London: May Fair Theatre, 16 March 1964 [24 performances]

New York [Off-Broadway]: Martinique Theatre, 10 November 1961 [141 performances]

Music by Jacques Urbont; book and lyrics by Bruce Geller

PC: *Lucy*: Annie Ross; *Mrs Malaprop*: Gwen Nelson; *Lydia Languish*: Mary Millar; *Sir Lucius O'Trigger*: Peter Gilmore; *Captain Jack Absolute*: James Fox; *Bob Acres*: Ronnie Barker; *Sir Anthony Absolute*: Peter Pratt

MN: To Bath Derry-O; Poor; What Can It Be?; Odds; I Love a Fool; A More than Ordinary, Glorious Vocabulary; Women Simple; The Lady Was Made to Be Loved; The Good Old Ways; Honour; I Found Him; Don't Ask Me; Why Wives?; To Arms; Quickly; All in Love

Ambassador

London [original production]: Her Majesty's Theatre, 19 October 1971 [86 performances]

New York [Broadway]: Lunt-Fontanne Theatre, 19 November 1972 [9 performances]

Music by Don Gohman; lyrics by Hal Hackady; book by Don Ettlinger, based on the novel *The Ambassadors* by Henry James

PC: *Lambert Strether*: Howard Keel; *Countess Marie de Vionnet*: Danielle Darrieux; *Jeanne de Vionnet*: Isobel Stuart; *Bilham*: Blain Fairman; *Amelia Newsome*: Margaret Courtenay; *Chadwick Newsome*: Richard Heffer

MN: A Man You Can Set Your Watch By; It's a Woman; Lambert's Quandary; Lilas; The Right Time the Right Place; Surprise; Charming; All of My Life; What Can You Do with a Nude?; Love Finds the Lonely; Tell Her; La Femme; Young with Him; I Thought I Knew You; What Happened to Paris?; La Nuit d'Amour; Am I Wrong?; Mama; That's What I Need Tonight; You Can Tell a Lady by Her Hat; This Utterly Ridiculous Affair; Not Tomorrow; Thank You, No

Annie Get Your Gun

London: Coliseum, 7 June 1947 [1,304 performances]
New York: Imperial Theatre, 16 May 1946 [1,147 performances]
Music and lyrics by Irving Berlin; book by Herbert and Dorothy Fields
PC: *Annie Oakley*: Dolores Gray; *Frank Butler*: Bill Johnson; *Tommy Keeler*: Irving Davies; *Winnie Tate*: Wendy Toye; *Buffalo Bill Cody*: Ellis Irving; *Charlie Davenport*: Hal Bryan; *Dolly Tate*: Barbara Babington
MN: Buffalo Bill; I'm a Bad, Bad Man; Doin' What Comes Naturally; The Girl that I Marry; You Can't Get a Man with a Gun; Show Business; They Say It's Wonderful; Moonshine Lullaby; I'll Share It All with You; Ballyhoo; My Defences Are Down; Wild Horse Ceremonial Dance; I'm an Indian Too; Adoption Dance; Lost in His Arms; Who Do You Love, I Hope?; Sun in the Morning; Anything You Can Do

Anything Goes

London: Palace Theatre, 14 June 1935 [261 performances]
New York: Alvin Theatre, 21 November 1934 [420 performances]
Music and lyrics by Cole Porter; book by Guy Bolton and P. G. Wodehouse, revised by Howard Lindsay and Russel Crouse
PC: *Reno Lagrange*: Jeanne Aubert; *Billy Crocker*: Jack Whiting; *Moonface Mooney*: Sydney Howard; *Hope Harcourt*: Adele Dixon; *Bonnie*: Betty Kean
MN: I Get a Kick Out of You; Bon Voyage; All Through the Night; Sailor's Chanty; Where Are the Men?; You're the Top; Anything Goes; Public Enemy Number One; Blow, Gabriel, Blow; Be Like the Bluebird; The Gypsy in Me

London: Saville Theatre, 18 November 1969 [15 performances]
PC: *Reno Sweeny*: Marion Montgomery; *Billy Crocker*: James Kenney; *Moonface Martin*: Michael Segal; *Bonnie*: Janet Mahoney
MN: You're the Top; Bon Voyage; Where Have You Been?; It's Delovely; Heaven Hop; Friendship; I Get a Kick Out of You; Let's Do It; Anything Goes; Public Enemy Number One; Let's Step Out; Let's Misbehave; Blow, Gabriel, Blow; All Through the Night; Be Like the Bluebird; Take Me Back to Manhattan

Applause

London: Her Majesty's Theatre, 16 November 1972 [382 performances]
New York: Palace Theatre, 30 March 1972 [898 performances]
Music by Charles Strouse; lyrics by Lee Adams; book by Betty Comden and Adolph Green, based on the film *All About Eve* and Mary Orr's story *The Wisdom of Eve*

PC: *Margo Channing*: Lauren Bacall; *Bill Sampson*: Eric Flynn; *Eve Harrington*: Angela
Richards; *Howard Benedict*: Basil Hoskins; *Buzz Richards*: Rod McLennan; *Duane Fox*:
Ken Walsh; *Sheila*: Sheila O'Neill
MN: Backstage Babble; Think How It's Gonna Be; But Alive; The Best Night of My Life;
Who's That Girl?; Applause; Hurry Back; Fasten Your Seat Belts; Welcome to the
Theatre; Inner Thoughts; Good Friends; She's No Longer a Gypsy; One of a Kind;
One Halloween; Something Greater

Belle Starr

London [only]: Palace Theatre, 30 April 1969 [12 performances]
Music by Steve Allen; lyrics by Steve Allen, Warren Douglas and Jerry Schafer; book by
Warren Douglas
PC: *Belle Starr*: Betty Grable; *Billy the Kid*: Blayne Barrington; *Jesse James*: Ray Chiarella;
Calamity Jane: Valerie Walsh; *Killer Malone*: Michael Hawkins
MN: Story Song; Belle; Happy Birthday to Vegas; We're Gonna Make History; The
Gunfighter's Ballad; A Lady Don't Do; Ladylike Lady Like Me; It Takes One to Know
One; Dirty, Rotten, Vicious, Nasty Guys; Dance Polka; Gee, You're Pretty; I'm a Lady;
The Biggest Pair of 38's in Town; Never Had This Feeling Before

Bells Are Ringing

London: Coliseum, 14 November 1957 [292 performances]
New York: Shubert Theatre, 29 November 1956 [924 performances]
Music by Jule Styne; book and lyrics by Betty Comden and Adolph Green
PC: *Ella Peterson*: Janet Blair; *Jeff Moss*: George Gaynes; *Gwynne Smith*: Allyn McLerie;
Sandor: Eddie Molloy; *Sue Summers*: Jean St. Clair; *Inspector Barnes*: Donald Stewart;
Francis: C. Denier Warren; *Carl*: Harry Naughton; *Larry Hastings*: Robert Henderson;
Blake Barton: Franklin Fox
MN: It's a Perfect Relationship; On My Own; You've Got to Do It; It's a Simple Little
System; Is It a Crime?; Hello, Hello, There; I Met a Girl; Long Before I Knew You;
Mu … Cha … Cha; Just in Time; Drop That Name; The Party's Over; Salzburg;
The Midas Touch; I'm Going Back

The Boys from Syracuse

London: Theatre Royal, Drury Lane, 7 November 1963 [100 performances]
New York: Alvin Theatre, 23 November 1938 [235 performances]; Theatre Four, 15 April
1963 [502 performances]
Music by Richard Rodgers; lyrics by Lorenz Hart; book by George Abbott, based on the
play *The Comedy of Errors* by Shakespeare
PC: *Antipholus of Syracuse*: Bob Monkhouse; *Adriana*: Lynn Kennington; *Luce*: Maggie
Fitzgibbon; *Luciana*: Paula Hendrix; *Antipholus of Ephesus*: Denis Quilley; *Dromio of
Syracuse*: Ronnie Corbett; *Dromio of Ephesus*: Sonny Farrar; *Courtesan*: Pat Turner
MN: I Had Twins; Dear Old Syracuse; What Can You Do with a Man?; Falling in Love
with Love; The Shortest Day of the Year; The Dance of Dilemma (Ballet); This Can't
be Love; Ladies of the Evening; He and She; You Have Cast Your Shadow on the Sea;
Come with Me; Big Brother; Sing for Your Supper; Oh Diogenes!

Brigadoon

London: His Majesty's Theatre, 14 April 1949 [685 performances]
New York: Ziegfeld Theatre, 13 March 1947 [581 performances]
Music by Frederick Loewe; book and lyrics by Alan Jay Lerner
PC: *Tommy Albright*: Philip Hanna; *Fiona MacKeith*: Patricia Hughes; *Meg Brockie*: Noele Gordon; *Jeff Douglas*: Hiram Sherman; *Harry Ritchie*: James Jamieson; *Charlie Cameron*: Bill O'Connor
MN: Once in the Highlands; Brigadoon; Down in MacConnachy Square; Waitin' for My Dearie; I'll Go Home with Bonnie Jean; The Heather on the Hill; The Love of My Life; Jeannie's Packin' Up; Come to Me, Bend to Me; Almost Like Being in Love; The Wedding Dance; Sword Dance; The Chase; There But for You Go I; My Mother's Weddin' Day; Funeral Dance; From This Day On

Bye Bye Birdie

London: Her Majesty's Theatre, 15 June 1961 [268 performances]
New York: Martin Beck Theatre, 14 April 1960 [607 performances]
Music by Charles Strouse; lyrics by Lee Adams; book by Michael Stewart
PC: *Rose* Grant: Chita Rivera; *Albert Peterson*: Peter Marshall; *Mae Peterson*: Angela Baddeley; *Conrad Birdie*: Marty Wilde; *Kim MacAfee*: Sylvia Tysick; *Mr MacAfee*: Robert Nichols; *Mrs MacAfee*: Mary Laura Wood
MN: An English Teacher; The Telephone Hour; How Lovely to Be a Woman; We Love You, Conrad; Put On a Happy Face; Normal American Boy; One Boy; Honestly Sincere; Hymn for a Sunday Evening; Ballet: How to Kill a Man; One Last Kiss; Act Two Prologue: The World at Large; What Did I Ever See in Him?; A Lot of Livin' to Do; Kids; Baby, Talk to Me; Shriners' Ballet; Spanish Rose; Rosie

Cabaret

London: Palace Theatre, 28 February 1968 [336 performances]
New York: Broadhurst Theatre, 20 November 1966 [1,165 performances]
Music by John Kander; lyrics by Fred Ebb; book by Joe Masteroff, based on *Berlin Stories* by Christopher Isherwood and John Van Druten's play *I Am a Camera*
PC: *Sally Bowles*: Judi Dench; *Clifford Bradshaw*: Kevin Colson; *Master of Ceremonies*: Barry Dennen; *Fräulein Schneider*: Lila Kedrova; *Herr Schultz*: Peter Sallis; *Fräulein Kost*: Pamela Strong; *Ernst Ludwig*: Richard Owens
MN: Willkommen; So What?; Don't Tell Mama; Telephone Song; Perfectly Marvellous; Two Ladies; It Couldn't Please Me More; Tomorrow Belongs to Me; Why Should I Wake Up?; The Money Song; Married; Meeskite; If You Could See Her; What Would You Do?; Cabaret

Call Me Madam

London: Coliseum, 15 March 1952 [485 performances]
New York: Imperial Theatre, 12 October 1950 [644 performances]
Music and lyrics by Irving Berlin; book by Howard Lindsay and Russel Crouse
PC: *Mrs Sally Adams*: Billie Worth; *Cosmo Contsantine*: Anton Walbrook; *Kenneth Gibson*: Jeff Warren; *Pemberton Maxwell*: Donald Burr; *Princess Marie*: Shani Wallis; *Senator Brockbank*: Arthur Lowe

MN: Mrs Sally Adams; The Hostess With the Mostes' on the Ball; Washington Square
    Dance; Lichtenburg; Can You Use Any Money Today?; Marrying for Love; The
    Ocarina; It's a Lovely Day Today; The Best Thing for You Would Be Me; Something to
    Dance About; Once Upon a Time Today; They Like Ike

Camelot

London: Theatre Royal, Drury Lane, 19 August 1964 [518 performances]
New York: Majestic Theatre, 3 December 1960 [873 performances]
Music by Frederick Loewe; book and lyrics by Alan Jay Lerner, based on the novel *The
    Once and Future King* by T. H. White
PC: *King Arthur*: Laurence Harvey; *Guenevere*: Elizabeth Larner; *Sir Lancelot*: Barry
    Kent; *Merlyn*: Miles Malleson; *Morgan LeFay*: Moyra Fraser; *Mordred*: Nicky Henson;
    King Pellinore: Cardew Robinson; *Sir Lionel*: Raymond Edwards; *Sir Dinadan*: Victor
    Flattery; *Nimue*: Josephine Gordon
MN: I Wonder What the King is Doing Tonight?; The Simple Joys of Maidenhood;
    Camelot; Follow Me; C'est Moi; The Lusty Month of May; Then You May Take
    Me to the Fair; How to Handle a Woman; The Jousts; Before I Gaze at You Again;
    If Ever I Would Leave You; The Seven Deadly Virtues; What Do the Simple Folk Do?;
    The Persuasion; Fie on Goodness!; I Loved You Once in Silence; Guenevere

Can-Can

London: Coliseum, 14 October 1954 [394 performances]
New York: Shubert Theatre, 7 May 1953 [892 performances]
Music and lyrics by Cole Porter; book by Abe Burrows
PC: *La Mome Pistache*: Irene Hilda; *Aristide Forestier*: Edmund Hockridge; *Boris
    Adzinidzinadze*: Alfred Marks; *Claudine*: Gillian Lynne; *Hilaire Jussac*: George Gee;
    Theophile: Warren Mitchell; *Étienne*: Alan Gilbert
MN: Maidens Typical of France; Never Give Anything Away; C'est Magnifique; Quadrille;
    Come Along with Me; Live and Let Live; I Am in Love; If You Loved Me Truly;
    Montmart'; The Garden of Eden [ballet]; Allez-Vous-En; Never, Never Be an Artiste;
    It's All Right with Me; Every Man is a Stupid Man; The Apaches; I Love Paris; Can-Can

Candide

London: Saville Theatre, 30 April 1959 [60 performances]
New York: Martin Beck Theatre, 1 December 1956 [73 performances]
Music by Leonard Bernstein; lyrics by Richard Wilbur, with other lyrics by John Latouche
    and Dorothy Parker; book by Lillian Hellman, assisted by Michael Stewart, based on
    Voltaire's satire
PC: *Dr Pangloss/Martin*: Laurence Naismith; *Candide*: Denis Quilley; *Cunegonde*: Mary
    Costa; *Governor of Buenos Aires*: Ron Moody; *Old Lady*: Edith Coates
MN: The Best of All Possible Worlds; Oh Happy We; It Must Be So; Oh What a Day for
    a Holiday; It Must Be Me; Mazurka; Glitter and Be Gay; You Were Dead, You Know;
    Pilgrims' Procession; I am Easily Assimilated; Quartet Finale; Eldorado; We Are
    Women; Bon Voyage; What's the Use?; I've Got Troubles; Make Our Garden Grow

Carnival

London: Lyric Theatre, 8 February 1963 [34 performances]
New York: Imperial Theatre, 13 April 1961 [719 performances]
Music and lyrics by Bob Merrill; book by Michael Stewart, based on the film *Lili* by Helen
    Deutsch
PC: *Lili*: Sally Logan; *Marco*: James Mitchell; *Paul Berthalet*: Michael Maurel; *Rosalie*:
    Shirley Sands; *Jacquot*: Bob Harris; *Schlegel*: Felix de Wolfe
MN: Direct from Vienna; A Very Nice Man; Fairyland; I've Got to Find a Reason; Mira;
    Sword, Rose and Cape; Humming; Yes My Heart; Magic, Magic; Tanz Mit Mir;
    Carnival Ballet; Theme from Carnival; Yum Ticky; The Rich; Beautiful Candy; Her
    Face; Grand Imperial Cirque de Paris; I Hate Him; Always Always You; She's My Love

Carousel

London: Theatre Royal, Drury Lane, 7 June 1950 [566 performances]
New York: Majestic Theatre, 19 April 1945 [890 performances]
Music by Richard Rodgers; book and lyrics by Oscar Hammerstein II, based on the play
    Liliom by Ferenc Molnár
PC: *Billy Bigelow*: Stephen Douglass; *Julie Jordan*: Iva Withers; *Carrie Pipperidge*: Margot
    Moser; *Enoch Snow*: Eric Mattson; *Nettie Fowler*: Marion Ross; *Jigger Craigin*: Morgan
    Davies; *Starkeeper*: William Sherwood; *Louise Bigelow*: Bambi Linn; *Mrs Mullin*:
    Marjorie Mars; *June Girl*: Mavis Ray
MN: Waltz Suite; You're a Queer One, Julie Jordan; When I Marry Mr Snow; If I
    Loved You; June is Bustin' Out All Over; When the Children Are Asleep; Blow
    High, Blow Low; Hornpipe; Soliloquy; This Was a Real Nice Clam Bake; Geraniums
    In the Winder; There's Nothing So Bad for a Woman; What's the Use of Wond'rin;
    You'll Never Walk Alone; The Highest Judge of All; Ballet

Cinderella

London [only]: Coliseum, 18 December 1958 [168 performances]
First shown on American TV
Music by Richard Rodgers; book and lyrics by Oscar Hammerstein II
PC: *Buttons*: Tommy Steele; *The King*: Jimmy Edwards; *Cinderella*: Yana; *The Prince*:
    Bruce Trent; *The Baron's Stepdaughters: Portia* (Kenneth Williams), *Joy* (Ted Durante);
    Fairy Godmother: Betty Marsden
MN: In My Own Little Corner; A Very Special Day; Do I Love You Because You're
    Beautiful?; The Prince is Giving a Ball; Stepsisters' Lament; Marriage Type Love;
    Your Majesties, a List of the Bare Necessities; When You're Driving Through the
    Moonlight; A Lovely Night; Impossible; Waltz for a Ball; Gavotte; No Other Love;
    Ten Minutes Ago

London: Adelphi Theatre, 22 December 1960 [101 performances]
PC: *Buttons*: Ted Rogers; *The King*: Jimmy Edwards; *Cinderella*: Jan Waters; *The Prince*:
    Bill Newman; *Fairy Godmother*: Betty Bowdon
MN: as above

Cindy

London: Fortune Theatre, 30 May 1968 [29 performances]
New York [Off-Broadway]: Gate Theatre, 19 March 1964 [closed 21 June 1964]
Music and lyrics by Johnny Brandon; book by Joe Sauter and Mike Sawyer, based on an
    idea by Johnny Brandon and Stuart Weiner
PC: *Zelda Kreller*: Hy Hazell; *Ruth Rosenfeld*: Rose Hill; *Cindy Kreller*: Geraldene
    Morrow; *Lucky*: Johnny Tudor; *Chuck Rosenfeld*: Dudley Stevens; *Golda Kreller*:
    Angela Darren; *Della Kreller*: Anna Stillman
MN: Once Upon a Time; Let's Pretend; Is There Something to What He Said?; Papa,
    Let's Do It Again; A Genuine Feminine Girl; Cindy; Think Mink; Tonight's the Night;
    Ballroom Music; Who Am I?; Shoe Music; If You've Got It, You've Got It; The Life I
    Planned for Him; If It's Love; Call Me Lucky; Laugh It Up; What a Wedding

Company

London: Her Majesty's Theatre, 8 January 1972 [344 performances]
New York: Alvin Theatre, 26 April 1970 [705 performances]
Music and lyrics by Stephen Sondheim; book by George Furth
PC [original American/takeover British]: *Robert*: Larry Kert/Eric Flynn; *Joanne*: Elaine
    Stritch/Marti Stevens; *Sarah*: Marti Stevens/Jill Martin; *David*: Lee Goodman/Paul
    Tracey; *Peter*: J. T. Cromwell/Phillip Hinton; *Jenny*: Teri Ralston/Barbara Tracey;
    Harry: Kenneth Kimmins/Robert Colman; *Kathy*: Donna McKechnie/Antonia Ellis;
    Larry: Robert Goss/Bob Sessions; *April*: Carol Richards/Julia McKenzie; *Paul*: Steve
    Elmore/Richard Owens; *Amy*: Beth Howland/Gracie Luck; *Marta*: Annie McGreevey/
    Julia Sutton; *Susan*: Joy Franz/Jenny Wren
MN: Company; The Little Things You Do Together; Sorry-Grateful; You Could Drive
    a Person Crazy; Have I Got a Girl for You; Someone is Waiting; Another Hundred
    People; Getting Married Today; Side by Side; What Would We Do Without You?; Poor
    Baby; Tick Tock; Barcelona; The Ladies Who Lunch; Being Alive

The Crystal Heart

London [original production]: Saville Theatre, 19 February 1957 [7 performances]
New York [Off-Broadway]: East 74th Street Theatre, 15 February 1960 [6 performances]
Music by Baldwin Bergersen; lyrics and book by William Archibald
PC: *Mistress Phoebe Ricketts*: Gladys Cooper; *Ted*: Laurie Payne; *Wellington Marchmount*:
    Harold Scott; *Miss Louisa Hatfield*: Julia Shelley; *The Captain*: Peter Sinclair; *Virtue*:
    Dilys Laye
MN: A Year is a Day; The Anchor's Down; Yes, Aunt; A Girl with a Ribbon; I Wanted to
    See the World; Hilltop Dance; A Monkey When He Loves; How Strange the Silence;
    Desperate; Lovely Island; Pretty Little Bluebird; Handsome Husbands; Agnes and
    Me; Madam, I Beg You; My Heart Won't Learn; When I Dance with My Love; Lovely
    Bridesmaids; It's So British; It Took Them

Dames at Sea

London: Duchess Theatre, 27 August 1969 [127 performances]
New York [Off-Broadway]: Bouwerie Lane Theatre, 20 December 1968 [575
    performances]

Music by Jim Wise; lyrics by Robin Miller and George Haimsohn; book by Robin Miller
and George Haimsohn
PC: *Mona Kent*: Joyce Blair; *Joan*: Rita Burton; *Hennessey*: Kevin Scott; *Ruby*: Sheila
White; *Dick*: Blayne Barrington; *Lucky*: William Ellis; *Captain*: Kevin Scott
MN: Wall Street; It's You; Broadway Baby; That Mister Man of Mine; Choo-Choo
Honeymoon; The Sailor of My Dreams; Singapore Sue; Good Times Are Here to Stay;
Dames at Sea; The Beguine; Raining in My Heart; There's Something About You;
The Echo Waltz; Star Tar; Let's Have a Simple Wedding

Damn Yankees

London: Coliseum, 28 March 1957 [258 performances]
New York: 46th Street Theatre, 5 May 1955 [1,019 performances]
Music and lyrics by Richard Adler and Jerry Ross; book by George Abbott and Douglas
Wallop, based on Wallop's novel *The Year the Yankees Lost the Pennant*
PC: *Applegate*: Bill Kerr; *Joe Boyd*: Phil Vickers; *Meg Boyd*: Betty Paul; *Joe Hardy*: Ivor
Emmanuel; *Lola*: Belita; *Gloria Thorpe*: Judy (Judith) Bruce; *Van Buren*: Donald
Stewart; *Rocky*: Robin Hunter
MN: Six Months Out of Every Year; Goodbye, Old Girl; Blooper Ballet; Heart;
Shoeless Joe from Hannibal, Mo; A Little Brains, A Little Talent; A Man Doesn't
Know; Who's Got the Pain?; The Game; Near to You; Those Were the Good Old Days;
Two Lost Souls

The Dancing Heiress

London: Lyric Opera House, Hammersmith, 15 March 1960 [15 performances]
Music and lyrics by Murray Grand; book by Jack Fletcher and Murray Grand
PC: *Marion La Verne*: Millicent Martin; *Tom Manning*: Irving Davies; *Libby Longtree*: Jill
Ireland; *Evelyn Longtree*: Lally Bowers; *Angela Longtree*: Pamela Strong
MN: The Lady is News; We're Out for Money; Life is Peaches and Cream; You're a Tonic;
I'm Going to Wind-Up with You; Youth and Beauty; Under-Tow of Love; Marion's on
the Make; The Internashnal [*sic*]; Zig-Zag; Morning, Noon, Evening and Night; That
Same Old Sensation; You; Song of the Shadows; Agua Caliente

The Desert Song

London: Theatre Royal, Drury Lane, 7 April 1927 [432 performances]
New York: Casino Theatre, 30 November 1926 [471 performances]
Music by Sigmund Romberg; lyrics by Otto Harbach and Oscar Hammerstein II; book by
Otto Harbach, Oscar Hammerstein II and Frank Mandel
PC: *Margot Bonvalet*: Edith Day; *Pierre Birabeau*: Harry Welchman; *Bennie Kidd*: Gene
Gerrard; *Azuri*: Phebe [*sic*] Brune; *Sid El Kar*: Sidney Pointer; *Captain Paul Fontaine*:
Barry Mackay; *Clementina*: Maria Minetti; *Susan*: Clarice Hardwicke
MN: Prelude and Drinking Song; Ho! – Riding Song of the Riffs; Margot; I'll Be a Buoyant
Girl; Why Did We Marry Soldiers?; French Marching Song; Romance; Then You Will
Know; I Want a Kiss; It; The Desert Song; Song of the Brass Key; One Good Boy Gone
Wrong; Eastern and Western Love [comprising: Let Love Go; One Flower; One Alone];
The Sabre Song; Farewell; Dance of Triumph

London: Alhambra, 8 June 1931 [29 performances]

PC: *Margot Bonvalet*: Sylvia Welling; *Pierre Birabeau*: Alec Fraser; *Bennie Kidd*: John E. Coyle; *Azuri*: Ruby Morriss; *Sid El Kar*: Sidney Pointer; *Captain Paul Fontaine*: Barry Mackay; *Clementina*: Nancy Eshelby; *Susan*: Elsa Palmer

MN: Prelude and Drinking Song; Ho! (Riding Song of the Riffs); French Marching Song; Romance; It; The Desert Song; Dance of the Brass Key; One Good Boy Gone Wrong; Eastern and Western Love [comprising: Let Love Go; One Flower in Your Garden; One Alone]; The Sabre Song; Farewell; Introduction Scenes; Dance of Triumph

London: Coliseum, 24 September 1936 [146 performances]

PC: *Margot Bonvalet*: Edith Day; *Pierre Birabeau*: Harry Welchman; *Bennie Kidd*: Frederic Bentley; *Azuri*: Lola Waring; *Sid El Kar*: Sidney Pointer; *Captain Paul Fontaine*: Walter Bird; *Clementina*: Maud Zimbla; *Susan*: Clarice Hardwicke

MN: Prelude and Drinking Song; Ho! Riding Song of the Riffs; Margot; I'll Be a Buoyant Girl; Why Did We Marry Soldiers?; French Marching Song; Romance; Then You Will Know; I Want a Kiss; It; The Desert Song; Song of the Brass Key; One Good Boy Gone Wrong; Eastern and Western Love [comprising: Let Love Go; One Flower in Your Garden; One Alone]; The Sabre Song; Farewell; Introduction Scenes; Dance of Triumph

London: Garrick Theatre, 29 June 1939 [75 performances]

PC: *Margot Bonvalet*: Doris Francis; *Pierre Birabeau*: Bruce Carfax; *Bennie Kidd*: Alexander Cameron; *Azuri*: Greta Buchanan; *Sid El Kar*: Rhys Thomas; *Captain Paul Fontaine*: Warwick Ashton; *Clementina*: Kathleen Fraser; *Susan*: Phyllis Bourke

MN: Ho Song; Drinking Song; Margot; I'll Be a Buoyant Girl; French Marching Song; Romance; My Passion; I Want a Kiss; It; The Desert Song; My Little Castagnet; Song of the Brass Key; One Good Boy Gone Wrong; Eastern and Western Love [comprising: Let Love Come [*sic*]; One Flower; One Alone]; Sabre Song; All Hail; Dance of Triumph

London: Prince of Wales Theatre, 16 January 1943 [86 performances]

PC: *Margot Bonvalet*: Eleanor Fayre; *Pierre Birabeau*: Harry Welchman; *Bennie Kidd*: Frederic Bentley; *Azuri*: Phyllis Baker; *Sid El Kar*: Sidney Pointer; *Captain Paul Fontaine*: Victor Standing; *Clementina*: Olive Rose; *Susan*: Helen Barnes

MN: Opening Chorus and Drinking Song; Riff Song; Drinking Song; Margot; I'll Be a Buoyant Girl; French Marching Song; Romance; My Passion; I Want a Kiss; It; The Desert Song; My Little Castagnet; Song of the Brass Key; One Good Boy Gone Wrong; Eastern and Western Love [comprising: Let Love Come; One Flower; One Alone]; Sabre Song; All Hail

London: Palace Theatre, 13 May 1967 [433 performances]

PC: *Margot Bonvalet*: Patricia Michael; *Pierre Birabeau*: John Hanson; *Benjamin Kidd*: Tony Hughes; *Azuri*: Lita Scott; *Sid El Kar*: Dermod Gloster; *Captain Paul Fontaine*: Raymond Duparc; *Clementina*: Carol Dorée; *Susan*: Doreen Kay

MN: Opening; The Riff Song; Pretty Maid of France; I'll Be a Buoyant Girl; French Military Marching Song; Romance; Then You Will Know; I Want a Kiss; It; The Desert Song; Finale Act One [includes: Soft As a Pidgeon]; Act Two Opening; Song of the Brass Key; One Good Boy Gone Wrong; Eastern and Western Love [comprises: Let Love Go; One Flower in Your Garden; One Flower Grows Alone in Your Garden; One Alone]; The Sabre Song; The Edge of the Desert; Dance of Triumph

Do Re Mi

London: Prince of Wales Theatre, 12 October 1961 [169 performances]
New York: St James Theatre, 26 December 1960 [400 performances]
Music by Jule Styne; lyrics by Betty Comden and Adolph Green; book by Garson Kanin
PC: *Hubert Cram*: Max Bygraves; *Kay Cram*: Maggie Fitzgibbon; *Tilda Mullen*: Jan
    Waters; *John Henry Wheeler*: Steve Arlen; *Fatso O'Rear*: Danny Green; *Brains Berman*:
    Harry Ross; *Skin Demopoulos*: David Lander
MN: Waiting, Waiting; All You Need is a Quarter; Take a Job; The Juke Box Hop; It's
    Legitimate; I Know About Love; The Auditions; Cry Like the Wind; Ambition; Success;
    Fireworks; What's New at the Zoo; Asking for You; The Late, Late Show; Adventure;
    Make Someone Happy; Dance: The Juke Box Trouble; V.I.P.; All of My Life ['Hey, Look
    Me Over' from the Cy Coleman – Carolyn Leigh *Wildcat* subsequently interpolated.]

DuBarry Was a Lady

London: His Majesty's Theatre, 22 October 1942 [178 performances]
New York: 46th Street Theatre, 6 December 1939 [408 performances]
Music and lyrics by Cole Porter; book by Herbert Fields and B. G. DeSylva
PC: *Louis Blore*: Arthur Riscoe; *May Daly*: Frances Day; *Alice Barton*: Frances Marsden;
    Charley: Jackie Hunter; *Alex Barton*: Bruce Trent; *Harry Norton*: Teddy Beaumont
MN: Every Day a Holiday; When Love Beckoned; Come on In; Dream Song; Mesdames
    et Messieurs; Gavotte; Picture Me Without You; You've Got Something; Danse
    Victoire; Danse Erotique; Du Barry was a Lady; Danse Tzigane; Give Him the Oo-la-la;
    It Was Written in the Stars; Katie Went to Haiti; Friendship

Fanny

London: Theatre Royal, Drury Lane, 15 November 1956 [347 performances]
New York: Majestic Theatre, 4 November 1954 [888 performances]
Music and lyrics by Harold Rome; book by S. N. Behrman and Joshua Logan, based on
    the trilogy of Marcel Pagnol
PC: *Panisse*: Robert Morley; *César*: Ian Wallace; *Fanny*: Janet Pavek; *Marius*: Kevin Scott;
    Honorine: Mona Washbourne; *The Admiral*: Michael Gough; *Escartifique*: C. Denier
    Warren; *Arab Dancing Girl*: Hameda; *M. Brun*: Julian Orchard
MN: Octopus Song; Restless Heart; Never Too Late for Love; Cold Cream Jar Song;
    Does He Know?; Why Be Afraid to Dance?; Shika, Shika; Welcome Home; I Like You;
    I Have to Tell You; Fanny; The Sailing; Oysters, Cockles and Mussels; Panisse and Son;
    Wedding Dance; First Act Finale; Birthday Song; To My Wife; The Thought of You;
    Love is a Very Light Thing; Other Hands, Other Hearts; Montage; Be Kind to Your
    Parents

The Fantasticks

London: Apollo Theatre, 7 September 1961 [44 performances]
New York [Off-Broadway]: Sullivan Street Playhouse, 3 May 1960 [17,162 performances]
Music by Harvey Schmidt; book and lyrics by Tom Jones, based on the play *Les
    Romanesques* by Edmund Rostand
PC: *Luisa*: Stephanie Voss; *El Gallo*: Terence Cooper; *Matt*: Peter Gilmore; *Bellamy*:
    Timothy Bateson; *Hucklebee*: Michael Barrington; *Henry Albertson*: John Wood;
    Mortimer: John Cater; *Prentice*: Melvyn Hayes

MN: Try to Remember; Much More; Metaphor; Never Say 'No'; It Depends on What
You Pay; Soon It's Gonna Rain; The Rape Ballet; Happy Ending; This Plum is Too Ripe;
I Can See It; Plant a Radish; Round and Round; They Were You

Fiddler on the Roof

London: Her Majesty's Theatre, 16 February 1967 [2,030 performances]
New York: Imperial Theatre, 22 September 1964 [3,242 performances]
Music by Jerry Bock; lyrics by Sheldon Harnick; book by Joseph Stein, based on various
stories by Sholom Aleichem, including *Tevye's Daughters*
PC: *Tevye*: Topol; *Golde*: Miriam Karlin; *Yente*: Cynthia Grenville; *Lazar Wolf*: Paul
Whitsun-Jones; *Perchik*: Sandor Eles; *Tzeitel*: Rosemary Nicols; *Hodel*: Linda Gardner;
Motel: Jonathan Lynn; *Chava*: Caryl Little
MN: Prologue; Tradition; Matchmaker, Matchmaker; If I Were a Rich Man; Sabbath
Prayer; To Life; Miracle of Miracles; The Tailor Motel Kamzoil; Sunrise, Sunset;
Wedding Dance; Now I Have Everything; Do You Love Me?; I Just Heard; Far from the
Home I Love; Chavaleh; Anatevka; Epilogue

Finian's Rainbow

London: Palace Theatre, 21 October 1947 [55 performances]
New York: 46th Street Theatre, 10 January 1947 [725 performances]
Music by Burton Lane; lyrics by E. Y. (Yip) Harburg; book by Harburg and Fred Saidy
PC: *Sharon McLonergan*: Beryl Seton; *Finian McLonergan*: Patrick J. Kelly; *Woody
Mahoney*: Alan Gilbert; *Og*: Alfie Bass; *Susan Mahoney*: Beryl Kaye; *Senator Billboard
Rawkins*: Frank Royde
MN: The Time of the Year; How Are Things in Glocca Morra?; Look to the Rainbow;
Old Devil Moon; Something Sort of Grandish; If This Isn't Love; Necessity; When the
Idle Poor Become the Idle Rich; Dance of the Golden Crock; Fiddle Faddle; The Begat;
When I'm Not Near the Girl I Love

Fiorello!

London: Piccadilly Theatre, 8 October 1962 [56 performances]
New York: Broadhurst Theatre, 23 November 1959 [795 performances]
Music by Jerry Bock; lyrics by Sheldon Harnick; book by Jerome Weidman and George
Abbott
PC: *Fiorello H. LaGuardia*: Derek Smith; *Marie Fischer*: Nicolette Roeg; *Thea LaGuardia*:
Marion Grimaldi; *Mitzi Travers*: Patricia Michael; *Dora*: Bridget Armstrong; *Ben
Marino*: Peter Reeves; *Floyd Macduff*: Simon Oates; *Morris Cohen*: David Lander
MN: On the Side of the Angels; Politics and Poker; Unfair; Marie's Law; The Name's
La Guardia; The Bum Won; I Love a Cop; Till Tomorrow; When Did I Fall In Love?;
Gentleman Jimmy; Little Tin Box; The Very Next Man

Flower Drum Song

London: Palace Theatre, 24 March 1960 [464 performances]
New York: St James Theatre, 1 December 1958 [600 performances]
Music by Richard Rodgers; lyrics by Oscar Hammerstein II; book by Hammerstein and
Joseph Fields, based on the novel by C. Y. Lee

PC: *Linda Low*: Yama Saki; *Mei Li*: Yau Shan Tung; *Wang Ta*: Kevin Scott; *Madam Liang*:
Ida Shepley; *Sammy Fong*: Tim Herbert; *Wang Chi Yang*: George Pastell; *Helen Chao*:
Joan Pethers; *Frankie Wing*: Leon Thau; *Nightclub Singer*: Ruth Silvestre

MN: You Are Beautiful; A Hundred Million Miracles; I Enjoy Being a Girl; I Am Going
to Like It Here; Like a God; Chop Suey; Don't Marry Me; Grant Avenue; Love, Look
Away; Fan Tan Fanny; Gliding through My Memoree; Ballet; The Other Generation;
Sunday; Wedding Parade

Follow the Girls

London: His Majesty's Theatre, 25 October 1945 [572 performances]
New York: New Century Theatre, 8 April 1944 [882 performances]
Music by Phil Charig; lyrics by Dan Shapiro and Milton Pascal; book by Guy Bolton,
Eddie Davis and Fred Thompson

PC: *Goofy Gale*: Arthur Askey; *Bubbles LaMarr*: Evelyn Dall; *Dinky Riley*: Jack Billings;
Spud Doolittle: Vic Marlowe; *Bob Monroe*: Hugh French; *Felix*: Charles Peters; *Betty
Deleaninnion*: Wendy Toye; *Phyllis Brent*: Sheila Douglas-Pennant

MN: At the Spotlight Canteen; Where You Are; You Don't Dance; Strip Tease Girl;
Thanks for a Lousy Evening; You're Perf; Story of a Girl [music by Freddie Bretherton;
dance arranged by Wendy Toye]; Twelve O'Clock; Inspection with the Feet; Going
Adrift; Beguine; Follow the Girls; Brave Jack Tar; The Debut [dance arranged by Wendy
Toye]; I Wanna Get Married; I Wanna Hang my Hat

Funny Girl

London: Prince of Wales Theatre, 13 April 1966 [112 performances]
New York: Winter Garden, 26 March 1964 [1,348 performances]
Music by Jule Styne; lyrics by Bob Merrill; book by Isobel Lennart from her original story

PC: *Fanny Brice*: Barbra Streisand; *Nick Arnstein*: Michael Craig; *Eddie Ryan*: Lee Allen;
Mrs Brice: Kay Medford; *Mrs Strakosh*: Stella Moray; *Emma*: Isabelle Lucas; *Florenz
Ziegfeld Jr*: Ronald Leigh-Hunt; *Tom Kenney*: Jack Cunningham

MN: If a Girl Isn't Pretty; I'm the Greatest Star; Cornet Man; Who Taught Her
Everything?; His Love Makes Me Beautiful; I Want to Be Seen with You Tonight;
Henry Street; People; You Are Woman; Don't Rain on My Parade; Sadie, Sadie; Find
Yourself a Man; Rat-Tat-Tat-Tat; Who Are You Now?; The Music that Makes Me Dance

A Funny Thing Happened on the Way to the Forum

London: Strand Theatre, 3 October 1963 [762 performances]
New York: Alvin Theater, 8 May 1962 [964 performances]
Music and lyrics by Stephen Sondheim; book by Burt Shevelove and Larry Gelbart, based
on the plays of Plautus

PC: *Prologus/Pseudolus*: Frankie Howerd; *Hysterium*: Kenneth Connor; *Lycus*: Jon
Pertwee; *Erronius*: Robertson Hare; *Senex*: 'Monsewer' Eddie Gray; *Philia*: Isla Blair;
Domina: Linda Gray; *Hero*: John Rye; *Miles Gloriosus*: Leon Greene

MN: Comedy Tonight; Love, I Hear; Free; The House of Marcus Lycus; Lovely; Pretty
Little Picture; Everybody Ought to Have a Maid; I'm Calm; Impossible; Bring Me my
Bride; That Dirty Old Man; That'll Show Him; Lovely; Funeral Sequence and Dance

Gentlemen Prefer Blondes

London: Princes Theatre, 20 August 1962 [223 performances]
New York: Ziegfeld Theatre, 8 December 1949 [740 performances]
Music by Jule Styne; lyrics by Leo Robin; book by Joseph Fields and Anita Loos, adapted
from the novel by Anita Loos
PC: *Lorelei Lee*: Dora Bryan; *Dorothy Shaw*: Anne Hart; *Sir Francis Beekman*: Guy
Middleton; *Henry Spoffard*: David Morton; *Gus Esmond*: Donald Stewart; *Gloria Stark*:
Valerie Walsh; *Mrs Ella Spoffard*: Bessie Love
MN: It's High Time; Bye Bye Baby; A Little Girl from Little Rock; I Love What I'm Doing;
Scherzo; Just a Kiss Apart; It's Delightful Down in Chile; Sunshine; You Say You Care;
Finaletto [Act One]; Mamie is Mimi; You Kill Me; Diamonds Are a Girl's Best Friend;
Homesick Blues; Keeping Cool with Coolidge; Button Up with Esmond; Gentlemen
Prefer Blondes

Godspell

London: Round House, 17 November 1971, then Wyndhams Theatre [1,128 performances]
New York [Off-Broadway]: Cherry Lane Theatre, 17 May 1971 [includes Broadway: 2,645
performances]
Music and lyrics by Stephen Schwartz; conceived and directed by John-Michael Tebelak,
based on St Matthew's Gospel
PC: [Programme does not specify roles] Jacquie-Ann Carr, Julie Covington, David Essex,
Neil Fitzwilliam, Jeremy Irons, Verity-Anne Meldrum, Deryk Parkin, Tom Saffery, Gay
Soper, Marti Webb
MN: Tower of Babble; Prepare Ye the Way of the Lord; Save the People; Day by Day;
Learn Your Lessons Well; Bless the Lord; All for the Best; All Good Gifts; Light of
the World; Turn Back, O Man; Alas for You; By My Side; We Beseech Thee; On the
Willows; Finale

Golden Boy

London: Palladium, 4 June 1968 [118 performances]
New York: Majestic Theatre, 20 October 1964 [569 performances]
Music by Charles Strouse; lyrics by Lee Adams; book by Clifford Odets and William
Gibson, based on Odets' play
PC: *Joe Wellington*: Sammy Davis Jnr; *Lorna Moon*: Gloria de Haven; *Eddie Satin*: Lon
Satton; *Lola*: Lola Falana; *Tom Moody*: Mark Dawson
MN: Workout; Colourful; Night Song; Everything's Great; Lorna's Here; There's a Party
Going On; Don't Forget 127th Street; Tour; This is the Life; Yes, I Can!; Trio; I Want to
Be with You; You're No Brother of Mine; No More; The Fight; What Became of Me?

Gone with the Wind

London: Theatre Royal, Drury Lane, 3 May 1972 [397 performances]
Music and lyrics by Harold Rome; book by Horton Foote, based on the novel by Margaret
Mitchell
Rhett Butler: Harve Presnell; *Scarlett O'Hara*: June Ritchie; *Melanie Hamilton*: Patricia
Michael; *Ashley Wilkes*: Robert Swann; *Mammy*: Isabelle Lucas; *Belle Watling*: Doreen
Hermitage; *Gerald O'Hara*: Harry Goodier

MN: Today's the Day; Cakewalk; We Belong to You; Tara; Bonnie Blue Flag; Bazaar
Hymn; Virginia Reel; Quadrille; Two of a Kind; Blissful Christmas; Tomorrow is
Another Day; Ashley's Departure; Where is my Soldier Boy?; Why Did They Die?;
Lonely Stranger; A Time for Love; Atlanta Burning; A Soldier's Goodbye; Which Way
is Home?; If Only; How Often, How Often; The Wedding; A Southern Lady; Marrying
for Fun; Strange and Wonderful; Blueberry Eyes; Little Wonders; Bonnie Gone;
It Doesn't Matter Now

The Great Waltz

London: Theatre Royal, Drury Lane, 9 July 1970 [605 performances]
New York: Center Theatre, 22 September 1934 [347 performances]
Musical adaptation by Erich Wolfgang Korngold, Julius Bittner, Robert Wright and
George Forrest; lyrics by Wright and Forrest; additional lyrics by Forman Brown; book
by Jerome Chodorov, based on the version by Moss Hart and Milton Lazarus; original
book and lyrics by Alfred Willner, Heinz Reichert and Ernst Marischka
PC: *Helene Vernet*: Sari Barabas; *Johann Strauss Snr*: Walter Cassel; *Resi*: Diane Todd;
Johann Strauss Jnr (Schani): David Watson; *Hartkopf*: Eric Brotherson; *Dommayer*:
Robert Dorning; *Ebeseder*: Gabor Baraker; *Hirsch*: David Tate
MN: Two by Two; He Owes It All to Me!; A Waltz with Wings; I'm in Love with Vienna;
My Philosophy of Life; Love and Gingerbread; Action in the Kitchen (Pepetuum
Mobile); Teeter-Totter Me; Where Would I Be?; State of the Dance; Radetzky
March; Of Men and Violins; An Artist's Life; Act One Finale; The Enchanted Wood;
Celebrated People; At Dommayer's; The Gypsy Told Me; The Put-On Polka (Tritsch-
Tratsch); No Two Ways; I Hate Music; The Blue Danube

Guys and Dolls

London: Coliseum, 28 May 1953 [555 performances]
New York: 46th Street Theatre, 24 November 1950 [1,200 performances]
Music and lyrics by Frank Loesser; book by Abe Burrows and Jo Swerling, based on the
story *The Idyll of Miss Sarah Brown* by Damon Runyon
PC: *Sky Masterson*: Jerry Wayne; *Miss Adelaide*: Vivian Blaine; *Nathan Detroit*: Sam
Levene; *Miss Sarah Brown*: Lizbeth Webb; *Arvide Abernathy*: Ernest Butcher; *Big Jule*:
Lew Herbert; *Nicely-Nicely Johnson*: Stubby Kaye; *Harry the Horse*: Tom Pedi; *Benny
Southstreet*: Johnny Silver; *Liver Lips Louie*: Lou Jacobi
MN: Fugue for Tinhorns; Follow the Fold; The Oldest Established; I'll Know; A Bushel
and a Peck; Adelaide's Lament; Guys and Dolls; Havana; The Elegant Dancers; If I
Were a Bell; My Time of Day; I've Never Been in Love Before; Take Back Your Mink;
More I Cannot Wish You; The Crap Game Ballet; Luck Be a Lady; Sue Me; Sit Down,
You're Rockin' the Boat; Marry the Man Today

Hair

London: Shaftesbury Theatre, 27 September 1968 [1,998 performances]
New York: Public Theatre, 29 October 1967 [94 performances]; Biltmore Theatre, 29 April
1968 [1,742 performances]
Music by Galt MacDermot; book and lyrics by Gerome Ragni and James Rado

302   West End Broadway   Appendix

PC: *Claude*: Paul Nicholas; *Berger*: Oliver Tobias; *Sheila*: Annabel Leventon; *Woof*: Michael Feast; *Jeannie*: Linda Kendrick; *Dionne*: Marsha Hunt; *Crissy*: Liz White; *Hud*: Peter Straker

MN: Aquarius; Donna; Hashish; Sodomy; Coloured Spade; Manchester; Ain't Got No; I Believe in Love; The Rally; Air; Initials; I Got Life; Going Down; Hair; My Conviction; Easy to Be Hard; Don't Put It Down; Frank Mills; Be-In; Where Do I Go?; Electric Blues; Black Boys; White Boys; Walking in Space; Abie Baby; Gettysburg Address; Three-Five-Zero-Zero; What a Piece of Work is Man; Good Morning Starshine; The Bed; Eyes Look Your Last; The Flesh Failures (Let the Sun Shine In)

Hello, Dolly!

London: Theatre Royal, Drury Lane, 2 December 1965 [794 performances]
New York: St James Theatre, 16 January 1964 [2,844 performances]
Music and lyrics by Jerry Herman; book by Michael Stewart, based on the play *The Matchmaker* by Thornton Wilder
PC: *Mrs Dolly Gallagher Levi*: Mary Martin; *Horace Vandergelder*: Loring Smith; *Irene Molloy*: Marilynn Lovell; *Minnie Fay*: Coco Ramirez; *Barnaby Tucker*: Johnny Beecher; *Cornelius Hackl*: Garrett Lewis; *Ermengarde*: Sonya Petrie; *Ambrose Kemper*: Peter Dixon; *Rudolph*: Gordon Clyde; *Ernestina*: Judith Drake; *Judge*: Vernon Rees
MN: I Put My Hand In; It Takes a Woman; Put on Your Sunday Clothes; Ribbons Down My Back; Motherhood; Dancing; Before the Parade Passes By; Elegance; The Waiters' Gallop; Hello, Dolly!; It Only Takes a Moment; So Long Dearie

High Button Shoes

London: Hippodrome, 22 December 1948 [291 performances]
New York: New Century Theatre, 9 October 1947 [727 performances]
Music and lyrics by Jule Styne and Sammy Cahn; book by Stephen Longstreet
PC: *Harrison Floy*: Lew Parker; *Sara Longstreet*: Kay Kimber; *Henry Longstreet*: Sidney James; *Oggle Ogglethorpe*: Jack Cooper; *Mr Pontdue*: Tommy Godfrey; *Fran*: Hermene French; *Nancy*: Joan Heal; *Uncle Willie*: Peter Felgate; *Stevie Longstreet*: Michael Nicholls; *Elmer Simpkins*: James Ramsay; *corps de ballet* included Audrey Hepburn
MN: He Tried to Make a Dollar; Can't You Just See Yourself in Love with Me?; There's Nothing Like a Model T; Next to Texas, I Love You; Security; Tango; Bird Watcher's Song; Get Away for a Day in the Country; A Summer Incident; Papa, Won't You Dance with Me?; On a Sunday by the Sea; Bathing Beauty Ballet; You're My Girl; I Still Get Jealous; You're My Boy; Nobody Ever Died for Dear Old Rutgers; Castle Walk

High Spirits

London: Savoy Theatre, 3 November 1964 [93 performances]
New York: Alvin Theatre, 7 April 1964 [375 performances]
Book, music and lyrics by Hugh Martin and Timothy Gray, based on the play *Blithe Spirit* by Noel Coward
PC: *Madame Arcati*: Cicely Courtneidge; *Ruth Condomine*: Jan Waters; *Charles Condomine*: Denis Quilley; *Elvira*: Marti Stevens; *Mrs Bradman*: Ann Hamilton; *Dr Bradman*: Peter Vernon; *Edith*: Denise Coffey

MN: Was She Prettier Than I?; The Bicycle Song; You'd Better Love Me; Where Is
the Man I Married?; The Sandwich Man; Go into Your Trance; Forever and a Day;
Something Tells Me; I Know Your Heart; Faster Than Sound; If I Gave You; Talking to
You; Home Sweet Heaven; Something Is Coming to Tea; The Exorcism; What In the
World Do You Want?

How to Succeed in Business without Really Trying

London: Shaftesbury Theatre, 28 March 1963 [520 performances]
New York: 46th Street Theatre, 14 October 1961 [1,417 performances]
Music and lyrics by Frank Loesser; book by Abe Burrows, Jack Weinstock and Willie
Gilbert, based on the book by Shepherd Mead
PC: *J. Pierpont Finch*: Warren Berlinger; *J. B. Biggley*: Billy De Wolfe; *Rosemary*: Patricia
Michael; *Smitty*: Josephine Blake; *Bud Frump*: David Knight; *Mr Twimble*: Bernard
Spear; *Hedy La Rue*: Eileen Gourlay; *Miss Jones*: Olive Lucius
MN: How To (Succeed); Happy to Keep His Dinner Warm; Coffee Break; The Company
Way; A Secretary is Not a Toy; Been a Long Day; Grand Old Ivy; Paris Original;
Rosemary; Cinderella Darling; Love from a Heart of Gold; I Believe in You; The Yo Ho
Ho (Pirate Dance); Brotherhood of Man

I and Albert

London [only]: Piccadilly Theatre, 6 November 1972 [120 performances]
Music by Charles Strouse; lyrics by Lee Adams; book by Jay Allen
PC: *Queen Victoria*: Polly James; *Albert*: Sven-Bertil Taube; *Lord Melbourne/Disraeli*:
Lewis Fiander; *Lord Palmerston/Gladstone*: Aubrey Woods; *Baroness Lehzen*: Silvia
Beamish
MN: It Has All Begun; Leave It Alone; I've 'Eard the Bloody 'Indoos 'As It Worse;
The Victoria and Albert Waltz; This Gentle Land; This Noble Land; I and Albert;
His Royal Highness; Enough!; Victoria; This Dear Paradise [subsequently cut]; Just You
and Me; All Glass; Draw the Blinds; The Widow at Windsor [lyric by Rudyard Kipling];
No One to Call Me Victoria; When You Speak with a Lady; Go It, Old Girl!

I Do! I Do!

London: Lyric Theatre, 16 May 1968 [116 performances]
New York: 46th Street Theatre, 15 June 1968 [561 performances]
Music by Harvey Schmidt; book and lyrics by Tom Jones, based on the play *The
Fourposter* by Jan de Hartog
PC: Ian Carmichael, Anne Rogers
MN: Prologue [comprises: All the Dearly Beloved; Together Forever; I Do! I Do!]; Good
Night; I Love My Wife; Something Has Happened; My Cup Runneth Over; Love Isn't
Everything; Nobody's Perfect; A Well Known Fact; Flaming Agnes; The Honeymoon
is Over; Where Are the Snows?; When the Kids Get Married; The Father of the Bride;
What is a Woman?; Someone Needs Me; Roll Up the Ribbons; This House

Irene

London: Empire Theatre, 7 April 1920 [399 performances]
New York: Vanderbilt Theater, 18 November 1919 [670 performances]
Music by Harry Tierney; lyrics by Joseph McCarthy; book by James Montgomery

PC: *Irene O'Dare*: Edith Day; *Mme Lucy*: Robert Hale; *Donald Marshall*: Pat Somerset; *Helen Cheston*: Margaret Campbell; *Mrs Marshall*: Maidie Hope
MN: Hobbies; Alice Blue Gown; Castle of Dreams; The Talk of the Town; To Be Worthy of You; We're Getting Away with It; Irene; To Love You; Sky Rocket; Last Part of Every Party; There's Something in the Air

London: His Majesty's Theatre, 21 March 1945 [166 performances]
PC: *Irene O'Dare*: Pat Taylor; *Mme Lucy*: Arthur Riscoe; *Donald Marshall*: Frank Leighton; *Jane Gilmour*: Doreen Duke; *H. P. Bowden*: Hugh French; *Helen Cheston*: Doreen Percheron; *Mrs Marshall*: Maidie Andrews
MN: The Art of Genealogy; Hobbies; Alice Blue Gown; Down Town East of Broadway [by Noel Gay]; Castle of Dreams; Talk of the Town; To Be Worthy; Broadway Jitterbug; Irene; We're Getting Away with It; Sky Rocket; The Last Part of Every Party

The King and I

London: Theatre Royal, Drury Lane, 8 October 1953 [926 performances]
New York: St James Theatre, 29 March 1951 [1,246 performances]
Music by Richard Rodgers; book and lyrics by Oscar Hammerstein II, based on *Anna and the King of Siam* by Margaret Landon
PC: *Anna Leonowens*: Valerie Hobson; *The King*: Herbert Lom; *Lady Thiang*: Muriel Smith; *The Kralahome*: Martin Benson; *Tuptim*: Doreen Duke; *Dancer*: Sonya Hana; *Lun Tha*: Jan Muzurus
MN: I Whistle a Happy Tune; My Lord and Master; Hello, Young Lovers!; March of the Siamese Children; A Puzzlement; The Royal Bangkok Academy; Getting to Know You; We Kiss in a Shadow; Shall I Tell You What I Think of You?; Something Wonderful; Western People Funny; I Have Dreamed; Ballet: The Small House of Uncle Thomas; Shall we Dance?

Kismet

London: Stoll Theatre, 20 April 1955 [648 performances]
New York: Ziegfeld Theatre, 3 December 1953 [583 performances]
Music and lyrics by Robert Wright and George Forrest, based on the music of Aleksandr Borodin; book by Charles Lederer and Luther Davis, based on the play by Edward Knoblock
PC: *Hajj*: Alfred Drake; *Marsinah*: Doretta Morrow; *Lalume*: Joan Diener; *Caliph*: Peter Grant; *Wazir*: Paul Whitsun-Jones; *Omar Khayyam*: Donald Eccles; *Princess Samaris*: Juliet Prowse
MN: Rhymes Have I; Fate; Bazaar of the Caravans; Not Since Nineveh; Baubles, Bangles and Beads; Stranger in Paradise; He's in Love!; Gesticulate; Night of My Nights; Was I Wazir?; Rahadlakum; And This is My Beloved; The Olive Tree; Presentation of Princesses

Kiss Me, Kate

London: Coliseum, 8 March 1951 [501 performances]
New York: New Century Theatre, 30 December 1948 [1,077 performances]
Music and lyrics by Cole Porter; book by Sam and Bella Spewack, based on *The Taming of the Shrew* by William Shakespeare

PC: *Fred Graham*: Bill Johnson; *Lilli Vanessi*: Patricia Morison; *Lois Lane*: Julie Wilson;
  Bill Calhoun: Walter Long; *Hattie*: Adelaide Hall; *Gangster*: Sidney James; *Gangster*:
  Danny Green; *Paul*: Archie Savage
MN: Another Op'nin', Another Show; Why Can't You Behave?; Wunderbar; So in Love;
  We Open in Venice; Tom Dick or Harry; I've Come to Wive It Wealthily in Padua;
  I Hate Men; Were Thine That Special Face; I Sing of Love; Kiss Me Kate; Too Darn
  Hot; Where Is the Life that Late I Led?; Always True to You (in My Fashion); Bianca;
  Brush Up Your Shakespeare; I Am Ashamed that Women Are So Simple

Lady, Be Good!

London: Empire Theatre, 14 April 1926 [326 performances]
New York: Liberty Theatre, 1 December 1924 [330 performances]
Music by George Gershwin; lyrics by Ira Gershwin; book by Guy Bolton and Fred
  Thompson
PC: *Dick Trevor*: Fred Astaire; *Susie Trevor*: Adele Astaire; *J. Watterson Watkins*:
  William Kent; *Rufus Parke*: Denier Warren [later C. Denier Warren]; *Bertie Bassett*:
  Ewart Scott; *Jeff*: Buddy Lee; *Jack Robinson*: George Vollaire; *Daisy Parke*: Glori [*sic*]
  Beaumont; *Shirley Vernon*: Irene Russell
MN: Buy a Little Button; We're Here Because –; Hang On to Me; Oh, What a Lovely
  Party; End of a String; Fascinating Rhythm; So Am I; Lady, Be Good; Linger in the
  Lobby; I'd Rather Charleston [lyric by Desmond Carter]; The Half of It Dearie Blues;
  Juanita; Ukelele Solo; Carnival Time; Swiss Miss

London: Saville Theatre, 25 July 1968 [155 performances]
PC: *Dick Trevor*: Lionel Blair; *Susie Trevor*: Aimi Macdonald; *Watty Watkins*: Joe Baker;
  Rufus Parke: Bernard Clifton; *Bertie Bassett*: Raymond Clarke; *Jeff*: Joe Chisolm; *Jack
  Robinson*: Patrick Rose; *Daisy Parke*: Pauline Garner; *Shirley Vernon*: Elizabeth Connor
MN: Nice Work If You Can Get It; Hang On to Me; Oh What a Lovely Party; On the
  End of a String; I've Got a Crush On You; Fascinating Rhythm; I'm Feeling I'm
  Falling; So Am I; Lady Be Good; Linger in the Lobby; For You, For Me, For Evermore;
  I'd Rather Charleston; The Half of It, Dearie, Blues [*sic*]; Juanita; Love Walked In; Swiss
  Miss; Little Jazz Bird

Let's Face It!

London: Hippodrome, 19 November 1942 [348 performances]
New York: Imperial Theatre, 29 October 1941 [547 performances]
Music and lyrics by Cole Porter; book by Herbert and Dorothy Fields, based on the play
  The Cradle Snatchers by Russell Medcraft and Norma Mitchell
PC: *Jerry Walker*: Bobby Howes; *Maggie Watson*: Joyce Barbour; *Frankie Burns*: Jack
  Stamford; *Winnie Potter*: Patricia Kirkwood; *Cornelia Abigail Pigeon*: Babette O'Deal;
  Nancy Collister: Noele Gordon; *Eddie Hilliard*: Leigh Stafford; *Jean Blanchard*: Pat
  Leonard
MN: Milk, Milk, Milk; A Lady Needs a Rest; Jerry, My Soldier Boy; Let's Face It; Farming;
  Ev'rything I Love; Ace in the Hole; You Irritate Me So; Baby Games; A Fairy Tale; Rub
  Your Lamp; Cuttin' a Rug; I've Got Some Unfinished Business with You; Let's Not Talk
  about Love; A Little Rumba Numba; Speciality Dance; I Hate You, Darling; Melody in
  Four F (music and lyrics by Sylvia Fine and Max Liebman)

Little Mary Sunshine

London: Comedy Theatre, 17 May 1962 [44 performances]
New York [Off-Broadway]: Orpheum Theatre, 18 November 1959 [1,143 performances]
Book, music and lyrics by Rick Besoyan
PC: *Little Mary Sunshine*: Patricia Routledge; *Captain Jim Warrington*: Terence Cooper;
    Corporal Billy Jester: Bernard Cribbins; *Nancy Twinkle*: Joyce Blair; *General Oscar
    Fairfax*: Erik Chitty; *Mme Ernestine Von Liebedich*: Gita Denise; *Chief Brown Bear*:
    Ed Bishop [The cast also included Anna Dawson, Patricia Michael, Judy Nash, Hilary
    Tindall and John Quayle.]
MN: The Forest Rangers; Little Mary Sunshine; Look for a Sky of Blue; You're the Fairest
    Flower; In Izzenschnooken on the Lovely Essenzook Zee; Playing Croquet; Swinging;
    How Do You Do?; Tell a Handsome Stranger; Once in a Blue Moon; Colorado Love
    Call; Every Little Nothing; Act One Finale; Such a Merry Party; Say Uncle; Me a Heap
    Big Injun; Naughty, Naughty Nancy; Mata Hari; Do You Ever Dream of Vienna?;
    A Shell Game [pantomime]; Coo Coo; Finale

Little Me

London: Cambridge Theatre, 18 November 1964 [334 performances]
New York: Lunt-Fontanne Theatre, 17 November 1962 [257 performances]
Music by Cy Coleman; lyrics by Carolyn Leigh; book by Neil Simon, based on a novel by
    Patrick Dennis
PC: *Noble Eggleston/Mr Pinchley/Val du Val/Fred Poitrine/Otto Schnitzler/Prince
    Cherny/Young Noble*: Bruce Forsyth; *Belle*: Eileen Gourlay; *Miss Poitrine*: Avril Angers;
    *Pinchley Jnr/Defence Lawyer/German Soldier/General Schreiber/Ship Captain/
    Assistant Director/Yulnick*: Bernard Spear; *George Musgrove*: Swen Swenson; *Patrick
    Dennis*: David Henderson-Tate; *Lady Eggleston*: Enid Lowe; *Benny Buxgrave*: Laurie
    Webb; *Bernie Buxgrave*: Jack Francois; *Mum Hoggsfather*: Bee Duffell
MN: The Truth; At the Very Top of the Hill; Birthday Party; I Love You; Deep Down
    Inside; Be a Performer; Dimples; Boom-Boom; I've Got Your Number; Real Live Girl;
    Poor Little Hollywood Star; Little Me; The Prince's Farewell; Here's to Us

The Love Doctor

London [only]: Piccadilly Theatre, 12 October 1959 [16 performances]
Music, book and lyrics by Robert Wright and George Forrest
PC: *The Tramp*: Ian Carmichael; *Toinette*: Joan Heal; *Polidore Argan*: Douglas Byng;
    Beline: Eleanor Drew; *Henrietta Argan*: Patricia Routledge; *Leander*: Peter Gilmore;
    Achille Diafoirus: Richard Wordsworth
MN: Bleed and Purge; Rich Man, Poor Man; Be-Angelled; Promised; Loose in the
    Foot; Who Is? You Are!; His Father's Son; She's Appalling, She's Alluring; I Would
    Love You Still; I Am Your Man; The Parade; Would I Were; Up; Formula, Formulae,
    Formulorum; The Carefree Heart; Anatomy; The Chase

Love from Judy

London [only]: Saville Theatre, 25 September 1952 [594 performances]
Music by Hugh Martin; lyrics by Hugh Martin and Jack Gray; book by Eric Maschwitz,
    based on the novel *Daddy-Long-Legs* by Jean Webster

PC: *Jerusha Abbott*: Jean Carson; *Jervis Pendleton*: Bill O'Connor; *Butterfly*: Adelaide Hall; *Sally McBride*: June Whitfield; *Jimmy McBride*: Johnny Brandon; *Mrs Grace Pritchard*: Linda Gray; *Julia Pendleton*: Audrey Freeman

MN: Mardi Gras; I Never Dream When I'm Asleep; It's Great to Be an Orphan; Goin' Back to School; Dumb, Dumb, Dumb; It's Better Rich; Daddy-Long-Legs; Love from Judy; A Touch of Voodoo; Skipping Rope Hornpipe; Here We Are; Go and Get Your Old Banjo; Kind to Animals; Aint Gonna Marry; My True Love; What Do I See in You?

Lute Song

London: Winter Garden Theatre, 11 October 1948 [24 performances]
New York: Plymouth Theatre, 6 February 1946 [142 performances]
Music by Raymond Scott; lyrics by Bernard Hanighen; book by Sidney Howard and Will Irwin, based on the Chinese play *Pi-Pa-Ki*

PC: *Tchao-ou-Niang*: Dolly Haas; *Tsai-Yong*: Yul Brynner; *Tsai*: George Manship; *Madame Tsai*: Margaret Halstan; *Princess Nieou-chi*: Iris Russell; *Youen-Kong*: Frank Forsyth; *Imperial Chamberlain/Genie*: Antony Eustrel

MN: Mountain High, Valley Low; North Road; Imperial March; Monkey See, Monkey Do; Where You Are; Eunuch Scene; Marriage Music; Willow Tree; Beggar's Music; Vision Song; Chinese Market Place and 'Bitter Harvest'; Dirge Song; Genie Music; Phoenix Dance; Lion Dance; Lute Song

Mame

London: Theatre Royal, Drury Lane, 20 February 1969 [443 performances]
New York: Winter Garden Theatre, 24 May 1966 [1,508 performances]
Music and lyrics by Jerry Herman; book by Robert E. Lee and Jerome Lawrence, based on their play from the novel by Patrick Dennis

PC: *Mame Dennis Burnside*: Ginger Rogers; *Agnes Gooch*: Ann Beach; *Vera Charles*: Margaret Courtenay; *Beauregard*: Barry Kent; *Dwight Babcock*: Guy Spaull; *Patrick Dennis*: Gary Warren; *Patrick Dennis age 19–29*: Tony Adams; *Ito*: Burt Kwouk

MN: St Bridget; It's Today; Open a New Window; The Man in the Moon; My Best Girl; We Need a Little Christmas; The Fox Hunt; Mame; Bosom Buddies; Gooch's Song; That's How Young I Feel; If He Walked into My Life

Man of La Mancha

London: Piccadilly Theatre, 24 April 1968 [253 performances]
New York: ANTA Washington Square Theatre, 22 November 1965 [2,328 performances]
Music by Mitch Leigh; lyrics by Joe Darion; book by Dale Wasserman

PC: *Don Quixote/Cervantes*: Keith Michell; *Aldonza*: Joan Diener; *Sancho*: Bernard Spear; *The Housekeeper*: Olive Gilbert; *The Padre*: Alan Crofoot; *Pedro*: Shev Rodgers; *Antonia*: Patricia Bredin; *Dr Carrasco*: Peter Arne; *The Innkeeper*: David King

MN: Man of La Mancha (I Don Quixote); It's All the Same; Dulcinea; I'm Only Thinking of Him; I Really Like Him; What Does He Want of Me?; Little Bird, Little Bird; Barber's Song; Golden Helmet of Mambrino; To Each His Dulcinea; The Quest (The Impossible Dream); The Combat; The Dubbing; The Abduction; Moorish Dance; Aldonza; The Knight of the Mirrors; A Little Gossip; The Psalm

London: Piccadilly Theatre, 10 June 1969 [118 performances]
PC: *Don Quixote/Cervantes*: Richard Kiley; *Aldonza*: Ruth Silvestre; *Sancho*: Bernard
    Spear; *The Housekeeper*: Olive Gilbert; *The Padre*: Gordon Wilcock; *Pedro*: John
    Larsen; *Antonia*: Ruth Llewellyn; *Dr Carrasco*: Johathan [*sic*] Burn; *The Innkeeper*:
    Charles West

Man with a Load of Mischief

London: Comedy Theatre, 9 December 1968 [26 performances]
New York [Off-Broadway]: Jan Hus Playhouse, 6 November 1966, transferred to
    Provincetown Playhouse, 17 May 1967 [241 performances]
Music by John Clifton; lyrics by John Clifton and Ben Tarver; book by Ben Tarver, based
    on the play by Ashley Dukes
PC: *Lady*: Roberta D'Esti; *Innkeeper*: Leon Eagles; *His Wife*: Julia McKenzie; *Nobleman*:
    Paul Dawkins; *His Servant*: Valentine Palmer
MN: Wayside Inn; The Rescue; Entrance Polonaise; Romance; Goodbye My Sweet; Man
    with a Load of Mischief; Once You've Had a Little Taste; Hulla-baloo-belay; Dinner
    Minuet; You'd Be Amazed; A Friend Like You; Come to the Masquerade; What Style;
    A Wonder; Make Way for My Lady; Forget; Any Other Way; Quartet

Previously presented at the Intimate, Palmers Green on 14 August 1968
PC: *Lady*: Roberta D'Esti; *Innkeeper*: John Gower; *His Wife*: Dilys Laye; *Nobleman*:
    Richard Todd; *His Servant*: David Kernan

The Most Happy Fella

London: Coliseum, 21 April 1960 [288 performances]
New York: Imperial Theatre, 3 May 1956 [676 performances]
Book, music and lyrics by Frank Loesser, based on the play *They Knew What They
    Wanted* by Sidney Howard
PC: *Tony*: Inia Wiata; *Rosabella*: Helena Scott; *Cleo*: Libi Staiger; *Herman*: Jack DeLon;
    Joey: Art Lund; *Marie*: Nina Verushka; *Postman*: William Dickie; *Doc*: Walter Midgley;
    Pasquale: Rico Froehlich; *Guiseppe*: Ralph Farnworth; *Ciccio*: John Clifford
MN: Ooh My Feet; I Know How It Is; Seven Million Crumbs; The Letter; Somebody,
    Somewhere; The Most Happy Fella; The Letter Theme; Standing on the Corner; Joey,
    Joey, Joey; Rosabella; Abbondanza; Plenty Bambini; Sposalizio; Special Delivery;
    Benvenuta; Aren't You Glad?; That Old Man; Don't Cry; Fresno Beauties (Cold and
    Dead); Love and Kindness; Happy to Make Your Acquaintance; I Don't Like This
    Dame; Big 'D'; How Beautiful the Days; Young People; Warm All Over; Old People;
    I Like Everybody; I Love Him; Like a Woman Loves a Man; My Heart is So Full of You;
    Hoedown; Mamma, Mamma; Goodbye, Darlin'; Song of a Summer Night; Please Let
    Me Tell You; Tony's Thoughts; She's Gonna Come Home with Me; I Made a Fist

The Music Man

London: Adelphi Theatre, 16 March 1961 [395 performances]
New York: Majestic Theatre, 19 December 1957 [1,375 performances]
Book, music and lyrics by Meredith Willson (book in association with Franklin Lacey)

PC: *Professor Harold Hill*: Van Johnson; *Marian Paroo*: Patricia Lambert; *Marcellus Washburn*: Bernard Spear; *Mrs Paroo*: Ruth Kettlewell; *Eulalie Shinn*: Nan Munro; *Winthrop Paroo*: Denis Waterman/Stephen Ashworth; *Mayor Shinn*: C. Denier Warren; *The Iowa Four*: Alan Thomas, Peter Rhodes, Frederick Williams, John Lloyd Parry

MN: Rock Island; Iowa Stubborn; Trouble; Piano Lesson; Goodnight My Someone; Seventy-Six Trombones; Sincere; The Sadder-but-Wiser Girl; Pickalittle; Goodnight Ladies; Marian the Librarian; My White Knight; Wells Fargo Wagon; It's You; Shipoopi; Lida Rose; Will I Ever Tell You?; Gary, Indiana; Till There Was You

My Fair Lady

London: Theatre Royal, Drury Lane, 30 April 1958 [2,281 performances]
New York: Mark Hellinger Theatre, 15 March 1956 [2,717 performances]
PC: *Henry Higgins*: Rex Harrison; *Eliza Doolittle*: Julie Andrews; *Alfred P. Doolittle*: Stanley Holloway; *Colonel Pickering*: Robert Coote; *Freddy Eynsford-Hill*: Leonard Weir; *Mrs Higgins*: Zena Dare; *Mrs Eynsford-Hill*: Linda Gray
MN: Why Can't the English?; Wouldn't It Be Loverly?; With a Little Bit of Luck; I'm an Ordinary Man; Just You Wait; The Rain in Spain; I Could Have Danced All Night; Ascot Gavotte; On the Street Where You Live; The Embassy Waltz; You Did It; Show Me; Get Me to the Church on Time; A Hymn to Him; Without You; I've Grown Accustomed to Her Face

No Strings

London: Her Majesty's Theatre, 30 December 1963 [151 performances]
New York: 54th Street Theatre, 15 March 1962 [580 performances]
Music and lyrics by Richard Rodgers; book by Samuel Taylor
PC: *David Jordan*: Art Lund; *Barbara Woodruff*: Beverly Todd; *Mollie Plummer*: Hy Hazell; *Comfort O'Connell*: Marti Stevens; *Mike Robinson*: David Holliday; *Louis de Pourtal*: Ferdy Mayne; *Jeanette Valmy*: Erica Rogers; *Luc Delbert*: Geoffrey Hutchings
MN: The Sweetest Sounds; How Sad; Loads of Love; The Man Who Has Everything; Be My Host; La La La; You Don't Tell Me; Love Makes the World Go; Nobody Told Me; Look No Further; Maine; An Orthodox Fool; Eager Beaver; No Strings

Oklahoma!

London: Theatre Royal, Drury Lane, 29 April 1947 [1,548 performances]
New York: St James Theatre, 31 March 1943 [2,212 performances]
Music by Richard Rodgers; book and lyrics by Oscar Hammerstein II, based on the play *Green Grow the Lilacs* by Lynn Riggs
PC: *Curly*: Howard (Harold) Keel; *Laurey*: Betty Jane Watson; *Aunt Eller*: Mary Marlo; *Will Parker*: Walter Donahue; *Jud Fry*: Henry Clarke; *Ali Hakim*: Marek Windheim; *Ado Annie Carnes*: Dorothea MacFarland
MN: Oh! What a Beautiful Mornin'; The Surrey with the Fringe on Top; Kansas City; I Cain't Say No; Many a New Day; It's a Scandal! It's an Outrage!; People Will Say We're in Love; Por Jud; Lonely Room; Out of My Dreams; The Farmer and the Cowman; All Er Nothin'; Oklahoma!

On the Town

London: Prince of Wales Theatre, 30 May 1963 [53 performances]
New York: Adelphi Theatre, 28 December 1944 [463 performances]
Music by Leonard Bernstein; book and lyrics by Betty Comden and Adolph Green, from
an idea by Jerome Robbins
PC: *Ozzie*: Elliott Gould; *Gabey*: Don McKay; *Chip*: Franklin Kiser; *Hildy*: Carol Arthur;
Ivy Smith: Andrea Jaffe; *Claire*: Gillian Lewis; *Madame Dilly*: Elspeth March; *Lucy
Schmeeler*: Rosamund Greenwood; *Judge Pitkin W. Bridgework*: John Humphry; *Pas de
Deux*: Tommy Merrifield; Sylvia Ellis
MN: I Feel Like I'm Not Out of Bed Yet; New York, New York; Miss Subways; Come
Up to My Place; Carried Away; Lonely Town; Pas de Deux; Barre; I Can Cook Too;
Lucky to Be Me; Times Square Ballet; So Long Baby; I Wish I Was Dead; You Got Me;
I Understand; Dream Coney Island; Some Other Time; Real Coney Island

Once Upon a Mattress

London: Adelphi Theatre, 20 September 1960 [38 performances]
New York: Alvin Theatre, 25 November 1959 [460 performances]
Music by Mary Rodgers; lyrics by Marshall Barer; book by Jay Thompson, Marshall
Barer and Dean Fuller, based on the story *The Princess and the Pea* by Hans Christian
Andersen
PC: *Princess Winnifred*: Jane Connell; *Lady Larken*: Patricia Lambert; *The Queen*: Thelma
Ruby; *Jester*: Max Wall; *Prince Dauntless*: Robin Hunter; *Wizard*: Bill Kerr; *The King*:
Milo O'Shea; *Sir Harry*: Bill Newman; *Sir Studley*: Peter Regan; *Minstrel*: Peter Grant;
The Nightingale of Samarkand: Meg Walter
MN: Many Moons Ago; An Opening for a Princess; In a Little While; Shy; The Minstrel,
The Jester and I; Sensitivity; Swamps of Home; Normandy; Spanish Panic; Song of
Love; Quiet; Happily Ever After; Man to Man Talk; Very Soft Shoes; Yesterday I Loved
You; Lullaby

110 in the Shade

London: Palace Theatre, 8 February 1967 [101 performances]
New York: Broadhurst Theatre, 24 October 1963 [330 performances]
Music by Harvey Schmidt; lyrics by Tom Jones; book by N. Richard Nash, based on his
play *The Rainmaker*
PC: *Lizzie Curry*: Inga Swenson; *Bill Starbuck*: Stephen Douglass; *File*: Ivor Emmanuel;
Jim Curry: Joel Warfield; *Snookie Updegraff*: Vanessa Howard; *H. C. Curry*: George
Hancock; *Noah Curry*: Max Latimer
MN: Another Hot Day; Lizzie's Coming Home; Love, Don't Turn Away; Poker Polka;
Hungry Men; The Rain Song; You're Not Foolin' Me; Raunchy; A Man and a Woman;
Old Maid; Everything Beautiful Happens at Night; Melisande; Simple Little Things;
Little Red Hat; Is It Really Me?; Wonderful Music; 110 in the Shade

Paint Your Wagon

London: Her Majesty's Theatre, 11 February 1953 [478 performances]
New York: Sam S. Shubert Theatre, 12 November 1951 [289 performances]
Music by Frederick Loewe; book and lyrics by Alan Jay Lerner

PC: *Ben Rumson*: Bobby Howes; *Jennifer Rumson*: Sally Ann Howes; *Julio Valveras*: Ken Cantril; *Jacob Woodling*: Ormonde Douglas; *Jake Whippany*: Laurie Payne; *Sandy Twist*: Kenneth Sandford; *Yvonne Sorel*: Sheila O'Neill; *Ed*: Terence Cooper; *Mike Mooney*: Liam Gaffney

MN: I'm on My Way; Rumson Town; What's Goin' on Here?; I Talk to the Trees; Lonely Men Dance; They Call the Wind Maria; I Still See Elisa; How Can I Wait?; Trio; In Between; Whoop-ti-ay!; Carino Mio; There's a Coach Comin' in; Coach Ballet; Hand Me Down That Can o' Beans; Rope Dance; Can-Can; Another Autumn; Movin'; All for Him; Wanderin' Star; Fandango's Farewell; Strike!

The Pajama Game

London: Coliseum, 13 October 1955 [588 performances]
New York: St. James Theatre, 13 May 1954 [1,063 performances]
Music and lyrics by Richard Adler and Jerry Ross; book by George Abbott and Richard Bissell, based on Bissell's novel *7½ Cents*
PC: *Sid Sorokin*: Edmund Hockridge; *Babe Williams*: Joy Nichols; *Hines*: Max Wall; *Gladys*: Elizabeth Seal; *Mabel*: Joan Emney; *Prez*: Frank Lawless
MN: The Pajama Game; Racing with the Clock; A New Town is a Blue Town; I'm Not at All in Love; I'll Never Be Jealous Again; Hey There; Her Is; Sleep-Tite; Once a Year Day; Small Talk; There Once Was a Man; Steam Heat; Think of the Time I Save; Hernando's Hideaway; Jealousy Ballet; 7½ Cents

Pal Joey

London: Princes Theatre, 31 March 1954 [245 performances]
New York: Ethel Barrymore Theatre, 25 December 1940 [374 performances]
New York [revival]: Broadhurst Theatre, 3 January 1952 [542 performances]
Music by Richard Rodgers; lyrics by Lorenz Hart; book by John O'Hara, based on his short stories
PC: *Joey Evans*: Harold Lang; *Vera Simpson*: Carol Bruce; *Linda English*: Sally Bazely; *Gladys Bumps*: Jean Brampton; *Ludlow Lowell*: Lou Jacobi; *Melba Snyder*: Olga Lowe; *Victor*: Malcolm Goddard; *The Kid*: Maureen Creigh
MN: You Mustn't Kick It Around; I Could Write a Book; Chicago; That Terrific Rainbow; What Is a Man?; Happy Hunting Horn; Bewitched, Bothered and Bewildered; Pal Joey; Joey Looks into the Future; The Flower Garden of My Heart; In Our Little Den; Plant You Now, Dig You Later; Do It the Hard Way; Take Him

Panama Hattie

London: Piccadilly Theatre, 4 November 1943 [308 performances]
New York: 46th Street Theatre, 30 October 1940 [501 performances]
Music and lyrics by Cole Porter; book by Herbert Fields and B. G. de Sylva, edited by Graham John
PC: *Eddy Brown*: Max Wall; *Hattie Maloney*: Bebe Daniels; *Vivian Budd*: Claude Hulbert; *Joe Briggs*: Jack Stanford; *Loopy Smith*: Richard Hearne; *Florrie*: Frances Marsden; *Speciality Dancer*: Diane Gardiner
MN: Join It Right Away; Visit Panama; I've Still Got My Health; Fresh as a Daisy; Welcome to Betty; Let's Be Buddies; I'm Throwing a Ball Tonight; I Detest a Fiesta; Who Would Have Dreamed; All I've Got to Get Now is My Man; You Said It; Loopy Teaches Budd to Dance

London: Adelphi Theatre, 25 January 1945 [100 performances; reopening of above production]
PC: *Eddy Brown*: Max Wall; *Hattie Maloney*: Bebe Daniels; *Vivian Budd*: Claude Hulbert; *Joe Briggs*: Jack Stanford; *Loopy Smith*: Fred Kitchen Jnr; *Florrie*: Frances Marsden; *Speciality Dancer*: Diane Gardiner
MN: as above, except that 'Loopy Teaches Budd to Dance' became 'Joe Teaches Budd to Dance'

Plain and Fancy

London: Theatre Royal, Drury Lane, 25 January 1956 [217 performances]
New York: Mark Hellinger Theatre, 27 January 1955 [461 performances]
Music by Albert Hague; lyrics by Arnold B. Horwitt; book by Joseph Stein and Will Glickman
PC: *Ruth Winters*: Shirl Conway; *Dan King*: Richard Derr; *Katie Yoder*: Grace O'Connor; *Papa Yoder*: Malcolm Keen; *Hilda Miller*: Joan Hovis; *Peter Reber*: Jack Drummond; *Emma Miller*: Virginia Somers; *Ezra Reber*: Reed de Rouen; *Samuel Zook*: Harry Naughhton; *Isaac Miller*: Bernard Spear [cast also included Ivor Emmanuel, Andy Cole and Terence Cooper]
MN: You Can't Miss It; It Wonders Me; Plenty of Pennsylvania; Young and Foolish; Why Not Katie?; By Lantern Light; It's a Helluva Way to Run a Love Affair; This is All Very New to Me; Plain We Live; How Do You Raise a Barn?; Follow Your Heart; City Mouse, Country Mouse; I'll Show Him; Carnival Ballet; Dance Hall; Take Your Time and Take Your Pick

Pocahontas

London [only]: Lyric Theatre, 14 November 1963 [12 performances]
Music, lyrics and book by Kermit Goell, based on his book *Pocahontas*
PC: *Pocahontas*: Anita Gillette; *Captain John Smith/John Rolfe*: Terence Cooper; *Winnuska*: Isabelle Lucas; *Tom Savage*: Steve Parry; *Captain Dale Wingfield*: Michael Barrington; *King James*: George Hancock; *Queen Anne*: Christene Palmer
MN: Prologue; The First Landing; Gold; She Fancied Me; Free as a Bird; You Have to Want to Touch Him; Too Many Miles from London Town; Eagle Dance; London Bridge is Falling Down; I Love You Johnnie Smith; Things; Virginia; Oranges and Lemons; I Want to Live with You; I Have Lost My Way; Give Me a Sign; Like My True Love Grows; Yes, I Love You; Fit for a Princess; You Can't Keep a Good Man Down; Masque of Christmas

Promises, Promises

London: Prince of Wales Theatre, 2 October 1969 [560 performances]
New York: Shubert Theatre, 1 December 1968 [1,281 performances]
Music by Burt Bacharach; lyrics by Hal David; book by Neil Simon, based on the film *The Apartment* by Billy Wilder and I. A. L. Diamond
PC: *Chuck Baxter*: Anthony Roberts; *Fran Kubelik*: Betty Buckley; *J. D. Sheldrake*: James Congdon; *Dr Dreyfuss*: Jack Kruschen; *Marge MacDougall*: Kelly Britt; *Jesse Vanderhoff*: Don Fellows; *Dobitch*: Ronn Carroll; *Eichelberger*: Ivor Dean; *Kirkeby*: Jay Denyer; *Vivien Della Hoya*: Donna McKechnie

MN: Half As Big As Life; Upstairs; You'll Think of Someone; Our Little Secret; She Likes Basketball; Knowing When to Leave; Where Can You Take a Girl?; Wanting Things; Turkey Lurkey Time; A Fact Can be a Beautiful Thing; Whoever You Are; A Young Pretty Girl Like You; I'll Never Fall in Love Again; Promises, Promises

Romany Love

London: His Majesty's Theatre, 7 March 1947 [90 performances]
New York: produced as *Gypsy Lady* at the New Century Theatre, 17 September 1946 [79 performances]
Music by Victor Herbert; lyrics by Robert Wright and George Forrest; book by Henry Myers, with additional dialogue by Fred Thompson
PC: *Musetta*: Helena Bliss; *Boris*: Melville Cooper; *Andre*: Eric Starling; *The Great Alvardo*: John Tyers; *Sandor*: George Britton; *Fresco*: Eddie Kelland Espinosa; *Valerie*: Jane Farrar
MN: Life is a Dirty Business; My Treasure; Andalusia; Romany Life; On a Wonderful Day Like To-day; The Facts of Life Backstage; I Love You, I Adore You; The World and I; Piff Paff; Bolero; Keepsakes; Young Lady a la Mode; Springtide; Ballet Divertissement; My First Waltz; Reality

Rose-Marie

London: Theatre Royal, Drury Lane, 20 March 1925 [851 performances]
New York: Imperial Theatre, 2 September 1924 [557 performances]
Music by Rudolf Friml and Herbert Stothart; book and lyrics by Oscar Hammerstein II and Otto Harbach
PC: *Rose-Marie La Flamme*: Edith Day; *Jim Kenyon*: Derek Oldham; *Hard-Boiled Herman*: Billy Merson; *Lady Jane*: Clarice Hardwicke; *Sgt Malone*: John Dunsmure; *Emile La Flamme*: Michael Cole; *Wanda*: Ruby Morriss
MN: Hard-Boiled Herman; Rose Marie; The Mounties; Lak Jeem; Indian Love Call; Pretty Things; Ballet Eccentric; Why Shouldn't We?; Totem Tom Tom [*sic*]; Act Two Opening Chorus; Only a Kiss; Empire March and Gavotte; Minuet of the Minute; Wandel Waltz; Bridal Procession and 'Door of My Dreams ['Wandel Waltz' omitted from subsequent programmes]

London: Theatre Royal, Drury Lane, 12 September 1929 [100 performances]
PC: *Rose-Marie La Flamme*: Edith Day; *Jim Kenyon*: Roy Russell; *Hard-Boiled Herman*: Gene Gerrard; *Lady Jane*: Clarice Hardwicke; *Sgt Malone*: Charles Meakins; *Emile La Flamme*: Barrie Livesey; *Wanda*: Hazel Gaudreau
MN: Not listed in theatre programme

London: Stoll Theatre, 16 July 1942 [149 performances]
PC: *Rose-Marie La Flamme*: Marjorie Browne; *Jim Kenyon*: Raymond Newell; *Hard-Boiled Herman*: George Lacy; *Lady Jane*: Phyllis Monkman; *Sgt Malone*: David Davies; *Emile La Flamme*: Paul Jackson; *Wanda*: Betty Frankiss
MN: Hard-Boiled Herman; Rose Marie; The Mountie [*sic*]; Lak Jeem; Indian Love Call; Cabin Pantomime; Pretty Things; Eccentric Ballet; Why Shouldn't We?; Totem Tom-Tom; Only a Kiss; The Minuet of the Minute; One Man Woman; Bridal Procession; The Door of My Dreams

London: Victoria Palace, 22 August 1960 [135 performances]

PC: *Rose-Marie La Flamme*: Stephanie Voss; *Jim Kenyon*: David Whitfield; *Hard-Boiled Herman*: Ronnie Stevens; *Lady Jane*: Maggie Fitzgibbon; *Sgt Malone*: Andy Cole; *Emile La Flamme*: James Sharkey; *Wanda*: Gillian Lynne

MN: Opening Chorus: Vive la Canadienne; Hard-Boiled Herman; Rose Marie I Love You; The Mounties Song; Like Jim; Indian Love Call; No Place for a Girl; I Want to Be Free; Totem Tom Tom; Why Shouldn't We?; I Have the Love; Pretty Things; Friendly Kisses; And I Love Her So; Quaint; The Door of My Dreams

Sail Away

London: Savoy Theatre, 21 June 1962 [252 performances]
New York: Broadhurst Theatre, 3 October 1961 [167 performances]
Music, book and lyrics by Noel Coward
PC: *Mimi Paragon*: Elaine Stritch; *Johnny Van Mier*: David Holliday; *Joe/Ali*: John Hewer; *Barnaby Slade*: Grover Dale; *Nancy Foyle*: Sheila Forbes; *Elinor Spencer-Bollard*: Dorothy Reynolds; *Mr Sweeney*: Sydney Arnold; *Mrs Sweeney*: Edith Day
MN: Come to Me; Sail Away; Where Shall I Find Him?; Beatnik Love Affair; Later than Spring; The Passenger's Always Right; Useless Useful Phrases; The Little Ones ABC; Go Slow Johnny; You're a Long, Long Way from America; The Customer's Always Right; Something Very Strange; Italian Wedding Ballet; Don't Turn Away from Love; Bronxville Darby and Joan; When You Want Me; Why Do the Wrong People Travel?

Sally *see* Wild Rose

1776

London: New Theatre, 16 June 1970 [168 performances]
New York: 46th Street Theatre, 16 March 1969 [1,217 performances]
Music and lyrics by Sherman Edwards; book by Peter Stone, based on the original concept by Edwards
PC: *John Adams*: Lewis Fiander; *Benjamin Franklin*: Ronald Radd; *John Dickinson*: Bernard Lloyd; *Stephen Hopkins*: Tony Steedman; *Richard Henry Lee*: David Morton; *Thomas Jefferson*: John Quentin; *Edward Rutledge*: David Kernan; *Martha Jefferson*: Cheryl Kennedy; *Abigail Adams*: Vivienne Ross
MN: Sit Down, John; Piddle, Twiddle and Resolve; Till Then; The Lees of Old Virginia; But, Mr Adams; Yours, Yours, Yours; He Plays the Violin; Cool, Cool, Considerate Men; Momma Look Sharp; The Egg; Molasses to Rum; Is Anybody There?

She Loves Me

London: Lyric Theatre, 29 April 1964 [189 performances]
New York: Eugene O'Neill Theatre, 23 April 1963 [302 performances]
Music by Jerry Bock; lyrics by Sheldon Harnick; book by Joe Masteroff, based on the play *Parfumerie* by Miklos Laszlo
PC: *Georg Nowack*: Gary Raymond; *Amalia Balash*: Anne Rogers; *Ilona Ritter*: Rita Moreno; *Steven Kodaly*: Gary Miller; *Ladislav Sipos*: Peter Sallis; *Arpad Laszlo*: Gregory Phillips; *Zoltan Maraczek*: Karel Stepanek

MN: Good Morning, Good Day; Sounds While Selling; Thank You, Madam; Days
  Gone By; No More Chocolates; Letters; Tonight at Eight; I Don't Know His Name;
  Perspective; Goodbye, Georg; Will He Like Me?; Ilona; Heads I Win; A Romantic
  Atmosphere; Tango Tragique; Dear Friend; Try Me; Where's My Shoe?; Ice Cream;
  She Loves Me; A Trip to the Library; Grand Knowing You; Twelve Days to Christmas

Show Boat

London: Theatre Royal, Drury Lane, 3 May 1928 [350 performances]
New York: Ziegfeld Theatre, 27 December 1927 [572 performances]
Music by Jerome Kern; book and lyrics by Oscar Hammerstein II, adapted from the novel
  by Edna Ferber
PC: *Gaylord Ravenal*: Howett Worster; *Julie La Verne*: Marie Burke; *Joe*: Paul Robeson;
  Magnolia Hawks Ravenal: Edith Day; *Cap'n Andy Hawks*: Cedric Hardwicke; *Ellie
  May Chipley*: Dorothy Lena; *Frank Schultz*: Leslie Sarony; *Parthy Ann Hawks*: Viola
  Compton; *Queenie*: Alberta Hunter
MN: Cotton Blossom; Only Make Believe; Old Man River; Can't Help Loving That Man;
  Life on the Wicked Stage; Till Good Luck Comes My Way; I Might Fall Back On You;
  C'mon Folks; You Are Love; At the Fair; Why Do I Love You?; In Dahomey; Bill [lyric
  by P. G. Wodehouse]; Good-bye My Lady Love; Dance Away the Night

London: Stoll Theatre, 17 April 1943 [264 performances]
PC: *Gaylord Ravenal*: Bruce Carfax; *Julie La Verne*: Pat Taylor; *Joe*: 'Mr Jetsam'; *Magnolia
  Hawks Ravenal*: Gwyneth Lascelles; *Cap'n Andy Hawks*: Mark Daly; *Ellie May Chipley*:
  Sylvia Kellaway; *Frank Schultz*: Leslie Kellaway; *Parthy Ann Hawks*: Hester Paton
  Brown
MN: as 1928 production above, but 'How'd You Like to Spoon with Me?' replaced
  'Good-bye My Lady Love'

London: Adelphi Theatre, 29 July 1971 [910 performances]
PC: *Gaylord Ravenal*: Andre Jobin; *Julie La Verne*: Cleo Laine; *Joe*: Valentine Pringle;
  Magnolia Hawks Ravenal: Lorna Dallas; *Cap'n Andy Hawks*: Derek Royle; *Ellie May
  Chipley*: Jan Hunt; *Frank Schultz*: Jeffrey Shankley; *Parthy Ann Hawks*: Pearl Hackney;
  Queenie: Ena Cabayo
MN: Cotton Blossom; Where's the Mate for Me?; Make Believe; Old Man River; Can't
  Help Loving That Man; Misery Music; I Might Fall Back on You; Queenie's Ballyhoo;
  You Are Love; Nobody Else But Me; The Wedding; The Cake Walk; At the Fair; Why
  Do I Love You?; Bill; How'd You Like to Spoon with Me?; Goodbye My Lady Love;
  After the Ball; Dance Away the Night

Simply Heavenly

London: Adelphi Theatre, 20 May 1958 [16 performances]
New York [Off-Broadway]: 85th Street Playhouse, 21 May 1957 [44 performances];
  transferred to Broadway at the Playhouse Theatre, 20 August 1957 [62 performances];
  transferred to Off-Broadway at the Renata Theatre, 8 November 1957
  [63 performances]. Total of 169 performances.
Music by David Martin; book and lyrics by Langston Hughes
PC: *Jessie B. Simple*: Melvin Stewart; *Miss Mamie*: Bertice Reading; *Melon*: John Bouie;
  Ananais Boyd: Earl Cameron; *Zarita*: Ilene Day; *Bodiddly*: Charles A. McRae.

MN: Prologue; Simply Heavenly; Watermelons; Let Me Take You for a Ride; The Broken
String Blues; He's a Great Big Bundle of Joy; Did You Ever Hear the Blues?; Deep In
Love with You; John Henry; Paddy's Bar; When I'm In a Quiet Mood; I Want Someone
to Come Home To; Let's Ball Awhile; Hunter and the Hunted; Good Ol' Girl.

Something for the Boys

London: Coliseum, 30 March 1944 [75 performances]
New York: Alvin Theatre, 7 January 1943 [420 performances]
Music and lyrics by Cole Porter; book by Herbert Fields and Dorothy Fields
PC: *Blossom*: Evelyn Dall; *Chiquita*: Daphne Barker; *Harry*: Bobby Wright; *Rocky*: Leigh
Stafford; *Laddie*: Jack Billings
MN: See That You're Born in Texas; When My Baby Comes to Town; Something for the
Boys; Home on the Range; Could It Be You?; He's a Right Guy; Hey Good Lookin';
Leader of the Band; I'm in Love with a Soldier Boy; Happy Land in the Sky; By the
Miss-iss-iss-iss-iss-iss-inewah

Song of Norway

London: Palace Theatre, 7 March 1946 [526 performances]
New York: Imperial Theatre, 21 August 1944 [860 performances]
Musical adaptation and lyrics by Robert Wright and George Forrest, from the music of
Edvard Grieg; book by Milton Lazarus from a play by Homer Curran
PC: *Louisa Giovanni*: Janet Hamilton-Smith; *Edvard Grieg*: John Hargreaves; *Rikard
Nordraak*: Arthur Servent; *Nina Hagerup*: Halina Victoria; *Count Peppi Le Loup*:
Bernard Ansell; *Mrs Grieg*: Olive Sturgess; *Father Grieg*: Colin Cunningham; *Freddy*:
Jan Lawski; *Adelina*: Moyra Fraser; *Tito*: John Pygram
MN: Prelude; The Legend; Hill of Dreams; Festival Dance; Freddy and His Fiddle;
Now; Strange Music; Midsummer's Eve; March of the Trollgers; Hymn of Betrothal;
Introduction Act Two (Papillon); Bon Vivant; Three Loves; Down Your Tea;
Nordraak's Farewell; Chocolate Pas des Trois; Waltz Eternal; Peer Gynt (Solveig's
Melody; Hall of the Mountain King; Anitra's Dance); I Love You; At Christmastime;
The Song of Norway

London: Palace Theatre, 11 July 1949
PC: *Louisa Giovanni*: Peggy Rowan; *Edvard Grieg*: Ivor Evans; *Rikard Nordraak*: Arthur
Servent; *Nina Hagerup*: Brenda Stanley; *Count Peppi Le Loup*: Frank Rydon; *Mrs
Grieg*: Olive Sturgess; Father *Grieg*: Dale Williams; *Freddy*: Guy Massey; *Adelina*:
Shelagh Day; *Tito*: Guy Massey

The Sound of Music

London: Palace Theatre, 18 May 1961 [2,385 performances]
New York: Lunt-Fontanne Theatre, 16 November 1959 [1,443 performances]
Music by Richard Rodgers; lyrics by Oscar Hammerstein II; book by Howard Lindsay and
Russel Crouse, based on a true story adapted from *The Trapp Family Singers* by Maria
Augusta Trapp
PC: *Maria Rainer*: Jean Bayless; *Captain Georg von Trapp*: Roger Dann; *The Mother
Abbess*: Constance Shacklock; *Liesl*: Barbara Brown; *Rolf Gruber*: Nicholas Bennett;
Max Detweiler: Harold Kasket; *Elsa Schraeder*: Eunice Gayson; *Sister Margaretta*:
Olive Gilbert

MN: Preludium; The Sound of Music; Maria; My Favourite Things; Do-Re-Mi; You Are
Sixteen; The Lonely Goatherd; How Can Love Survive?; So Long, Farewell; Climb
Every Mountain; No Way to Stop It; Ordinary Couple; Processional; Edelweiss

South Pacific

London: Theatre Royal, Drury Lane, 1 November 1951 [802 performances]
New York: Majestic Theatre, 7 April 1949 [1,925 performances]
Music by Richard Rodgers; lyrics by Oscar Hammerstein II; book by Hammerstein and
Joshua Logan, based on the *Tales of the South Pacific* by James Michener
PC: *Ensign Nellie Forbush*: Mary Martin; *Emile De Becque*: Wilbur Evans; *Bloody Mary*:
Muriel Smith; *Luther Billis*: Ray Walston; *Lt Joseph Cable*: Peter Grant; *Stewpot*: Bill
Nagy; *Liat*: Betta St. John [company also included Ivor Emmanuel, Larry Hagman,
Andrew (later Andy) Cole, June Whitfield and Joyce Blair]
MN: Dites-Moi Pourquoi; A Cockeyed Optimist; Twin Soliloquies; Some Enchanted
Evening; Bloody Mary is the Girl I Love; There's Nothing Like a Dame [*sic*]; Bali Ha'i;
I'm Gonna Wash That Man Right Outa My Hair; Younger than Springtime; Soft Shoe
Dance; Happy Talk; Honey Bun; You've Got to Be Carefully Taught; This Nearly Was
Mine

The Student Prince

London: His Majesty's Theatre, 3 February 1926 [96 performances]
New York: Al Jolson Theater, 2 December 1924 [608 performances]
Music by Sigmund Romberg; book and lyrics by Dorothy Donnelly, based on Rudolf
Bleichman's play *Old Heidelberg*
PC: *Prince Carl Franz*: Allan Prior; *Kathie*: Ilse Marvenga; *Dr Engel*: Herbert Waterous;
Lutz: Oscar Figman; *Princess Margaret*: Lucyenne Herval; *Captain Tarnitz*: John
Coast; *Detlef*: Raymond Marlowe
MN: By Our Bearing So Sedate; Golden Days; Garlands Bright; Drinking Song; To the
Inn We're Marching; You're in Heidelberg; Welcome to Prince; Deep in My Heart,
Dear; Serenade; Farmer Jacob; Students' Life; Farewell, Dear; Waltz Ensemble; Just We
Two; Gavotte; What Memories; Sing a Little Song; Come Boys

London: Stoll Theatre, 23 May 1944 [48 performances]
PC: *Prince Carl Franz*: Bruce Trent; *Kathie*: Marion Gordon; *Dr Engel*: Harry Brindle;
Lutz: Cyril James; *Princess Margaret*: Marjorie Macklin; *Captain Tarnitz*: Arthur
Clarke; *Detlef*: Bernard Albrow
MN: Golden Days; Drinking Song; To the Inn We're Marching; You're in Heidelburg [*sic*];
Welcome to Prince; Deep in My Heart; Serenade; Student Life [*sic*]; By Our Bearing So
Sedate; Waltz Ensemble; Just We Two; Gavotte; What Memories; Sing a Little Song;
Let's All be Gay Boys

London: Cambridge Theatre, 8 June 1968 [282 performances]
PC: *Prince Carl Franz*: John Hanson; *Kathie*: Barbara Strathdee; *Dr Engel*: George
Hancock; *Gretchen*: Virginia Courtney; *Lutz*: Kenneth Henry; *Princess Margaret*: Clare
Herbert; *Captain Tarnitz*: Colin Thomas; *Detlef*: Richard Loring
MN: Golden Days; Garlands Bright; To the Inn We're Marching; Drinking Song; Come
Boys; Heidelberg Fair; Deep In My Heart, Dear; Serenade; Student Life; Parting Scene;
By Our Bearing So Sedate; Just We Two; Vision Scene; I Like You More and More;
Do You Love Me?

Sunny River

London: Piccadilly Theatre, 18 August 1943 [86 performances]
New York: St. James Theatre, 4 December 1941 [36 performances]
Music by Sigmund Romberg; book and lyrics by Oscar Hammerstein II
PC: *Lolita/Marie Sauvinet*: Evelyn Laye; *Jean Gervais*: Dennis Noble; *Cecilie Marshall*:
    Ena Burrill; *Madeleine Caresse*: Edna Proud; *Daniel Marshall*: Don Avory; *Emma*:
    Marion Wilson
MN: Bow-Legged Gal; My Girl and I; Call It a Dream; It Can Happen to Anyone; Observe
    the Bee; Duet; Eleven Levee Street; Madam; Along the Winding Road; Bundling;
    Somebody Ought to Be Told; Can You Sing?; Making Conversation; Finale Act One;
    Mah Bow-Legged Gal [sic]; Sunny River; The Duello; She Got Him; Time is Standing
    Still

Sweet Charity

London: Prince of Wales Theatre, 11 October 1967 [476 performances]
New York: Palace Theatre, 29 January 1966 [608 performances]
Music by Cy Coleman; lyrics by Dorothy Fields; book by Neil Simon, based on the film
    Nights of Cabiria by Federico Fellini, Tullio Pinelli and Ennio Flaiano
PC: *Charity Hope Valentine*: Juliet Prowse; *Oscar Lindquist*: Rod McLennan; *Nickie*:
    Josephine Blake; *Helene*: Paula Kelly; *Vittorio Vidal*; John Keston; *Johann Sebastian
    Brubeck*: Fred Evans; *Good Fairy*: Joyanne Delancey; *Fritzie*: Sheila O'Neill
MN: You Should See Yourself; The Rescue; Big Spender; Rich Man's Frug; If My Friends
    Could See Me Now; Too Many Tomorrows; There's Gotta be Something Better than
    This; I'm the Bravest Individual; Rhythm of Life; Baby Dream Your Dream; Sweet
    Charity; Where am I Going?; I'm a Brass Band; I Love to Cry at Weddings

The Threepenny Opera

London: Royal Court Theatre, 9 February 1956, then Aldwych Theatre 21 March
    [140 performances]
New York: Theatre de Lys, 10 March 1954 for 95 performances; reopened at same theatre
    20 September 1955 [2,611 performances]
Music by Kurt Weill; book and lyrics by Bertolt Brecht in an English adaptation by Marc
    Blitzstein
PC: *Macheath (Mack the Knife)*: Bill Owen; *Polly Peachum*: Daphne Anderson; *Jenny*:
    Maria Remusat; *Lucy*: Georgia Brown; *Mr J. J. Peachum*: Eric Pohlmann; *Mrs Peachum*:
    Lisa Lee; *Tiger Brown*: George A. Cooper; *Street Singer*: Ewan MacColl
MN: Prologue: Ballad of Mack the Knife; Morning Anthem; Instead-of Song; Wedding
    Song; The Bide-a-Wee in Soho; Army Song; Love Song; Ballad of Dependency;
    1st Threepenny Finale: The World is Mean; Polly's Song; Pirate Jenny; Ballad of the
    Fancy Man; Ballad of the Easy Life; Barbara Song; Jealousy Duet; 2nd Threepenny
    Finale: How to Survive; Useless Song; Solomon Song; Calls from the Grave; Death
    Message; 3rd Threepenny Finale: The Mounted Messenger

London: Prince of Wales Theatre, 10 February 1972; transferred to Piccadilly Theatre,
    10 April 1972
PC: *Macheath (Mack the Knife)*: Joe Melia; *Polly Peachum*: Vanessa Redgrave (replaced
    for the Piccadilly Theatre transfer by Helen Cotterill); *Jenny*: Annie Ross; *Lucy*: Barbara
    Windsor; *Mr J. J. Peachum*: Ronald Radd; *Mrs Peachum*: Hermione Baddeley; *Tiger
    Brown*: Dan Meaden; *Street Singer*: Lon Satton

The Vagabond King

London: Winter Garden Theatre, 19 April 1927 [480 performances]
New York: Casino Theatre, 21 September 1925 [511 performances]
Music by Rudolf Friml; lyrics by Brian Hooker; book by Brian Hooker, Russell Janney and
   W. H. Post, based on Justin Huntly McCarthy's play *If I Were King*, itself based on the
   novel by R. H. Russell
PC: *François Villon*: Derek Oldham; *Guy Taborie*: Mark Lester; *Katherine de Vaucelles*:
   Winnie Melville; *Louis XI*: H. A. Saintsbury; *Huguette du Hamel*: Norah Blaney; *Lady
   Mary*: Betty Eley
MN: Opening Chorus; Love for Sale; Drinking Song; Song of the Vagabonds; Some
   Day; Only a Rose; Fight Music and Finaletto; Opening Second Act; Hunting; Scotch
   Archer's Song; To-Morrow; Nocturn [*sic*]; Ballet; Serenade; Huguette Waltz; Love Me
   To-night

London: Coliseum, 18 March 1937 [40 performances]
PC: *François Villon*: Harry Welchman; *Guy Taborie*: George Graves; *Katherine de
   Vaucelles*: Maria Elsner; *Louis XI*: H. A. Saintsbury; *Huguette du Hamel*: Sylvia Welling;
   Lady Mary: Nancy Neale
MN: as above

London: Winter Garden Theatre, 22 April 1943 [94 performances]
PC: *François Villon*: Webster Booth; *Guy Taborie*: Syd Walker; *Katherine de Vaucelles*:
   Anne Ziegler; *Louis XI*: Henry Baynton; *Huguette du Hamel*: Tessa Deane; *Lady Mary*:
   Sara Gregory
MN: The Tavern Song; Love for Sale; Drinking Song; Song of the Vagabonds; Some
   Day; Only a Rose; Hunting; Archer's Song; Tomorrow; Nocturne; Ballet; Serenade;
   Huguette Waltz; Love Me To-night; Te Deum; The Song of Victory

The Wayward Way

London: Vaudeville Theatre, 27 January 1965 [36 performances]
Music by Lorne Huycke; lyrics by Bill Howe; based on the play *The Drunkard* by W. H.
   Smith and 'A Gentleman'
PC: *William Dowton*: Jim Dale; *Mary*: Roberta D'Esti; *Squire Cribbs*: John Gower; *Edward
   Middleton*: David Holliday; *Agnes*: Cheryl Kennedy; *Mrs Wilson*: Stella Courtney
MN: Haven that is Graven on My Heart; It's Old to Some But New to Me; Oh Sweet
   Revenge; Nobody's Making Sense; Everybody on Earth Loves a Wedding; Molly;
   Brotherhood; Goodbye for Good; A Curlicue; He's Wayward in a Way; The Foul D.T.'s;
   Every Soul You Save

West Side Story

London: Her Majesty's Theatre, 12 December 1958 [1039 performances]
New York: Winter Garden, 26 September 1957 [734 performances]
Music by Leonard Bernstein; lyrics by Stephen Sondheim; book by Arthur Laurents,
   based on *Romeo and Juliet* by William Shakespeare and an idea by Jerome Robbins
PC: *Tony*: Don McKay; *Maria*: Marlys Watters; *Anita*: Chita Rivera; *Riff*: George
   Chakiris; *Bernardo*: Ken LeRoy; *Velma*: Susan Watson; *Anybodys*: Sylvia Tysick; *Doc*:
   David Bauer; *Rosalia*: Francesca Bell

MN: Prologue; Jet Song; Something's Coming; The Dance at the Gym; Maria; Tonight; America; Cool; One Hand, One Heart; The Rumble; I Feel Pretty; Somewhere; Gee, Officer Krupke; A Boy Like That; I Have a Love; Taunting

Where's Charley?

London: Palace Theatre, 20 February 1958 [404 performances]
New York: St. James Theatre, 11 October 1948 [792 performances]
Music and lyrics by Frank Loesser; book by George Abbott, based on the play *Charley's Aunt* by Brandon Thomas
PC: *Charley Wykeham*: Norman Wisdom; *Amy Spettigue*: Pip Hinton; *Donna Lucia D'Alvadorez*: Marion Grimaldi; *Sir Francis Chesney*: Jerry Desmonde; *Jack Chesney*: Terence Cooper; *Kitty Verdun*: Pamela Gale; *Mr Spettigue*: Felix Felton
MN: The Years Before Us; Better Get Out of Here; The New Ashmolean Marching Society and Students' Conservatory Band; My Darling, My Darling; Make a Miracle; Serenade with Asides; Lovelier than Ever; The Woman in His Room; Pernambuco; Where's Charley?; Once in Love with Amy; The Gossips; At the Red Rose Cotillion

Wild Rose

London: Princes Theatre, 6 August 1942 [205 performances]
Music by Jerome Kern; lyrics by Clifford Grey and others; book by Guy Bolton, based on an unproduced musical, *The Little Thing*, by P. G. Wodehouse; book revised by Frank Eyton and Richard Hearne
PC: *Sally*: Jessie Matthews; *Maxie*: Richard Hearne; *Gaston de Frey*: André Randall; *Tom Blair*: Frank Leighton; *Rosie Roxie*: Elsie Percival; *Diamond Jim Brady*: Jack Morrison; *Lillian Russell*: Linda Gray
MN: No musical numbers listed in theatre programme

Wish You Were Here

London: Casino, 10 October 1953 [282 performances]
New York: Imperial Theatre, 25 June 1952 [598 performances]
Music and lyrics by Harold Rome; book by Arthur Kober and Joshua Logan, based on the play *Having Wonderful Time* by Kober
PC: *Teddy Stern*: Elizabeth Larner; *Chick Miller*: Bruce Trent; *Fay Tomkin*: Shani Wallis; *Dickie Fletcher*: Dickie Henderson Jnr; *Pinky Harris*: Christopher Hewett; *Harry 'Muscles' Green*: Joe (Tiger) Robinson; *Lou Kandel*: Mark Baker
MN: Camp Karefree; Goodbye Love; Social Director; Shopping Around; Bright College Days; Mix and Mingle; Could Be; Tripping the Light Fantastic; Where Did the Night Go?; Certain Individuals; They Won't Know Me; Summer Afternoon; Don Jose of Far Rockaway; Everybody Love Everybody; Wish You Were Here; Relax; Flattery

Wonderful Town

London: Princes Theatre, 23 February 1955 [207 performances]
New York: Winter Garden, 25 February 1953 [559 performances]
Music by Leonard Bernstein; lyrics by Betty Comden and Adolph Green; book by Joseph Fields and Jerome Chodorov, based on their play *My Sister Eileen*, and adapted from the stories of Ruth McKinney

PC: *Ruth Sherwood*: Pat Kirkwood; *Robert Baker*: Dennis Bowen; *Eileen Sherwood*: Shani Wallis; *Wreck*: Sidney James; *Appopolous*: David Hurst; *Frank Lippencott*: Christopher Taylor; *Chick Clark*: Colin Croft; *Speedy Valente*: Stanley Robinson; *Violet*: Judy (Judith) Bruce

MN: Christopher Street; Ohio; Conquering New York; One Hundred Easy Ways; What a Waste; 'Story Vignettes by Miss Comden and Mr Green'; A Little Bit In Love; Pass the Football; Conversation Piece; A Quiet Girl; Conga!; My Darlin' Eileen; "Swing!"; It's Love; Wrong Note Rag

Your Own Thing

London: Comedy Theatre, 6 February 1969 [42 performances]
New York [Off-Broadway]: Orpheum Theatre, 13 January 1968 [937 performances]
Music and lyrics by Hal Hester and Danny Apolinar; book by Donald Driver, based on the play *Twelfth Night* by Shakespeare
PC: *Seb*: Gerry Glasier; *Viola*: Leland Palmer; *Orson*: Les Carlson; *Danny*: Danny Apolinar; *Olivia*: Marcia Rodd
MN: No One's Perfect, Dear; The Flowers; I'm Me! (I'm Not Afraid); Baby! Baby!; Come Away, Death; I'm on My Way to the Top; Let It Be; She Never Told Her Love; Be Gentle; What Do I Know?; The Now Generation; The Middle Years; When You're Young and in Love; Hunca Munca; Don't Leave Me; Do Your Own Thing

You're a Good Man, Charlie Brown

London: Fortune Theatre, 1 February 1968 [117 performances]
New York: Theatre 80 St. Marks, 7 March 1967 [1,597 performances]
Music and lyrics by Clark Gesner; book by John Gordon [Clark Gesner]
PC: *Linus*: Gene Kidwell; *Charlie Brown*: David-Rhys Anderson; *Patty*: Courtney Lane; *Schroeder*: Gene Scandur; *Snoopy*: Don Potter; *Lucy*: Boni Enten
MN: You're a Good Man, Charlie Brown; Schroeder; Snoopy; My Blanket and Me; Kite; Dr. Lucy (The Doctor is In); Book Report; The Red Baron; T.E.A.M. (The Baseball Game); Glee Club Rehearsal; Little Known Facts; Suppertime; Happiness

Notes

Introduction

1 For a more expansive, and alternative, outline of the first stirrings of American musical theatre a dependable source is Gerald Bordman's *American Musical Theatre*, pp. 1–17.

2 Certainly, the London production seen at the Apollo Theatre in 1968 was presented as a musical.

3 Rick Besoyan may have had this title in mind when writing the song 'Naughty, Naughty Nancy' for his pastiche of American operetta, *Little Mary Sunshine*. In 1910 Victor Herbert's operetta *Naughty Marietta* and its title song celebrated the attraction of mischievousness.

4 Proving that there was nothing new in musical theatre, the 1955 *Damn Yankees* also used Faust for its inspiration.

5 Lyric by Leo Robin for 'We're All in the Same Boat' from *The Girl in Pink Tights*.

1939–45

1 Moss Empires comprised a nationwide chain of theatres created by the 1898 merging of properties owned by Sir Edward Moss and Sir Oswald Stoll.

2 Quoted in Robert Hewison, *Under Siege: Literary Life in London, 1939–45* (London: Weidenfeld & Nicolson, 1977), p. 23.

3 Wilson, *Post-War Theatre*, p. 7.

4 *Observer*, 19 July 1942.

5 *Sunday Times*, 9 August 1942.

6 *The Times*, 23 October 1942.

7 *The Times*, 30 June 1939.

8 *Observer*, 2 July 1939.

9 *Observer*, 27 September 1936.

10 *The Times*, 25 September 1936.

11 *The Times*, 19 April 1943.

12 *The Times*, 24 April 1943.

13 Agate, *Immoment Toys*, p. 60.

14 The cast included Marion Gordon as Kathie, Bryan Johnson as Asterberg and Bobbie Pett as Gretchen. Twenty years later Johnson played the title role in a second-drawer touring production. Bobbie Pett became Roberta Pett, a saucer-eyed comedienne who regularly played principal boy in pantomime and appeared in seaside summer shows.

15 *The Times*, 24 May 1944.

16 Uncredited press cutting in Victoria and Albert Theatre Museum archive.

17 Philip Page, *Daily Mail*, undated clipping in Victoria and Albert Theatre and Performance Collections.

18 *The Times*, undated clipping in the Victoria and Albert Theatre and Performance Collections.

19 *Sunday Times*, 25 March 1945.

20 *Evening Standard*, 23 March 1945.

21 *The Brains Trust* was a BBC radio programme of the 1940s, with regular panellists Julian Huxley, C. E. M. Joad and A. B. Campbell.

22 *New Statesman and Nation*, 11 October 1941.

23 Mass-Observation Diarist 5353, 7 May 1945.

24 *The Times*, 26 October 1945.

25 *New York Sun*, unidentified clipping in the Victoria and Albert Theatre and Performance Collections.

26 The British musical *Belle or the Ballad of Dr Crippen*, book by Wolf Mankowitz, songs by Monty Norman, opened at the Strand Theatre in London for a brief run in 1961.

1946

1 *Stage*, 14 March 1946.

2 *Theatre World*, August 1949, p. 32.

1947

1 Quoted in David Kynaston, 'The Austerity Issue: Don't Panic', *Independent*, 2 November 2008.

2 George Orwell, 'The Lion and the Unicorn: Socialism and the English Genius'.

3 *Theatre World*, November 1946, p. 25.

4 *Stage*, 13 March 1947.

5 Wilson, *Post-War Theatre*, p. 101.

6 Vivian Ellis, *I'm on a See-Saw* (London: Michael Joseph, 1953), p. 15.

7 Edward Fox in conversation with the author.

8 Wilson, *Post-War Theatre*, pp. 101–2.

9 *The Times*, 4 May 1947.

10 *Daily Telegraph*, 4 May 1947.

11 *Everybody's*, 21 October 1950.

12 *Stage*, 24 April 1947.

13 *Stage*, 8 May 1947.

14 *Recorder*, 14 June 1947.

15 *Weekly Sporting Review*, 14 June 1947.

16 Unidentified newspaper clipping in Victoria and Albert Theatre and Performance Collections.

17 *Sunday Times*, 22 June 1947. An interesting statement from a writer whose contributions to the British musical had been and would continue to be rooted in the utterly conventional.

18 *Tatler and Bystander*, 25 June 1947.

19 *New Statesman*, 14 June 1947.

20 *Daily Worker*, 14 June 1947.

21 *Sphere*, 8 November 1947.

22 *Observer*, 26 October 1947.

23 *Tatler*, 5 November 1947.

24 *Evening Standard*, 24 October 1947.

1948

1 *Stage*, 13 October 1948.

2 *Stage*, 31 December 1948.

3 *Theatre World*, February 1949, p. 6.

4 Robert Nesbitt, 'Broadway Musicals Reviewed', *Stage*, 27 May 1948.

5 *Land of Promise: The British Documentary Movement, 1930–1950* (London: British Film Institute, n.d.), p. 57.

6 *I Do! I Do!* did much the same thing in a sweeter way in the 1960s, spanning only fifty years or so.

1949

1 By Friedrich Gerstäcker (1816–72).
2 *Tribune*, 22 April 1949.
3 *Spectator*, 22 April 1949.
4 Alan Bendle, *Manchester Evening News*, 26 March 1949.
5 *Punch*, 27 April 1949.
6 *Tatler*, 27 April 1949.
7 *Sunday Times*, 17 April 1949.
8 *Reynolds News*, 24 April 1949.
9 *Stage*, 27 April 1949.
10 Unidentified newspaper clipping in Victoria and Albert Theatre and Performance Collections.

1950

1 Book by S. J. Perelman and Ogden Nash, music by Kurt Weill, lyrics by Ogden Nash.
2 Book by David Thompson, music and lyrics by John Kander and Fred Ebb.
3 Directed by Frank Borzage, the American film of *Liliom* had a screenplay by S. N. Behrman. Charles Farrell played Liliom, and Rose Hobart Julie.
4 *Theatre World*, July 1950, pp. 10 and 35. In the course of her review, Frances Stephens also thought it necessary to explain to British readers that 'carousel' meant 'roundabout'.
5 *Theatre World Annual* no. 2 (London: Rockcliff, 1951), p. 3.
6 *Stage*, 15 June 1950.
7 *Daily Telegraph*, 8 June 1950.
8 *Guardian*, 8 June 1950.
9 Even Eastmancolor could not save the tepid movie, despite competent performances from Gordon Macrae as Billy and Shirley Jones as Julie. Leslie Halliwell pronounced it 'hollow and boring, a humourless whimsy in which even the songs seem an intrusion': Leslie Halliwell, *Halliwell's Film Guide*, 6th edn (London: Grafton, 1987), p. 171.

1951

1 The characters of Fred Graham and Lilli Vanessi were in part inspired by the American actors Alfred Lunt and Lynn Fontanne.
2 *Theatre World*, April 1951, p. 32.
3 *Stage*, 15 March 1951.
4 *Socialist Leader*, 9 March 1951.
5 *Guardian*, 28 December 1970.
6 Sydney Edwards, *Evening News*, n.d.
7 *Times Literary Supplement*, February 1987, n.d.
8 Note in theatre programme for *Kiss Me, Kate* at Norwich Playhouse, 1996.
9 *Post*, 8 April 1949.
10 Reviews of the original Broadway production cited in Steven Suskin's *Opening Night on Broadway*.
11 *Stage*, 8 November 1951.

12 *Queen*, 21 November 1951.
13 *The Times*, 2 November 1951.
14 *Daily Express*, 2 November 1951.
15 *Evening Standard*, 2 November 1951.
16 *Daily Telegraph*, 2 November 1951.
17 *Illustrated London News*, 24 November 1951.
18 Note by Richard Rodgers in the souvenir brochure programme for the 1951 London production.
19 *Scapa!*, book, music and lyrics by Hugh Hastings, based on his play *Seagulls Over Sorrento*, seen at the Adelphi Theatre in 1962.
20 *Evening Standard*, 2 November 1951.
21 *Stage*, undated newspaper clipping in the Victoria and Albert Theatre and Performance Collections.

1952

1 Walbrook's dalliance with musical theatre included his playing the lead in the British *Wedding in Paris* in London opposite Evelyn Laye in 1954.
2 *Theatre World*, July 1952, p. 32.
3 *Stage*, 27 March 1952.
4 The motel was *Crossroads*, the setting of a popular television soap opera in which Miss Gordon appeared.
5 *Guardian*, 17 March 1952.
6 *Queen*, 9 April 1952.
7 Unidentifiable and undated newspaper clipping in Victoria and Albert Theatre and Performance Collections.
8 *Theatre World*, May 1952, p. 6
9 *Stage*, 24 March 1983.
10 *Stage*, 2 October 1952.
11 *Stage*, 16 October 1952.
12 *Evening Standard*, 26 September 1952.
13 *Punch*, 15 October 1952.
14 *Everybody's*, 8 November 1952.

1953

1 *Tatler*, 18 March 1953.
2 *Manchester Guardian*, 13 February 1953.
3 William Alwyn, *Ariel to Miranda* (unpublished MS), entry for 23 March 1956.
4 *Evening Standard*, 29 May 1953.
5 *Punch*, 10 June 1953.
6 *Sunday Telegraph*, 31 May 1953.
7 Secrest, *Somewhere for Me*, pp. 306–7.
8 Ibid.
9 *Plays and Players*, November 1953, p. 13.
10 *Stage Yearbook*, 1954.
11 *Plays and Players*, November 1953, p. 16.
12 Ornadel, *Reach for the Moon*, pp. 103–4.

1954

1 Bordman, *American Musical Theatre*, p. 588.
2 *Plays and Players*, May 1954, p. 10.
3 *Daily Mail*, 15 October 1954.
4 *Daily Express*, 15 October 1954.
5 *Tatler*, 27 October 1954.
6 Anthony Cookman, *Tatler*, 27 October 1954.
7 *Punch*, 20 October 1954.

1955

1 The 1947 *Bonanza Bound* had music by Saul Chaplin. It closed *en route* to Broadway.
2 *Plays and Players*, April 1955, p. 19.
3 Kenneth Tynan, *Observer*, 27 February 1955.
4 *Stage*, 3 March 1955.
5 *The Times*, 24 February 1955.
6 Philip Hope-Wallace, *Guardian*, 25 February 1955.
7 *Plays and Players*, April 1955, p. 19.
8 Pat Kirkwood, *The Time of My Life*, p. 191.
9 Ibid, p. 196.
10 'Fabulous Drake', *Plays and Players*, May 1955, p. 11.
11 *Plays and Players*, May 1978, p. 33.
12 *Sketch*, 4 May 1955.
13 *Punch*, 27 April 1955.
14 *Plays and Players*, May 1978, p. 33.
15 Philip Hope-Wallace, *Manchester Guardian*, 21 April 1955.
16 *Sunday Times*, 24 April 1955.
17 *Independent*, 18 June 2007.
18 *Observer*, 1 July 2007.
19 Ibid.
20 Edward Seckerson, *Independent*, 29 June 2007.
21 *Daily Mail*, 5 October 1999.
22 *Independent*, 5 October 1999.
23 *Daily Mail*, 5 October 1999.
24 BBC News, 29 November 1999.
25 Talk given by Vivian Ellis to the Arts Theatre Club in December 1955, quoted in *Stage*, 8 December 1955.

1956

1 *Plays and Players*, March 1956, p. 7.
2 Quoted in Suskin, *Opening Night on Broadway*, p. 557.
3 *Tatler*, 8 February 1956.
4 J. C. Trewin, *Illustrated London News*, 11 February 1956.
5 *Punch*, 1 February 1956.
6 *Stage*, 2 February 1956.
7 Alfred Lunt (1892–1977) and Lynn Fontanne (1887–1983), a famous husband and wife acting partnership.
8 Edward Goring, *Daily Mail*, 22 March 1957.

9 Ivor Brown wrote 'Texts which are out of copyright can be legally plundered: but there is such a thing as courtesy: the programme contained names in plenty, down to providers of 'cigar-holder' and 'step-ladder'. But there was no room for a three letter word, Gay.' *Theatre 1955–6*, p. 61.

10 Sanders, *The Days Grow Short*, pp. 400–1.

11 In his final years Goldschmidt's compositions attracted attention after years of neglect. He was the subject of the BBC radio programme *Desert Island Discs* in 1994.

12 Brown, *Theatre 1955–6*, p. 62.

13 *Theatre World*, March 1956, p. 8.

14 *Plays and Players*, March 1956, p. 7.

15 Walter Kerr, *Herald Tribune*, 5 November 1954.

16 'The Hippopotamus Song' by Michael Flanders and Donald Swann.

17 A brand of theatrical make-up.

18 Peter Hepple, *Stage*, 20 June 1957. Returning to the show so long after its opening, Hepple suggested that the musical had been underrated at its London premiere.

19 Raimu (Jules Auguste Muraire), the French actor who created the role of César on stage and on film.

20 *Plays and Players*, Christmas 1956, p. 13.

21 *Observer*, 18 November 1956.

22 *Sunday Express*, 18 November 1956.

23 *Tatler*, 28 November 1956.

24 *Sketch*, 5 December 1956.

25 R. B. Marriott, *Stage*, 22 November 1956.

1957

1 *Stage*, 21 February 1957.

2 *Stage*, 31 January 1957.

3 *Stage*, 21 February 1957.

4 *Plays and Players*, April 1957, p. 13.

5 *Plays and Players*, April 1957, p. 20.

6 Unidentified newspaper clipping in Victoria and Albert Theatre and Performance Collections.

7 Review by Frank Jackson in *Reynolds News*, 31 March 1957.

8 *Financial News*, 29 March 1957.

9 In 1953 Paul had appeared on Broadway in the title role of *Maggie*, an adaptation of J. M. Barrie's play *What Every Woman Knows*.

10 Not that short. In all, with rehearsals and out-of-town dates, the company had almost a year's work out of it.

11 *Manchester Evening Chronicle*, 26 October 1957.

12 *Stage*, 31 October 1957.

13 *Manchester Guardian*, 28 October 1957.

14 Reported in *Daily Mail*, 15 November 1957.

15 *Manchester Guardian*, 16 November 1957.

16 *Sunday Times*, 17 November 1957.

17 *The Times*, 15 November 1957.

18 *Observer*, 17 November 1957.

19 Cecil Wilson, *Daily Mail*, 15 November 1957.

20 *Evening Standard*, 15 November 1957.

21 But obviously not charming enough to be retained for the film version.

22 *Plays and Players*, June 1958, pp. 23–4. The reviewer is referring not only to *Damn Yankees* but *The Pajama Game*.

23 The creator of this work insisted on its lower-case title *archy and mehitabel*, leaving any future writers who mention it liable to be accused of bad proof-reading. Ethan Mordden has already broken convention by giving the title as it appears in the main text of this book.

1958

1 By Wisdom and June Tremayne.

2 Mordden, *Beautiful Mornin'*, p. 248.

3 *Plays and Players*, April 1958, p. 15.

4 *Bell, Book and Candle*, a play by John Van Druten, produced in London in 1954.

5 J. W. Lambert 'London Theatre', *International Theatre Annual No. 3* (London: John Calder, 1958), p. 31.

6 *Plays and Players*, June 1958, p. 7.

7 As reported in the *Sunday Times*, 7 December 1958.

8 Uncredited feature in *The Times*, 12 December 1958.

9 Robert Wraight [*sic*] in *Star*, 13 December 1958.

10 *The Times*, 13 December 1958.

11 *Daily Mail*, 7 November 1958.

12 *Financial Times*, 13 December 1958.

13 *Sunday Times*, 14 December 1958.

14 *Observer*, 14 December 1958.

15 Letter from Hugh Beaumont of H. M. Tennent to Lord Chamberlain's Office, 13 November 1958.

16 Philip Hope-Wallace, *Guardian*, 22 December 1958.

17 *The Times*, 19 December 1958.

18 *Observer*, 21 December 1958.

19 *Daily Herald*, 10 September 1958.

20 Undated clipping from the *Slough Observer* in Victoria and Albert Theatre and Performance Collections.

1959

1 *Theatre World*, June 1959, p. 8.

2 Not *Wonderful Time* as mentioned by Humphrey Burton in his programme note for the National Theatre revival.

3 Voltaire, *Letters on England*.

4 Moody, *A Still Untitled (But Not Quite) Autobiography*, p. 139.

5 *Star*, 17 October 1959.

6 *Daily Express*, 17 October 1959.

7 *Daily Telegraph*, 17 October 1959.

8 *Stage*, 3 September 1959.

9 *Stage*, 15 October 1959.

10 *Daily Telegraph*, 26 October 1959.

11 *Manchester Guardian*, 14 October 1959.

12 *Evening Standard*, 14 October 1959.

13 W. A. Darlington, *Daily Telegraph*, 18 December 1959.

14 *The Times*, 18 December 1959.

15 *Observer*, 20 December 1959.
16 Playwright and actor and creator of shell fine art. Perhaps best known for his role as Paul Temple in the BBC radio series.
17 *Queen*, 5 January 1960.

1960

1 *Plays and Players*, April 1960, p. 33.
2 R. B. Marriott, *Stage*, 17 March 1960.
3 Ibid.
4 *The World of Suzie Wong*, a play by Paul Osborn from the novel by Richard Mason, produced in London in 1959.
5 *The Times*, 25 March 1960.
6 *Daily Telegraph*, 22 April 1960.
7 Ibid.
8 Anthony Cookman, *Tatler*, 11 May 1960.
9 J. C. Trewin, *Illustrated London News*, 11 May 1960.
10 *Daily Mail*, 13 August 1960.
11 *Daily Mail*, 23 August 1960.
12 *Daily Telegraph*, 23 August 1960.
13 *Evening Standard*, 21 September 1960.
14 *Guardian*, 22 September 1960.
15 *Sunday Times*, 25 September 1960.
16 *Illustrated London News*, 1 October 1960.
17 *Daily Mail*, 21 September 1960.
18 Email from Patricia Michael to author 1 August 2011.

1961

1 *Theatre World*, April 1961, p. 14.
2 *Theatre World*, June 1961, p. 51.
3 The nineteenth-century American evangelists Dwight Lyman Moody and Ira David Sankey were composers of Christian songs.
4 Robert Muller, *Daily Mail*, 19 May 1961.
5 Ibid.
6 Harold Conway, *Sunday Dispatch*, 21 May 1961.
7 *Sunday Times*, 21 May 1961.
8 Poulenc's opera was first seen at La Scala in 1957. In the final scene one by one the persecuted and condemned nuns climb the scaffold singing the *Salve regina*.
9 *The Times*, 19 May 1961.
10 *Tatler*, 7 June 1961.
11 *The Sound of Music*, Palace Theatre programme note.
12 *Plays and Players*, March 1960, p. 20.
13 *Plays and Players*, August 1961, p. 11.
14 Brian Reece died the following year, aged 49.
15 *Housewives' Choice*, a BBC radio programme in which gramophone records were requested by housewife listeners.
16 John Mapplebeck, *Guardian*, 26 May 1961.
17 *Sunday Telegraph*, 10 September 1961. Julian Slade and Dorothy Reynolds were the composers of the record-breaking British musical *Salad Days*.

18 Robert Muller, *Daily Mail*, 8 September 1961.
19 Milton Shulman, *Evening Standard*, 8 September 1961.
20 *Play Away*, a BBC television programme for children which ran from 1971 to 1984.
21 West End Whingers review of second preview of 2010 production of *The Fantasticks*, 26 May 2010.
22 *Guardian*, 10 June 2010.
23 *Daily Telegraph*, 10 June 2010.
24 *Show Pictorial*, 9 September 1961.
25 *Plays and Players*, December 1961, p. 17.
26 *Spectator*, 20 October 1961.
27 Jan Waters in conversation with the author, 30 March 2012

1962

1 Eric Shorter, *Daily Telegraph*, 18 May 1962.
2 *Daily Express*, 18 May 1962.
3 *The Times*, 18 May 1962.
4 Email from Patricia Michael to the author, 1 March 2012.
5 *Theatre World*, October 1962, p. 6.
6 Letter from Antony Howard in *Stage*, 6 September 1962. The London programme for *Gentlemen Prefer Blondes* credited 'Musical direction and orchestrations by Alyn Ainsworth'.
7 *Daily Mail*, 9 October 1962.
8 Graham Samuel, *Western Mail*, 13 October 1962.
9 Harold Hobson, *Sunday Times*, 14 October 1962.
10 *The Times*, 9 October 1962.
11 *Daily Telegraph*, 9 October 1962.

1963

1 Caryl Brahms, *Time and Tide*, 21 February 1963.
2 Letter from Peter W. Burton, *Stage*, 28 February 1963.
3 *Theatre World*, March 1963, pp. 9–10.
4 Ibid, p. 16.
5 Ibid.
6 *Stage*, 14 February 1963.
7 Ibid.
8 *Hendon Times*, 15 February 1963.
9 *Manchester Saturday Chronicle*, 16 February 1963.
10 *Daily Mail*, 9 February 1963. Horrible Henry was one of the puppets – the green walrus – who befriended Lili.
11 *Daily Express*, 9 February 1963.
12 *Daily Mail*, 6 October 1962.
13 Formerly the Princes Theatre, the theatre had been closed for refurbishment and reopened as the Shaftesbury Theatre with this production.
14 *Theatre World*, May 1963, pp. 30–1.
15 Email from Patricia Michael, 1 March 2012.
16 *Theatre World*, May 1963, p. 12.
17 *Daily Telegraph*, 31 May 1963.
18 Although you will be lucky to find them even there.

19 *Daily Mail*, 31 May 1963.
20 Ibid.
21 *Guardian*, 31 May 1963.
22 *Illustrated London News*, 15 June 1963.
23 *London Evening Standard*, 31 May 1963.
24 *London Evening Standard*, 4 October 1963.
25 Julian Slade had written one, seen at the Arts Theatre in London in 1956. The musical had first been presented on BBC television two years earlier.
26 Pat Wallace, *Tatler*, 7 November 1963.
27 Bernard Levin, *Daily Mail*, 8 November 1963.
28 *Daily Telegraph*, 31 October 1963.
29 *Daily Mail*, 11 November 1963.
30 *The Times*, 8 November 1963.
31 B. A. Young, *Punch*, 13 November 1963.
32 *Stage*, 21 November 1963.
33 W. A. Darlington, *Daily Telegraph*, 15 November 1963.
34 Bernard Levin, *Daily Mail*, 15 November 1963.
35 Michael Kenyon, *Guardian*, 15 November 1963.
36 *The Times*, 15 November 1963.
37 W. A. Darlington, *Daily Telegraph*, 31 December 1963.
38 *The Times*, 31 December 1963.
39 *Sunday Times*, 5 January 1963.
40 Ibid.
41 *The Times*, 31 December 1963.
42 Bernard Levin, *Daily Mail*, 31 December 1963.
43 *Theatre World*, February 1964, p. 6.

1964

1 Bernard Levin, *Daily Mail*, 17 March 1964.
2 Philip Hope-Wallace, *Guardian*, 17 March 1964.
3 Eric Shorter, *Daily Telegraph*, 17 March 1964.
4 *Stage*, 19 March 1964.
5 Bernard Levin, *Daily Mail*, 30 April 1964.
6 Eric Shorter, *Daily Telegraph*, 30 April 1964.
7 *Stage*, 16 April 1964.
8 R. B. Marriott, *Stage*, 27 August 1964.
9 *Daily Telegraph*, 20 August 1964.
10 *The Times*, 20 August 1964.
11 *Daily Mail*, 20 August 1964.
12 Ibid.
13 *The Times*, 20 August 1964.
14 *Daily Mail*, 21 August 1964.
15 Ibid.
16 Ibid.
17 David Shipman, *The Great Movie Stars: The International Years* (London: Angus & Robertson, 1972), p. 210.
18 *Daily Mail*, 20 August 1964.
19 *Theatre World*, September 1964, p. 13.
20 Lees, *The Musical Worlds of Lerner and Loewe*.

21 In the 1945 film of *Blithe Spirit*, directed by David Lean.
22 Johns, *Dames of the Theatre*, p. 175.
23 *Illustrated London News*, 14 November 1964.
24 W. A. Darlington, *Daily Telegraph*, 4 November 1964.
25 Michael Thornton, *Sunday Express*, 8 November 1964.
26 *Sunday Times*, 8 November 1964.
27 Bernard Levin, *Daily Mail*, 4 November 1964.
28 Author in conversation with Jan Waters, 30 March 2012.
29 Philip Hope-Wallace, *Guardian*, 19 November 1964.
30 Michael Thornton, *Evening Standard*, 22 November 1964.
31 *The Times*, 19 November 1964.
32 Philip Hope-Wallace, *Guardian*, 19 November 1964.

1965

1 Eckley claimed it had first been produced by P. T. Barnum four years earlier.
2 W. A. Darlington, *Daily Telegraph*, 28 January 1965.
3 The 'Olio' is an American term for an entertainment made up of disparate items, as in British music-hall or variety.
4 Winston Churchill died 24 January 1965.
5 *The Times*, 3 December 1965.
6 Citron, *Jerry Herman: Poet of the Showtune*.
7 *Plays and Players*, February 1966, p. 13.
8 *Daily Telegraph*, 8 December 1965.
9 Peter Lewis, *Daily Mail*, 3 December 1965.
10 Milton Shulman, *Evening Standard*, 3 December 1965.
11 Harold Hobson, *Sunday Times*, 5 December 1965.

1966

1 *Funny Girl*, theatre programme for Prince of Wales production, p. 25.
2 *Jewish Bulletin of Northern California*, 5 January 1996.
3 *Funny Girl*, theatre programme for Prince of Wales production, p. 25.
4 *Plays and Players*, June 1966, p. 15.

1967

1 *Sunday Telegraph*, 12 February 1967.
2 *Plays and Players*, April 1967, p. 21.
3 *Stage*, 23 February 1967.
4 'The Milkman Cometh: Jeremy Rundall talks to Topol', *Plays and Players*, March 1967, pp. 48–9.
5 'The Feast of the Fiddler', *Plays and Players*, April 1967, p. 15.
6 *Sunday Express*, n.d.
7 *Plays and Players*, July 1967, p. 19.
8 Ibid.
9 *Evening News*, 15 May 1967.
10 *Punch*, 24 May 1967.
11 Email from Patricia Michael to the author, 1 March 2012.
12 John Peter, *The Times*, 12 October 1967.

13 Peter Lewis, *Daily Mail*, 12 October 1967.
14 *Guardian*, 12 October 1967.
15 *Stage*, 19 October 1967.

1968

1 *Tatler*, March 1968.
2 *Daily Mail*, 2 February 1968.
3 *Plays and Players*, May 1968, pp. 14–17, 64.
4 *Daily Mail*, 29 February 1968.
5 *Daily Telegraph*, 29 February 1968.
6 Gillian Lynne, *Stage*, 24 July 1968.
7 Charles Spencer, *Stage*, 24 July 1968.
8 *Londoner*, 4 May 1968.
9 Souvenir brochure for the London production of *Man of La Mancha*.
10 Ibid.
11 *Evening Standard*, 25 April 1968.
12 *The Times*, 25 April 1968.
13 *Tatler*, June 1968.
14 *Daily Mail*, 25 April 1968.
15 *Illustrated London News*, 4 May 1968.
16 *Sunday Times*, 27 April 1968.
17 *Stage*, 12 June 1969.
18 J. C. Trewin, *Illustrated London News*, 21 June 1969.
19 Helen Dawson, 'Talent Wasting', *Plays and Players*, July 1968, p. 18.
20 *Tatler*, July 1968.
21 *Guardian*, 17 May 1968.
22 *Stage*, 6 June 1968.
23 Harold Clurman's introduction to script of *Golden Boy* published in *Famous Plays of 1938–39* (London: Victor Gollancz, 1939), p. 101.
24 Strouse, *Put On a Happy Face*, p. 155.
25 Hugh Leonard, *Plays and Players*, August 1968, p. 54.
26 Martin's leading roles in British musicals included *The Water Gipsies*, *Oliver!*, *The Matchgirls*, *Joey Joey* and *Queenie*.
27 *Evening Standard*, 5 June 1968.
28 J. C. Trewin, *Illustrated London News*, 20 June 1968.
29 *Daily Mail*, 5 June 1968.
30 Interview with John Hanson, *Sunday Times*, 2 June 1968.
31 *Daily Telegraph*, 10 June 1968.
32 *Illustrated London News*, 22 June 1968.
33 *Evening Standard*, 26 July 1968.
34 *The Times*, 26 July 1968.
35 Reader's report from the Lord Chamberlain's Correspondence Files, 10 June 1968.
36 Ibid, 11 July 1968.
37 *The Times*, 28 September 1968.
38 *Daily Telegraph*, 28 September 1968.
39 *Daily Express*, 28 September 1968.
40 *Sunday Times*, 29 September 1968.
41 *Lady*, 17 October 1968.
42 *Daily Telegraph*, 23 November 1971.

43 *Guardian*, 21 December 1971.
44 *Daily Telegraph*, 16 February 1973.
45 Alan Brien, *Plays and Players*, October 1974, p. 39.
46 'Taking Off: Michael Coveney on London's new sexual musical', *Plays and Players*, September 1974, p. 23. Both *Irene* and *No, No, Nanette* had recently been revived on Broadway (in 1973 and 1971 respectively).
47 *Guardian*, 10 December 1968.
48 *Evening Standard*, 10 December 1968.
49 *Lady*, 26 December 1968.
50 Henry Raynor, *Daily Telegraph*, 10 December 1968.

1969

1 *The Times*, 1 February 1969.
2 *Daily Mail*, 7 February 1969.
3 *Daily Telegraph*, 7 February 1969.
4 *Financial Times*, 7 February 1969.
5 *Sun*, 7 February 1969.
6 *Evening Standard*, 21 February 1969.
7 *Daily Mail*, 21 February 1969.
8 *Lady*, 13 March 1969.
9 *Daily Telegraph*, 21February 1969.
10 *The Times*, 21 February 1969.
11 On Broadway, she had earned a reputation for missing a good many when playing in *Hello, Dolly!*
12 J. C. Trewin, *Lady*, 15 May 1969.
13 Philip Howard, *Daily Telegraph*, 28 February 1969.
14 Irving Wardle, *The Times*, 2 May 1969.
15 *Stage*, 1 May 1969.
16 J. C. Trewin, *Illustrated London News*, 10 May 1969.
17 Eric Shorter, *Daily Telegraph*, 2 May 1969.
18 Barry Norman, *Daily Mail*, 2 May 1969.
19 *Daily Mail*, 12 May 1969.
20 *The Times*, 28 August 1969.
21 *Daily Telegraph*, 28 August 1969.
22 *Guardian*, 28 August 1969.
23 *Tatler*, October 1969.
24 *Daily Telegraph*, 3 October 1969.
25 *Sunday Times*, 5 October 1969.
26 *Guardian*, 19 November 1969.
27 *Illustrated London News*, 29 November 1969.

1970

1 *Daily Telegraph*, 17 June 1970.
2 *The Times*, 17 June 1970.
3 *Stage*, 16 July 1970.

1971

1 *Daily Telegraph*, 30 July 1971.
2 *Sunday Times*, 1 August 1971.
3 *Guardian*, 30 July 1971.
4 *Stage*, 28 October 1971.
5 *Punch*, 24 November 1971.
6 *The Times*, 18 November 1971.
7 *Daily Telegraph*, 18 November 1971.
8 *Guardian*, 18 November 1971.

1972

1 *The Times*, 19 January 1972.
2 *Tatler*, June 1972.
3 *Daily Telegraph*, 19 January 1972.
4 'Say it with Music', *Guardian*, 22 January 1972.
5 *His Monkey Wife*, a musical by Sandy Wilson based on John Collier's novel, produced at Hampstead Theatre Club in 1971.
6 Email from Patricia Michael to the author, 1 March 2012.
7 Strouse, *Put on a Happy Face*, pp. 200–1.
8 The London production of the Canadian musical *Anne of Green Gables* (New Theatre, 16 April 1969).
9 *Daily Telegraph*, 7 November 1972.
10 *Guardian*, 7 November 1972.
11 *The Times*, 7 November 1972.
12 *Plays and Players*, December 1972, pp. 48–9.
13 'Tin Pan Alley W1: Joan Buck goes down memory lane with Charles Strouse and Lee Adams of *I and Albert* and *Applause* fame', *Plays and Players*, December 1972, pp. 23–5.
14 *Plays and Players*, January 1973, pp. 46–7.
15 *London Evening News*, 17 November 1972.
16 *Lady*, 30 November 1972.

Select Bibliography

Agate, James, *Immoment Toys: A Survey of Light Entertainment on the London Stage, 1920–1943* (London: Jonathan Cape, 1945)

Billington, Michael, *State of the Nation: British Theatre since 1945* (London: Faber & Faber, 2007)

Bordman, Gerald, *American Musical Comedy: From Adonis to Dreamgirls* (New York: Oxford University Press, 1982)

—— *American Musical Theatre: A Chronicle* (New York: Oxford University Press, 2001)

—— *American Operetta: From HMS Pinafore to Sweeney Todd* (New York: Oxford University Press, 1981)

—— *Days to Be Happy, Years to Be Sad* (New York: Oxford University Press, 1982)

Brown, Ivor, *Theatre, 1955–6* (London: Max Reinhardt, 1956)

Burton, Humphrey, *Leonard Bernstein* (London: Faber & Faber, 1994)

Carmichael, Ian, *Will the Real Ian Carmichael ...* (London: Macmillan, 1979)

Carner, Mosco, *Puccini: A Critical Biography* (London: Duckworth, 1958)

Citron, Stephen, *Jerry Herman: Poet of the Showtune* (New Haven: Yale University Press, 2004)

—— *Noel and Cole: The Sophisticates* (London: Sinclair-Stevenson, 1992)

—— *The Wordsmiths: Oscar Hammerstein II and Alan Jay Lerner* (Oxford: Oxford University Press, 1995)

Comden, Betty, and Adolph Green, *The New York Musicals of Comden and Green: On the Town, Wonderful Town, Bells Are Ringing* (New York: Applause, 1997)

Everett, William A., *Sigmund Romberg* (New Haven: Yale University Press, 2007)

Everett, William A., and Paul R. Laird (eds), *The Cambridge Companion to the Musical*, 2nd edn (Cambridge: Cambridge University Press, 2008)

Filichia, Peter, *Broadway Musicals: The Biggest Hit and the Biggest Flop of the Season 1959 to 2009* (Milwaukee: Applause Theatre and Cinema Books, 2010)

Fordin, Hugh, *Getting to Know Him: A Biography of Oscar Hammerstein II* (New York: Da Capo Press, 1995)

Gänzl, Kurt, *The Blackwell Guide to the Musical Theatre on Record* (Oxford: Blackwell Reference, 1990)

Gardiner, Juliet, *Wartime Britain, 1939–1945* (London: Headline, 2004)

Green, Stanley, *Broadway Musicals Show by Show*, 6th edn (New York: Applause, 2008)

—— *Encyclopaedia of the Musical* (London: Cassell, 1976)

—— *The World of Musical Comedy* (South Brunswick: Yoseloff, 1974)

Hirschhorn, Clive, *The Hollywood Musical* (London: Octopus Books, 1981)

Hischak, Thomas, *The Oxford Companion to the American Musical* (New York: Oxford University Press, 2008)

Hughes, Gervase, *Composers of Operetta* (London: Macmillan, 1962)

Jablonski, Edward, *Alan Jay Lerner: A Biography* (New York: Henry Holt, 1996)

Johns, Eric, *Dames of the Theatre* (London: W. H. Allen, 1974)

Kimball, Robert (ed.), *Cole* (Woodstock: Overlook Press, 2000)

Kirkwood, Patricia, *The Time of My Life* (London: Robert Hale, 1999)

Kislan, Richard, *The Musical: A Look at the American Musical Theater* (New York: Applause, 1995)

Knapp, Raymond, *The American Musical and the Formation of National Identity* (Princeton: Princeton University Press, 2005)

Kynaston, David, *Austerity Britain, 1945–51* (London: Bloomsbury, 2007)

Lambert, Philip, *To Broadway, to Life!: The Musical Theater of Bock and Harnick* (New York: Oxford University Press, 2011)

Lees, Gene, *The Musical Worlds of Lerner and Loewe* (London: Robson, 1991)

Lewis, Robert, *Slings and Arrows* (New York: Stein & Day, 1984)

Macqueen-Pope, W., *Pillars of Drury Lane* (London: Hutchinson, 1955)

Mandelbaum, Ken, *Not Since Carrie: Forty Years of Broadway Musical Flops* (New York: St. Martin's Press, 1991)

Mander, Raymond, and Joe Mitchenson, *Musical Comedy: A Story in Pictures* (London: Peter Davies, 1969)

Marwick, Arthur, *British Society since 1945* (London: Penguin, 1982)

McBrien, William, *Cole Porter: The Definitive Biography* (London: HarperCollins, 1998)

Moody, Ron, *A Still Untitled (Not Quite) Autobiography* (London: J. R. Books, 2010)

Mordden, Ethan, *Beautiful Mornin': The Broadway Musical in the 1940s* (New York: Oxford University Press, 1999)

—— *Coming Up Roses: The Broadway Musical in the 1950s* (New York: Oxford University Press, 1998)

—— *The Happiest Corpse I've Ever Seen: The Last Twenty-Five Years of the Broadway Musical* (New York: Palgrave Macmillan, 2004)

—— *Open a New Window* (New York: Palgrave Macmillan, 2001)

—— *Rodgers and Hammerstein* (New York: Harry N. Abrams, 1992)

Norton, Richard C., *A Chronology of American Musical Theater*, 3 vols (New York: Oxford University Press, 2002)

Ornadel, Cyril, *Reach for the Moon* (Brighton: Book Guild, 2007)

Peyser, Joan, *Leonard Bernstein* (London: Bantam, 1987)

Plays and Players journal

Raymond, Jack, *Show Music on Record: The First 100 Years* (Washington, DC: Smithsonian Institution Press, 1992)

Riis, Thomas L., *Frank Loesser* (New Haven: Yale University Press, 2008)

Rodgers, Richard, *Musical Stages: An Autobiography* (London: W. H. Allen, 1976)

Ross, Robert, *The Complete Frankie Howerd* (London: Reynolds & Hearn, 2001)

Sandbrook, Dominic, *Never Had It So Good: A History of Britain from Suez to the Beatles* (London: Little, Brown, 2005)

—— *State of Emergency: The Way We Were: Britain, 1970–1974* (London: Allen Lane, 2010)

Sanders, Ronald, *The Days Grow Short: The Life and Music of Kurt Weill* (Los Angeles: Silman-James Press, 1991)

Secrest, Meryle, *Somewhere For Me: A Biography of Richard Rodgers* (London: Bloomsbury, 2001)

—— *Stephen Sondheim: A Life* (London: Bloomsbury, 1998)

Seeley, Robert, and Rex Bunnett, *London Musical Shows on Record, 1889–1989* (Harrow: General Gramophone Publications, 1989)

Shellard, Dominic, and Steve Nicholson, *The Lord Chamberlain Regrets …: A History of Theatre Censorship* (London: British Library, 2004)

Sondheim, Stephen, *Finishing the Hat: Collected Lyrics (1954–1981) with Attendant Comments, Principles, Heresies, Grudges, Whines and Anecdotes* (London: Virgin Books, 2010)

The Stage (weekly issues and *Stage Yearbooks*)

Stempel, Larry, *Showtime: A History of the Broadway Musical Theater* (New York: W. W. Norton, 2010)

Steyn, Mark, *Broadway Babies Say Goodnight: Musicals Then and Now* (London: Faber, 1997)

Strouse, Charles, *Put on a Happy Face: A Broadway Memoir* (New York: Union Square Press, 2008)

Suskin, Steven, *Opening Night on Broadway: A Critical Quotebook of the Golden Era of the Musical Theatre* (New York: Schirmer Books, 1990)

—— *Second Act Trouble: Behind the Scenes at Broadway's Big Musical Bombs* (New York: Applause, 2006)

—— *Show Tunes: The Songs, Shows, and Careers of Broadway's Major Composers*, 4th edn (New York: Oxford University Press, 2010)

Taylor, Theodore, *Jule: The Story of Composer Jule Styne* (New York: Random House, 1979)

Theatre World journal

Traubner, Richard, *Operetta: A Theatrical History* (London: Gollancz, 1984)

Who's Who in the Theatre, various editions

Wilson, A. E., *Post-War Theatre* (London: Home and Van Thal, [1949])

Winer, Deborah Grace, *On the Sunny Side of the Street: The Life and Lyrics of Dorothy Fields* (New York: Schirmer Books, 1997)

Wright, Adrian, *A Tanner's Worth of Tune: Rediscovering the Postwar British Musical* (Woodbridge: Boydell Press, 2010)

Index of Musical Works

General Index